BUSINESS LAW

 W9-CFJ-595

HARCOURT BRACE JOVANOVICH COLLEGE OUTLINE SERIES

BUSINESS LAW

Darryl L. Webb

College of Commerce and Business Administration
The University of Alabama

Books for Professionals
Harcourt Brace Jovanovich, Publishers
San Diego   New York   London

Copyright © 1984 by Books for Professionals, Inc.

All rights reserved. No part of this publication may be reproduced or transmitted in any form or by any means, electronic or mechanical, including photocopy, recording, or any information storage and retrieval system, without permission in writing from the publisher.

Requests for permission to make copies of any part of the work should be mailed to:

Permissions
Harcourt Brace Jovanovich, Publishers
Orlando, Florida 32887

Printed in the United States of America

Library of Congress Cataloging in Publication Data

Webb, Darry L.
    Business law.

    (Harcourt Brace Jovanovich college outline series)
(Books for professionals)
    Includes index.
    1. Business law—United States.   I. Title.
II. Series.   III. Series: Books for professionals.
KF889.3.235   1984   346.73'07   83-22473
ISBN 0-15-600003-2   347.3067

First edition

A   B   C   D   E

PREFACE

The purpose of this book is to present a complete course in business law in the clear, concise format of an outline. Although comprehensive enough to be used by itself for independent study, this outline is specifically designed to be used as a supplement to college courses and textbooks on the subject. Notice, for example, the Textbook Correlation Table that begins on the inside of the front cover. This table shows how the pages of this outline correspond by topic to the pages of five of the leading textbooks on business law currently in use at major colleges and universities. So, should the sequence of topics in this outline differ from the sequence of topics in your textbook, you can easily locate the material you want by consulting the table.

Regular features at the end of each chapter are also specially designed to supplement your textbook and course work in business law:

RAISE YOUR GRADES   This feature consists of a checkmarked list of open-ended thought questions to help you assimilate the material you have just studied. By inviting you to compare concepts, interpret ideas, and examine the whys and wherefores of chapter material, these questions help you to prepare for class discussions, quizzes, and tests.

SUMMARY   This feature consists of a brief restatement of the main ideas in each chapter, including definitions of key terms. Because it is presented in the efficient form of a numbered list, you can use it to refresh your memory quickly before an exam.

RAPID REVIEW   Like the summary, this feature is designed to provide you with a quick review of the principles presented in the body of each chapter. Consisting of true-false questions, it allows you to test your retention and reinforce your learning at the same time. Should you have trouble answering any of these questions, you can locate and review the relevant sections provided.

SOLVED PROBLEMS   Each chapter of this outline concludes with a set of practical problems and their step-by-step solutions. Undoubtedly the most valuable feature of the outline, these problems allow you to apply your knowledge of business law to numerous real-life situations. Along with the sample midterm and final examinations, they also give you ample exposure to the kinds of problems that you are likely to encounter on a typical college exam. To make the most of these problems, try writing your own solutions first. Then compare your answers to the detailed solutions provided in the book.

Of course, there are other features of this outline that you will find very helpful too. One is the format itself, which serves both as a clear guide to important ideas and as a convenient structure upon which to organize your knowledge. A second is the careful attention devoted to contract law and sales contracts, as regulated by the Uniform Commercial Code. Practically every transaction conducted in today's marketplace involves contracts, whether for personal or business purposes. Yet a third is the handy glossary provided at the back of the book, which should be helpful in comprehending the many terms that are used throughout the book as they apply to business law.

Business law is a subject that everyone, particularly business people, should be familiar with for its practical applications. The case problems in this book are designed to make these practical applications clear. Understanding these applications and the legal principles behind them will be an invaluable aid to you throughout your business career.

CONTENTS

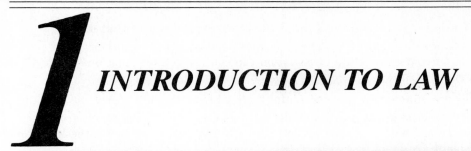

1 INTRODUCTION TO LAW

THIS CHAPTER IS ABOUT

☑ **Definitions of Law**
☑ **Common Law**
☑ **Sources of U.S. Law**
☑ **Classifications of Law**
☑ **Court Systems in the United States**
☑ **Judicial Proceedings in a Civil Lawsuit**

1-1. Definitions of Law

The term *law* has several acceptable meanings. A *law* in general is any rule that has been established and must be obeyed. The term *law* is also used to describe a system of principles and rules of human conduct. In addition, *law* can mean a rule or other enactment of a governmental law-making body. Finally, *law* can also mean the principles, rules, and standards that apply to a particular field, such as "business law."

1-2. Common Law

The U.S. legal system is based primarily on the English system of *jurisprudence* (law).

The English court system began developing following the Norman Conquest in 1066. The early courts were known as the "King's Court" (*Curia Regis*). At first, judges resolved cases by applying their knowledge of customs and traditions to the disputes brought before them. In the thirteenth century, decisions of the judges began to be published in "Year Books," and these published case decisions came to serve as guides for the judges when new cases arose that were similar to prior ones. For each new case, judges would refer to the published cases to determine whether or not a *precedent* had been established in a prior decision. If there was indeed such a precedent, the judge would follow it in the current case. This practice became known as the doctrine of *stare decisis* ("let the decision stand").

Reliance on precedent gave certainty, stability, and predictability to the system of jurisprudence. Precedent is still the basis of the U.S. legal system. Precedents are followed unless a valid reason exists for changing the law and establishing a new precedent.

1-3. Sources of U.S. Law

In the U.S. legal system, there are six important sources of law.

A. The United States Constitution is the basic law of the land.

The U.S. Constitution is the foundation for most laws in the United States. Any law that contradicts the provisions of the U.S. Constitution is null and void.

B. Statutes are enacted by governmental bodies.

Both federal and state governments have legislative branches that establish numerous laws. These laws are known as *statutes* and comprise a large portion of the total body of law known as *statutory law*.

C. The constitution of each state sets forth the fundamental law of that state.

State constitutions establish the basic principles pertaining to the authority and power of the state. Of course, no state constitution can contradict the provisions of the U.S. Constitution.

D. Ordinances are enacted by governmental bodies below the state level.

Laws passed by local governmental bodies such as city councils are called *ordinances*. Ordinances are enforceable if they do not exceed the legislative power of the local governmental body.

E. Governmental agencies establish administrative rules and regulations.

There are numerous administrative agencies at both the federal and state levels, such as the National Labor Relations Board, the Internal Revenue Service, and hundreds of others. These agencies establish many rules and regulations to carry out their assigned tasks. These rules and regulations become part of what is known as *administrative law*.

F. Case decisions handed down by federal and state courts are a tremendously important source of law.

Judges pronounce new legal principles continually as disputes are resolved in court. When no previously existing statutory law is involved, this creation of case law by judicial decision is known as the creation of *common-law principles*. Judges also make decisions concerning the application and interpretation of various statutes. The resulting very large body of case law serves as a vital and primary source of our law.

1-4. Classifications of Law

Law is classified in a variety of ways.

A. A common way of classifying law is to distinguish substantive law from procedural law.

Substantive law deals with the creation, definition, and regulation of legal rights and obligations. Some examples are

- contract law
- tort law
- property law

Procedural law is concerned with the enforcement of rights existing by reason of substantive law. Some examples are

- civil procedure
- criminal procedure
- administrative procedure

B. Another way of classifying law is to distinguish public law from private law.

Public law deals with the rights and powers of the state. Some examples are

- constitutional law
- criminal law
- administrative law

Private law is concerned with individuals in their relations with each other. Most of business law falls within this category. Some examples are

- contract law
- tort law
- property law

These categories can be further subdivided.

1. *Criminal law* deals with acts considered as wrongs against society. The three main classifications of crimes are

   (a) *treason*—providing aid and comfort to enemies of the United States

(*b*) *felonies*—crimes punishable by penitentiary imprisonment or death
(*c*) *misdemeanors*—crimes punishable by fine or local jail confinement

A crime committed by a business or against a business is sometimes called a *white-collar crime*. Technically, the term *white-collar crime* does not refer to a specific legal category of crime. Instead, it is used to describe nonviolent violations of specific state criminal statutes or of the federal criminal code, generally committed by an individual or business in order to obtain an economic advantage. Some examples are

- commercial bribery
- mail fraud
- tax fraud
- false advertising
- computer theft
- commercial disparagement
- embezzlement

2. *Tort law* is concerned with civil wrongs.
   A *tort* is a civil wrong as opposed to a criminal wrong. The purpose of tort law is to compensate an injured party. The party causing the injury is called the *tortfeasor*. The three requirements for the existence of a tort are a duty, a breach of that duty, and an injury that imminently results from that breach of duty. Some examples are

   (*a*) intentional torts such as assault and battery (some acts are both crimes and torts), false imprisonment, defamation of character, and invasion of privacy
   (*b*) negligent torts such as personal injury automobile accident cases
   (*c*) torts resulting from strict liability in cases involving extremely hazardous activity such as dynamite blasting or keeping wild and vicious animals that escape and cause injury (some states currently allow the court to apply strict liability standards against manufacturers of dangerously unsafe products)

1-5. Court Systems in the United States

The United States has a dual judicial system consisting of the federal court system and the various state court systems. Within each system there are two kinds of courts: trial courts and appellate courts. *Trial courts* have original jurisdiction, which means that it is to these courts that cases are initially brought for resolution. The evidence is presented and the judge or jury must determine the facts in the case. After the facts are determined, the law is applied to the facts and a judgment is rendered. *Appellate courts* exist to hear appeals from trial courts. At the appellate level, however, the case is not just tried again in the same manner as at the trial court. Instead, appellate courts provide a forum where the trial court *litigants* (parties in the case) can present arguments about what occurred during the original trial. The litigants usually argue that errors occurred during the original trial, and the appellate court judges respond to the argument by referring to the record of the trial court proceedings.

A. The federal judicial system is divided into three main kinds of courts.

1. *District courts* (trial courts). Each state has at least one federal district court, which has original jurisdiction over federal criminal cases and the following civil cases:

   (*a*) suits between citizens of different states ("diversity of citizenship") where the value of the matter in controversy exceeds $10,000
   (*b*) suits involving a "federal question" (an issue concerning the U.S. Constitution, statutes, or treaties of the United States) where the value of the matter in controversy exceeds $10,000
   (*c*) suits brought under various federal statutes

2. *Courts of appeal* (appellate courts). The United States is divided into "judicial circuits," and each circuit contains one court of appeals. Each federal court of appeals has appellate jurisdiction over final decisions of the federal district courts within its judicial circuit and also over most decisions of federal administrative agencies.

   3. *U.S. Supreme Court.* The Supreme Court is the highest appellate court in the country. Cases are brought before this court either by appeal or *certiorari* ("discretionary review").

B. State judicial systems are likewise divided into three main kinds of courts.

   1. *Trial courts.* These are courts of original jurisdiction. Some of them have general jurisdiction over any type of subject matter, whereas others, such as *small claims courts*, have limited jurisdiction.
   2. *Intermediate appellate courts.* Most states have appellate courts at the intermediate level that function like the federal courts of appeal in that they are not the highest level of appeal.
   3. *Highest-level appellate courts.* These courts are called supreme courts in some states. Regardless of the title, however, these courts function as the courts of last resort within the various states.

1-6. Judicial Proceedings in a Civil Lawsuit

The best way to understand the procedure involved in a civil (noncriminal) lawsuit is to divide the entire process into four essential aspects: initiation of the suit, pretrial preparation, trial, and appeal.

A. Initiation of the suit

A lawsuit begins with the filing of a summons and complaint, usually with the clerk of the appropriate court. The *complaint* contains the names and addresses of the *plaintiff* (the party bringing the suit) and the *defendant* (the party being sued). In addition, the complaint contains a statement of the jurisdictional facts, the cause of action (the basis of the suit: breach of contract, negligence, etc.), and a demand for some type of relief (money, damages, injunction, etc.). The suit may be served personally (served directly on the defendant) or by publication (notice of suit advertised somewhere, such as in a newspaper). The *summons* informs the defendant that a response to the suit is necessary; otherwise, a judgment can be entered against the defendant (this kind of judgment is called a *default judgment*). The defendant, after proper service, may *demur* (object) to the complaint (a defendant who wishes to demur files a *demurrer*, which is a response to the effect that the complaint has failed to state a cause of action sufficient to justify legal action). In many jurisdictions, the demurrer has been replaced by a motion to dismiss for failure to state a cause of action. Instead of demurring, the defendant may file an answer denying the allegations in the complaint and setting up grounds for defense. Sometimes a defendant will file an answer and counterclaim against the plaintiff.

B. Pretrial preparation

Prior to the trial, both plaintiff and defendant may utilize certain discovery procedures to attempt to find out as much as possible about the other's case. Each especially tries to find out what testimony will be given at the trial in order to avoid being surprised. The most important pretrial discovery tool is the deposition. A *deposition* is a sworn statement consisting of answers to questions put to a prospective witness.

C. Trial

When a case comes to trial, the first order of business is to resolve any *pleading* questions that may exist. If the defendant has filed a demurrer or a motion to dismiss the case due to insufficient facts, then the judge must decide if the complaint does in essence state a valid cause of action. Should the judge uphold the demurrer, the plaintiff must amend the complaint (if possible) to state a cause of action. Should the plaintiff be unable to properly amend, then the defendant would "win" on the pleadings. However, if the judge overrules the demurrer, then the defendant can file an answer denying the allegations. At this point the parties are said to be *at issue*, and the trial can now proceed according to the following steps:

   1. *Jury selection.* The attorneys conduct *voir dire*, which is an examination of prospective jurors to determine their ability to serve impartially. The attorneys are allowed *chal-*

lenges for cause (a reason for challenge is required) and are granted *peremptory challenges* (a reason for challenge is not required). States usually do not set limits for the number of challenges for cause allowed, but usually do set limits for the number of peremptory challenges allowed.

2. *Opening statement.* Each attorney, starting with the plaintiff's attorney, is allowed the opportunity to make a statement of what he or she expects the evidence to show.

3. *Plaintiff's case in chief.* The plaintiff calls her or his witnesses, who are allowed to testify. Each witness is subjected to *direct examination, cross-examination,* and, in some instances, re-direct and re-cross-examination. Acceptable exhibits are presented. The court takes judicial notice of matters of common knowledge, meaning that such matters need not be proved. When the plaintiff's case is concluded, the defendant may file a motion for nonsuit or for a directed verdict. In a directed verdict, the court dictates the jury's verdict, thereby withdrawing the case from the jury.

4. *Defendant's case in reply.* The same procedure is followed as in the plaintiff's case. Proof is offered in support of the defendant's answer and counterclaim, if one was filed. Following the defendant's case in reply, the plaintiff may file for a directed verdict.

5. *Summation.* Each attorney is allowed to make final arguments to the jury.

6. *Instructions.* The judge then provides instructions to the jury, informing them of the law pertinent to the case. The judge also tells the jury all the different verdicts that they may render, depending on how they ascertain the facts in the case. Each way in which the facts are judged requires a specific verdict.

7. *Jury verdict.* The jury resolves all questions of fact (not questions of law) and returns a verdict.

8. *Decision.* The jury's verdict coupled with the law in the particular case, determines the outcome of the *litigation.* The judge gives a judgment in the case and grants appropriate relief, if any.

D. Appeal

A party to the suit may wish to appeal the decision. The first step in this process is to file a *notice of appeal* and to serve it on the adversary party. Also, the *appellant* (party that appeals) must put up bond for the costs of the other party. An application for a *stay of judgment* must be made that prevents the original judgment from being carried out immediately. A record of the trial must then be forwarded to the appellate court. This record consists of the original documents and exhibits along with a transcript of the proceedings. Attorneys for the appellant and *appellee* (party that receives notice of appeal) file legal briefs. Sometimes they orally argue these briefs, and sometimes they orally argue only the legal propositions contained in the briefs. The appellate court reaches a decision and files a written opinion that either affirms the original judgment, reverses it, or reverses and remands it for further proceedings.

RAISE YOUR GRADES

Can you explain . . . ?

☑ the various definitions of *law*

☑ the development of the English common-law system of jurisprudence

☑ the meaning of *stare decisis*

☑ the main sources of law in the U.S. legal system

☑ the various classifications of law, with examples of each

☑ the difference between a trial court and an appellate court

☑ the three main categories of federal courts and state courts

☑ how to carry a case through the various steps from filing to appeal

SUMMARY

1. A *law* in general is any rule that has been established and must be obeyed. The term is also used to describe a system of principles and rules of human conduct.
2. The term *law* can also mean a rule or other enactment of a governmental law-making body.
3. The term *law* can also mean the principles, rules, and standards that apply to a particular field, such as "business law."
4. The U.S. legal system is based primarily on the English common-law system of jurisprudence.
5. The doctrine of *stare decisis* ("let the decision stand") developed under the common law and established the concept of legal precedents.
6. The doctrine of *stare decisis* endows our legal system with certainty, stability, and predictability.
7. The main sources of law in the U.S. legal system are constitutions, statutes and ordinances, administrative rules and regulations, and case decisions.
8. *Substantive law* deals with the creation, definition, and regulation of legal rights and obligations.
9. *Procedural law* is concerned with the enforcement of rights existing by reason of substantive law.
10. *Public law* deals with the rights and powers of the state.
11. *Private law* is concerned with individuals in their relations with each other.
12. Criminal law deals with acts considered as wrongs against society. The three main classifications of crimes are treason, felonies, and misdemeanors.
13. *White-collar crime* is a term used to describe nonviolent violations of specific state criminal statutes or of the federal criminal code, generally committed by an individual or business in order to obtain an economic advantage.
14. A *tort* is a civil wrong as opposed to a criminal wrong.
15. The three requirements for the existence of a tort are a duty, a breach of that duty, and an injury that imminently results from that breach of duty.
16. Torts are divided into three categories: intentional torts, negligent torts, and torts resulting from strict liability.
17. The United States has a dual court system consisting of the federal court system and the various state court systems.
18. The two main kinds of courts are trial courts and appellate courts.
19. In the federal court system, the district court is the trial court and has original jurisdiction over federal criminal cases and certain civil cases.
20. The three types of civil cases under federal district court jurisdiction are suits between citizens of different states ("diversity of citizenship"), suits involving a federal question, and suits brought under various federal statutes.
21. In the state court systems, the trial court is the court of original jurisdiction.
22. In appellate courts, cases are not simply tried again in the same manner as in trial or district courts.
23. The four main steps in a civil trial are initiation of the suit, pretrial preparation, trial, and appeal.
24. A lawsuit begins with the filing of a summons and complaint with the clerk of the appropriate court.
25. The most important pretrial discovery tool is the deposition (a sworn statement consisting of answers to questions put to a prospective witness).
26. The first order of business at the trial is to resolve any pleading questions.
27. Attorneys conduct *voir dire*, which consists of asking prospective jurors questions to determine their ability to serve impartially.
28. Judges provide instructions to the jury informing them of the law pertinent to the case.
29. The jury resolves all questions of fact and returns a verdict.
30. A judgment is given by the judge after the jury's verdict.

RAPID REVIEW	**Answers**

True or False?

1. Customs and traditions were of little significance to the decisions of English common-law judges. [Section 1-2] — *False*

2. The doctrine of *stare decisis* is one of the most important principles developed from English common law. [Section 1-2] — *True*

3. The doctrine of *stare decisis* requires that judges *never* contradict prior case decisions. [Section 1-2] — *False*

4. Any U.S. law that contradicts the provisions of the U.S. Constitution is null and void. [Section 1-3] — *True*

5. Laws passed by local governmental bodies are called *statutes*. [Section 1-3] — *False*

6. The only important source of law in the United States is the large body of case law resulting from case decisions at the state and federal levels. [Section 1-3] — *False*

7. Substantive law deals with the creation, definition, and regulation of legal rights and obligations. [Section 1-4] — *True*

8. Tort law is an example of substantive law. [Section 1-4] — *True*

9. Most of business law falls into the category of public law. [Section 1-4] — *False*

10. White-collar crime is a specific, legally defined category of crime. [Section 1-4] — *False*

11. Embezzlement is one kind of white-collar crime. [Section 1-4] — *True*

12. A tort is a criminal wrong as opposed to a civil wrong. [Section 1-4] — *False*

13. At the appellate court level, cases are retried in exactly the same manner as at the trial court level. [Section 1-5] — *False*

14. Federal district courts have original jurisdiction in suits where the value of the matter in controversy exceeds $5000. [Section 1-5] — *False*

15. Federal district courts have original jurisdiction in suits involving a "state question." [Section 1-5] — *False*

16. Cases can be brought before the U.S. Supreme Court by appeal but not by *certiorari*. [Section 1-5] — *False*

17. The most important pretrial discovery tool is the deposition. [Section 1-6] — *True*

18. The examination of prospective jurors is called *voir dire*. [Section 1-6] — *True*

SOLVED PROBLEMS

PROBLEM 1-1   Define and explain fully the doctrine of *stare decisis*.

Answer: *Stare decisis* means "let the decision stand." This doctrine evolved from the precepts of English common law. It established the concept of *precedent*. Under this doctrine, judges are to follow the precedents set down in prior cases unless a valid reason exists for not doing so. The importance of the doctrine of *stare decisis* is that it gave certainty, stability, and predictability to our legal system. [Section 1-2]

PROBLEM 1-2   List the five main sources of U.S. law.

Answer: 1. U.S. Constitution
2. state constitutions
3. statutes and ordinances
4. administrative rules and regulations
5. case decisions
[Section 1-3]

PROBLEM 1-3   Explain the difference between substantive law and procedural law.

Answer: Substantive law deals with the creation, definition, and regulation of legal rights and obligations. Procedural law involves the methods of enforcing rights existing by reason of substantive law. [Section 1-4]

PROBLEM 1-4   Plaintiff Jones, while employed as a waitress by defendant Walsh, was told by Walsh in front of several customers, "You are not ringing up the cash in the cash register." Jones asked, "Are you accusing me of stealing?" Walsh replied, "Well, you're not ringing up the cash." At a later time the missing cash was located. On what grounds could Jones sue Walsh?

Answer: Jones could sue Walsh on the grounds that Walsh had committed a tort against her. Specifically, the tort would be the intentional tort of *slander* (a type of defamation of character). Walsh is the tortfeasor, the party causing the injury. If Jones sues, she would seek compensation for the injury to her reputation resulting from Walsh's public, oral accusation that Jones had been stealing the restaurant's money. [Section 1-4]

PROBLEM 1-5   Johnson was a purchasing agent for Digitex Corporation. Smith was a sales agent for Quarty, Inc. Smith offered Johnson $2,000 a year if Johnson would purchase all of Digitex's supplies from Quarty. Johnson accepted the offer. Did this transaction constitute a crime on Smith's part? If so, what crime was committed?

Answer: Smith committed the crime of commercial bribery. In violation of criminal law, Smith gave Johnson $2,000 a year for the corrupt purpose of inducing Johnson to buy Quarty's goods. Smith illegally sought a business advantage by bribing Johnson. Smith's commercial bribery can also be categorized as a white-collar crime—a nonviolent violation of the law for economic gain. [Section 1-4]

PROBLEM 1-6   Williams was employed by the Federal Farm Insurance Company to collect premiums from policy holders. One holiday weekend he felt the need for some gambling action, so he took $500 in premium money and flew to Las Vegas. Unfortunately, he soon lost all the money at the blackjack tables. Did he commit a crime in taking the money?

Answer: By taking other people's money that was in his care and converting it to his own use, Williams committed the crime of embezzlement. *Embezzlement* is the fraudulent appropriation of property, in this case money, by a person to whom it has been entrusted. Williams had been entrusted with $500 in premium money—money that should have gone to the Federal Farm Insurance Company—but he appropriated it for his own use. Embezzlement is categorized as a white-collar crime because it is a nonviolent violation of the law in order to obtain an economic advantage. [Section 1-4]

PROBLEM 1-7   Wilcox, a resident of Alabama, drove her car to Knoxville, Tennessee. There she was involved in a serious automobile accident with Andrews, a Tennessee resident. Andrews claimed that Wilcox was negligent and sued her for $50,000. Can Andrews sue Wilcox in federal court? Explain your answer.

Answer: Andrews can sue Wilcox in federal district court. Federal district courts have original jurisdiction over federal criminal cases and various civil cases, one being suits between citizens of different states where the value of the matter in controversy exceeds $10,000. These requirements are met in this instance: Wilcox and Andrews are residents of different states and the suit is for $50,000. [Section 1-5]

PROBLEM 1-8   Describe the difference between a trial court and an appellate court.

Answer: The trial court has original jurisdiction, while the appellate court hears only appeals. This means that cases are initially brought to and resolved by the trial court. Here the case is presented, the jury or judge returns a verdict, and a judgment is rendered. If a party to the suit is unsatisfied with the outcome, the case can be taken to the appellate court, which exists to hear appeals from the trial court. At the appellate court, the case is not tried again in the same fashion as at the trial court. Rather, arguments are presented about what occurred during the original trial. [Section 1-5]

2 INTRODUCTION TO CONTRACTS

☑ **Definition of Contract**
☑ **Classification of Contracts**

2-1. Definition of *Contract*

A. Contract law is about promises and, more precisely, what kinds of promises are enforceable at law.

A promise enforceable at law is perhaps the simplest definition of a *contract*. In the Restatement of the Law of Contracts, Section 1, the following definition is provided: "a *contract* is a promise or a set of promises for the breach of which the law gives a remedy, or the performance of which the law in some way recognizes as a duty." (The Restatements of Law are publications of the American Law Institute that provide commentary on legal matters. The Restatements, though not actual law, are taken into consideration in many judicial decisions.) It is clear from this definition that the study of contracts is concerned primarily with promises and their enforceability. If a promise is determined to be a contractual promise, then it is generally enforceable at law. Conversely, if a promise is determined to be a noncontractual promise, then it is generally not enforceable at law.

B. A valid contract has four essential elements.

A *contractual promise* is defined as any promise contained in an agreement between legally competent parties, supported by consideration, and in pursuance of a lawful purpose. Therefore, the four essential elements of a valid contract are

1. valid offer and acceptance (mutual assent)
2. consideration
3. legally competent parties
4. lawful purpose

Each of these essential elements will be the subject of more detailed treatment in separate chapters to follow.

2-2. Classification of Contracts

Contracts can be classified in a number of different ways. The significance of these classifications will become clearer as this discussion proceeds.

A. Express versus implied-in-fact contracts

An *express contract* is one in which the parties demonstrate mutual assent through their *words*, either spoken or written. An *implied-in-fact contract* is one in which the parties demonstrate mutual assent through their *conduct*.

EXAMPLE 2-1: Alex took a seat in a barber's chair and gave the barber directions concerning his haircut. After the hair had been cut according to specfications, Alex was bound to pay the barber's fee, even though Alex never promised in words to do so. Alex, by his conduct, implied a promise to pay. This example clearly illustrates an implied-in-fact contract.

B. Quasi contracts (*implied-in-law contracts*)

A *quasi contract* is one that a court may consider implied in law when in reality there is no express contract or implied-in-fact contract. This kind of contract is usually imposed by the law on the parties as a way of preventing one party from being unjustly enriched at the expense of the other.

EXAMPLE 2-2: Diane, a doctor, encountered Albert, an unconscious victim of an auto accident. Diane rendered treatment to Albert. Diane subsequently billed Albert for her services. A court would find Albert liable to Diane on the basis of quasi contract even though Albert never promised to pay nor by his conduct implied a contract.

C. Bilateral versus unilateral contracts

A *bilateral contract* is one in which a promise is given in exchange for another promise. In other words, a bilateral contract is an exchange of mutual promises. (Jack promises Mike $15 if Mike promises to mow Jack's lawn.) A *unilateral contract* is one in which a promise is given in exchange for a requested act. (Jack promises to give Mike $15 for mowing Jack's lawn.)

D. Valid, unenforceable, void, and voidable contracts

A *valid contract* is one that meets all legal prerequisites and is therefore enforceable at law.

An *unenforceable contract* is one that meets all the requirements of mutual assent, consideration, and competency of parties, and is in fact in pursuance of a lawful purpose, but because it does not meet some other legal requirement, it is not enforceable. For example, the Statute of Frauds requires that certain contracts be in written form. Should a contract that must comply with this statute fail to do so, it would be declared unenforceable.

A *void contract* is one that never had any validity. Sometimes a court will decide that a contract is void *ab initio*, meaning that from the very beginning the contract had no validity.

A *voidable contract* is one that is binding on one party but not on the other. The contract is enforceable unless the party that has the option to withdraw rejects the contract. Grounds for rejecting a contract include fraud, lack of legal capacity to contract, mutual mistake, misrepresentation, and lack of free will.

EXAMPLE 2-3: Pete had a contract with Jane. However, instead of living up to the contract terms, Pete defrauded Jane. In such a case, Jane could rescind the contract and not be bound. The contract would be voidable at Jane's election and Jane's only. Pete would have no legal right to rescind the contract.

E. Executed versus executory contracts

An *executed contract* is one that is completely performed by both parties. There are no remaining promises to be fulfilled. An *executory contract* is one that contains promises still unperformed.

F. Entire versus severable contracts

An *entire contract*, sometimes called a *whole contract*, is one in which no provision could be separated and severed from the rest without destroying the basic intent of the parties. In other words, the entire contract situation is such that every provision must be carried out in order for the parties' basic intent to be satisfied. A *severable contract*, on the other hand, is one in which one or more parts or provisions could be severed from the rest without destroying the basic intent of the parties. This distinction is particularly relevant to the concept of "lawful purpose" (see Chapter 7).

RAISE YOUR GRADES

Can you explain . . . ?

☑ the definition and the essential elements of a valid contract

☑ the difference between an express and an implied contract
☑ the difference between a contract implied in fact and a contract implied in law (quasi contract)
☑ the difference between a bilateral and a unilateral contract
☑ the difference between valid, unenforceable, void, and voidable contracts
☑ the difference between an executed and an executory contract
☑ the difference between an entire and a severable contract

SUMMARY

1. The Restatement of the Law of Contracts defines *contract* as "a promise or a set of promises for the breach of which the law gives a remedy, or the performance of which the law in some way recognizes as a duty."
2. A contractual promise is enforceable at law.
3. A *contractual promise* is defined as any promise contained in an agreement between legally competent parties, supported by consideration, and in pursuance of a lawful purpose.
4. An *express contract* is one in which the parties demonstrate mutual assent through their *words*, either spoken or written.
5. An *implied-in-fact contract* is one in which the parties demonstrate mutual assent through their *conduct*.
6. A *quasi contract*, also called an *implied-in-law contract*, is one that a court may consider implied in law when in reality there is no express contract or implied-in-fact contract. A quasi contract is usually imposed by a court to prevent one party from being unjustly enriched at the expense of another.
7. A *bilateral contract* is one in which a promise is given in exchange for another promise.
8. A *unilateral contract* is one in which a promise is given in exchange for a requested act.
9. A *valid contract* is one that meets all the necessary legal prerequisites and thus is enforceable at law.
10. An *unenforceable contract* is one that meets all the requirements of mutual assent, consideration, and competency of parties, and is in fact in pursuance of a lawful purpose, but because it does not meet some other legal requirement, it is not enforceable.
11. A contract that is declared void *ab initio* is considered to have been void from the beginning.
12. A *voidable contract* is one that is binding on one party but not on the other.
13. An *executed contract* is one that has been completely performed by both parties.
14. An *executory contract* is one that contains promises still unperformed.
15. An *entire contract* is one in which no provision could be separated and severed from the rest without destroying the basic intent of the parties.
16. A *severable contract* is one in which one or more parts or provisions could be severed from the rest without destroying the basic intent of the parties.

RAPID REVIEW   Answers

True or False?

1. The law gives a remedy in the courts for the fulfillment of a contract. [Section 2-1]   *False*

2. All promises are enforceable at law. [Section 2-1]   *False*

3. A contract must be supported by consideration. [Section 2-1]   *True*

4. A contract may be made and is enforceable by the courts even if the contract is for an illegal purpose. [Section 2-1]   *False*

5. An express contract can never be made orally. [Section 2-2]   *False*

6. The mutual assent element of a contract may be satisfied by words or conduct. [Section 2-2]   *True*

7. A court has the power to imply a contract in law to prevent one party from being unjustly enriched at the expense of another. [Section 2-2]   *True*

8. A unilateral contract is formed when one promise is exchanged for another. [Section 2-2]   *False*

9. An unenforceable contract is one that is made in pursuance of an illegal object. [Section 2-2]   *False*

10. A void contract is one that was valid in the beginning but for some reason later became unenforceable. [Section 2-2]   *False*

11. A voidable contract is one that is binding on both parties and rescindable by both parties. [Section 2-2]   *False*

12. An entire contract is one in which one or more parts or provisions can be severed from the rest without destroying the basic intent of the parties. [Section 2-2]   *False*

SOLVED PROBLEMS

PROBLEM 2-1   A contract has been defined as a promise enforceable at law. To be enforceable at law, a contract must meet four requirements. Name and describe them.

Answer: 1. *Valid offer and acceptance (mutual assent)*. Mutual assent consists of an offer by one party and the acceptance of that offer by another party.
2. *Consideration.* Consideration is the requested acts or promises that the parties exchange.
3. *Legally competent parties.* The parties must have the legal capacity to enter binding contracts. (Minors, insane persons, and intoxicated persons do not have legal capacity.)
4. *Lawful purpose.* The contract and its performance must not violate the law or public policy.
[Section 2-1]

PROBLEM 2-2   Describe the differences between (a) an express contract, (b) a contract implied in fact, and (c) a contract implied in law.

Answer: (a) An express contract is one in which the parties have manifested their mutual assent by *words*, either spoken or written.
(b) A contract implied in fact is one in which the mutual assent of the parties is shown by the parties' conduct.
(c) A contract implied in law is one that may be judged to exist in situations where there is no existing express contract or implied-in-fact contract. In such situations, a court may impose a contract implied in law if it is needed to prevent one party from being enriched unjustly at the expense of another.
[Section 2-2]

PROBLEM 2-3   Define the terms (a) *valid contract*, (b) *unenforceable contract*, (c) *void contract*, and (d) *voidable contract*.

Answer: (a) A *valid contract* is one that meets all legal requirements and is therefore enforceable at law.
(b) An *unenforceable contract* is one that meets the four basic requirements of a valid contract, but because it does not meet some other legal requirement, it is unenforceable at law.
(c) A *void* or *void ab initio* contract is one that never was valid.

(d) A *voidable contract* is one that binds only one of the parties to the promise involved. The other party can rescind the contract at any time.
[Section 2-2]

PROBLEM 2-4   Moore walked outside her house and encountered Smith, a paint contractor. Smith told Moore that he was there to paint Moore's house. Moore had not requested Smith's services. However, Moore did nothing to prevent Smith from completing the job. After the job was finished, Moore told Smith that he had painted the wrong house. In fact, Smith should have gone three houses further down the street to the home of another individual named Moore. Smith brought suit against Moore. Can he obtain a judgment against Moore?

Answer: Smith can obtain a judgment against Moore even though there was no written or oral contract between them. By her conduct—that is, by doing nothing to halt the painting—Moore entered into a contract implied in fact with Smith. She knew that Smith was painting her house and that he expected compensation; therefore, the court will most likely direct her to pay him. The important point in this case is that the conduct by which Moore entered into the implied contract was not any overt act; it was simply doing nothing. A court would construe that as assent.

The court might also rule that a quasi contract exists. Smith is entitled to compensation because otherwise, Moore would be unjustly enriched at Smith's expense. [Section 2-2]

PROBLEM 2-5   Moore returned from a month-long vacation and found out that Smith had painted her house during her absence. Moore had no prior contact whatsoever with Smith. Smith had simply noticed that Moore's house could use a paint job and decided to do it while Moore was on vacation. Can Smith recover any money from Moore on the basis of a breach of contract?

Answer: There is no way that Smith could recover any money. No contract of any sort existed between Smith and Moore. There was no express contract between the two parties. Nor had Moore by her conduct done anything that could be construed as the basis for a contract implied in fact. Nor was there any basis for a quasi contract. For a court to impose a quasi contract upon Moore and Smith in this case would only give blanket permission to anyone to impose similar services on unsuspecting citizens. [Section 2-2]

PROBLEM 2-6   Williams contacted White and offered to pay White $5,000 to place hydrochloric acid in a few bottles of mouthwash located on the shelves of Joe's Pharmacy. Williams was angry with Joe and believed that this action would severely curtail Joe's business. White accepted Williams's offer and placed the acid in the mouthwash. Is this a valid contract between Williams and White, or is it unenforceable, or void?

Answer: Any court would hold that this is not a valid contract. The reason that it is not valid is that it fails to fulfill one of the four basic requirements for a valid contract: it is not in pursuance of a lawful purpose. Also, it is not simply an unenforceable contract, merely violating some lesser legal requirement. This contract is void, and furthermore, it is void *ab initio;* it had no validity from the very beginning. [Section 2-2]

3 VALID OFFER AND ACCEPTANCE

THIS CHAPTER IS ABOUT

- ☑ **Requirement of a Contract: Valid Offer and Acceptance (Mutual Assent)**
- ☑ **Elements of a Valid Offer**
- ☑ **Termination of an Offer**
- ☑ **Offers Under the Uniform Commercial Code**
- ☑ **Elements of a Valid Acceptance**
- ☑ **Acceptance Under the Uniform Commercial Code**

3-1. Requirement of a Contract: Valid Offer and Acceptance (Mutual Assent)

A necessary element to the formation of a contract consists of an offer by one party (the *offeror*) and an acceptance of that offer by another party (the *offeree*). Several elements must be present in order to have a valid offer and a valid acceptance.

3-2. Elements of a Valid Offer

An *offer* is a proposal by an offeror to an offeree for the purpose of forming a contract. When an offer is made and acceptance is given, there is mutual assent (see Chapter 4) and if all necessary contractual elements are present, a contract is formed. The offeree is given the power to create a contract by accepting the offer in appropriate fashion. Three elements are essential to a valid offer.

A. There must be a *clear intention* to contract.

The offeror's conduct or words must indicate a genuine intention to form a contract. If the offeree knows or should know that the offeror has no intention of entering into a contract, there is no valid offer.

1. *Reasonable person standard.* The "reasonable person" standard is the objective test used to determine whether or not an offer is valid. That is, would a reasonable person believe that the offeree's acceptance of the offer would create a complete contract, and that nothing further would remain to be discussed between the parties in order to bind them both? An offer made in jest, for example, would not be a valid offer if the offeree knew or should have known that the offeror was joking.

2. *Invitation to trade.* A common exception to the element of intention is the invitation to trade. Invitations to trade include advertisements, price lists, circulars, and catalogs. Unless they are worded specifically enough to be deemed valid offers, these items are considered to be no more than invitations to negotiate. For exceptions to this rule, see Section 3-4.

EXAMPLE 3-1: Antique dealer Jones passed out a price list in which he noted that genuine eighteenth-century oak tables could be purchased in his store at prices ranging from $300 to $600. Babcock showed up at the store one day, selected an unusually fine eighteenth-century oak table, and demanded that Jones sell it to him for $300 because that was the price Jones had listed on his price list. Jones refused, saying that his price list was not a firm offer, but rather a range within which customers could expect to negotiate. Babcock sued. Did he win?

Babcock did not win. Jones's price list was not a firm offer; it was an invitation to trade within a specified price range, a solicitation of offers from potential customers.

EXAMPLE 3-2: Jack Roeder, a clothing merchant, advertised in a local newspaper that on April 6, he would sell a valuable fur coat for $1 to the first customer who arrived in the store after 9 A.M. and asked for the coat. A customer arrived on the appointed day at the indicated time and demanded to buy the coat for $1. Roeder refused to sell it, so the would-be customer sued. What happened?

The customer won because the court ruled that the wording of Roeder's advertisement made it a valid offer rather than an invitation to trade.

B. The second element is *definiteness*.

The court must be able to determine the actual intent of the parties, so the terms of the offer must be clear and complete. An offer that contains indefinite terms, like the one in Example 3-1, does not create a valid contract. Note that the courts will not rewrite an offer that is indefinite; they will simply declare it invalid.

C. The third element is *communication*.

An offer must be communicated to the offeree so that the offeree can know of its existence and be able to accept the offer.

EXAMPLE 3-3: A mail-order company sent a postcard to its best customer, Jackson, stating that the company had just received a blue sweater in which she had shown an interest. The card said that the sweater would be sent to Jackson unless she telephoned to stop the order. Jackson no longer wanted the sweater. However, the card from the mail-order company never reached her, so she did not call to cancel the order. When the sweater arrived, she refused to accept it. The company then brought suit against Jackson for breach of contract. What happened?

The court ruled that there was no contract since the offer had never been communicated to the offeree. Hence, the mail-order company lost the suit.

3-3. Termination of an Offer

An offer is not an open-ended proposal; that is, it does not remain open forever. It may be terminated either by law or by the actions of the parties involved.

A. An offer automatically terminates by law under five conditions.

1. *Specified time period.* If an offer includes a specified time period and if the offeree does not accept within that period, the offer terminates.
2. *Reasonable time.* If an offer does not include a specific time period, the offer lapses after a reasonable time has elapsed.
3. *Death or insanity.* If either the offeror or the offeree becomes insane or dies during the duration of an offer, the offer is terminated.
4. *Destruction of property.* If property that is part of an offer is destroyed, the offer is terminated.
5. *Illegality.* If the subject matter of the offer becomes illegal after the offer is made, due to enactment of a new law, the offer then becomes invalid.

B. An offer terminates by the actions of the parties involved under three conditions.

1. *Rejection of an offer.* The offeree may terminate an offer by rejecting it. A rejection is not effective until the offeror receives it through any means—mail, telegraph, telephone, messenger, or the like. Moreover, up until the time that rejection is actually received, the offeree retains the power of acceptance. This fact can be important if the offeree has a change of heart, as in the following example.

EXAMPLE 3-4: Adams offered to sell Brown 100 tons of coal for $3,000 and asked Brown to accept or reject the offer within ten days. Brown decided that the price was too high, so on the second day he mailed a rejection. On the third day, though, Brown decided that he really wanted the coal after all, so he drove over to Adams's place of business and told Adams that he accepted the offer. The mail—with the rejection letter in it—arrived two hours later on the same day. On the fourth day, however, Adams received a higher bid from Crawford, so he decided to claim that Brown's rejection terminated the original offer, and that Brown therefore had no claim on the coal. Would a court let him do this?

A court would disagree with Adams's view and remind him that a rejection is not effective until communicated to the offeror. Since Brown's acceptance came before the arrival of the rejection letter, Brown's acceptance is valid.

> Once the offeror receives a rejection, any attempt by the offeree to accept the offer will be treated as a new offer, which the original offeror can then either reject or accept.

EXAMPLE 3-5: Jones wrote Carnavale and offered to sell him a boat for $2,000. Carnavale replied that he was not interested. A week later, Carnavale telephoned Jones that he had had a change of heart and wanted to buy the boat after all. Jones refused. Did Jones have the right to refuse?

Jones had a perfect right to refuse. Carnavale had terminated Jones's original offer by rejecting it, and Carnavale's change of heart legally constituted a new offer that Carnavale was now making to Jones. Jones could accept or reject this new offer as he saw fit.

> **2.** *Counteroffer.* An offer is terminated if a counteroffer is made. A *counteroffer* is a proposal by the offeree that changes the terms of the original offer. However, if the offeree merely asks whether or not the offeror will consider some other terms, the act of asking is not a counteroffer and does not terminate the offer. The offeree can still accept the original offer.

EXAMPLE 3-6: Jones wrote Carnavale and offered to sell him a boat for $2,000. Carnavale replied that he would pay $1,800 for the boat. Jones told him that $1,800 was not enough. Carnavale then offered to accept the original terms and pay $2,000 for the boat. Jones immediately told Carnavale that he had changed his mind and did not want to sell the boat, Carnavale said, "We have a binding contract. You can't back out." Was Carnavale correct?

Carnavale was not correct because he had made a counteroffer of $1,800 for the boat. That counteroffer terminated the original offer; hence, Carnavale no longer had the power to accept the original offer of a $2,000 sale price.

EXAMPLE 3-7: Adams offered to sell Gonzales 1,000 boxes of paper plates at $5.25 per box. Gonzales told Adams that he would think about the $5.25 offer, but asked Adams if she would consider selling the plates at $5.00 per box. Adams said that she would not change the price. Can Gonzales still accept the original offer?

Gonzales can still accept the original offer. Gonzales's initial response was only an inquiry, not a counteroffer. Therefore, the original offer remained open, and Gonzales can still accept it.

> **3.** *Revocation of an Offer.* An offer can be revoked any time prior to acceptance. An offeror can revoke an unaccepted offer at any time even if the offer states that it will be open for a specified time period, except for firm offers made by merchants selling goods (see Section 3-4). If, for example, an offeror states that the offer is open for ten days, the offeror can still revoke the offer before the ten-day period is over. The revocation goes into effect when communicated to the offeree. If the offeree accepts the offer prior to revocation, then a binding contract exists.

EXAMPLE 3-8: Johnson offered to sell his camera to Simmons for $300. Johnson told Simmons that the offer would be open for ten days. After three days, however, Johnson phoned Simmons and revoked the offer. Simmons objected, contending that the offer had to remain open for ten days. Is Simmons correct?

Simmons is not correct. Johnson can revoke the offer before the end of the ten days, provided he has not received money or any other form of consideration (see Chapter 5). Therefore, Johnson has the right to revoke the offer after only three days.

> The law provides an exception for unilateral contracts. A *unilateral contract* binds the offeree to perform or refrain from performing some act, usually in return for consideration from the offeror. Strictly speaking, a unilateral contract is not considered formed (i.e., the offer is not "accepted") until the requested act is fully performed. However, in many cases it would be unfair to the offeree if the usual rule of

revocation were followed—that is, if the offeror were allowed to revoke the offer any time prior to final acceptance, especially if the offeree had already substantially performed the requested act. Therefore, most courts allow the offeror to revoke only if the offeree has not yet substantially performed the requested act. Even then, the revocation must be in good faith and not merely an attempt by the offeror to avoid payment.

EXAMPLE 3-9: Apton offered Bailey $200 to cut down ten trees located on Apton's property. Bailey immediately started cutting down the trees. After Bailey had cut down nine trees, Apton said, "I take back my offer; don't expect any payment." Can Apton revoke the offer in this manner?

Apton cannot revoke the offer because Bailey had substantially performed the requested act. Apton, therefore, cannot refuse Bailey's claim for payment, and the terms of the offer must be carried out in full.

3-4. Offers Under the Uniform Commercial Code

A. The Uniform Commercial Code (UCC) applies to contracts for the sale of goods.

Any contract for the sale of goods must conform to the UCC.

B. Several sections of the UCC differ notably from common law in their treatment of contracts.

1. *Indefiniteness.* Under Section 2-204 of the UCC, the terms of a contract will not be considered indefinite even if one or more terms are left open, provided that the parties intended to make a contract and have arranged a reasonable remedy for the indefiniteness. In other words, indefinitenes does not automatically invalidate a contract.
2. *Revocation.* Under Section 2-205 of the UCC, a firm, written offer by a merchant cannot be revoked during the time stipulated in the offer or, if no time is stipulated, until a reasonable time (but never longer than three months) has passed. Consideration is not required (see Chapter 5). A merchant's offer that is not in writing can be revoked before any stipulated time expires.

3-5. Elements of a Valid Acceptance

An *acceptance* occurs when an offeree, by appropriate action, agrees to be bound by the conditions of the offeror's proposal. Just as an offer must be absolute and unconditional in order to be valid, an acceptance also must be absolute and unconditional and must conform to the terms of the offer. As noted earlier, any acceptance that does not conform to the terms of an offer becomes a counteroffer and thereby terminates the offer.

A. In a unilateral contract, acceptance occurs by performance of the requested act.

1. *Substantial performance* of the act constitutes acceptance.
2. *Partial performance* prior to withdrawal of an offer still makes the offeror liable on the basis of a quasi contract. The offeror must pay a reasonable price for any benefits received prior to revocation.

B. Silence of the offeree does not constitute acceptance.

In general, an offeree's silence in response to an offer cannot be construed as acceptance. This will hold true even if the offeror states in the offer that the offeree's silence will be construed as acceptance. However, there are exceptions:

1. When both parties have used silence as acceptance in prior dealings, the silence of the offeree is considered acceptance of the offer. Should the offeree decide not to accept the offer, the offeree must convey rejection of the offer to the offeror.
2. When an offer has been solicited by the offeree, the offeree's silence may be interpreted as acceptance.

EXAMPLE 3-10: Hobbs sent rabbit skins to the Furcoat Company on four occasions. Each time, Furcoat accepted the skins without comment and sent Hobbs a check for them. The fifth time that Hobbs sent skins to Furcoat, the company kept the skins but sent no check. After several months, Hobbs asked for his money, but Furcoat refused to pay, claiming that the skins had never been accepted. Hobbs sued for payment for the skins. Did he win?

Hobbs won. The court held that silence on the part of Furcoat, which it had used as acceptance in four previous dealings, coupled with the retention of the skins for an extended length of time, amounted to acceptance by Furcoat of Hobbs's offer.

C. Acceptance may be determined by applying the deposited-acceptance rule.

According to the *deposited-acceptance rule*, an offer is considered accepted the moment the offeree places the acceptance into the same (or better) channel of communication as was used for the offer. The offer is accepted as soon as the acceptance leaves the control of the offeree. Note how this differs from a rejection or a revocation, both of which must be received before they are considered valid.

If the offeree does not use the specified channel of communication, the acceptance is not effective until the offeror receives it.

1. The offeror's power to revoke is terminated at the precise moment that the offeree deposits the acceptance into the specified channel of communication.

EXAMPLE 3-11: O'Reilly extended an offer by mail for Fox to buy 100 shares of stock for $100 a share. O'Reilly then changed his mind, so he wrote a note revoking the offer and sent a messenger to deliver the note to Fox. Before the messenger delivered the note, Fox placed a letter accepting the offer into an official United States Postal Service box. Did Fox complete a valid acceptance?

Since the letter of acceptance had left the control of Fox and had been placed in the same channel of communication as was used for the offer, Fox did complete a valid acceptance. Therefore, the contract was valid since an offer had been extended and accepted before it was revoked.

2. An offeror can avoid the deposited-acceptance rule by stating in the offer that an acceptance will not be effective until actually received. In addition, an offeror can specify in the offer that a certain channel of communication must be used, and that the acceptance will not be effective until it is received if a different channel is used.

3-6. Acceptance Under the Uniform Commercial Code

A. New terms put forth by the offeree are treated as an acceptance.

Under Section 2-207 of the UCC, new terms put forth by the offeree are considered proposals for additions to the contract, and in fact become part of the contract unless they are inconsistent with terms in the original offer or are rejected by the original offeror within a reasonable amount of time. A contract is still formed, but the inconsistent terms will be disregarded unless the offeror agrees to the changes. This is in contrast to contracts not regulated by the UCC, where new terms are considered a counteroffer and therefore a rejection. An exception occurs when the original offer expressly forbids new terms by limiting acceptance to the terms of the offer.

B. An offer to purchase goods is treated as a unilateral offer.

A seller can accept an offer to purchase goods either by shipping the goods or by promising to ship them. A seller who ships goods that do not conform with the terms of the offer has still accepted the offer. However, this is also a breach of contract unless the seller notifies the buyer that the shipment is being offered as an accommodation or substitution.

C. Any reasonable means of communication may be used to accept an offer in a sale-of-goods contract.

The deposited-acceptance rule still applies except that the offeree does not have to place the acceptance in the same or better channel of communication as was used for the offer.

EXAMPLE 3-12. Smith offered Brooks 100 boxes of nails for $300 and sent the offer by wire. As in prior dealings with Smith, Brooks promptly returned his acceptance by overnight mail. In the meantime, Smith decided to raise the price of his nails, and received an order from another customer to buy the nails at the higher price. He refused to sell the 100 boxes of nails to Brooks for $300. Brooks sued Smith. Did he win?

Brooks won because he replied promptly and by a reasonable means of communication; one, in fact, that he had used in prior dealings with Smith.

RAISE YOUR GRADES

Can you explain . . . ?

☑ the three elements of a valid offer
☑ the five conditions under which an offer terminates by law
☑ the two conditions under which an offer terminates by the actions of the parties involved
☑ under what conditions an offeror may or may not revoke an offer
☑ the differences between the UCC and common law regarding offers and acceptances
☑ under what conditions an acceptance is deemed valid
☑ when an offer is considered accepted under the deposited-acceptance rule
☑ the time period in which an offer can be revoked
☑ the conditions of acceptance of a unilateral contract

SUMMARY

1. A contract consists of a valid offer by one party (the offeror) and a valid acceptance of that offer by another party (the offeree).
2. An offer is a proposal by an offeror to an offeree for the purpose of forming a contract.
3. Three essential elements are necessary to create a valid offer: intention, definiteness, and communication.
4. The "reasonable person" standard is a test of intention to determine whether or not a reasonable person would believe an offer was valid.
5. A new offer is created if an offeree attempts to accept an offer after having rejected it.
6. An offeror can limit the duration of an offer.
7. The death or insanity of either party terminates the offer.
8. The destruction of offered property terminates an offer.
9. A change in the law that would make the subject matter of an offer illegal terminates the offer.
10. The rejection of an offer by an offeree terminates the offer.
11. Under common law, a counteroffer terminates an offer.
12. An offeror can revoke an offer prior to its specified time limit, except in the case of UCC-regulated firm offers.
13. A unilateral offer cannot be revoked after the offeree has substantially performed the requested act.
14. Under the UCC, a contract can be created even though the terms are indefinite provided that the parties intended to make a contract and have provided a reasonable remedy for the indefiniteness.
15. Under the UCC, a firm, written offer by a merchant cannot be withdrawn during the time stipulated in the offer or, if no time is stated, until a reasonable time has passed.
16. An acceptance occurs when an offeree, by appropriate action, agrees to be bound by the conditions of the offeror's proposal.
17. Under common law, an acceptance must conform to the terms of the offer to be valid.
18. A unilateral contract may be accepted by performing the requested act.
19. Except in certain cases, silence cannot be interpreted as an acceptance.
20. According to the deposited-acceptance rule, an offer is considered accepted as soon as the acceptance leaves the control of the offeree and enters the same (or better) channel of communication as was used for the offer.
21. An offeror's power to revoke is terminated as soon as an acceptance is deposited into the specified channel of communication.
22. Under the UCC, new terms or additions put forth by the offeree are not considered a counteroffer and may become part of the contract, with certain exceptions.

23. Under the UCC, an offer to purchase goods may be accepted by the shipment of the goods or by a promise to ship the goods.
24. Under the UCC, any reasonable means of communication may be used to accept an offer in a sale-of-goods contract.

RAPID REVIEW   Answers

True or False?

1. After a valid offer is made, the power to create a contract resides in the offeree. [Secton 3-2]	*True*	
2. An offer made in jest is not a valid offer if the offeree should have known that the offeror was joking. [Section 3-2]	*True*	
3. The courts will rewrite an offer that is indefinite in order to make the offer clear. [Section 3-2]	*False*	
4. Before an offer is deemed valid, the offeror must actually communicate the offer to the offeree. [Section 3-2]	*True*	
5. The death or insanity of the offeror terminates an offer. [Section 3-3]	*True*	
6. If an offer is extended but a law is then passed making the subject matter of that offer illegal, the offer is still valid. [Section 3-3]	*False*	
7. In general, silence by an offeree constitutes acceptance of an offer. [Section 3-5]	*False*	
8. An inquiry by an offeree about the possibility of considering other terms is legally regarded as a counteroffer. [Section 3-3]	*False*	
9. Even if an offeror extends an offer for a stated period of time, under common law, he or she may revoke the offer before the end of that period by communicating the revocation to the offeree. [Section 3-3]	*True*	
10. An offeror may revoke an offer even after the offeree has accepted it, provided the offeror has not actually received the acceptance. [Section 3-3]	*False*	
11. In an offer to create a unilateral contract, the offeror may revoke the offer even after the offeree has substantially performed the requested act, provided the revocation is made in good faith and is not merely an attempt to avoid payment. [Section 3-3]	*False*	
12. Under the UCC, a contract will not be created if any condition or term is not clearly stated within the document. [Section 3-4]	*False*	
13. After a counteroffer has been made and the original offeror has rejected it, the original offeree can still accept the original offer. [Section 3-3]	*False*	
14. In a unilateral contract, acceptance can occur when the offeree substantially performs the requested act. [Section 3-5]	*True*	
15. An offeror's power to revoke is terminated when the offeree deposits an acceptance into a specified channel of communication. [Section 3-5]	*True*	
16. An offeree's silence may be interpreted as acceptance if the offeree directly solicited the offer. [Section 3-5]	*True*	

17. Under the deposited-acceptance rule, an acceptance becomes effective upon deposit into a specified channel of communication. [Section 3-5]   *True*

18. An offeror can avoid the deposited-acceptance rule by stating in the offer that an acceptance will not be effective until actually received. [Section 3-5]   *True*

19. Under the UCC, acceptance of an offer for a sale-of-goods contract must be communicated by the same delivery channel as was used for the offer. [Section 3-6]   *False*

20. Under the UCC, an acceptance is always invalid if it contains terms in addition to or different from the terms of the offer. [Section 3-6]   *False*

SOLVED PROBLEMS

PROBLEM 3-1   Discuss the three essential elements of a legally valid offer.

Answer: The three essential elements of a legally valid offer are intention, definiteness, and communication.

First, there must be an outward showing of an intention to contract before an offer can be considered valid. The test used is whether a reasonable person would believe that acceptance of the proposal would create a complete contract and whether there would be nothing further to discuss between the parties in order to bind them both to the contract.

Second, an offer must be explicitly clear and complete, enough so that a court could determine the actual intent of the parties. The parties to the offer must make sure that the terms of the offer are definite, because the courts will declare an indefinite offer invalid.

Third, an offer must be communicated in order to satisfy the contractual requirement of mutual assent. If one party has no knowledge of the offer, there is no mutual assent and thus no contract. [Section 3-2]

PROBLEM 3-2   Under what conditions can an offeror revoke an offer, and what must the offeror do for a revocation to be effective?

Answer: An offeror may revoke an offer at any time prior to acceptance, except in the case of UCC-regulated firm offers. This is true even if the offer states that it will be open for a specified time period. However, when the offer is for a unilateral contract, the offerer may not revoke the offer after the offeree has substantially performed the requested act.

A revocation becomes effective when communicated to the offeree. If the offeree accepts the offer prior to revocation, then a binding contract exists. [Section 3-3]

PROBLEM 3-3   In what ways can an offer be terminated?

Answer: An offer may be limited to a specified time; if so, then the offer terminates when the time limit passes. If no time limit is stated, an offer terminates after a reasonable length of time. The death or insanity of either party also terminates an offer. If an offer is made for a specified item and this item is destroyed, then the offer is terminated. If some aspect of an offer becomes illegal because of the passage of a new law, the offer terminates when the law is passed. Finally, the parties themselves, through rejection, counteroffer, or revocation, may terminate an offer. [Section 3-3]

PROBLEM 3-4   In what ways does an offer governed by the UCC differ from an offer governed by common law?

Answer: Under the UCC, an offer will not fail if certain terms or conditions are indefinite, provided that both parties intended to make a contract and have arranged a reasonable remedy for the indefiniteness. Also, an offer that is in writing and that states a specified time period for acceptance cannot be revoked before this period passes or before a reasonable time period has passed if no specific time is stated. [Section 3-4]

PROBLEM 3-5   When do acceptances and rejections become legally effective?

Answer: An acceptance becomes legally effective when the offeree, by appropriate action, agrees to be bound by the terms of the offer. In a unilateral contract, acceptance may become effective by performance of the requested act. According to the deposited-acceptance rule, acceptance occurs at the moment the acceptance leaves the control of the offeree and is placed in the control of the same (or better) channel of communication as was used for the offer or the channel requested by the offeror. If an offeree does not use the proper channel, an acceptance is not effective until the offeror receives it. Under the UCC, any reasonable channel of communication may be used.

A rejection, on the other hand, must be received to be effective. It can be delivered by any means. [Sections 3-5 and 3-6]

PROBLEM 3-6   Walker, a college professor, wrote to James on May 1, offering to sell his television set to James for $100. In the letter, Walker told James that the offer would remain open until 5 P.M. on May 10. On May 5, Walker found a buyer, Henry, who was willing to pay $125, so Walker sold the set to Henry on that date. Then Walker mailed a letter to James on May 5 revoking the offer. James received the letter on May 7 and immediately wrote to Walker, stating that he accepted Walker's offer of May 1. Walker, having already sold the television set, refused to do anything. James then filed suit against Walker. What probably happened and why?

Answer: There was a judgment for Walker. Walker had the right to revoke his offer any time prior to acceptance by James, even though the specified time period had not elapsed. [Section 3-3]

PROBLEM 3-7   Consider again the situation described in Problem 3-6, but suppose Walker was a merchant engaged in the business of selling television sets. What would be the judgment?

Answer: James would win the suit in this situation. Under the UCC (2-205), a merchant who makes a firm, written offer must keep the offer open for the stipulated period of time or, if no time is stipulated, for a reasonable time. In this case the offer had to be kept open until May 10 at 5:00 P.M. [Section 3-4]

PROBLEM 3-8   Sands, an avid golfer, was performing poorly during a round of golf. He told Bell, his playing partner, "If I don't score a par on the next hole, then I'll give you $500 to throw my clubs in the lake!" On the next hole, Sands three-putted the green for a double bogey (two strokes over par). Bell immediately took Sands's clubs and threw them into the lake, telling Sands, "You owe me $500!" Could Bell recover the money from Sands?

Answer: Most likely, Bell could not recover the money. Applying the "reasonable person" standard, we could conclude that Sands's offer was made in jest and therefore was not a valid offer. [Section 3-2]

PROBLEM 3-9   Rhodes decided to add a line of garden hoses to her hardware store inventory. She wrote to the Pontiac Hose Company, stating, "Ship me 2,000 garden hoses at $3 each." Pontiac replied, "We accept your offer to purchase 2,000 hoses, but the price is now $3.25 each. The hoses will be shipped today." When the hoses arrived, Rhodes accepted them but refused to pay more than $3 per hose. Was there a valid contract between the parties?

Answer: There was a valid contract, although Rhodes only had to pay $3 per hose. Under the UCC (2-207), new terms put forth by the offeree become part of the contract *unless* they are inconsistent with the original offer. Since the new price was inconsistent with the price contained in the original offer, Rhodes only had to pay the originally stated price and could disregard the new terms. The Pontiac Hose Company could have avoided this situation by requiring that Rhodes accept or reject the new terms before shipping the merchandise. By shipping the goods, the company displayed acceptance of Rhodes' terms. [Section 3-6]

PROBLEM 3-10   Best Mix Tobacco Company sent out hundreds of catalogs advertising several blends of tobacco. Thomas received one of the catalogs, but lost it. Some time later, he found his catalog and sent a check with an order for Tropical Blend, which was listed in the catalog at $14 a pound. Best Mix returned Thomas's check and order with a letter informing him that the price was now $16 a pound. Thomas sued for breach of contract. Did he win?

Answer: Thomas did not win because catalogs, price lists, and fliers are not considered real offers. Instead, they are considered to be invitations to trade—mere invitations to open negotiations. Thus, there was no offer for Thomas to accept. [Section 3-2]

PROBLEM 3-11   Lee and White were standing outside White's house when Jackson approached and said, "Lee, I'll sell you my ticket to the ballgame this weekend for $5." Lee declined, but White said, "I'll take it." Jackson refused to sell the ticket to White. White claimed breach of contract. Was he correct?

Answer: White was not correct. Jackson made the offer to Lee, not to White. Since White had not received an offer, no contract could exist between White and Jackson. [Section 3-2]

PROBLEM 3-12   Hirsch wrote to Andrews and offered to sell Andrews a movie projector for $200. Hirsch gave Andrews ten days to accept the offer. On the fifth day, Hirsch had a fatal heart attack. When Andrews learned of the heart attack, he decided to make a claim against Hirsch's estate for the sale of the movie projector, since the offer was still open at the time of Hirsch's death. Was Andrews successful?

Answer: Andrews was not successful because an offer is automatically terminated by the death of either party. This type of termination is called a termination by law and is automatic; that is, neither party has to act in order to terminate the offer. [Section 3-3]

PROBLEM 3-13   Davidson, a merchant, telephoned Marley and offered to sell Marley a motorcycle for $750. Davidson said that Marley had three days in which to accept the offer. On the second day, Davidson telephoned Marley and revoked the offer. Marley replied that Davidson had to keep the offer open for three days since Davidson was a merchant and the offer was therefore regulated by the UCC rather than by common law. Was Marley correct?

Answer: Davidson's offer was, in fact, subject to regulation by the UCC since it involved a sale of goods; however, under the UCC, an offer is not considered "firm" unless it is in writing. While Davidson's offer was firm in all other respects, it was not in writing, so he still retained his right to revoke the offer before the time period had expired. [Section 3-4]

PROBLEM 3-14   Carpenter was concerned about the increase in vandalism in her neighborhood, so she offered a reward of $500 to any person who furnished information leading to the arrest and conviction of any vandals in her area. Notice of the reward was printed in a local newspaper on October 15. On October 17, unaware of the offer, Mason gave the police evidence that led to the arrest and conviction of a vandal. Mason later learned about the reward and tried to claim it. Is Mason entitled to the reward?

Answer: Mason is not entitled to the reward for two reasons. First, Mason did not go to the police with the intention of fulfilling the terms of the offer. Second, Mason had no knowledge of the offer. So although one of the three elements of a valid offer—definiteness—was present, the other two elements that are essential for agreement were lacking. [Section 3-2]

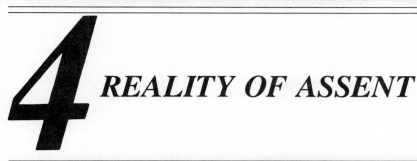

4 REALITY OF ASSENT

THIS CHAPTER IS ABOUT

☑ **The Need for Mutual Assent**
☑ **Lack of Mutual Assent Because of a Mistake**
☑ **Lack of Mutual Assent Because of Misrepresentation**
☑ **Lack of Mutual Assent Because of Duress**
☑ **Lack of Mutual Assent Because of Undue Influence**

4-1. The Need for Mutual Assent

One of the essential elements of a contract is genuine and mutual assent. *Mutual assent*—a "meeting of the minds"—is the unconditional agreement between parties to a contract. An agreement that lacks mutual assent may be void, voidable, or unenforceable. Thus, it is essential that you understand the circumstances in which mutual assent is lacking.

In general, lack of mutual assent results from the following:

• mistake
• misrepresentation
• duress
• undue influence

4-2. Lack of Mutual Assent Because of a Mistake

In contract law, a *mistake* is an erroneous belief about the existence, condition, quality, identity, or some other material fact concerning the subject matter of a contract. Some mistakes have no effect on the validity of a contract, while others render a contract void or voidable. Ordinarily, a mistake that involves an erroneous opinion or judgment, rather than an erroneous belief about a material fact, does not void a contract. A mistake can be either bilateral or unilateral.

A. Bilateral mistake

A *bilateral*, or *mutual*, *mistake* occurs when both parties to a contract err about a material fact relating to the subject matter. In such a case, the contract is void or voidable since there never was mutual assent between the parties.

EXAMPLE 4-1: Harry, a used-car dealer, purchased a foreign car for $500 and placed it for sale for $2,000 at his car lot. Janet saw the car and thought it was a collector's item worth at least $10,000, so she paid Harry the $2,000 for the car. After the sale, Harry learned that the car, although not a collector's item as Janet had thought, was worth $3,000. Harry felt that because both he and Janet were mistaken about the car's value, the contract is void. Is he correct?

Harry is not correct. Janet and Harry were both mistaken, but they were mistaken about the car's *value*, and a mistake that involves an opinion of value or quality rather than a material *fact* does not ordinarily void a contract.

B. Unilateral mistake

A *unilateral mistake* is one made by only one party to the contract and does not generally make the contract voidable.

1. *Reasonable person standard.* In determining whether a unilateral mistake results in a voidable contract, the courts are guided by the "reasonable person" standard; that is, if someone mistakenly believes a material fact about the subject matter that a reasonable person would not believe, then he or she has no grounds for voiding the contract. (The reasonable person standard was discussed in Chapter 3.)
2. *Palpable unilateral mistake.* Particularly in business situations, when a unilateral mistake is made and the other party knows or should have known about it, the contract can be voidable. This kind of unilateral mistake is sometimes called a *palpable unilateral mistake.* When such mistakes occur, the contract may be judged voidable because the courts will not permit the party who realizes, or should realize, the mistake to take unfair advantage of the party who made the mistake.

EXAMPLE 4-2: Clarke secured bids from several contractors for construction of a shopping center. Most of the bids ranged from $24 million to $30 million. Karson submitted a bid of $10 million, by far the lowest bid. Clarke awarded the contract to Karson. Karson then realized that he had failed to include the cost of solar heating panels when he calculated his bid. Karson believed that because of his mistake, the contract was voidable and therefore he should be released from the agreement. Is he correct?

In this case, Karson is correct. Ordinarily, a unilateral mistake does not make a contract voidable. However, Karson's mistake resulted in a bid that was so low that Clarke should have realized a mistake had been made. Thus, Karson committed a palpable unilateral mistake, and the contract is voidable.

4-3. Lack of Mutual Assent Because of Misrepresentation

In contract law there are two kinds of misrepresentation. The first is *fraud,* which is the knowing and intentional or reckless misrepresentation of the subject matter of a contract. The second is *innocent misrepresentation,* which is unknowing and unintentional.

A. Four elements generally must be present for a misrepresentation to be fraudulent.

1. *Intentional misrepresentation.* The party committing the misrepresentation must do so knowingly; this is sometimes called *scienter.*
2. *Misrepresentation of a material fact.* The misrepresentation must be of a material fact rather than just a false opinion. Often, however, the courts have ruled that false opinions are fraudulent when offered by persons considered experts in their field. This is also the case in a *fiduciary relationship;* that is, a relationship in which one party has a special reason to believe the opinion of the other party because he or she is in a position of trust or confidence. Examples of fiduciary relationships are lawyer and client, physician and patient, and financial advisor and client.

   It is not fraudulent for a salesperson to engage in "puffing," which is nothing more than a general kind of bragging about the subject matter.

EXAMPLE 4-3: Harry, a horse breeder, in an attempt to get Betty to buy a horse, told her, "This horse is one of the finest animals I have ever bred." Betty later found out that Harry had bred several horses of better lineage and ability, so she sued to void the contract on grounds that she had been defrauded. Is she correct?

Betty is not correct. Harry was merely "puffing," or bragging about, the horse, and Betty should have realized this.

3. *Sole reliance on misrepresentation.* The party to whom the misrepresentation was made must rely solely on it. If the innocent party did not or should not justifiably rely on the misrepresentation, then no fraud has occurred.
4. *Injury due to misrepresentation.* The party to whom the misrepresentation was made must be injured by his or her reliance on the misrepresented fact.

EXAMPLE 4-4: Cane sold Williams an abandoned mine by telling him that nickel had been discovered in the mine. In reality, Cane knew that the mine contained no nickel. Williams later learned of this, but during the first day of mining, he struck gold. Is the contract void because of fraudulent misrepresentation?

The contract is not void by fraudulent misrepresentation because Williams was not injured by the misrepresentation.

B. Silence or concealment can also constitute fraud.

The rules of fraud may apply if one party has failed to disclose information so important that with it, there would have been no contract, or if one party has taken active steps to prevent an innocent party from discovering the truth about the subject matter. An agreement in which one party reveals only half-truths about the subject matter may also constitute fraud.

EXAMPLE 4-5: Jason owned a race horse that had won several important races. In its last race, however, the horse had injured its leg. Jason had a veterinarian examine the horse's leg and was told that the horse would never again be able to race. Knowing that Paul was in the market for a race horse, Jason told him that the horse was a fine, strong animal with an outstanding racing record. Paul purchased the horse, but then learned of its injury. He sued on the grounds that the sale was fraudulent. Did he win?

Paul won the suit. Jason had withheld information that, had it been disclosed, would have kept Paul from buying the horse.

C. An innocent misrepresentation occurs when knowledge of the misrepresentation is lacking.

Like a fraudulent misrepresentation, an innocent misrepresentation is a false statement of fact that the victim relies on as being true. However, a party committing an innocent misrepresentation does so unknowingly and without intending to deceive.

D. Remedies for fraud differ from remedies for innocent misrepresentation.

1. A victim of fraud can either ask that the contract be rescinded or sue for damages.
2. A victim of innocent misrepresentation can ask only that the court rescind, or cancel, the contract. When a contract is rescinded, both parties are restored to their original, precontract state, and any benefits either has received are returned.

EXAMPLE 4-6: Patricia inherited her grandmother's engagement ring. Her grandmother once told her that the diamond in the ring was genuine and very valuable. Later Patricia needed money, so she sold the ring to John for $500, based on her belief that the diamond was genuine. However, John had the ring appraised and discovered that the diamond was an imitation and worth far less than $500. John sued for damages. Did he win?

John did not win damages because Patricia's grandmother had told her that the diamond was real, and Patricia had innocently misrepresented it as such to John. John was able to have the contract rescinded; he returned the ring to Patricia and she refunded his money.

4-4. Lack of Mutual Assent Because of Duress

Duress is the exercise of a threat that deprives a person of free will and forces that person to enter into a contract that he or she would not otherwise have entered into. One who enters a contract under duress can have the contract voided because mutual assent is lacking.

A. The courts apply a subjective test to determine if duress has occurred.

In cases involving duress, the courts seek to determine the following: Has the victim been deprived of free will and has this caused the victim to enter the contract involuntarily? The courts must also consider the victim's background, including the victim's physical and mental health, education, and occupation. The "reasonable person" standard does not apply in cases of duress.

B. Duress results from one of three kinds of threat.

1. Threat of physical harm to one's person, family, or property
2. Threat of criminal prosecution
3. Threat of economic loss

EXAMPLE 4-7: Roberts, the owner of a cargo ship, refused to unload 100 tons of goods belonging to Johnson. Roberts told Johnson that the goods would be kept on board until Johnson signed a contract giving Roberts the exclusive right to ship Johnson's goods for 20 years. Johnson signed because he needed the goods to meet business commitments. Later Johnson sued to have the contract voided, claiming that he had signed the contract under duress. Did he win?

Johnson won. He had signed the contract under threat of economic loss.

C. The threat of a civil suit is generally not considered duress for two reasons.

   1. The person who threatens the suit may merely be exercising a legal right.
   2. The person who is threatened with a civil suit can always defend against the suit.

4-5. Lack of Mutual Assent Because of Undue Influence

Undue influence occurs in unusually close or confidential relationships when a person in a position of trust coerces another person into entering a contract. Examples of confidential relationships are parent and child, guardian and ward, attorney and client, and doctor and patient. If undue influence is used to obtain a contract agreement, then mutual assent is lacking and the contract is voidable.

The same subjective test that is used to determine duress is also used to determine undue influence; that is, has the victim been deprived of free will and has this caused the victim to enter the contract involuntarily?

EXAMPLE 4-8: Attorney Douglas convinced Simpson, a 90-year-old client, that she was no longer capable of handling her own financial affairs and advised her to grant him the right to act on her behalf. Douglas persuaded Simpson to pay him an exorbitant fee for his services. After they made the agreement, Simpson sued Douglas, claiming undue influence. Did she win?

Simpson won. Douglas used his position of trust to coerce Simpson into making the agreement and therefore had exerted undue influence over her.

RAISE YOUR GRADES

Can you explain . . . ?

☑ the difference between a bilateral mistake and a unilateral mistake
☑ the difference between fraud and innocent misrepresentation
☑ the kinds of threat that may result in duress
☑ why the threat of a civil suit is not generally considered duress
☑ the types of relationships in which undue influence usually occurs

SUMMARY

   1. Mutual assent is the unconditional agreement between parties to a contract.
   2. In contract law, a mistake is an erroneous belief about a material fact or facts concerning the subject matter of a contract.
   3. Mistakes can be either bilateral (mutual) or unilateral. A bilateral mistake is one made by both parties and results in the contract being void or voidable. A unilateral mistake is one made by only one party and usually does not cause the contract to be voidable.
   4. A palpable unilateral mistake occurs when one party knows or should know that the other party has made a mistake. In these cases, a contract will not be binding on the mistaken party.
   5. In contract law there are two kinds of misrepresentation: fraud and innocent misrepresentation.
   6. Fraud is the knowing or intentional misrepresentation of a material fact that is relied upon by and causes injury to another party. Silence, concealment, and half-truths also may constitute fraud. In some cases, false opinions are fraudulent when offered by persons considered experts in their field.
   7. An innocent misrepresentation has all the elements of a fraudulent misrepresentation except that knowledge of the misrepresentation is lacking.

8. A victim of fraud can either ask that a contract be rescinded or sue for damages, whereas a victim of innocent misrepresentation can ask only that the court rescind the contract.
9. Duress is the exercise of a threat that deprives a person of free will and forces that person to enter into a contract that he or she would not otherwise have entered into.
10. Duress may result from the threat of physical harm, criminal prosecution, or economic loss. The threat of a civil suit is not generally considered duress.
11. Undue influence occurs in unusually close or confidential relationships when a person in a position of trust coerces another person into entering a contract.

RAPID REVIEW   Answers

True or False?

1.	A mistake involving an erroneous opinion or judgment can usually void a contract. [Section 4-2]	*False*
2.	A "palpable" unilateral mistake occurs when a reasonable person should have known that a mistake was made by the other party. [Section 4-2]	*True*
3.	All the following are elements of fraud: unintentional misrepresentation of a material fact; failure to disclose a fact that would cause someone not to enter a contract; justifiable reliance by the innocent party on the misrepresentation; injury to the innocent party as a result of relying on the misrepresentation. [Section 4-3]	*False*
4.	Nondisclosure or concealment of a fact never constitutes fraud. [Section 4-3]	*False*
5.	A victim of innocent misrepresentation can sue for damages. [Section 4-3]	*False*
6.	If one party makes an innocent misrepresentation of fact and gets another party to enter into a contract, the *first* party can rescind the contract. [Section 4-3]	*False*
7.	The threat of a civil suit is generally considered duress. [Section 4-4]	*False*
8.	To decide whether a person signed a contract under duress, the courts apply the "reasonable person" standard. [Section 4-4]	*False*
9.	If undue infuence is used to obtain a contract agreement, the contract is voidable. [Section 4-5]	*True*
10.	The same subjective test that is used to determine duress is also used to determine undue infuence. [Section 4-5]	*True*

SOLVED PROBLEMS

PROBLEM 4-1   Compare and contrast a bilateral mistake and a unilateral mistake in contract law, and describe the remedy for each.

Answer: A bilateral mistake occurs when both parties to a contract are mistaken as to one or more material facts regarding the subject matter of the contract. A mistake must occur with regard to a material fact and not simply because an erroneous opinion, especially one about the quality or value of an object, was given. When a bilateral mistake has occurred, the contract is void since there never was mutual assent between the parties.

A unilateral mistake occurs when only one party to a contract is in error about some material fact relating to the subject matter of the contract. Generally, a unilateral mistake does not make a contract voidable. The courts apply the "reasonable person" standard in determining whether a unilateral mistake results in a voidable contract. This means that if someone mistakenly believes a material fact about the subject matter that any reasonable person would not believe, then the contract is still valid. Sometimes, though, a contract in which there is a unilateral mistake is set aside. This usually occurs in business situations where one party has made a mistake and the other party realizes, or should realize, that a mistake has been made. A mistake of this type is called a "palpable" unilateral mistake. When such mistakes occur, the courts will not permit the party who realizes, or should realize, the mistake to take unfair advantage of the party who made the mistake. [Section 4-2]

PROBLEM 4-2   Describe the four elements that must be present for a contract to be fraudulent, and tell how fraud differs from innocent misrepresentation.

Answer: A contract is formed fraudulently (1) when there has been a false representation of a material fact relating to the subject matter of the contract, (2) when one party misrepresented the material fact knowingly or recklessly and with the intent to deceive the other party, (3) when the innocent party has justifiably relied on the misrepresentation, and (4) when the innocent party has suffered an injury as a result of having relied on the misrepresentation. Concealment, silence, and half-truths also may be considered fraudulent if there was intent to deceive.

Innocent misrepresentation involves all of the above elements except that the party that misrepresents a fact does so unintentionally.

Fraud also differs from innocent misrepresentation in the type of remedy that is afforded the injured party. In innocent misrepresentation, the injured party can ask to have the contract rescinded, whereas in a fraud misrepresentation, the injured party can either ask for rescission or can sue for damages. [Section 4-3]

PROBLEM 4-3   Compare and contrast contracts formed as a result of duress and undue influence.

Answer: Both duress and undue influence are similar in that they are forms of coercion that cause one party to enter a contract involuntarily or because his or her free will has been overcome. In both cases, the injured party may ask that the contract be rescinded.

In cases of duress, the victim becomes party to a contract because he or she has been threatened in one of several ways. The focus is on the fear felt by the victim. Duress might consist of a threat of physical harm, a threat of economic loss, or a threat of criminal prosecution. Even if a crime has been committed, a person cannot use the threat of criminal prosecution in order to pressure someone into signing a contract that he or she would not otherwise sign. The threat of a civil suit does not constitute duress, however, since the threatened party can always defend against the suit and also because the person threatening to sue may merely be exercising a legal right.

Undue influence is similar to duress, but it is more subtle and lacks the element of threat. The focus is on the feelings of trust the victim has toward the other party. In undue influence, one party who is in a special position of trust in relation to another party coerces that party into signing a contract. Special positions of trust include fiduciary relationships where one party would normally be expected to rely on the advice and opinions of another party; examples are the professional bond that exists between an attorney and client or a physician and patient. A personal relationship of trust might be between a parent and a young child, a guardian and a child, or even between an elderly parent who was unduly influenced by an adult child. [Sections 4-4 and 4-5]

PROBLEM 4-4   Thompkins decided to sell his small farm. Ten days later he negotiated a deal with Williams in which both parties agreed that Williams would purchase the land, including all mineral and water rights, for $10,000 to be paid upon delivery of the deed. The deal was closed when Thompkins delivered the deed to Williams and Williams then paid the $10,000 to Thompkins. A year later Williams allowed a geology class from the local university to make a geological survey of her land for their class project. While performing their tests, the students determined that a large coal deposit lay under the land, and possibly an accompanying natural-gas reserve. Williams contacted a major oil company, which agreed to lease the gas rights and hold an option to mine the coal for $20,000 a month plus 2 percent of all profits from extracted minerals and gas. Thompkins heard about the deal and felt cheated, so he brought suit to rescind the contract, claiming that a bilateral mistake had been made regarding the value of the property. Did he win?

Answer: Thompkins did not win. A bilateral mistake that involves an erroneous opinion or judgment, particularly about value or quality, does not ordinarily void a contract and is not cause for rescission. [Section 4-2]

PROBLEM 4-5   Hank, a limited partner in Wildcat Oil Drilling Company, induced Charles to buy his interest in the partnership. Hank told Charles that Wildcat had 14 producing wells, owned leases on 1,400 acres of land that had been rated AAA for gas production by a well-known geologist, and had 37 percent return on investment for each limited partner during the previous year. In reality, Wildcat had only one producing well, owned oil leases to 800 acres of land that had not been rated for gas production, and had less than a 5 percent return on investment for each partner during the previous year. When Charles discovered the true state of Wildcat's affairs, he sued to have his contract rescinded. Did he win?

Answer: Charles won. This is a clear case of fraud by Hank. Hank either knowingly misrepresented Wildcat's financial position or he should have known, since as a partner he had access to the company's records. Furthermore, Charles relied on Hank's statements and was subsequently injured as a result. Thus, all of the requirements of fraud were met. The contract would be rescinded by a court at Charles's option, or Charles could sue for damages. [Section 4-3]

PROBLEM 4-6   Sally, an experienced horse trainer, went to Wayne's ranch to purchase a horse. After looking at Wayne's horses, Sally found one that she felt would make a good race horse. She examined the horse but failed to notice that its leg joints were swollen. Wayne told her that the horse was a strong, healthy animal and a fine runner. Sally bought the horse and began training it for racing. She soon noticed, however, that the horse seemed to be in pain whenever it ran. Upon closer examination, she realized that the horse had arthritis in its leg joints and would never make a good race horse. Sally sued Wayne to have the contract rescinded, claiming fraud. What happened?

Answer: The court probably would not rescind this contract because one of the four elements of fraud was missing. It is true that Wayne knowingly misled Sally about material facts relating to the horse, and that Sally was injured because of his misrepresentation. However, as an experienced horse trainer, Sally could not claim to have relied solely on Wayne's misrepresentation in buying the horse. Justifiable reliance is the element of fraud that is missing from this contract, and a court probably would not rescind it. [Section 4-3]

PROBLEM 4-7   Sally is an accountant who wanted to buy a horse so that she could learn to compete in jumping contests at local horse shows. Sally went to Wayne's ranch and asked Wayne to recommend a good jumping horse. Wayne showed her a horse that he said was an excellent jumper and was in fine health. Sally bought the horse but was later told by her riding instructor that the horse had arthritis and would not be a suitable jumper. Sally sued Wayne to have the contract rescinded, claiming fraud. What happened?

Answer: The court rescinded the contract. In this case, unlike the one in Problem 4-6, Sally was not an experienced horse trainer and thus had to rely solely on Wayne's statements about the horse's condition. Wayne knowingly misled Sally about the condition of the horse, and she was injured as a result of his misrepresentation. [Section 4-3]

PROBLEM 4-8   Peter decided to buy a car from Joe's Used Cars. To be sure that he purchased a car that was in good working order, Peter asked Don, a mechanic, to go with him and help him select a car. Joe showed Peter several cars, which Don then inspected. Don chose a brown sedan, telling Peter that it was the best car on the lot and was in perfect condition. Peter bought the car, but the next day he discovered oil seeping from a crack in the engine. Peter sued Joe to have the contract rescinded. Did he win?

Answer: Peter did not win. In making the purchase, Peter relied on Don's, not Joe's advice. Thus he cannot claim that Joe defrauded him because the element of justifiable reliance is missing. For a contract to be fraudulent, all elements of fraud must have occurred between the parties to the contract. Peter might be able to sue Don for giving a false opinion, since in some circumstances, the courts will hold that a false opinion offered by an expert is fraudulent. [Section 4-3]

PROBLEM 4-9   Martinez, a contractor, was awarded a contract to build two movie theaters. One theater was to be completed by March 18, the date of a scheduled movie premiere. The other theater was to be built several months later. The contract stipulated that severe penalties would be assessed against Martinez should he fail to complete the theaters on schedule. Martinez awarded a subcontract to Duval to supply 500 seats for the first theater. Several weeks later, Duval learned of Martinez's plans to build the second theater. On March 14, Duval told Martinez that he wanted to supply the seats for the second theater. Martinez replied that he was not yet ready to make a decision about seats for that theater. Duval then told Martinez that he would not supply seats for the first theater unless Martinez agreed to give him a contract to supply seats for the second theater. Martinez checked with other suppliers but found none that could provide seats for the first theater in time for its scheduled opening. Martinez then agreed to award a subcontract to Duval to provide seats for the second theater. After the first theater was completed, Martinez sued to have the second contract voided. On what grounds did he base his suit? Did he win?

Answer: Martinez based his suit on economic duress, claiming that he had been forced to sign the second subcontract in order to meet his commitments on the first theater and thus avoid being penalized. The circumstances clearly support his contention, showing that Martinez signed the second subcontract against his will. Martinez won the suit, and the second subcontract was voided. [Section 4-4]

PROBLEM 4-10   Murdock owned a large collection of guns, including two pistols from the Revolutionary War. One of the pistols had been completely restored, while the other still required much work. Murdock decided to sell the second pistol and mentioned this to Hardy, another gun collector. Hardy had never seen this pistol but had seen the restored one; he did not know that Murdock owned two such pistols. Murdock offered the pistol to Hardy for $500. Hardy accepted, thinking he was purchasing the restored pistol. When Murdock delivered the gun, Hardy refused to accept it and demanded that Murdock deliver the other pistol. Murdock refused. Hardy then sued Murdock, claiming they had an enforceable contract. Is he correct?

Answer: Hardy is not correct. Both Hardy and Murdock were mistaken as to the identity of the subject matter. Contracts involving a bilateral (mutual) mistake of material fact are void. [Section 4-2]

PROBLEM 4-11   Lee owned a large fishing boat equipped with sonar, radar, and other expensive electronic equipment. While deep-sea fishing, Lee ran into a sudden squall and his boat capsized. Lee was left clinging to the overturned hull, which was drifting out to sea. Twelve hours later, Flynn, a salvage operator who happened to be working in the area, spotted Lee and the boat. Flynn offered to rescue Lee and tow his boat to shore if Lee promised to turn over to Flynn all salvage rights to Lee's boat. Lee agreed to Flynn's offer. Back on shore, Lee offered to reward Flynn for rescuing him but refused to grant Flynn salvage rights to the boat. Flynn sued Lee for the salvage rights, claiming that they had a valid contract. Lee countersued, claiming that he had been forced into the agreement under duress. Who is correct?

Answer: Lee is correct. At the time of the rescue, Lee had seen Flynn's offer as the only way to save his life, a situation that constitutes physical duress. Flynn had taken advantage of Lee's predicament in order to extract the agreement from him. Thus, Lee had been deprived of free will in agreeing to the offer, and the agreement is void. [Section 4-4]

PROBLEM 4-12   Lavalle purchased some video cassettes from a distributor to sell in her store, Video City. Cabot, another distributor, also tried to sell video cassettes to Lavalle. Lavalle declined to purchase cassettes from Cabot because his prices were too high. While looking over Lavalle's stock of cassettes, Cabot noticed that some had been illegally duplicated, or "pirated." Cabot mentioned this to Lavalle, who knew nothing about it. Cabot then threatened to have Lavalle arrested unless she signed a contract to purchase all of her video cassettes solely from Cabot. Lavalle signed, but later changed her mind and sought to void the contract. Can she do this? If so, on what grounds?

Answer: Lavalle can sue to have the contract voided on the ground that she signed under duress induced by the threat of criminal prosecution. Cabot's threat deprived Lavalle of her free will and forced her to enter the contract involuntarily. Note that threats of criminal prosecution are treated differently from threats of civil action. [Section 4-4]

PROBLEM 4-13 Norwood, an 83-year-old man in ill health, received a substantial inheritance from his wife upon her death. On hearing of the inheritance, Stockman, Norwood's nephew who for years had looked after Norwood and his wife, convinced Norwood that he was no longer capable of handling his own affairs. At Stockman's considerable urging, Norwood agreed to turn over control of his finances to Stockman. After signing the agreement, Norwood learned that Stockman was using money from the inheritance for his own purposes and was exacting a large fee for managing Norwood's financial affairs. Norwood asked Stockman to return control of his finances to him. Stockman refused, saying they had a contract. Norwood sued to void the contract on the ground that Stockman had exerted undue influence over him. Stockman contended that Norwood signed of his own free will. Who is correct?

Answer: Norwood is correct. Stockman used his position of trust to take advantage of Norwood and coerce him into the agreement. In this way Stockman exerted undue influence over Norwood, which in effect deprived Norwood of his free will. [Section 4-5]

PROBLEM 4-14 Arnie, owner of Arnie's Auto Repair Shop, ordered a compressor from A-1 Equipment Supply. The compressor arrived as ordered. However, Arnie realized that the compressor, though in perfect working order, did not produce enough air pressure to meet the needs of his auto shop. Arnie took the compressor back to A-1 and demanded that they return his money. A-1 refused, so Arnie brought suit. Did he win?

Answer: Arnie lost the suit. A-1 did not misrepresent the compressor to Arnie; rather, Arnie made a mistake when he chose that particular model. In cases involving a unilateral mistake, the mistaken party generally has no grounds for voiding the contract. [Section 4-2]

PROBLEM 4-15 Crawford promised to buy a camper from Doherty. Several weeks later, Crawford changed her mind. Doherty, who had already made arrangements for the sale, threatened to sue if Crawford did not sign a contract to complete the sale. Crawford signed, but then she sued to have the contract voided, claiming that she had signed under duress. Is she correct?

Answer: Crawford is not correct. The threat of a civil suit is not generally considered duress. There are two reasons for this: (1) the person who threatens the suit may merely be exercising a legal right, and (2) the person who is threatened with a civil suit can always defend against the suit. Thus, Doherty's threat to sue Crawford did not constitute duress. [Section 4-4]

5 CONSIDERATION

THIS CHAPTER IS ABOUT

☑ **Definition of Consideration**
☑ **Situations Where No Consideration Exists**
☑ **Contracts That Are Enforceable Without Consideration**
☑ **Consideration Under the Uniform Commercial Code**

5-1. Definition of Consideration

Consideration is the price, cause, motive, or influence that induces a party to enter into a contract. It is something of value that is given in exchange for a promise. Under the terms of that promise, usually each party gets something—a benefit—and in return, each party gives up something—a detriment. In general, consideration is required for a contract to be enforceable.

A. A legal benefit or detriment need not be tangible.

A legal benefit or detriment need not involve cash, property, service, or any other tangible asset. In some cases, it may be nothing more than a promise to give up or take on a legal obligation that one would not otherwise relinquish or assume.

EXAMPLE 5-1: Donald promised his brother Allen that he would reimburse all of Allen's tuition if Allen would attend the state university and major in commerce. Donald hoped that Allen would subsequently join the family computer-software business. Allen attended the university and took the degree in commerce. In the meantime, however, Donald's business suffered a downturn, and Donald, no longer wishing to hire his brother, refused to reimburse the tuition. Allen sued, claiming that there had been consideration and therefore an enforceable contract. What happened?

Allen won the suit. Allen, to his legal if not actual detriment, had surrendered his right to choose a university and a field of study. In return, he expected to receive the legal benefit of having his brother reimburse his tuition. Donald's legal benefit was choosing his brother's university and field of study; his detriment was incurring the bill for tuition. Whether or not the family business did well had no bearing on the terms of the contract.

B. Legal benefits are assignable to a third party.

In general, a person who is not a party to a contract has no legal right to receive a benefit. An exception exists, however, if the parties enter a contract with the *intent* of benefiting a third party. This third-party beneficiary can enforce the contract in court.

EXAMPLE 5-2: For fifteen years, Collier, a sea captain, had traveled back and forth to the Far East for Brown, who made a fortune selling the goods that Collier brought back. One day Collier decided to retire. Brown told Collier that if he would make one more trip, Brown would reward him by paying $100 a month to each of his two daughters for as long as they lived. Collier accepted the offer and made the final voyage. Brown paid the $100 a month to Collier's two daughters during Collier's lifetime. After Collier's death, however, Brown suspended payments to the last living daughter. She sued to reinstate the payments and to obtain the back payments she had not received. Did she win?

The court awarded the back payments to the daughter and insisted that Brown resume paying her $100 a month for the rest of her life. It ruled that Collier had carried out his part of the contract—to his legal detriment—by making the final voyage, and that Brown had received the benefits of that voyage. Brown, therefore, had to carry out his part of the mutual consideration, even though it involved a third party.

C. Consideration need not involve equal value.

The courts usually do not evaluate the adequacy or equality of consideration, but only whether consideration exists. An exception occurs, however, when the free will of one of the parties is overborne, or when one party receives consideration grossly and obviously disproportionate to that received by the other party.

5-2. Situations Where No Consideration Exists

A. Preexisting obligations are not consideration.

If a party to a contract does or refrains from doing something he or she is already bound to do or not to do, there is no legal detriment and hence, no consideration.

EXAMPLE 5-3: Murray, a shopping-center developer, needed a shopping center completed and ready to open by a particular date. Fletcher, the head of the construction company that was building the shopping center, informed Murray that building costs had risen so much that he could not complete the work by the date stated in the contract unless he was paid an extra $10,000. Murray agreed to pay the money, but only if the work was completed on schedule. Fletcher finished on time, but Murray refused to pay the bonus. Fletcher sued to enforce the contract. What happened?

Fletcher lost the case because he did only what he had promised to do and was in fact obligated to do under the terms of the original contract. Murray did not owe him the bonus. Had Murray offered to pay Fletcher a bonus to finish the project at an earlier date than the one stated in the contract, Fletcher would have won the case on grounds that the contract had been modified and that he had taken on a new obligation.

B. The preexisting obligation rule applies to debts in special ways.

1. *Payment in a manner not prescribed.* The payment of a debt in a manner or form different from that prescribed in the debt agreement may amount to consideration. The reason is that the revised manner or form of the payment may significantly alter the debtor's position and/or obligation. Some examples:

   • early payment of the debt
   • partial payment along with something else of value to make up the balance of the debt

2. *Undisputed debts.* For an *undisputed debt*, offering or even actually making partial timely payment is not valid consideration. The reason is that the debtor already owes the entire amount of the debt and thus suffers no additional legal detriment by offering partial timely payment.

3. *Disputed debts.* For a *disputed debt*, partial payment does constitute consideration if made in return for the creditor's promise to forget the balance of the debt. Courts emphasize that the dispute must be genuine.

EXAMPLE 5-4: Wiley, a grocer, contracted to buy 100 cases of grade A tomatoes from Rizzuto, a produce wholesaler. According to the terms of the contract, Wiley was to pay 50 percent of the amount upon signing, 30 percent upon receiving the tomatoes, and 20 percent one month after receipt. When the tomatoes were delivered, Wiley noticed that some of the crates appeared to contain grade B tomatoes. After inspecting the shipment, Rizzuto agreed that some of the tomatoes were grade B. Wiley offered to accept and pay for the shipment if Rizzuto would forgo the final payment that was due a month later. Rizzuto accepted this offer, but later sued Wiley for failure to make the final payment. What happened?

Wiley did not have to make the final payment. He had in good faith disputed the quality of the tomatoes he received, so the partial payment he offered Rizzuto—and which Rizzuto accepted—constituted consideration for a disputed debt.

C. Past benefits are not consideration for a present contract.

A party who makes a promise in return for benefits that have already been supplied has not received adequate consideration. The basic nature of consideration requires a bargained-for exchange, so a performance that has already occurred cannot be bargained for in a present contract.

EXAMPLE 5-5: Klein told Gilman, "Because you helped me paint my house last week, I will pay you $100." Gilman quickly agreed, and demanded payment. Klein replied that he had changed his mind. Gilman sued Klein for $100 for his services in painting the house. Did he win?

Gilman did not win. Klein owed Gilman nothing, since Gilman had already painted the house at the time that Klein offered him $100. There was no bargained-for consideration.

D. Illusory promises are not consideration.

1. An *illusory promise* is one in which the promisor does not actually promise to do anything. There is no consideration, since the promisor has offered to perform only if he or she wants to do so but is not under any obligation to do so.

EXAMPLE 5-6: Williams, the owner of a craft boutique, spotted Walker's hand-carved bookends at a crafts fair. She told Walker that the bookends were just what she was looking for, and promised to buy as many as she could for her boutique. After the fair, Walker sent Williams his entire stock of bookends. Williams refused the shipment, saying that she had never ordered the bookends. Walker sued, claiming that Williams had made a contract with him. Did he win?

Walker did not win. Williams's promise to buy as many bookends "as she could" was not consideration, since she had promised to perform only at her own discretion. Thus, she had made an illusory promise and was under no obligation to purchase the bookends from Walker since there was no contract.

2. Some contracts appear to consist of illusory promises but in fact, do not. All of the following contracts are valid:
   - *output contract*, in which one party agrees to either sell or purchase the other party's entire production.
   - *requirements contract*, in which one buyer agrees to buy all that he or she needs of a certain product from a seller.
   - *exclusive dealing contract*, in which two parties (a seller and a buyer) agree to deal exclusively with one another with regard to a certain product.

   Each of these contracts involves mutual obligation and, therefore, consideration.

EXAMPLE 5-7: Steuben, who owns a company that manufactures washing machines, agreed to sell his entire stock to the At Ease Hardware chain. Steuben was then offered a better price by a discount hardware chain, so he sold that chain 100 machines. When At Ease Hardware learned of the sale, they sued Steuben for breach of contract, claiming they had an output contract with Steuben that limited his right to sell to anyone else. What happened?

The court ruled in favor of At Ease Hardware. Steuben had agreed to sell his entire stock (output) to At Ease, an agreement that constitutes an output contract.

E. A gift is not consideration.

A gift is not consideration even if the recipient must take certain steps or make certain arrangements in order to receive it. There is consideration, however, when an action is requested by the promisor of the gift, and both the promisor and the promisee agree that the action is the bargained-for price of the agreement.

EXAMPLE 5-8: Howard wanted to finance his daughter Zelda's education by giving her some stocks, which she could then use to pay her tuition. He gave Zelda $40,000 worth of stocks, and in return she paid him $1. Did they form a legal contract?

Although Howard and Zelda appeared to form a contract since each seemingly had obtained a benefit from the agreement, a court would probably find that Howard's real intention was to give Zelda a gift, and thus there was no consideration involved.

5-3. Contracts That Are Enforceable Without Consideration

In some special situations, promises are binding even though they are not supported by consideration.

A. Under the doctrine of promissory estoppel, a contract is valid even though consideration is lacking.

Three elements are necessary in order to apply the *doctrine of promissory estoppel:*

1. The promise must be one that the promisor knew or should have known the promisee would rely on.
2. The promisee must have acted on that promise.
3. The promisee must have suffered financial injury as a result of acting on that promise.

EXAMPLE 5-9: Ralph promised that one day he would sell his farm to his son Philip. Relying on that promise, Philip built a house on his father's land. At a later date, however, Ralph received a lucrative offer from a corporation to build a factory on his property, so he decided to sell the farm to the corporation. Philip threatened to sue his father for breach of contract, but Ralph claimed that there was no mutual consideration. Who would win this suit?

Philip would win because he believed his father's promise to sell him the farm, acted on it, and was financially injured as a result of his reliance on the promise (he lost the money he had put into his house). Thus, the courts would apply the doctrine of promissory estoppel and rule that no consideration is required in this case.

B. A promise to pay a debt discharged by bankruptcy is valid without consideration.

A bankruptcy normally terminates all the debts of a party. However, if the party then agrees in writing to pay the debt, even though that party receives nothing in exchange for this promise, the courts will still enforce the contract. A similar situation arises when a new written promise has been made to repay a debt after the statute of limitations has run out. The contract is enforceable without consideration.

C. Contracts under seal are valid without consideration.

A *contract under seal* is one in which the promisor affixes a seal on the written contract. Under common law, the use of a seal precludes the requirement for consideration. Most states, however, have abolished the doctrine of contracts under seal.

5-4. Consideration Under the Uniform Commercial Code

Under the UCC, some sale-of-goods contracts that would otherwise fail for lack of consideration are enforceable.

A. A claim or breach can be settled without consideration.

If the aggrieved party agrees in writing to renounce or waive any further claim, then the dispute can thus be settled without consideration (UCC Section 1-107).

EXAMPLE 5-10: Greenfields, a grocer, agreed to buy 100 watermelons from Short, a produce wholesaler. Short was able to deliver only 50 melons, so she asked Greenfields to sign a waiver releasing her of the obligation to deliver any more melons. Greenfields signed the waiver but later reconsidered and sued Short, claiming that he had not received any consideration for the waiver. Did Greenfields win?

Greenfields lost the suit because the original contract involved the sale of goods and thus fell under the UCC. While it is true that Greenfields received no consideration for the waiver, no consideration was required in this situation. Under the UCC, the waiver would be considered a binding contract.

B. An agreement modifying a written contract needs no consideration.

No consideration is necessary for modification of a written contract if the change is mutually agreeable to all parties involved (UCC Section 2-209).

RAISE YOUR GRADES

Can you explain . . . ?

☑ the definition of consideration
☑ some situations where no consideration exists
☑ the difference between an undisputed debt and a disputed debt and how this affects consideration
☑ why past benefits are not consideration for a present contract
☑ the circumstances under which a gift may involve consideration
☑ when the doctrine of promissory estoppel may be applied
☑ the effects of the UCC on the rules of consideration

SUMMARY

1. Consideration is the price, cause, motive, or influence that induces a party to enter a contract. It is something of value that is given in exchange for a promise. Usually, each party gets something—a benefit—and gives up something—a detriment.
2. In general, consideration is required for a contract to be enforceable.
3. A legal benefit or detriment need not be tangible.
4. Legal benefits are assignable to a third party.
5. Consideration need not involve equal value. Courts do not usually evaluate the adequacy or equality of consideration, but only whether consideration exists.
6. A gift is not consideration, nor are preexisting obligations. Past benefits are not consideration for a present contract.
7. The payment of a debt in a manner or form different from that prescribed in the debt agreement may amount to consideration.
8. Offering, or actually making, partial payment for an undisputed debt is not consideration.
9. Partial payment of a disputed debt is consideration if made in return for the creditor's promise to forget the balance of the debt.
10. An illusory promise—one in which the promisor does not actually promise to do anything—is not consideration.
11. Under the doctrine of promissory estoppel, a contract is valid even though consideration is lacking.
12. A promise to pay a debt that has been discharged by bankruptcy is enforceable even though consideration is lacking.
13. Contracts under seal are valid without consideration in a few states only. Most states have abolished this doctrine.
14. Under the UCC, some sale-of-goods contracts that would otherwise fail for lack of consideration are enforceable.
15. Under UCC Section 1-107, a claim or breach can be settled without consideration if the aggrieved party agrees in writing to renounce or waive any further claim.
16. Under UCC Section 2-209, an agreement modifying a written contract needs no consideration if the change is mutually agreeable to all parties involved.

RAPID REVIEW   Answers

True or False?

1. A legal benefit or detriment must be tangible. [Section 5-1]   *False*

2. As a general rule, courts do not evaluate the adequacy or equality of consideration. [Section 5-1]   *True*

3. There is no consideration if a party to a contract does something that he or she is already bound to do. [Section 5-2]   *True*

4. Offering partial payment for an undisputed debt is valid consideration. [Section 5-2]   *False*

5. A party who makes a promise in return for benefits that have already been supplied has not received consideration. [Section 5-2]   *True*

6. An illusory promise is one in which the promisor does not actually promise to do anything. [Section 5-2]   *True*

7. A gift is consideration if the recipient has taken certain steps or made certain arrangements in order to receive the gift. [Section 5-2]   *False*

8. Some contracts are enforceable even though they are unsupported by consideration. [Section 5-3]   *True*

9. Under the UCC, an agreement modifying a written contract always requires additional consideration. [Section 5-4]   *False*

SOLVED PROBLEMS

PROBLEM 5-1   Describe consideration and explain its importance in contract law. Discuss typical situations where there can be no consideration.

Answer: In general, consideration must be present for a contract to be enforceable. Consideration is something of value that is given in exchange for a promise. Usually, each party gains a legal benefit and suffers a legal detriment. The courts do not ordinarily concern themselves with whether the consideration exchanged is of equal value, except when one party's free will is overborne, or when there exists a gross, obvious discrepancy between the levels of consideration exchanged.

There are several situations where there can be no consideration. For example, there is no consideration when a party does something he or she is already obligated to do. Similarly, past benefits are not consideration. An illusory promise, one in which nothing is really promised, also is not consideration. [Section 5-1]

PROBLEM 5-2   Discuss the role of consideration in an undisputed versus a disputed debt. Explain why these two types of debts are treated differently.

Answer: In an undisputed debt, offering or even actually making partial payment is not valid consideration to settle the debt. The reason is that the debtor already owes the entire amount of the debt and thus suffers no additional legal detriment by offering partial payment. In fact, the obligation to pay the debt was a preexisting one. If, however, the debtor does create some additional obligation along with the offer of partial payment, there can be adequate consideration for the return promise to forget the balance of the payment. A possible additional obligation might be to offer early payment of the debt or to give something extra to the creditor. When a debt is disputed, an offer of partial payment in return for settling the debt can be valid consideration. The dispute must be real and not merely an attempt to avoid paying a debt. [Section 5-2]

PROBLEM 5-3   Discuss the differences between an output contract, a requirements contract, and an exclusive dealings contract, and tell how they are different from an illusory promise.

Answer: An output contract is one in which one party agrees to purchase all the production of another party. A requirements contract is one in which one party agrees to purchase all that he or she needs or requires of a certain product from a seller. An exclusive-dealings contract is one in which both parties mutually agree to deal with one another with regard to a certain product. The courts hold that these contracts are all valid even though there is no consideration. Actually, in an exclusive-dealings contract, there is mutual obligation, since one party agrees to supply the needs or requirements of another party, and the other party in return agrees to promote the sale of the product. In an illusory promise, there is no consideration because the promisor has not actually promised to do anything. Typically, in an illusory promise, one party offers to buy all he or she wants or wishes of a product, but with no obligation to do so, whereas in an output or requirements contract, a party agrees specifically to buy all of the production or all that he or she needs or requires. Unlike an illusory promise to buy what one wants, there is usually some basis (previous sales, for example) for determining what the party needs or requires. A contract involving an illusory promise is not enforceable. [Section 5-2]

PROBLEM 5-4 Discuss the three situations in which the courts will hold that a contract is enforceable even though there is no consideration.

Answer: These three situations are promises to pay a discharged debt, promises where the doctrine of promissory estoppel applies, and contracts made under seal.

A promise to pay a debt that is no longer owed because it was discharged by bankruptcy or by the statute of limitations is enforceable even though there is no consideration. Under the doctrine of promissory estoppel, a contract in which there is no consideration is still enforceable if the promisee relied on the promise, acted on it, and was financially injured as a result of having acted on it. If the promisor knew or should have known that the promisee would rely on the promise, then the promisor will be required to fulfill the promise. Under common law, the use of a seal on a written contract precludes the requirement for consideration. Today, however, most states have abolished contracts under seal. [Section 5-3]

PROBLEM 5-5 Maria agreed to sell her car to Loretta if Loretta would pay Maria's daughter $7,000. Loretta paid Maria's daughter, but Maria refused to deliver the car, claiming that she had not received any legal benefit, and therefore no consideration, in return for her promise to sell the car. She demanded $500 for delivery of the car to Loretta. Loretta refused to pay, and sued Maria. What happened?

Answer: Loretta won the suit. The contract is enforceable even though the legal benefit of $7,000 was paid to Maria's daughter rather than to Maria. A legal benefit can be assigned to a third party. [Section 5-1]

PROBLEM 5-6 Harper, a horse breeder, owned a horse named Thunder that Jameson wanted to buy. Harper was asking $15,000 for Thunder, but Jameson did not have the money. Instead, Jameson paid Harper $10 for a one-year option on Thunder. Three months later, Jameson's aunt died, leaving him $15,000 in her will. Jameson went to Harper, $15,000 in hand, to buy Thunder. Harper refused to sell, however, since he had recently received another offer of $20,000 for the horse. Harper claimed the $10 option was inadequate consideration, so he was not bound by the option contract. Jameson sued. Did he win?

Answer: Jameson won the suit and the right to purchase Thunder for $15,000 based on his option contract. Except where gross and obvious disproportionality exists, the courts do not usually evaluate the adequacy of the consideration when evaluating a contract. The court only examines whether consideration was present (it was in this case) and whether it was mutual (which it also was, since Harper gave up the legal right to sell his horse for one year in exchange for $10). [Section 5-1]

PROBLEM 5-7 Simon wanted to go to an out-of-state college, but his Uncle Herbert was concerned about the possible corruption of Simon's morals since the school Simon had chosen had a bad reputation. Herbert told Simon that if Simon promised not to drink or smoke during his four years of college, he would pay Simon $5,000 upon graduation. Simon accepted his uncle's offer and abstained from alcohol and tobacco for four years. After he was graduated, Simon tried to collect from his uncle. Herbert acknowledged that he believed Simon had indeed abstained, but refused to pay the money. Herbert contended that Simon had not experienced any real detriment and thus consideration was lacking. Simon sued his uncle. Did he win?

Answer: Simon won the case. A legal detriment need not be a tangible detriment. The fact that Simon might actually have benefited by abstaining from these substances has nothing to do with the legal detriment he experienced, which was to relinquish his right to indulge if he so wished. The court ruled that there had been valid consideration and that Herbert had to pay Simon $5,000. [Section 5-1]

PROBLEM 5-8 Walters signed an agreement to sell his house to Lansing on May 15 for $40,000. On May 15, Lansing paid the $40,000, but Walters refused to turn over the deed and possession of the house unless Lansing paid him another $5,000. Lansing paid the money because she wanted the house badly. Later, she decided that she shouldn't have had to pay, so she sued Walters to recover her $5,000. Did she win?

Answer: Lansing won the suit and recovered the $5,000. Walters had signed an agreement to sell the house for $40,000. When he demanded the extra $5,000, he did not promise to do any additional act that he was not already bound to perform. Therefore, Walters gave no consideration for the additional $5,000, and thus is not entitled to the money. [Section 5-2]

PROBLEM 5-9 Assume the same situation as Problem 5-8 except that Lansing asked Walters to leave a chandelier in the dining room and replace some broken window frames and screens in return for the $5,000. Would Lansing win her suit under these circumstances?

Answer: Lansing will probably lose this one. Typically, an additional promise, no matter how trivial, amounts to consideration. Therefore, the chandelier and replaced frames and screens were consideration for the $5,000. Remember that the courts do not usually examine the actual value in determining the validity of the consideration. [Sections 5-1 and 5-2]

PROBLEM 5-10 Calloway contracted to sell Howe, the owner of a movie theater, two tons of popcorn for 30 cents a pound. Howe was to pay Calloway upon delivery Tuesday at Howe's theater. On Monday Calloway told Howe that he would have to pay 33 cents a pound because of an increase in transportation costs. Howe agreed in writing to the 3-cents-a-pound increase. On Tuesday Calloway delivered the popcorn, but Howe insisted on paying 30 cents a pound. Calloway sued Howe. Did he win?

Answer: Calloway won the suit. Howe is liable for the extra 3 cents a pound even though he received no additional consideration for the additional promise. Under the UCC (2-209), any modification of a contract for the sale of goods is enforceable with or without consideration. [Section 5-4]

PROBLEM 5-11 Prather promised to purchase two cords of firewood from Irwin "sometime next fall, when I get around to it." One day in October, Irwin arrived at Prather's house with the firewood and demanded payment. Prather refused to accept or pay for the delivery, so Irwin sued. What happened?

Answer: Prather won because his promise to buy the wood "sometime next fall, when I get around to it" was merely an illusory promise and not real consideration. [Section 5-2]

PROBLEM 5-12 Dorset helped Brewer chop wood and clear brush on Brewer's ranch. Several weeks later, Brewer, feeling grateful, offered to pay Dorset $300 for his work. Dorset, however, felt that his services were worth $500, so he sued Brewer for that amount. Did he win?

Answer: Dorset did not win since he performed the work before Brewer offered to pay him for it. Past actions cannot be used as consideration; thus, Brewer was not offering to pay consideration due under a contract, he was offering to make a gift. [Section 5-2]

PROBLEM 5-13 Jansen agreed to buy 100 boxes of toys from Olsen for $1,200 on an open-account arrangement. Upon delivery, Jansen claimed that many of the toys were defective. He estimated the total worth of the shipment at $800 and sent Olsen a check for that amount. On the back of the check, Jansen had written: "Paid in full for all accounts owed." Olsen endorsed and cashed the check and then brought suit against Jansen for the $400 he felt he was still owed. Did he win?

Answer: Olsen did not win. Since this involved a disputed debt, partial payment constituted consideration from the debtor. When Olsen signed the check, marked "Paid in full for all accounts owed," he provided consideration in the form of forgiveness for the remaining portion of the debt. [Section 5-2]

6 LEGAL CAPACITY

6-1. Introduction to Legal Capacity

In general, a person entering into a contract must possess a certain legally defined level of rationality or mental competency—called *legal capacity*—or the contract will be voidable.

A. There are two major categories of persons who lack legal capacity to contract.

The two major categories of persons who do not have legal capacity to contract are

- minors
- persons who are incompetent due to insanity, intoxication, or any other condition that causes severe mental impairment

In some states, convicts and aliens also lack legal capacity to contract.

B. Persons who lack legal capacity have the right to void a contract.

The law is framed to protect persons who lack the legal capacity to contract. In most cases, a contract involving a person who does not have legal capacity is voidable by that person. Thus, one who enters a contract with a person who lacks legal capacity does so at his or her own risk.

1. The right to void a contract exists regardless of how fair or favorable a contract may be.
2. The right to void a contract exists even if the person who had legal capacity did not know that he or she entered into a contract with someone who lacked capacity.

EXAMPLE 6-1: Judy, age 12, wanted to buy an expensive violin. Manny's Music Store agreed to sell Judy a violin worth $350 for only $10 a month—an amount she could afford to pay from her allowance. Upon learning of the agreement, Judy's parents protested because they feared her interest in music was only a passing fancy. At their request, Judy asked to be released from the contract. The store owner sued, maintaining that because he realized he was dealing with a minor, he created a contract that was especially favorable to her. What happened?

Judy was released from the contract. The fact that the contract was especially favorable to Judy—that the instrument dealer went out of his way not to take advantage of a minor—does not affect her right to void the contract.

6-2. Legal Definition of Minors

A. A *minor* is anyone under the legal age of majority.

Traditionally, the legal age of majority was 21. Today, however, the age of majority in most states is 18.

The legal status of a minor is determined solely by age, not by degree of competency or ability. Thus, a minor can still void a contract even though he or she possesses an appropriate degree of maturity or experience.

B. Some minors are legally emancipated.

In certain states, some minors can be legally *emancipated*—that is, no longer under parental protection or control. Often, emancipated status is granted to minors who are married. Under certain circumstances, emancipated minors do possess legal capacity to contract.

EXAMPLE 6-2: Joanna and Jeremy, both 17, got married after graduating from high school. After they married, they purchased some living-room furniture, signing a contract in which they agreed to pay $30 a month over two years. The marriage broke up after three months, however, and Jeremy returned the furniture, stating that he wished to void the contract because he was a minor. The store sued to enforce the contract on the grounds that Jeremy was subject to a state statute that held married minors to be emancipated and therefore responsible for their contracts. Did the store win?

The store won because Jeremy was married when he purchased the furniture and, by state statute, had relinquished his right as a minor to void the contract. Therefore, he was liable for the furniture payments.

6-3. Minors' Right to Ratify a Contract

Ratification is the affirmation that a contract will be considered valid. A contract involving a minor can be ratified only after the minor reaches the age of majority.

• Ratification may be *express* (oral or written) or *implied* (such as a show of intention).

EXAMPLE 6-3: John, age 17, signed a contract to buy a car. For the next eight months, until he reached his legal majority, John drove the car and made his monthly car payments. On his eighteenth birthday, John's father gave him a sports car. John kept his other car for another four months and continued his payments during that time. Then he returned the car to the dealer and said that he was voiding the contract and would make no further payments. The dealership sued, claiming breach of contract. What happened?

The dealership won. Although John had contracted to buy the car when he was a minor, he ratified the contract by continuing to make payments after reaching majority. Thus, the contract was enforceable. (Some states allow a minor to void a contract within a reasonable time after reaching majority. This is discussed in Section 6-4.)

6-4. Minors' Right to Void a Contract

A. Minors can void contracts in most situations.

1. A minor can void, or *disaffirm*, a contract any time prior to reaching majority. As with ratification, disaffirmation may be either express or implied.
2. In some states, minors can void a contract within a reasonable length of time after reaching majority. In general, this means within two years.
3. In most states, a minor who misrepresents his or her age in order to enter a contract can still void the contract. Usually, however, the minor must return or pay for any consideration already received.

   • Some states consider such misrepresentation to be fraudulent and hold that the other party also has the right to void the contract.

EXAMPLE 6-4: Albert, age 17, signed a contract to purchase a sailboat from the Barnacle Boat Company. Albert used the boat for three months and made payments in each of those months. At the beginning of the fourth month, Albert, still 17, returned the boat to Barnacle and said that he was voiding the contract. Barnacle sued Albert, claiming that the contract was enforceable because Albert had used and paid for the boat for three months. Did they win?

Barnacle Boats did not win because Albert was a minor and thus had the right to void the contract any time during his minority.

EXAMPLE 6-5: Barbara, age 16, signed a contract to purchase a stereo system from Stereo World. On the contract she wrote that her age was 18, the legal age of majority in her state. The following week, the manager of the store ran a credit check and discovered Barbara's true age. Not wanting to contract with a minor, the store manager called Barbara and asked her to return the stereo. Barbara refused, saying that she had a valid contract. Stereo World sued to void the contract, claiming that, according to state statute, Barbara had committed fraud by misrepresenting her age. Did the store win?

If the state had such a statute, then the store won the suit and could void the contract.

B. Minors cannot void contracts in some situations.

1. A minor who has entered into a contract cannot void that contract after reaching majority if he or she has shown an intention to carry out the terms of the contract since reaching the age of majority.
2. Some states deny minors the right to void contracts for life insurance, medical care, or student loans and other bank transactions.

C. Minors cannot void contracts for necessaries.

A *contract for necessaries* is enforceable against a minor.

1. The courts have broadly defined *necessaries* as those items that are reasonably or absolutely necessary to sustain one's existence.

   • The courts have been flexible in deciding which items are necessaries, usually basing their judgment on the conditions of the case under consideration.
   • In general, necessaries include food, shelter, clothing, medical services, and schooling (including, in many cases, a college education). A car is not usually considered a necessary.

2. In a contract for necessaries, a minor's liability is governed by quasi-contract theory. Accordingly, the minor must pay only the reasonable value of necessaries actually received and is not bound by terms for necessaries not yet received.
3. A minor can disaffirm a contract for necessaries only by returning any consideration or by compensating the other party for consideration already received.

EXAMPLE 6-6: Sally, a minor, enrolled in a computer programming school. The two-year course cost $2,500. Sally paid $500 to begin classes and contracted with the school to pay the balance over the two years of the course. After the first month, Sally realized that she was not interested in computers, so she dropped out of the school and requested that her $500 be refunded. The school informed Sally that it would not refund her money and that she still owed the remaining $2,000. Sally maintained that because she was a minor, she had a right to void the contract at any time during her minority. Who was right?

Sally was obligated to compensate the school, but only for the actual amount of the value she received. Thus, she probably could recover only part of her $500 down payment. Most courts have decided that education falls into the classification of necessaries.

D. The legal effect of a minor's voidance.

Usually, a minor who voids a contract must be returned to his or her precontract status.

1. Most states require a minor to return any consideration that he or she has received, regardless of its condition. In some cases, however, a minor can still void a contract even if he or she is unable to return any consideration.
2. Some states do not permit a minor to benefit from a voidance or to void a contract unless the minor can return the other party to precontract status. The minor must either return in good condition any consideration received or compensate the other party. If the minor is unable to do this, the contract may not be disaffirmed.

6-5. Legal Capacity and Incompetent Persons

A person can be deemed legally *incompetent* to enter a contract if he or she is temporarily or permanently unable to comprehend his or her own actions with regard to forming the contract. Such incompetence may be due to insanity, abuse of alcohol or narcotics, senility, or anything else that causes severe mental impairment. Under the law, a person who is in a state of incompetence lacks the capacity to contract.

Whether or not a person is incompetent at the actual time of contract determines the validity of the contract.

A. The effect of temporary insanity differs from the effect of permanent insanity.

1. A person judged by a court to be permanently insane cannot contract for anything; all contracts with such a person are void.
2. Contracts formed by a person who was temporarily insane at the time of forming the contract are voidable. A person who enters a contract while temporarily insane must fully restore the other party to the precontract state when disaffirming. The only exception to this obligation occurs when the other party has taken unfair advantage of the insane person; in that case, the temporarily insane person has no legal obligation to return the consideration if the contract is voided.
3. Contracts formed at the time a person is of sound mental ability are valid, even though the person may not be competent at other times.

EXAMPLE 6-7: After thirty years as a successful stockbroker, William Harper began to exhibit very peculiar behavior. For example, over his wife's protests he bought a 60-foot yacht and quit his job to sail around the world. This act worried all his friends because not only had he never before shown any interest in sailing, but also he had always become seasick during previous ocean voyages. Shortly thereafter, however, it was discovered that a brain tumor was causing Harper's strange behavior. Surgery was then performed and the tumor was removed. After the operation, Harper realized he did not want to sail around the world, and he attempted to disaffirm the contract for the yacht on grounds of temporary insanity. The yacht dealer sued, claiming that Harper had shown no signs of mental disability during the negotiations. Who won?

Harper was able to disaffirm the contract on the grounds that he had been temporarily insane when he bought the yacht. However, he had to return the yacht to the dealer in good condition, and he had to compensate the dealer for the time that the yacht had been in his possession.

B. An intoxicated person is afforded the same legal protection as a person who is temporarily insane.

Under the law, a person will be deemed incompetent due to intoxication only if that person was so intoxicated when forming a contract that he or she did not understand the nature or consequences of the contract.

EXAMPLE 6-8: Jeanne Smith, age 35, owned her own cosmetics firm. She was very successful, but the stress of business led her into heavy drug use. She hoarded amphetamines and was unable to get through the day without them. She also used tranquilizers to counteract the effects of the amphetamines. One day, after taking an especially heavy dose of both medications, she had a business meeting with an acquaintance named Paul Carter. Carter pressed Smith to sell him her company. Completely unable to grasp what she was doing, Smith agreed to sell and accepted a $50,000 down payment from Carter. Later, Smith recovered from the effects of the drugs and was shocked at what she had done. She sued Carter for the return of her company, claiming that she had been incompetent at the time of the transaction. Did she win?

Smith's company was restored to her. The court ruled that she was incompetent at the time of the contract because of her drug intoxication. As a result, she had only to disaffirm the contract.

RAISE YOUR GRADES

Can you explain . . . ?

☑ why a contract is voidable if one party lacks the legal capacity to contract
☑ how being a minor affects a person's contractual ability
☑ when a minor can and cannot void a contract
☑ how temporary and permanent insanity affect a person's contractual capacity

SUMMARY

1. Contracts formed with a person who lacks legal capacity are voidable.
2. The right to void rests with the person who does not have legal capacity.
3. A person who does not have legal capacity to contract can void a contract regardless of how fair or favorable a contract may be. Also, the right to void exists even if the person who had legal capacity did not know that the other party lacked legal capacity.
4. Minors lack the legal capacity to contract, and therefore they have the right not to be bound by a contract even though they have voluntarily agreed to it.
5. Under certain circumstances, emancipated minors possess legal capacity to contract.
6. Upon reaching legal majority, a person has the right to ratify any contract entered into as a minor.
7. In general, a minor has the right to disaffirm a contract at any time before reaching majority or within a reasonable time after reaching it.
8. In most states, a minor who misrepresents his or her age in order to form a contract can still void the contract, but he or she may be held liable for any consideration already received.
9. Minors are held liable for the reasonable value of necessaries received under the terms of a contract. In general, necessaries include food, shelter, clothing, medical services, and schooling.
10. Usually, a minor who voids a contract must be returned to his or her precontract status.
11. Persons who are deemed legally incompetent lack the capacity to contract.
12. All contracts with a person who has been adjudged permanently insane are voidable.
13. Contracts formed by a person who was temporarily insane at the time of forming the contract are voidable.
14. In general, persons who are incompetent because of intoxication lack legal capacity and are given the same legal protection as persons who are temporarily insane.

RAPID REVIEW   Answers

True or False?

1. No category of persons is afforded extra protection under contract law. [Section 6-1]   *False*
2. A fair contract cannot be voided by anyone. [Section 6-1]   *False*
3. The legal status of a minor is determined by degree of competency. [Section 6-2]   *False*
4. A minor may ratify a contract at any time during his or her minority. [Section 6-3]   *False*
5. Ratification of a contract by a minor must be in writing. [Section 6-3]   *False*
6. A minor who has fraudulently misrepresented his or her age in order to enter into a contract may not void the contract. [Section 6-4]   *False*
7. A contract for necessaries is enforceable against a minor. [Section 6-4]   *True*
8. Most states require a minor who disaffirms a contract to return any consideration that he or she received. [Section 6-4]   *True*
9. If a person has been temporarily insane, any contract made by that person is void. [Section 6-5]   *False*
10. A person who enters a contract while temporarily insane must restore the other party to the precontract state when disaffirming, unless the other party has taken unfair advantage of the insane person. [Section 6-5]   *True*

11. A person with a history of alcoholism who is sober at the time   *False*
    of entering a contract can disaffirm the contract. [Section
    6-5]

SOLVED PROBLEMS

PROBLEM 6-1 Frank Wilson had a drinking problem. He had sober periods, but when he was drunk, he often did things he couldn't remember. One night, during a drinking bout, he decided to go on an ocean voyage. The idea still seemed attractive to him the next morning when he was sober. He went to his travel agent, Jane Dilling, and signed up for a South Seas cruise, paying an $800 deposit. That afternoon, he started a long drinking bout again. His family became so concerned that they had him placed in a hospital for treatment. While he was in the hospital, Wilson's family called Dilling and canceled the trip. When Wilson was released from the hospital several months later, he was sober and went to ask Dilling for his money back. Dilling refused, saying that even though the trip had been canceled, she and Wilson had made a valid contract under which she was entitled to keep any deposit for a trip canceled less than one week before departure, which had been the case when his family canceled the trip. Wilson sued Dilling to get his $800 back, claiming that the contract was void because he had been incompetent due to alcoholism, and citing his recent hospitalization as proof. What happened?

Answer: Wilson lost his suit. His right to void contracts as an alcoholic extended only to those contracts he had signed while intoxicated—so intoxicated that he could not understand that a contract was being formed. Wilson, however, was sober at the time of contract. Therefore, he was legally competent to contract and not entitled to the return of his $800 deposit. [Section 6-5]

PROBLEM 6-2 Robert, age 17 but legally emancipated, enrolled in a 20-lesson exercise class that cost $250. He took three lessons, decided he did not need the exercise, and attempted to disaffirm the contract on the grounds that he was a minor. The manager of the exercise studio refused to refund Robert's $250, and Robert sued. What was the outcome?

Answer: The court ruled that the exercise studio was not required to return the $250 to Robert. As an emancipated minor, Robert had the legal capacity to contract. Therefore, Robert did not have the right to disaffirm the contract even though he was below the age of majority. [Section 6-2]

PROBLEM 6-3 Delilah, age 17, bought herself a personal computer on credit. In a contract with the computer dealer, she agreed to make monthly payments of $200 for a period of two years. She made the payments for five months; the most recent payment was made four days after she reached majority. After making the fifth payment, she saw another personal computer she liked better than the one she had bought. Delilah had heard that a contract made by a minor could be disaffirmed, so she returned her computer to the dealer and asked for her money back. Did the dealer have to return Delilah's money?

Answer: The dealer did not have to return Delilah's money. By making a payment after she reached the age of majority, Delilah had shown intent to carry out the terms of the contract, thus ratifying the contract by implication. Delilah did not have to do anything overt, such as calling or writing the store, to ratify. All she had to do was demonstrate that she intended to honor the contract terms. [Sections 6-3 and 6-4]

PROBLEM 6-4 Sean, age 16, contracted with Bill's Appliances to buy a television set. The contract called for Sean to pay a $100 deposit and ten monthly payments of $30 each. Before the first payment was due, however, Bill learned that Sean was a minor. He was worried since he knew a minor could disaffirm a contract at any time. Bill feared that he might possibly get stuck with a used television, which would be worthless to him since he sold only new appliances. Bill immediately called Sean and demanded that he return the television. He said that he would return Sean's deposit and that he would not accept any payment checks. Sean refused to return the television and promptly mailed in his first monthly payment. Could Bill disaffirm the contract?

Answer: Bill could not disaffirm the contract and had to let Sean keep the television. The contract remained in force because, except in certain states when a minor has committed fraudulent misrepresentation, the contracts of minors are voidable only at the minor's option. An adult cannot disaffirm a contract entered into with a minor simply because he or she fears the minor will disaffirm later. In this case, Sean had not committed any misrepresentation, so that argument was not available to Bill as cause for voiding the contract. [Sections 6-1 and 6-4]

PROBLEM 6-5   Jane, a minor, bought a $700 racing bicycle from a local cycle shop. Two months later she had an accident in a bicycle race, and the bicycle's frame was bent severely out of shape. Deciding that she didn't want the broken bicycle, Jane returned it to the shop and demanded a full refund of the purchase price on the grounds that as a minor, she had the right to disaffirm the purchase contract and be returned to her precontract status. The bicycle dealer, however, refused to accept Jane's demand unless she returned her bicycle in perfect condition or paid the dealer for the cost of the repairs. Did Jane have to meet the dealer's conditions in order to get her refund?

Answer: The answer depends on the state in which the sale was made. In most states, a minor has the right to disaffirm a contract like Jane's and return the consideration received in any condition or even not return it at all. In other states, however, a minor is not permitted to benefit from a disaffirmation and must either return the consideration in good condition or provide compensation for any damage to it. If the minor is unable to do this, the contract may not be disaffirmed. [Section 6-4]

PROBLEM 6-6   Don, a minor, wanted to buy a car from Happy Harry, a used-car dealer. Harry, having had contracts voided by minors in the past, exercised extreme caution in his dealings with anyone who looked young. He asked for identification, and Don produced a driver's license that belonged to his older brother. This fooled Harry, who then sold the car to Don. Later, Don had trouble with the car and, invoking a minor's right to disaffirm a contract, tried to return it to Harry for a full refund. Did Harry have to accept the car and refund Don's money?

Answer: The answer depends on the state where the sale took place. Most states permit a minor to disaffirm a contract even if the minor has misrepresented his or her age in order to enter the contract. In cases of misrepresentation, the minor usually must return the consideration or provide compensation when disaffirming the contract. In a few states, Don would have lost the right to disaffirm when he misrepresented his age to enter the contract. Don would not have been entitled to return the car in those states. [Section 6-4]

PROBLEM 6-7   David, a minor with no income, borrowed $500 from his uncle Larry, promising to repay the money in one month. David then spent all of the money on a ski trip to Colorado. One month later, when Larry tried to collect the money he was owed, David refused to pay on the grounds that he was a minor and was disaffirming the contract. Did Larry have a legal right to collect on the debt?

Answer: In most states, Uncle Larry would not have a legal right to collect the money he was owed. As a minor, David had a perfect right to disaffirm this kind of contract, and moreover, he could do so even though he was unable to return any consideration. [Section 6-4]

PROBLEM 6-8   Charles, age 17, took a six-week job in a lumber camp. At the start of that period, he entered into a contract with Sally, the operator of a boarding house, for six weeks of room and board for $480, payable at the end of the six weeks. When the six weeks were up, however, Charles refused to pay, stating that he was disaffirming the contract under his rights as a minor. Sally sued Charles for the $480. What happened?

Answer: Sally won the case. Contracts for necessaries are enforceable against minors, and room and board most definitely fall into the classification of necessaries. Thus, Charles was obligated to pay Sally but, according to quasi-contract theory, he had to pay only the reasonable value of necessaries received. In this case, the court would probably rule that the $80 a week for room and board was a fair price, so Charles would owe Sally the entire $480. [Section 6-4]

PROBLEM 6-9 The night before his wedding, Jeremy was drinking very heavily. Late in the evening, when barely able to sit upright, he agreed to sell his two-seater sports car to a friend for $1,000. The friend paid Jeremy, bought a final round of drinks, and then drove the car home, dropping off Jeremy on the way. The next morning, Jeremy remembered nothing about the deal and panicked when he could not find the car. His friend then called and refreshed Jeremy's memory. Jeremy demanded the return of the car, but his friend refused. Jeremy, very upset, said that he had been too drunk to realize what he was doing. Who owned the car?

Answer: Jeremy still owned his car because he was plainly incompetent to enter a contract at the time of the agreement. His intoxication at that moment had been so extreme that he had not understood that a contract was being formed. The friend would have to return the car, and Jeremy would have to return the $1,000 because a person who enters into a contract while incompetent due to intoxication, like one who does so while temporarily insane, must return any consideration received or compensate the other party if the contract is voided. [Section 6-5]

7 ILLEGAL CONTRACTS

THIS CHAPTER IS ABOUT

☑ **Legality of Purpose**
☑ **Agreements That Are Contrary to Public Policy**
☑ **Agreements That Violate Statutory or Common Law**
☑ **Effects of Illegality on a Contract**

7-1. Legality of Purpose

The final element that must be present for an agreement to be valid is *legality of purpose*. An agreement has legality of purpose *except* when it is considered to be

• contrary to public policy
• in violation of statutory or common law

7-2. Agreements That Are Contrary to Public Policy

The definition of what is contrary to public policy varies over time and from state to state; however, certain broad categories of agreements are generally held to be contrary to public policy.

A. Unconscionable agreements are contrary to public policy.

An *unconscionable agreement* is one in which one party, through its superior bargaining power, has compelled the other party to accept terms that are grossly unfair.

1. Agreements that are unconscionable because one party has unfairly exercised superior bargaining power over another occur most often:
   • between employers and their employees, especially when the agreement has an extremely restrictive or broadly worded clause prohibiting the employee from competing with the employer after the employment is terminated—such agreements may also be contrary to public policy because they restrain competition (see Section 7-2C)
   • between finance companies and consumer borrowers
   • between landlords and their tenants
   • between insurance companies and their clients
   • between quasi-public monopoly institutions such as utility companies and their customers

2. One type of unconscionable agreement occurs when a party with superior bargaining power claims the protection of an exculpatory clause.
   • An *exculpatory clause* is one that disclaims liability even if the person or institution that is doing the disclaiming is actually at fault.
   • If the parties to a contract have comparable bargaining power, if there is no element of surprise, and if no personal injury is at issue, the courts will sometimes accept an exculpatory clause.

EXAMPLE 7-1: The automobile claim ticket that the Lazy-Day Parking Lot company issued to its customers contained an exculpatory clause disclaiming liability for any damage done to cars by company employees. One morning, Linda left her car with the lot attendant, took a claim ticket, and placed it in her purse without reading it. That afternoon, she returned to retrieve her car and found a scrape on one side that had not been there in the morning. She complained to the lot attendant, but he showed her the exculpatory clause on her claim ticket and informed her that even though she had not bothered to read it, the ticket was a valid contract. He further told Linda that the exculpatory clause protected the company from any liability. Linda sued for damages anyway. Did she win and, if so, why?

Linda won her suit. The court ruled that the claim ticket was issued primarily for identification, and that the exculpatory clause on the ticket was compelled upon Linda from an unequal bargaining position (she had to accept the ticket in order to claim her car and was given no notice that the exculpatory clause was on the ticket). Furthermore, the exculpatory clause was contrary to public policy in that the garage served a public purpose for a fee to provide attendant parking which could be expected to include reasonable care exercised in the protection of property.

B. Contracts that interfere with a public process may be contrary to public policy.

The "public process" in this case refers to the judicial and legislative processes; the process of protecting the public's health, safety, or morals; and the licensing process. Examples of contracts that interfere with a public process include the following:

- a contract that pays a public official to vote a certain way or that otherwise exerts undue influence on him or her. (Often in such cases, not only is the contract invalid, but also the parties are committing the crime of bribery.)
- a contract that impedes or suppresses a criminal investigation or that otherwise limits a person's civil rights.
- a contract whereby a person who lacks the necessary license promises to provide legal, medical, or other services for which a license is required. (*Note:* this rule refers only to licensing requirements that are intended to protect the public; if licensing requirements strictly intended to raise revenue are lacking, the contract is usually enforceable.)

EXAMPLE 7-2: Janet's company transferred her from California to New York, so Janet needed to sell her house in a hurry. Having had no previous dealings with real estate brokers—her house had been inherited—Janet took a friend's advice and called Sam, a local accountant, who reportedly maintained a part-time real estate practice. Sam had Janet sign an exclusive listing agreement whereby, in return for a promised commission, Sam had the exclusive right to seek a buyer for the house. Janet then left for New York, confident that the house would soon be sold. After five months, however, Sam had found no buyers, and Janet began to regret signing the exclusive agreement. She consulted a lawyer, who told her that such exclusive agreements were not standard in the industry. Moreover, on a trip back to California, Janet checked with the state real estate commission and learned that there were no records to indicate that Sam had ever obtained a real estate license. Janet then informed Sam that she was terminating the agreement. Sam, however, threatened to sue for breach of contract. Did Sam have a case?

Sam did not have a case for suing Janet. The fact that Sam lacked a California real estate license made the agreement voidable from the start. The real estate licensing requirement is definitely one that is designed to protect the public (rather than merely raise revenue), so any agreement whereby a person who lacks a real estate license promises to provide real estate agency services is voidable since it interferes with a public process.

C. Contracts containing clauses that unduly restrain trade or competition may be contrary to public policy.

1. A contract formed solely for the purpose of restraining trade or competition is illegal.
2. A contract that contains a "non-compete clause" may be considered legal if the primary purpose of the contract is not to restrain trade or competition.
   - A *non-compete clause* is a clause whereby one party agrees not to compete with the other in a designated activity, usually in business. Non-compete clauses are legal if they are considered "reasonable." The courts judge what is reasonable based on how long the clause will be in effect (the "time" test), what physical area it covers (the "geography" test), and whether it is truly necessary to protect the legitimate interests of a party to the contract.
   - A *sale-of-business contract*, particularly one involving a professional practice, can legally include a non-compete clause whereby the seller promises not to enter the

same business again for a reasonable time period and/or within a reasonably limited geographic area.

- An *employment contract* can legally include a non-compete clause whereby the employee promises not to enter into business competition with the employer if the employment terminates. However, the clause must contain a reasonable time limit and/or geographic area limit, and the employer must have a valid claim that the employee's access to the employer's business secrets, customer lists, and the like would give the employee an unfair competitive advantage.
- A *real estate contract* can legally include a non-compete clause if the clause is reasonable and necessary to protect a legitimate property interest of the seller or lessor.

EXAMPLE 7-3: Albert, a bright, young student just out of college, went to work for Silicon Software, a company in Northern California, as a software writer. On his first day on the job, he signed an employment contract that contained a clause whereby Albert pledged that if for any reason his employment at Silicon ended, then for one year thereafter he would not join or start another software business in California. Six months later, however, Albert left Silicon and started his own software company nearby. Silicon sued Albert for breach of contract, and Albert countersued to have the contract set aside. Who won?

Silicon won the suit, and Albert had to give up his software company. The court noted that the non-compete clause in Albert's employment contract met the tests of time and geography that are used to determine if such clauses are reasonable. The period of one year was not considered excessive, although the court commented that the period might well have been shorter considering the speed of technological change in the software industry. The geographical restriction to California was also considered reasonable given the nature of the industry. Finally, the court ruled that the non-compete clause was reasonable on the grounds that Albert's access to Silicon's technological secrets and customer lists would give Albert an unfair competitive advantage.

EXAMPLE 7-4: Thomas, a promising young chef, took a job as second chef at Chez Pierre, a famous Miami restaurant. The day that he began work, he signed an employment contract containing a clause whereby he pledged that if for any reason his employment at Chez Pierre ended, for one month thereafter he would not work in any other Florida restaurant. A year later, however, he was offered a better job in an Italian restaurant in Tampa, but only if he could start work there immediately. He therefore sued to be released from his contract with Chez Pierre. Did he succeed?

Thomas succeeded in having his employment contract set aside. The court ruled that even though the one-month restriction was reasonable, the geographical restriction was not because the typical Chez Pierre customer in Miami was not likely to desert that restaurant for the one in Tampa just to continue enjoying Thomas's cooking.

7-3. Agreements That Violate Statutory or Common Law

Contracts often lack legality of purpose if they violate statutory or common law regarding criminal activities or laws designed to uphold the public morality.

A. A contract is illegal if its execution requires the performance of a criminal act.

1. A contract formed solely for the purpose of executing a criminal act or civil wrong is illegal.
2. A contract formed for an otherwise legal purpose can still be legal even if a criminal act is performed as part of its execution. The test of the contract's legality is whether or not the criminal act was necessary to its execution.

EXAMPLE 7-5: Martin, a construction contractor, had done business for many years with Great Northern Lumber Company. One year when lumber prices rose sharply, he requested special treatment from Great Northern as a long-time customer. Great Northern offered him a special low price on a single shipment of lumber, and Martin gratefully accepted. When the shipment arrived, however, so did a federal agent who informed Martin that the logs had been stolen from federal lands by one of Great Northern's subcontractors. The logs were then seized for use as evidence. Martin had already paid for the shipment, so he threatened to sue Great Northern if the company failed to fulfill the order legally at the agreed-upon low price. However, Great Northern's president rejected his claim, arguing that the sales contract had been illegal because it involved a criminal activity. The best Martin could do, said the company president, was to reorder at a higher price. Martin sued. Did he win?

Martin was able to enforce the original sales contract. That contract could certainly have been carried out in a legal fashion, and Martin had had no way of knowing that it would actually be executed in an illegal manner. Great Northern was ordered to execute the contract by legal means.

B. A contract is illegal if its execution violates laws designed to uphold the public morality.

Most litigation regarding such laws involves those against usury and gambling.

1. *Usury laws.* Most states have usury laws that set a legal limit on the annual rate of interest that lenders can charge.

   • A loan agreement that specifies a usurious rate of interest is illegal.
   • In some states, if an interest rate is judged to be usurious, the lender must forfeit all interest. In other states, the lender must forfeit just the excess interest. Still other states prescribe remedies somewhere between these two extremes.
   • If the lender imposes a service charge for the loan, that charge is added to the amount of interest when determining whether the loan is usurious.
   • In many states the usury laws do not apply to interest charged on loans made to corporations. In consequence, lenders can charge corporations whatever interest rate the market will bear.

2. *Antigambling laws.* Most states have antigambling laws under which almost all types of gambling are illegal.

   • *Gambling* is a transaction in which a person gives up something of value (consideration) in order to try to win a prize.
   • Any contract that involves gambling normally is illegal.
   • Some states make exceptions to permit regulated gambling on horse races, bingo, and the like.
   • *Lotteries* are generally illegal unless operated by the state. Lottery-like procedures used in sales promotions are legal only if at least one of the three lottery elements—consideration, chance, or prize—is missing. If the consumer can enter simply by filling out a form (i.e., without giving any consideration) or by submitting a short qualifying statement (i.e., removing, at least in part, the element of chance), then the procedure is legal.

7-4. Effects of Illegality on a Contract

A. A contract that is illegal is void and usually unenforceable.

The court may or may not provide relief to the parties to an illegal contract, depending in part on whether relief is necessary to prevent injustice.

1. *Parties equally at fault.* If both parties to the contract are deemed equally at fault (*in pari delicto*), the court will provide no relief for either party. Neither party can sue the other for breach of contract or for damages, and neither party can ratify the contract.
2. *Parties not equally at fault.* If the parties are not *in pari delicto*, the court may provide relief for the less guilty party, especially if doing so is in the public interest. Under this rule, persons who form illegal contracts because of duress or fraud may be allowed to recover any consideration given.
3. *Party belonging to protected class.* If the law that the contract violates is meant to protect a particular segment of society (say, a given class of consumers) to which one party to the contract belongs, the court may permit that party to recover any consideration given and will sometimes even enforce the contract.
4. *Party having change of heart.* If one party knowingly provides another with money or property to be used for an illegal purpose but later has a change of heart, the court may permit the first party to recover that money or property (provided it has not been spent). The doctrine applied in this case is called *locus poenitentiae* ("place of repentence").

B. A contract may be partially legal and partially illegal.

In a multipart contract, some parts may be legal and others illegal. When this is the case, if the court can clearly distinguish the legal part or parts from the illegal part or parts, it may enforce the legal part or parts while declaring the rest void.

RAISE YOUR GRADES

Can you explain . . . ?

☑ how to apply the tests of time and geography to a non-compete clause in a contract

☑ when a contract formed between parties who have unequal bargaining power would be unconscionable

☑ when an exculpatory clause may be enforceable and when it may not be enforceable

☑ why a former employee who went into business competition with his or her former employer might have an unfair advantage

☑ how sales promotions that resemble lotteries can be legal in spite of the antigambling laws

☑ how the *in pari delicto* doctrine helps a court determine whether or not to provide relief to a party to an illegal contract

☑ how the *locus poenitentiae* doctrine applies when a party who knowingly provides another with money or property to be used for an illegal purpose has a change of heart

SUMMARY

1. Legality of purpose is necessary for a contract to be valid and enforceable.
2. A contract that is contrary to public policy is illegal.
3. Three kinds of contracts that are generally held to be contrary to public policy are unconscionable agreements, agreements that interfere with the public process, and agreements in restraint of trade or competition.
4. An unconscionable agreement is one in which one party uses superior bargaining power to compel the other party to accept grossly unfair terms.
5. Examples of interference with the public process include tampering with the legislative or judicial process; with the public health, safety, or morals; or with licensing laws intended to protect the general public.
6. Any agreement formed solely for the purpose of restraining trade or competition is illegal.
7. A contract that contains a non-compete clause may be considered legal if the primary purpose of the contract is not to restrain trade or competition. Reasonable non-compete clauses often appear as part of a sale-of-business contract, an employment contract, and certain real estate contracts.
8. A contract that violates statutory or common law is illegal.
9. A contract formed solely for the purpose of executing any criminal act or civil wrong is illegal.
10. A contract is illegal if its execution violates laws designed to uphold the public morality. Most litigation regarding such laws involves those against usury and gambling.
11. A contract that is illegal is void and usually unenforceable unless enforcement is necessary to prevent injustice.
12. If both parties to an illegal contract are deemed equally at fault ("*in pari delicto*"), the court will provide no relief for either party.

13. If the parties to an illegal contract are not *in pari delicto*, the court may provide relief for the less guilty party.
14. In a multipart contract, some parts may be legal and others illegal. If the court can clearly distinguish the legal parts from the illegal ones, it may enforce the legal parts and declare the others void.

RAPID REVIEW — Answers

True or False?

1. As long as two parties enjoy equal bargaining power, they may contract to restrain competition in any manner desired. [Section 7-2] — *False*

2. An exculpatory clause is one that disclaims liability even if the party doing the disclaiming is actually at fault. [Section 7-2] — *True*

3. Exculpatory clauses are always valid. [Section 7-2] — *False*

4. Usury laws set a legal maximum on the annual interest rate chargeable on a loan. [Section 7-3] — *True*

5. All states have laws against usury. [Section 7-3] — *False*

6. A non-compete clause is always illegal. [Section 7-2] — *False*

7. A contract formed for a legal purpose will always become void if a criminal act is performed as part of its execution. [Section 7-3] — *False*

8. If two parties to an illegal contract are *in pari delicto*, one is more at fault than the other. [Section 7-4] — *False*

9. When the parties to an illegal contract are *in pari delicto*, the court typically provides no relief to them. [Section 7-4] — *True*

10. If any part of a multipart contract is deemed illegal, the whole contract is automatically illegal. [Section 7-4] — *False*

11. State antigambling laws do not apply to lotteries. [Section 7-3] — *False*

SOLVED PROBLEMS

PROBLEM 7-1 Sally, a legal secretary, needed to make some extra money, so as a sideline, she began drawing up wills for her friends. She charged $50 for each will. After she wrote a will for her neighbor, however, he refused to pay her. Sally then threatened to sue him. If she did, would she win?

Answer: Sally could not win since, technically speaking, she was practicing law without a license. Under the law, whenever a license is required for a given activity in order to protect the public (rather than merely to raise revenue), no person who lacks that license can form a legal contract to perform the given activity. Any such contract formed by such a person is automatically invalid since it interferes with a public process. The license to practice law is definitely one that is required to protect the public, so this rule would apply in Sally's case. [Section 7-2]

PROBLEM 7-2 Anthony operated a messenger service in the city. The city required such businesses to pay a $10 license fee, but Anthony had never done so, so technically his business was unlicensed. One day Anthony contracted with Noreen to deliver one hundred packages for $3 each. After Anthony's messengers had delivered the packages, Noreen noticed that the delivery van lacked the usual business license sticker. Fearful of violating the law by dealing with an unlicensed delivery service, Noreen refused to pay Anthony, claiming that their agreement was illegal since he lacked the proper license. Anthony sued to collect his fee. Did he win?

Answer: Anthony won his case. Under the law, when a person who lacks the proper license contracts to perform an activity for which that license is required, that contract is illegal and void if the reason for that licensing requrement is to protect the public. If, however, the license is required strictly to raise revenue, the contract is enforceable. In this case, the city license requirement for messenger services was obviously imposed to raise revenue, so even though Anthony lacked the proper license, his contract was still enforceable. [Section 7-2]

PROBLEM 7-3   Henry, a third-year medical student, found Simon lying injured on the side of the road. Without hesitation, Henry rushed to Simon's aid and, in the critical moments before the ambulance arrived, provided the care that probably saved Simon's life. Some days later, Henry sent Simon a bill for his medical services. Simon, however, refused to pay, pointing out that Henry was not a licensed physician. Henry then sued for the amount he believed he was owed. Did he win?

Answer: Henry did not win. The license requirement to practice medicine is intended to protect the public, not to raise revenue; therefore, under the law, a person who lacks a physician's license cannot form a legal contract to provide medical services. Any such contract formed by such a person is void and unenforceable because it interferes with a public process. Henry might have exerted every bit of his medical skill in saving Simon's life, but only a licensed physician has the right to charge a fee for medical services. [Section 7-2]

PROBLEM 7-4   Sharon bought a television at a bargain price from her local appliance store. A few days later, however, a police officer came to her door, told her that the television was stolen property, and confiscated it. Can Sharon get her money back from the appliance store?

Answer: Sharon should be able to get her money back or get another television from the store. Her sales agreement with the appliance retailer was a valid one even though its execution involved a criminal act. The agreement could easily have been carried out lawfully, and Sharon had no way of knowing that a criminal act was involved. [Section 7-3]

PROBLEM 7-5   Pam, the owner of a popular bookstore in a suburban town, agreed to sell her business to Frank for $100,000. Frank insisted, however, that the sales agreement include a clause prohibiting Pam from opening another bookstore in the same town for a period of one year. Pam duly signed this agreement. A month later she opened a hobby shop, but that business faltered. For a few weeks she tried running a card shop, but that business also failed to prosper. Finally, she decided to go back into the bookstore business, hoping to attract her old customers. She recalled her agreement with Frank not to do so, but reasoned that it was not enforceable since its purpose was to restrain competition. Could Frank sue Pam?

Answer: Frank had an excellent case for suing Pam. A non-compete clause like the one he had insisted on is legal in a sale-of-business contract as long as it meets the time and geography criteria for reasonableness. Its primary purpose was not merely to restrain trade or competition. Pam's opening another bookstore in the same town within a year and drawing her old customers to her new business would constitute unfair competition. [Section 7-2]

PROBLEM 7-6   Dave sought a loan from Money Investors, Inc., a privately owned loan company. Because Dave's credit rating was very poor, however, the company charged him what he considered to be an exorbitant rate of interest. Dave suspected that the terms of the loan were usurious, so he decided to check the state usury laws. If Dave's suspicions are correct, what might Money Investors have to do?

Answer: Depending on the laws of the state where the loan was made, if the interest rate is usurious, Money Investors might have to forfeit all interest on the loan, or it might have to forfeit just the excess interest, or a court might prescribe another remedy somewhere between those two extremes. [Section 7-3]

PROBLEM 7-7   Maxwell Industries, Inc., needed money for new machinery, so it obtained a loan from Money Investors, the same company that made the loan in Problem 7-6. The interest rate on the loan to Maxwell Industries was the same charged to Dave, the individual borrower described in Problem 7-6. If Dave obtained a judgment for usury against Money Investors, could Maxwell Industries do so too?

Answer: In many states, Maxwell Industries could not charge a lender like Money Investors with usury, even though that lender's interest rate might be deemed usurious if it were imposed on a loan made to an individual borrower. The reason is that Maxwell Industries is a corporation, and in many states the usury laws do not apply to loans made to corporations. In those states, lenders can charge corporations whatever interest rate the market will bear. [Section 7-3]

PROBLEM 7-8   The Galaxy Record Shop began losing customers when a new record store opened nearby, so as a desperate measure, it launched a widely publicized contest designed to boost sales. To enter, a person had to buy a record. For each purchase, the salesclerk would drop an entry card bearing the purchaser's name into a large container on the checkout counter. Eventually, a drawing would be held, and the winner would receive $5,000. Before the contest was a few days old, however, the district attorney charged Galaxy with conducting an illegal lottery. On what grounds was the case based?

Answer: The grounds for the case were that Galaxy's contest met all three criteria in the legal definition of a lottery—that is, there was a prize, it was to be awarded according to chance, and to enter the contest a person had to turn over some form of consideration; in this case, the purchase price of a record. Sales promotions of this kind can be legal only so long as they do not meet all three criteria, so usually either no purchase is required to enter (removing the element of consideration) or the contest winner is selected on some basis other than chance. [Section 7-3]

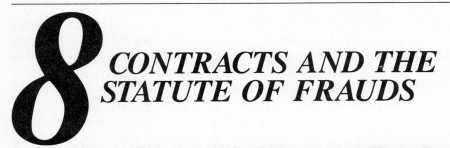

8 CONTRACTS AND THE STATUTE OF FRAUDS

THIS CHAPTER IS ABOUT

☑ **Definition of the Statute of Frauds**
☑ **Contracts That Must Comply With the Statute of Frauds**
☑ **Sufficiency of the Written Terms**
☑ **The Parol Evidence Rule**

8-1. Definition of the Statute of Frauds

Although oral contracts are generally enforceable, each state has a statute under which certain types of contracts are enforceable only if they are in writing. A statute of this type is called a *Statute of Frauds*, and it is intended to provide protection against fraud and perjury in contracts. It is important to note the following items about the Statute of Frauds:

- Any contract that must comply with the Statute of Frauds must be in writing to be enforceable.
- When a contract that should comply with the Statute of Frauds is not in writing, that contract is not void, but it is enforceable between the parties.
- An executed contract need not comply with the Statute of Frauds.

8-2. Contracts That Must Comply With the Statute of Frauds

Five categories of contracts must comply with the Statute of Frauds.

A. Collateral contracts must comply with the Statute of Frauds.

A *collateral contract* is one whereby a person promises to answer for the debt, default, or miscarriage of another person. A collateral contract is thus a *secondary* contract, formed following an original promise between the original parties to a contract. The requirement that collateral contracts comply with the Statute of Frauds and be in writing is intended to prevent any person from testifying falsely that another person has promised to pay a debt.

EXAMPLE 8-1: Robert, a free-lance record producer, owed $10,000 to the Good Tunes Recording Studio for a recording session. Unable to pay the debt, he asked Judy, his sister, for help. Judy telephoned Good Tunes and offered to pay the balance of Robert's debt. If Judy then failed to pay, could Good Tunes sue her to collect?

An agreement like that between Judy and Good Tunes is a collateral contract and must comply with the Statute of Frauds by being in writing. If it is not in writing, it is not enforceable, and if Judy were sued for nonpayment, she could plead this noncompliance as a defense. However, if the agreement were in writing, it would be a valid contract and could be enforced.

Certain promises to assume the debt of another person are not true collateral contracts, even though they may appear to be so, and consequently do not have to be in writing to be enforceable.

- A promise that is made to the debtor rather than to the creditor is not a collateral contract.
- A promise to assume the debt of a different party from the original debtor is not a collateral contract. That kind of promise is simply a new promise, and as such, it need not necessarily comply with the Statute of Frauds.

- A promise to assume the debt of another person that is made for the main purpose of benefitting the promisor rather than for the benefit of the debtor is not a collateral contract. The test applied to determine whether a given promise falls into this category is known as the *main purpose* or *leading object* doctrine.

EXAMPLE 8-2: Geoffrey telephoned the Quali-Tee Department Store, where he was a well-known customer, and told Jane, the manager of the college menswear department, that he was sending his son to be outfitted for school. Geoffrey asked Jane to forward the bill to him. When the bill arrived, however, it was far more than Geoffrey expected, so Geoffrey refused to pay it on the grounds that his telephoned promise to pay his son's debt did not comply with the Statute of Frauds and was therefore unenforceable. Was this a valid argument?

Geoffrey's argument would not be considered valid by a court since his promise was not a true collateral agreement. His call to Jane was not a secondary promise to pay his son's debts if his son couldn't pay; instead, that call was an original promise by Geoffrey to pay a bill that his son happened to incur. Since that was the case, Geoffrey could not plead noncompliance with the Statute of Frauds as a reason for nonpayment.

EXAMPLE 8-3: Reliable Medical Services, a surgical supply company, gave notice to Metro Hospital that it would discontinue service if Metro did not pay a certain outstanding bill within ten days. Philip, the president of the hospital and, not coincidentally, the holder of 30 percent of its stock, telephoned Reliable and promised that he himself would pay the bill if the hospital failed to do so. When the bill was still unpaid ten days later, however, Reliable cut off service to Metro and threatened suit against Philip on the grounds that it had a collateral contract with him. Philip's defense was that his telephoned promise failed to comply with the Statute of Frauds and thus the collateral contract was unenforceable. Would this defense hold up in court?

Philip's defense most likely would not hold up in court since, as a major holder of hospital stock, he himself was likely to benefit from any promise to pay Reliable's bill. Under the law, a promise to assume the debt of another party that is made to financially benefit the promisor is not a true collateral contract and therefore need not comply with the Statute of Frauds. Hence, Philip's noncompliance defense would not be acceptable. Furthermore, since the promise was not a collateral agreement, it would be classified as an original promise and would therefore be enforceable even though it was not in writing.

B. Contracts involving the sale or transfer of any interest in real property must comply with the Statute of Frauds.

Real property is land and its improvements (including buildings), the land rights (timber, minerals, and the like), and land uses that can be severed from the land itself and sold separately.

- *Physical severance.* Any physical part of a real property that can be severed—such as a part of a building, rocks taken from the ground, and so forth—automatically changes from real property into personal property at the time of severance, with all the implications this entails for contract law.
- *Severance by contract.* In a few instances, real property can be changed into personal property not just by physical severance, but through the signing of a contract that entails severance. For example, if a person buys the rights to mine and remove minerals from the real property of another person, those minerals are considered personal property from the time of the signing of the contract, even though they have not yet been physically severed from the real property.

1. Contracts involving real property that do not involve the transfer of any interest in that property do not necessarily have to comply with the Statute of Frauds. For example, a contract to build a house may be enforceable even if it is not in writing.
2. Most states have extended the definition of real property so that the following must also comply with the Statute of Frauds:

   - *Easements.* An easement is a grant of the right to use someone else's real property for a stipulated purpose.
   - *Leases.* A lease is an agreement by which a real property owner gives a tenant the right to occupy the property in exchange for rent.
   - *Life estates.* A life estate is a grant of ownership interest in real property made to a person for the duration of that person's life.

- *Conveyances.* A conveyance is an instrument, such as a deed, that transfers title to real property from one party to another.
- *Mortgages.* A mortgage is a lien against a borrower's real property as security for the payment of a debt.

3. Sometimes the courts enforce oral contracts involving the sale of real property when there has been partial performance since not to do so would be overly harsh on the buyer.

   - Where the partial performance is that the buyer has not only paid at least part of the purchase price, but has also taken possession of the property and/or made valuable improvements to it, an oral contract may be enforced.
   - Where the partial performance consists only of partial or complete payment of the purchase price for the real property, an oral contract will not be enforced, and the Statute of Frauds may be used as a defense. The court would rule that the partial or complete payment be returned.

EXAMPLE 8-4: Essie and Jacqueline, two longtime friends, made an oral agreement for Jacqueline to purchase Essie's summer cottage. A week later, Jacqueline paid the full purchase price of $50,000. However, before Jacqueline could take possession of the cottage, Essie sued to block the sale, using the argument that the agreement failed to comply with the Statute of Frauds and was therefore unenforceable. Would Essie's argument be accepted by a court?

Essie's argument probably would be accepted by a court. Jacqueline had neither taken possession of the cottage nor made valuable improvements to it, so the fact that she had paid the full purchase price was not sufficient to prevent Essie from arguing successfully that the agreement failed to comply with the Statute of Frauds and was therefore unenforceable. Essie would be required by the court to return the money.

C. Contracts that cannot be performed within one year must comply with the Statute of Frauds.

1. To determine the time taken for an oral contract to be performed, the courts measure from the time of the oral promise to the time when the promise is fully performed.
2. The courts also take into account whether a long-term oral contract could possibly be performed within one year. If it can, it need not comply with the Statute of Frauds.

EXAMPLE 8-5: Chuck, the director of a major research foundation, hired Susan, a research scientist, to undertake a three-year study of the effects of smoking on teenagers. Their agreement was strictly verbal. Chuck and Susan settled on its terms during the course of Susan's final job interview. Six months later, however, Chuck fired Susan without giving any reason. Could Susan sue Chuck to enforce the terms of their agreement?

Susan most likely could not have a court enforce the terms of her agreement with Chuck. By definition, her three-year study could not be performed in less than one year, so her employment agreement would have had to comply with the Statute of Frauds to be enforceable. Thus, since the agreement was never in writing, it would not be enforceable.

3. A contract that calls for continuous performance of some activity running indefinitely into the future generally must comply with the Statute of Frauds. The reason is that such a contract envisions performance of the specified activity beyond one year following the contract date.

EXAMPLE 8-6: The Elegance Button Company made an oral agreement with the Triton Shirt Company to supply all the buttons Triton needed for as long as Triton needed shirt buttons. Six months later, however, Triton became displeased with the quality of the buttons and asked to break the contract. Triton claimed that the contract was unenforceable because it was not in writing and could not be performed within a year and thus failed to comply with the Statute of Frauds. Could Triton break the contract on these grounds?

Triton could probably break the contract in this case. A court would most likely rule that a contract for continued performance, such as Triton's with Elegance, envisions performance of the specified activity beyond one year from the contract date, so the contract would need to comply with the Statute of Frauds and would not be enforceable if it were not in writing.

D. Contracts for the sale of goods for $500 or more must comply with the Statute of Frauds.

For this category of contracts, the requirement to be in writing is not in state laws but rather in Statute of Frauds provisions in the Uniform Commercial Code (UCC).

The UCC Statute of Frauds specifies several exceptions under which an oral contract for the sale of goods for $500 or more is enforceable. These exceptions are as follows:

- if the goods have been specifically manufactured for the buyer
- if the oral contract is confirmed in writing by one party and not objected to by the other party in writing within ten days
- if the buyer accepts all or part of a shipment of the goods
- if the buyer makes partial payment

E. Several miscellaneous categories of contracts must comply with the Statute of Frauds.

These categories are as follows:

- contracts to sell securities for $5,000 or more
- bilateral contracts to sell personal property other than goods or securities, such as patents, royalties, or rights, if the amounts involved are $5,000 or more
- contracts by an estate executor to pay the debts of the deceased

8-3. Sufficiency of the Written Terms

For a written contract to be valid under the Statute of Frauds, it need not be a formal document.

A. A written contract can be in various forms.

A written contract can be a memo, any type of written correspondence, or a notation on some other significant document.

B. A written contract must contain certain specific terms.

A written contract does not have to contain all the terms of the agreement; however, certain essential terms must be present, as follows:

- the names of the parties
- a description of the subject matter of the agreement
- a description of the material terms and conditions of the agreement

C. A written contract must be signed by the party who is charged to do something.

The party who is charged to do something is the only party whose signature must appear on the written contract. This signature need not appear in the formal close of the contract. It may appear anywhere in the writing.

8-4. The Parol Evidence Rule

A. Written contracts are protected by the parol evidence rule.

Under the *parol evidence rule,* oral testimony cannot be used in a lawsuit to change, vary, or modify a written contract or to contradict the terms of a written contract. Some oral testimony is exempted from the parol evidence rule; notably:

- testimony that demonstrates that terms or modifications, even if oral, were added later
- testimony that clarifies ambiguities in the written contract
- testimony that proves that a contract was signed under duress or because of fraud

---

RAISE YOUR GRADES

Can you explain . . . ?

- ☑ why certain types of contracts are required to be in writing
- ☑ what happens when a contract that should comply with the Statute of Frauds is not in writing

☑ the difference between an original promise and a collateral contract
☑ why a court may sometimes enforce an oral contract for the sale of real property
☑ what specific terms must always be included in a written contract
☑ the parol evidence rule

SUMMARY

1. Each state has a Statute of Frauds that requires certain types of contracts to be in writing.
2. When a contract that should comply with the Statute of Frauds is not in writing, it is not void, but it is unenforceable between the parties.
3. A party to a contract that should comply with the Statute of Frauds can use noncompliance as a defense if sued for not fulfilling the contract terms.
4. A collateral contract, which is a secondary promise to a creditor to assume the debt if an original promisor does not pay, must comply with the Statute of Frauds.
5. A promise to assume the debt of another party is not a collateral contract if its main purpose is to provide a benefit to the promisor.
6. A promise to assume the debt of another party is not a collateral contract if it is made to the debtor rather than to the creditor.
7. Contracts involving the sale or transfer of any interest in real property must comply with the Statute of Frauds.
8. Sometimes oral contracts for the sale of real property are enforced when there has been partial performance since not to do so would be overly harsh on the buyer.
9. Contracts that cannot be performed within one year must comply with the Statute of Frauds.
10. Contracts for the sale of goods for $500 or more must comply with the Statute of Frauds (with certain exceptions).
11. Several other specific kinds of contracts must comply with the Statute of Frauds.
12. For a written contract to be valid under the Statute of Frauds, it need not be a formal document.
13. The party who is charged to do something in a contract is the only party whose signature absolutely must appear on the written contract.
14. Under the parol evidence rule, oral testimony cannot be used in a lawsuit to change, vary, modify, or contradict a written contract.
15. Oral testimony is exempted from the parol evidence rule when it clarifies ambiguous terms in the contract, demonstrates that a term was added later, or proves that the contract was signed under duress or fraud.

RAPID REVIEW   Answers

True or False?

1. If an oral contract does not belong to a category that must comply with the Statute of Frauds, it is enforceable provided all of the essential elements of a contract exist. [Section 8-1]   *True*

2. Any contract that must comply with the Statute of Frauds is automatically void if it is not in writing. [Section 8-1]   *False*

3. A collateral contract is one whereby a debtor promises to pay all of his or her outstanding debts. [Section 8-2]   *False*

4. A promise to assume another person's debt must be made to that person's creditor in order to be a collateral contract. [Section 8-2]   *True*

5. A promise to assume another person's debt is not a collateral contract if its main purpose is to benefit the promisor. [Section 8-2]

True

6. A promise to a debtor to assume that person's debt must be in writing to be enforceable. [Section 8-2]

False

7. Any contract involving real property must be in writing to be enforceable. [Section 8-2]

False

8. A contract for the sale of land must be in writing to be enforceable. [Section 8-2]

True

9. Sometimes oral contracts for the sale of real property are enforced when the buyer has made partial payment. [Section 8-2]

False

10. For a written contract to be valid under the Statute of Frauds, all parties must sign it. [Section 8-3]

False

11. Under the parol evidence rule, oral testimony can be used in a lawsuit to modify the terms of a written contract. [Section 8-4]

False

12. An oral promise to build someone a garage involves real property and therefore must be in writing to be enforceable. [Section 8-2]

False

SOLVED PROBLEMS

PROBLEM 8-1 Barbara owed Marie $500, payable at the end of April. On April 15, Barbara's father, John, telephoned Marie to promise that he would pay the debt if his daughter did not do so. However, April passed and so did May, and neither Barbara nor John ever paid Marie. What would most likely happen if Marie sued John to collect on this promise?

Answer: Marie could sue, but it is very unlikely that she would win. John's oral promise to pay Barbara's debt is classified as a collateral contract, and as such it must comply with the Statute of Frauds and be in writing in order to be enforceable. [Section 8-2]

PROBLEM 8-2 The Tri-County Power Company wished to place a power line across Bill's property. A company representative made an oral agreement with Bill to pay him $10 per foot for the privilege. Tri-County then brought in its construction crew and attempted to start work. Bill, however, refused to let the crew onto his property and claimed the company did not have a valid contract. The company threatened suit. If it sued, would it win?

Answer: If the company brought suit, it most likely would not win. The contract described is one for an easement, which is the right to use someone else's property for a stipulated purpose. In most states, any agreement covering the sale or transfer of any interest in real property, including easements, must comply with the Statute of Frauds and be in writing to be enforceable. Bill and Tri-County had only an oral agreement, so their agreement was probably not enforceable. [Section 8-2]

PROBLEM 8-3 On Monday, Bob agreed in writing to buy Louise's late-model car for $3,000, payable on delivery of the car in ten days. On Tuesday, however, Bob telephoned Louise and, after some discussion, they both agreed that the contract would be valid only if the car was not damaged prior to delivery. Ten days after the contract was made, Louise delivered the car. However, Bob refused to accept it or pay for it because there was a large dent on its hood that he had never seen before. Louise sued, claiming that she and Bob had a valid, written contract. In his defense, Bob wished to describe in court his telephone discussion with Louise. Would the rules protecting written contracts permit him to do so?

Answer: Bob would be permitted to testify about the telephone conversation. Under the law, written contracts are protected by the parol evidence rule, whereby oral testimony cannot be used in a lawsuit to modify, change, or contradict the terms of a written contract. However, some kinds of oral testimony are exempted from this rule, including testimony demonstrating that a new term or condition was added, even orally, after a written agreement had already been signed. Bob's testimony falls into this category, so it would be exempted from the parol evidence rule. If the court accepted this evidence, Louise would probably lose her suit, and her written contract with Bob would not be enforced. [Section 8-4]

PROBLEM 8-4   When Jennifer died, she left an $8,000 debt owed to John. Jennifer's son, Don, was the executor of her estate. Examining her finances, he soon realized that the estate could pay only a part of the $8,000 debt. Don therefore promised John orally that he would pay the balance of the debt himself, out of his own pocket. After two years had gone by with no payment, however, John sued Don for the money. Will John win this case?

Answer: John is not likely to win this case. Don's promise to him—a promise by an estate executor to pay a debt of the deceased—falls into the category of collateral contracts that must comply with the Statute of Frauds and be in writing to be enforceable. Since Don made only an oral promise, that promise is not likely to be enforced. [Section 8-2]

PROBLEM 8-5   On July 15, Yvonne and Mary formed a written contract whereby Yvonne agreed to sell Mary five acres of land for $8,000. Delivery of the deed and payment of the $8,000 were scheduled for August 25. On that date, Mary arrived at Yvonne's lawyer's office with the money, but Yvonne refused to hand over the deed. Mary decided to sue Yvonne for breach of contract. Could she win this case?

Answer: Mary could win the case. Her contract is for the sale of land and must therefore comply with the Statute of Frauds and be in writing to be enforceable. Since it is in writing, it does comply, and thus Yvonne cannot use noncompliance as a defense. [Section 8-2]

PROBLEM 8-6   On March 1, in the course of a streetcorner conversation, Al agreed to hire Ken as a gardener for a period of eight months, starting on the following September 1. Ken started work on time and did everything he was told, but on November 1, Al fired him without giving any reason. If Ken sued Al for breach of contract, could he win the suit?

Answer: Ken most likely could not win the suit. His contract would be deemed one that had to comply with the Statute of Frauds under the rule requiring compliance by contracts that cannot be performed within one year. Although the actual working period envisioned was only eight months, the courts determine the time taken for an oral contract to be performed from the time of the oral promise to the time when that promise would be fully performed—in this case, the period from March 1 to the date eight months after the following September 1, or a total of fourteen months. Therefore, since Ken's contract should have complied with the Statute of Frauds, but did not because it was not in writing, it would not be enforceable. [Section 8-2]

PROBLEM 8-7   Fran, a farmer, made an oral agreement to sell Bob her entire soybean crop for $350. Later, she received an offer of $600 for the crop from Sal. Reasoning that her oral agreement with Bob was unenforceable, she sold all her soybeans to Sal at the higher price. Bob then sued Fran for breach of contract. Could he win this case?

Answer: Bob is likely to be able to enforce his contract, even though it was only an oral one. Fran could not use noncompliance with the Statute of Frauds as a defense since only contracts for the sale of goods for $500 or more must comply with that Statute, and Bob's contract was for only $350. Bob's contract can therefore be an oral one and still be enforceable. [Section 8-2]

PROBLEM 8-8   In a telephone conversation on Friday, Warren and Rick, two ranchers, agreed that Warren would let Rick graze his cattle on Warren's land and, in return, Rick would pay Warren $50 as consideration. On Saturday, Rick realized that an easement like the one he was obtaining from Warren had to comply with the Statute of Frauds in order to be enforceable. Rick therefore decided to confirm his and Warren's oral agreement in writing by sending Warren a letter that read: "This is to confirm our Friday agreement whereby you promise to let me graze my cattle on your land and, in return, I promise to pay you $50 as consideration." Rick signed the letter and sent it off to Warren. On Monday, Rick called Warren to make final arrangements, but Warren said that he had changed his mind about the easement. Rick threatened to sue for breach of contract, claiming that the agreement between them was enforceable since he had confirmed it in writing. Is he right?

Answer: Rick could not win this case. Even though he confirmed the easement in writing, only he signed the confirming letter. Warren never signed the letter, and since Warren is the party who is charged to do something under the terms of the agreement, his signature must be on the written document if the agreement is to be valid. [Section 8-3]

PROBLEM 8-9 Andrew, a wholesaler, agreed to sell Gideon, a discounter, 40 cartons of ski parkas. The two merchants then drew up a written contract clearly stating the price—$600—and the condition of sale—that the parkas would be slightly flawed. Andrew and Gideon both signed the agreement. A few days later, however, Gideon looked at the contract again and realized that it failed to mention that he wanted the parkas in assorted colors. He then called Andrew, and Andrew assured him that there would be no problem: assorted colors would be delivered. When the parkas arrived, however, all of them were black. Gideon refused to accept or pay for them. Andrew then sued for breach of contract, claiming that the contract never mentioned the color of the parkas. How might Gideon best defend himself?

Answer: Gideon might defend himself by describing in court how he and Andrew had added the additional condition to the contract during their telephone conversation. Testimony about oral conditions added later to a written contract is accepted in court even though the parol evidence rule forbids most other kinds of oral testimony that might be used to modify or contradict the terms of a written contract. [Section 8-4]

9 *THIRD-PARTY RIGHTS*

THIS CHAPTER IS ABOUT

☑ **Assignments**
☑ **Conditions of an Assignment**
☑ **Form of an Assignment**
☑ **Effects of an Assignment of Rights**
☑ **Effects of an Assignment of Duties**
☑ **Assignments Under the Uniform Commercial Code**
☑ **Third-Party Beneficiary Contracts**

9-1. Assignments

In any contract, both parties have specified rights and duties. In certain circumstances, the rights or duties of one contracting party may be transferred to a third party. This transfer of rights or duties is known as an *assignment*. Strictly speaking, duties are "delegated," but many contracts speak of "assigning" duties as well as rights. Here we will use the word *assignment* for both purposes.

A. Any party to a contract may assign rights or duties to a third party.

Any party to a contract may assign rights or duties of that contract, unless there is some express reason prohibiting him or her from doing so.

B. When rights or duties are assigned, the parties to the contract enter into new relationships.

1. The party making the assignment is the *assignor*.
2. The third party to whom the assignment is made is the *assignee*.
3. The remaining original party to the contract is the *obligor* or *obligee*, depending on whether he or she is to perform for or receive performance from the assignee, respectively.

9-2. Conditions of an Assignment

A. Most contractual rights or duties are assignable.

Rights or duties may be assigned either in full or in part, including those for claims of money due or about to be due.

B. Some contractual rights or duties are not assignable.

Various types of contractual rights or duties are not assignable unless the obligor agrees to the assignment. Others are not assignable because they are limited by law.

1. Rights or duties under a personal services contract are not assignable unless agreed to by both parties. In these cases, the rights or duties are unique to the person who would receive or perform them. Examples are the right to collect for a personal injury and the right to the services of an artist or surgeon.
2. The right to purchase goods on credit is generally not assignable. This is because the right is granted based on the credit of the original party.

3. Rights or duties are not assignable if the assignment would materially change the burden or risk of the obligor.
4. The rights or duties of a contract that contains a clause specifically prohibiting assignment usually are not assignable. Sometimes, the courts will allow the assignment of rights for reasons of equity and justice, despite a prohibitive assignment clause.
5. Rights or duties for which a statute exists restricting or prohibiting their assignment are not assignable. These statutes vary from state to state.

EXAMPLE 9-1: Curtis gave Jeanette, a well-known portrait artist whose work he admired, a prepaid fee of $2,000 to paint a portrait of his wife from a favorite photograph. When Curtis saw the completed portrait, however, he did not like it and noticed that the style was nothing like Jeanette's. When Curtis questioned Jeanette, she informed him that her work load had been heavy when she agreed to paint the portrait, so she had let one of her students paint it for her. She refused to return the $2,000. Curtis sued to recover the prepaid fee, claiming that he had hired only Jeanette and no one else to paint the portrait. Could Curtis win his suit?

Curtis could win the suit. Portrait painting by a recognized artist is not an assignable duty because the party who contracts with the artist presumes to have bought a special or unique skill that no one else has. In theory at least, Jeanette's artistic skill could not be duplicated by anyone else, so she had no right to assign her duty to paint the portrait without the express knowledge and consent of Curtis.

EXAMPLE 9-2: John's Auto Supply had a contract with Belted Tire Company to purchase 50 tires a month at a specified price. Belted Tire Company was to deliver the tires to John's Auto Supply on the 15th of each month. After several months, John's Auto Supply sold its right to purchase the tires to a body shop in a town that was 60 miles away, which meant that Belted Tire Company would have to drive 60 miles further (or 120 miles round-trip) to deliver the tires. Belted Tire Company could not do this and maintain its schedule of other delivery commitments, so it sued John's Auto Supply to have the assignment overturned. John's Auto Supply responded that it had the right to transfer its right to purchase to a third party. Who won?

Belted Tire Company won the case. John's Auto Supply did have the right to assign its right to purchase to a third party, but not if it would materially change the burden of the obligor. In effect, Belted Tire Company would have been required to give a performance different from that which it contracted to make; therefore, the assignment was not allowable.

9-3. Form of an Assignment

A. An assignment generally may be expressed in any form.

An assignment may be written or spoken, *except* in cases where the original contract falls under statutory regulation. Examples of such contracts are real estate contracts and contracts that must comply with the Statute of Frauds.

B. Consideration is not required for an assignment.

A new contract is not formed when rights or duties are assigned. A third party merely substitutes for one of the original parties, with the contract remaining the same. Therefore, no new consideration is required.

C. The assignee should give notice to the obligor of an assignment of rights.

To protect his or her rights, an assignee should always give notice to the obligor. Notification protects the assignee both by preventing further performance for the assignor and by avoiding the risk that the assignor may attempt to make a second assignment of the contract rights. Should an assignor attempt to assign his or her rights more than once, the majority position in the United States is that the first person to whom a right to performance is assigned has the right to receive that performance, even though the second assignee was first to notify the obligor. This is called the *American First in Time* rule. Some states, however, still follow an English practice called the *English First to Notify* rule. Under this rule, the first assignee to notify the obligor of the assignment has the right to receive performance.

9-4. Effects of an Assignment of Rights

A. The relationship between an assignor and an assignee is one of implied warranty.

The assignor makes an implied promise that the rights being assigned are valid, that he or she is the owner of those rights, and that he or she will not interfere with the assignee's enforcement of those rights. The assignor does not, however, make any promise that the obligor will in fact pay or perform as required. In other words, the assignor relinquishes not only the rights, but any liability that may result from a lack of performance on the obligor's part.

B. The relationship between an obligor and an assignee is the same as between the original parties.

The assignee is said to "stand in the shoes" of the assignor. This phrase means that the assignee can seek to enforce his or her rights in court if performance is not fulfilled by the obligor, and that the assignee assumes the liabilities of the assignor should the obligor have cause to seek damages.

EXAMPLE 9-3: Carson Manufacturing had a contract with Casco Company to receive shipments of machine tools every month for a period of one year. After two months, Carson Manufacturing found it necessary to cut back its operations, so it assigned its right to receive the machine tool shipments to Bessemer, Inc. Bessemer, Inc., notified the Casco Company that further shipments were to be made to their warehouse. For three months, Casco Company made the deliveries, but then it went out of business. Bessemer, Inc., was unable to find another supplier, so it brought suit to have Carson Manufacturing find them another supplier, claiming that Carson Manufacturing bore the ultimate responsibility for Casco Company's failure to fulfill the contract. Would Bessemer, Inc., win the suit?

Bessemer, Inc., would not win the suit. Carson Manufacturing would not be held liable for the failure of Casco Company to fulfill the contract. When rights are assigned, an implied warranty exists between the assignor and assignee, but that warranty does not extend to any liability for the performance or lack of performance of the obligor. Bessemer, Inc., however, "stands in the shoes" of the assignor (Carson Manufacturing) and would be allowed to seek any damages from Casco Company.

9-5. Effects of an Assignment of Duties

The assignment of duties differs somewhat from an assignment of rights.

A. The assignor remains liable for the performance of an assigned duty.

Unlike an assignment of rights, when a duty is assigned to a third party, the assignor is not relieved of the ultimate responsibility for satisfactory performance of the duty. If performance is unsatisfactory, the obligee can sue either the assignee or the assignor. The assignor can, in turn, sue the assignee for failure to perform the assigned duty properly.

B. Only duties that are nonpersonal in nature may be assigned.

A duty that is personal in nature can never be assigned without the consent of the other party to the contract.

C. Some contracts may prohibit the assignment of duties.

As a general rule, a contract clause prohibiting the assignment of duties will be enforced.

EXAMPLE 9-4: Bilt-OK Construction contracted with Willa to remodel her kitchen. Willa wanted custom-built cabinets of oak. Bilt-OK did not normally build custom cabinets, so it assigned that part of the job to an independent carpenter. As work progressed on the cabinets, Willa decided that she was displeased with the carpentry work—grains did not match and the doors were hung unevenly. She complained to a Bilt-OK representative who disclaimed liability, explaining that she would have to take her complaint to the independent carpenter. Willa decided to sue Bilt-OK anyway to have her money refunded, claiming that Bilt-OK was the party that had assigned the carpentry job to the independent carpenter. Shortly thereafter, Bilt-OK filed suit against the carpenter. Would either of these lawsuits succeed?

Both of these lawsuits would succeed. Bilt-OK assigned the carpentry work to the independent carpenter, but that assignment did not relieve Bilt-OK of ultimate responsibility for satisfactory performance of the job. In this situation, Willa had the option of suing the carpenter directly or of suing

Bilt-OK as the assignor. Since Willa opted to sue Bilt-OK, that company's only recourse was to sue the carpenter for an amount at least equivalent to whatever damages Willa may collect.

D. An assignor can only be released from liability through the formation of a novation.

A *novation* is an agreement between all parties of a contract that cancels an existing contract and creates a new one. Only through a novation can an assignor be released from liability for the satisfactory performance of duties.

9-6. Assignments Under the Uniform Commercial Code

The UCC generally approves of the assignment of rights or duties so long as they do not contradict certain guidelines. Remember that the UCC applies only to the sale of goods.

- Rights cannot be assigned that would materially affect the burden or risk of the remaining original party, without that party's consent. [Section 2-210]
- A contract containing a clause prohibiting assignment of the contract is interpreted to bar only delegation of duties, not rights, unless it specifically includes rights also. [Section 2-210]
- An assignment made using the wording "an assignment of all my rights under the contract" or "an assignment of the contract" is interpreted to include both the rights and duties unless the contrary is stated. [Section 2-210]
- An assignor can require proof of performance by an assignee. [Section 2-210]

9-7. Third-Party Beneficiary Contracts

Contracts are often made that include an express intent by either party of providing a benefit to a third person who is not an actual party to the contract. Such a contract is known as a *third-party beneficiary contract*. The third person is known as the *third-party beneficiary* or *beneficiary*. An example of a third-party beneficiary contract is a life insurance policy that names a third person as its beneficiary.

A. There are two categories of third-party beneficiary contracts.

1. A *donee-beneficiary contract* is formed when one party to a contract provides that the proceeds of the contract be conferred upon a third party as a gift.
2. A *creditor-beneficiary contract* is formed when one party to a contract provides that the proceeds of the contract be used to pay a prior debt to a third party.

B. The beneficiary may sue to enforce a third-party beneficiary contract.

The beneficiary must establish that the contract was formed with the express intent of providing a benefit to him or her. The beneficiary need not be named specifically in the contract in order to receive a benefit.

EXAMPLE 9-5: Esther bought a life insurance policy for $50,000 from a vending machine in an airport lounge just before she boarded a flight. In her hurry, she forgot to name a beneficiary on the insurance form before turning it in. Unfortunately, an hour after takeoff, the plane crashed and Esther was killed. Some of her belongings were found and sent to her daughter, Joanna. Among them was a copy of the insurance policy. Joanna contacted the insurance company and claimed the money on the grounds that she was Esther's only living relative. However, the insurance company refused to pay her, claiming that she was not named as a beneficiary on the policy. Would the company's argument be upheld in court?

The company's argument would not be upheld in court. Joanna could make a valid claim to be the third-party beneficiary of the insurance policy even though she was not named in the policy. The policy could only have been taken out for the benefit of someone other than Esther herself and, even though no beneficiary was expressly named, there clearly was intended to be a beneficiary. As Esther's only living relative, Joanna is entitled to the money.

C. Incidental beneficiaries cannot sue to enforce a contract.

Contracts often provide unintended benefits to a third party without that being their specific intent. Such a party is an *incidental beneficiary* and is not allowed to sue for enforcement of the contract. For instance, a contract to pay a person for services might be incidentally beneficial to that person's creditors since the debtor could use payment to settle debts. The specific intent of the contract, however, might be solely to benefit the original parties themselves. In that case, a creditor would be an incidental beneficiary and not be allowed to sue to enforce the contract.

D. A third-party beneficiary contract generally cannot be rescinded without the beneficiary's consent.

If the beneficiary has been notified of a third-party beneficiary contract, has agreed to it, or has somehow relied on it, then the original parties cannot rescind the contract without the beneficiary's consent. Rescission is possible if the beneficiary has not been notified of the terms. An exception occurs with infants, who are presumed to have accepted the terms of any contract that is favorable to them from the moment of execution.

RAISE YOUR GRADES

Can you explain . . . ?

☑ the legal relationships between parties when an assignment of rights or duties is made
☑ the kinds of rights or duties that are generally not assignable and why
☑ the difference between the *American First in Time* rule and the *English First to Notify* rule
☑ the nature of the implied warranty between an assignor and assignee in an assignment of rights
☑ what is meant when it is said that the assignee "stands in the shoes" of the assignor in an assignment of rights
☑ the two categories of third-party beneficiary contracts and the rights of the beneficiaries of these contracts
☑ what an incidental beneficiary is and the rights of such a beneficiary

SUMMARY

1. Both parties to a contract have specified rights and duties.
2. An assignment is the transfer of rights or duties, either in full or in part, from one contracting party to a third party.
3. Either party to a contract may assign rights or duties to a third party, provided there are no restrictions on such assignments.
4. The party making the assignment is the assignor, the third party to whom the assignment is made is the assignee, and the remaining party is the obligor or obligee, depending on whether he or she is to perform for or receive performance from the assignee, respectively.
5. Most contractual rights or duties are assignable.
6. Rights or duties under a personal services contract are not assignable.
7. The right to purchase goods on credit is generally not assignable.
8. Rights or duties are not assignable without the obligor's consent if the assignment would materially alter the burden or risks of the obligor.
9. The rights or duties of a contract that contains a clause prohibiting assignment usually are not assignable.
10. Rights or duties for which a statute exists restricting or prohibiting their assignment are not assignable.
11. An assignment may be written or spoken, except in cases where the original contract falls under statutory regulation that requires it to be in a specific form.

12. Consideration is not required for an assignment.
13. The assignee should give notice of an assignment of rights to the obligor.
14. In an assignment of rights, the relationship between an assignor and an assignee is one of implied warranty.
15. In an assignment of rights, the relationship between an obligor and an assignee is the same as between the original parties.
16. In an assignment of duties, the assignor remains responsible for the ultimate satisfactory performance of the duty.
17. Contracts may contain a clause prohibiting the assignment of duties.
18. An assignor can only be released from liability for the satisfactory performance of duties through the formation of a novation.
19. The UCC generally approves of the assignment of rights or duties under certain conditions.
20. A third-party beneficiary contract exists when the contracting parties intend for the proceeds or performance of the contract to go to a third person who is not an actual party to the contract.
21. There are two categories of third-party beneficiary contracts—donee-beneficiary contracts and creditor-beneficiary contracts.
22. The beneficiary may sue to enforce a third-party beneficiary contract.
23. A contract that is incidentally beneficial to a third person does not give that person the right to sue for enforcement of the contract.
24. A third-party beneficiary contract cannot be rescinded except under certain conditions.

RAPID REVIEW | Answers

True or False

1. There are three categories of situations in which a transfer of rights or duties to a third party may take place. [Section 9-1]

    True

2. The legal relationships between the original parties to a contract remain the same after an assignment of rights or duties is made. [Section 9-1]

    False

3. A clause within a contract that specifically prohibits the assignment of rights or duties is always upheld in court. [Section 9-2]

    False

4. An assignment may be expressed in any form. [Section 9-3]

    False

5. Notification of an assignment of rights must always be given by the assignee to the obligor. [Section 9-3]

    False

6. Consideration is not required for an assignment. [Section 9-3]

    True

7. An assignment of rights carries with it an implied warranty by the assignor that the rights being assigned are valid, that the assignor is the owner of those rights, and that the assignor will not interfere with the assignee's enforcement of those rights. [Section 9-4]

    True

8. An assignor of rights remains liable for the ultimate satisfactory fulfillment of those rights. [Section 9-4]

    False

9. An assignor of duties remains liable for the ultimate satisfactory performance of those duties. [Section 9-5]

    True

10. A novation is an agreement between all parties of a contract that cancels an existing contract and creates a new one. [Section 9-5]

    True

11. An assignment of personal duties may be made without the consent of the obligee. [Section 9-5]

    False

12. If an obligee is not satisfied with the performance of duties under a contract, and assignment of those duties was made to a third party, the obligee may sue either the assignor or the third party to enforce the contract. [Section 9-5]   *True*

13. The UCC approves of the assignment of rights or duties under a contract for the sale of goods in all circumstances. [Section 9-6]   *False*

14. A donee-beneficiary contract is formed when one party to a contract provides that the proceeds of the contract be given to a third party as a gift. [Section 9-7]   *True*

15. A creditor-beneficiary contract is formed when one party to a contract promises a creditor that he or she will use the proceeds of the contract to pay off a debt. [Section 9-7]   *False*

16. Third-party beneficiaries must be named in a contract in order to sue for enforcement of the contract. [Section 9-7]   *False*

17. A third-party beneficiary contract can never be rescinded without the beneficiary's consent. [Section 9-7]   *False*

SOLVED PROBLEMS

PROBLEM 9-1   Alice, a young lawyer, bought a home in the historic district of Appledale to renovate for use as her law office. She contracted with Jacob, a local architect who specialized in restoring historic structures, to draw blueprints for the renovation. Jacob planned to start the blueprints in September, but in August, he received a grant to study in Europe, so without first seeking Alice's permission, he sold the right to perform to Sam, another architect. Sam drew up some blueprints, but Alice was disappointed in them and refused to pay for them, arguing that her contract for the work had been with Jacob. Sam sued to force Alice to pay for the blueprints. Will Sam win?

Answer: It is doubtful that a court would make Alice pay for Sam's blueprints. A contract to draw blueprints for renovation of a historic structure would most likely be considered a contract to perform a unique, personal service requiring special skills and experience on the part of the person undertaking it. A court would not consider this duty assignable unless Jacob sought Alice's permission to do so. In fact, Alice could sue Jacob since he remained ultimately responsible for the satisfactory performance of the contract. Sam's only recourse would be to sue Jacob for reimbursement for his time. [Section 9-5]

PROBLEM 9-2   Reuben sold his car to Carol for $2,000, payable in six months. In three months, however, Reuben needed cash, so he sold the right to collect this debt to Sam for $1,500. When the six months were up, Sam wrote to Carol requesting the $2,000, but his letter was returned, marked "Moved, Left no Address." Sam then sued Reuben for payment of the $2,000. Could Sam collect?

Answer: Sam could not collect any money from Reuben. The assignment of a right does not carry with it any warranty that the obligor will perform. When Reuben assigned his right to collect the debt to Sam, he was absolved of any liability resulting from Carol's failure to live up to the contract. However, Sam does have the right to try to locate Carol and sue to enforce his right to collect the debt from her. [Section 9-5]

PROBLEM 9-3   Suppose that in the situation described in Problem 9-2, Carol had paid Reuben the $2,000 before she was notified that Reuben had sold Sam the right to collect the debt. Could Sam sue Carol to collect the debt under these circumstances?

Answer: Sam could not sue Carol to collect the debt under these circumstances. An assignment of a right is binding on the obligor only if the obligor is notified of the assignment. Since Carol paid Reuben the $2,000, believing that Reuben still had the right to collect the debt, she would not be required to pay the money twice. Sam would have the right, however, to sue Reuben for the $2,000 if Reuben refused to turn it over to him. Sam could have protected himself from this type of situation by notifying Carol of the assignment. [Section 9-5]

PROBLEM 9-4 Arthur, a wheat farmer, contracted with Jack to deliver 10,000 tons of wheat to Jack's mill. Later, however, Arthur sold his duty to deliver the wheat to Doug, another wheat farmer. When Doug delivered the wheat to Jack's mill, Jack refused it, claiming that only Arthur's wheat was acceptable. Could Jack refuse Doug's wheat on these grounds?

Answer: Jack could not refuse to accept Doug's wheat just because it wasn't Arthur's. Wheat is typically considered a uniform product, so the duty to deliver it can be assigned to anyone capable of delivering wheat of the contracted kind and quantity. Jack could refuse Doug's wheat only if Jack could prove that the original contract had called for a special kind of wheat that only Arthur was growing. [Section 9-2]

PROBLEM 9-5 Martha sold her house trailer to Agnes for $10,000, payable in 90 days. One Monday, soon afterwards, Martha needed cash, so she sold the right to collect this debt to James for $9,500, On the next day, Tuesday, Martha dishonestly sold the right to collect the same debt to Charles for $9,000. On Wednesday, Charles notified Agnes that the right to collect the debt was now his. On Thursday, however, James notified Agnes that he, too, had the right to collect the debt. To whom should Agnes pay the $10,000?

Answer: The majority position on this question in the United States is that the first person to whom a debt is assigned has the right to collect it. This is called the "American First in Time" rule. Under this rule, James would have the right to collect the debt since he was the first one to whom Martha assigned that right. A few states, however, still follow an English practice called the "English First to Notify" rule. Under this rule, the first assignee who notifies the debtor of the assignment has the right to collect the debt. If this rule were applied in this case, Charles would have the right to collect Agnes's debt. [Section 9-3]

PROBLEM 9-6 Larry sold his motorcycle to Hal in exchange for Hal's promise to pay the outstanding note on Larry's car. When the note came due, however, Hal failed to pay it, so the bank that held the loan sued Larry to collect on the note. Larry refused to pay on the grounds that he had assigned the note to Hal. Would Larry's argument be upheld in court?

Answer: Larry's argument would not be upheld in court. The right to purchase goods on credit is not an assignable right. The bank relied solely on Larry's credit standing when it granted him the loan, and is not obligated to relieve Larry of his liability for the debt, even though Larry assigned it to Hal. Larry would have to pay the note himself, but he could then sue Hal for not fulfilling his agreement. [Section 9-2]

PROBLEM 9-7 Tom, a painter, contracted with Sally, a friend, to paint three rooms of Sally's house. In exchange, Sally agreed to pay $200 to Tom's mother, Irma. Tom did not owe the money to Irma; he simply wanted her to have the money as a gift. Tom painted the rooms, but Sally did not pay Irma the $200. Could Irma sue Sally to collect the money?

Answer: Irma could sue Sally to collect the $200. Irma was not an original party to the contract, but she was a third-party beneficiary. More specifically, a donee-beneficiary contract was formed between Tom and Sally, in that Tom expressly intended when entering the contract that the $200 owed for his services be given to Irma as a gift. So long as Irma can prove that the contract was formed with this intent that she receive a benefit, she has the right as the beneficiary to sue Sally to enforce the contract. [Section 9-7]

PROBLEM 9-8 Suppose that in the situation described in Problem 9-7, Tom owed Irma the $200. Could Irma sue Sally to collect the money?

Answer: Even if Tom owed Irma the $200 instead of giving it to her as a gift, Irma could still sue Sally to collect the money. In these circumstances, a creditor-beneficiary contract would have been formed between Tom and Sally, in that Tom would have expressly intended when entering the contract that the $200 owed for his services be used to pay a debt to Irma. Again, so long as Irma could prove that the contract was formed with this intent that she receive a benefit, she would have the right as the beneficiary to sue Sally to enforce the contract. [Section 9-7]

PROBLEM 9-9   Levi, a potter, had a contract to provide The Pottery Place store with two sets of handcrafted canister sets in exchange for $200. He happened to be overdue on a payment of $100 that he owed to Artisan's Supply Shop for clay he had purchased on credit. Levi assured Artisan's Supply Shop that as soon as he received the $200 for his canister sets, he would pay them the $100. As it turned out, when Levi received the $200 from The Pottery Place, he used the money as part of his rent payment and did not pay the debt he owed to Artisan's Supply Shop. He informed Artisan's Supply Shop later that he had spent the $200 and could not pay them till he sold more of his work. Artisan's Supply Shop contacted The Pottery Place and demanded the $100, claiming that the contract between Levi and The Pottery Place had been a creditor-beneficiary contract and, as such, they were entitled as the beneficiary to seek payment of the $100 from The Pottery Place. The Pottery Place denied that there had been such an agreement. Artisan's Supply Shop sued The Pottery Place for the $100 anyway. Would Artisan's Supply Shop win the suit?

Answer: Artisan's Supply Shop would not win the suit. When the contract was formed between the original parties (The Pottery Place and Levi), it did not include the express intent that the proceeds of the contract be used to pay the debt Levi owed to Artisan's Supply Shop. Despite Levi's oral commitment to Artisan's Supply Shop, the contract was clearly formed for the mutual benefit of the original parties themselves, making Artisan's Supply Shop only an incidental beneficiary to the contract. Levi's oral declaration of intent made to Artisan's Supply Shop was therefore not binding on The Pottery Place. Artisan's Supply Shop could sue only Levi to collect the debt. [Section 9-7]

10 DISCHARGE AND REMEDIES

THIS CHAPTER IS ABOUT

- ☑ **Discharge of Contracts**
- ☑ **Discharge by Conditions of a Contract**
- ☑ **Discharge by Performance**
- ☑ **Discharge by Agreement**
- ☑ **Discharge by Impossibility**
- ☑ **Discharge by Operation of Law**
- ☑ **Discharge by Breach of Contract**
- ☑ **Remedies for Breach of Contract**

10-1. Discharge of Contracts

Usually, the parties to a contract eventually perform as specified. When this occurs, the obligations of the parties are said to be *discharged* by full performance. Full performance, however, is not the only method by which the parties may be discharged from further liability under the contract. There are some instances when a party may be excused, and thereby discharged, from a contract even though that party's obligations have not been performed.

10-2. Discharge by Conditions of a Contract

A *condition* is an expressly stated or implied situation or event upon which the performance of a contract is dependent. If the conditions set forth by a contract are not present, the parties can be discharged from their obligations to perform. There are several categories of contractual conditions.

A. Performance can be based on a condition precedent.

A condition in a contract that provides that a party's obligation to perform is dependent on some fact or event taking place is called a *condition precedent*.

EXAMPLE 10-1: John and Marilyn agreed that he would buy her car for $2,500 on August 31. On June 1, however, Marilyn delivered the car to John, stating that she was moving across country in less than a week and urgently needed the money. John refused to accept the car or pay the $2,500. Marilyn sued John for not fulfilling the contract. Did she win?

Marilyn did not win. The August 31 date was a condition precedent to John's obligation to perform. Although Mary performed her obligations under the contract, John was not required to perform until the condition precedent had occurred.

B. Performance can be based on a condition subsequent.

A condition in a contract that provides that a party is obligated to perform some act, but also provides that the party will be relieved of that obligation if some fact or event takes place is called a *condition subsequent*.

EXAMPLE 10-2: Sean, a gardener, had a contract with the O'Toole Company to take care of the company grounds for five years. The contract also stated that if the company should move to another location within that five-year period, Sean would be released from his obligation to care for the grounds.

After four years, the O'Toole Company relocated to another state. Sean quit, but the company threatened to sue him for not fulfilling the contract terms of providing service for five years. Would the O'Toole Company win the suit?

The O'Toole Company would not win the suit. The company's relocation was a condition subsequent that released Sean from the obligation to continue caring for the grounds. Sean would therefore be discharged from performing the last year of service based on the condition subsequent.

C. Performance can be based on concurrent conditions.

A *concurrent condition* exists when the performance of one party is conditioned upon the performance of the other party, and both are intended to occur at approximately the same time. One party may not hold the other party liable for performance unless he or she is willing and able to perform also.

D. Performance can be based on an implied-in-fact condition.

A condition that is not stated in a contract, but is understood or inferred under the circumstances, is an *implied-in-fact condition*. For example, a contract to buy goods contains the implied-in-fact condition that the promisor has the goods to sell in the first place.

E. Performance can be based on an implied-in-law condition.

An *implied-in-law condition* is understood to exist in any contract in that it is understood that no performance or means of performance will violate the law. For example, a contract to sell goods is understood to contain an implied-in-law condition that the goods involved are not stolen.

10-3. Discharge by Performance

Most contracts are discharged by full performance by both parties of its terms. Disputes can arise, however, as to whether there has been full performance. There are several principles that are applied to determine if performance is sufficient to discharge either party from its obligations.

A. A tender of performance can discharge a party to a contract.

A good faith offer to perform is known as a *tender*. If one party makes a tender of performance, that party can be discharged from the contract if the tender of performance is not accepted by the other party. An exception occurs when a tender of performance is given to pay a debt. If the tender is refused, the party is still obligated to pay the debt.

B. Substantial performance can discharge a party to a contract.

Substantial performance occurs when a party essentially performs all of his or her obligations under the contract with only minor deviations. When substantial performance has been given, the performing party can be discharged from the contract and the other party cannot refuse to compensate for performance. However, the performing party can be held liable for the minor deviations. The substantial performance rule is most often applied to construction contracts.

If it is determined that less than substantial performance was given by a party, then that party is not entitled to the performance of the other party, and the other party may sue for any damages caused by the partial performance of the contract. A court may require, however, that the other party pay for any partial performance received.

EXAMPLE 10-3: The Coopers saw a model of a house built by Lummox Construction Company. They contracted with Lummox Construction to build the same house for them for $85,000. When the house was completed, however, they noticed that the air-conditioning unit had been placed directly below their bedroom window on the back of the house. On the model house, the unit had been placed next to the garage on the side of the house. The house was like the model in every other respect, but they were upset about the placement of the unit because they would be able to hear it running below their bedroom window. The Coopers refused to pay for the house unless Lummox Construction Company would move the unit to the side of the house. The company refused to move the unit and sued the Coopers for payment of the house, claiming that substantial performance had been given. Would Lummox Construction Company win the suit?

Lummox Construction Company would win the suit. It would be clear that substantial performance was given since the house was like the model in every respect except for the placement of the air-conditioning unit. Lummox Construction Company could be held liable for the minor deviation, however, since the unit would indeed be noisy if left below the bedroom window.

C. A time of performance can discharge a party to a contract if not met.

Many contracts state a specific *time of performance* when performance must be completed. When no time of performance is stated, performance must be completed within a *reasonable amount of time*. It is important to note that even if a specific time of performance is stated, it must be shown to be vital or *of the essence* to be strictly enforceable. For example, if a performing party is unable to meet a specified time of performance for legitimate reasons, and can show that the time factor was not truly *of the essence*, then the other party would not be allowed to discharge the contract for violation of the time specification.

D. Satisfactory performance can discharge a party to a contract.

A contract may contain a *personal satisfaction clause* stating that the party receiving performance must be satisfied with it in order for the contract to be discharged. The courts recognize that a personal satisfaction clause could be easily abused, so two approaches are generally applied when determining if satisfactory performance has been given.

1. *Objective satisfaction.* If the standard for satisfaction applies to mechanical utility, merchantability, or operative fitness, such as a piece of machinery, the reasonable person standard is applied. Payment may not be refused if a reasonable person would accept the performance.
2. *Subjective satisfaction.* If the standard for satisfaction applies to matters of personal taste or preference, such as a painting, the reasonable person standard is not applied. Payment may be refused even if a reasonable person would accept the performance.

EXAMPLE 10-4: Jason and Karen, who were about to be married, contracted with Ellen, a jeweler, to have custom wedding bands made of gold. They provided clear and detailed drawings of exactly what they wanted for Ellen to follow. The contract also provided that the rings must meet with their personal satisfaction. When the rings were completed, Jason and Karen were pleased that the rings did look exactly like the detailed drawings they had provided. When Karen tried hers on, however, she felt that it was too heavy and rejected it on the grounds that it did not meet with her personal satisfaction. Jason rejected his also, since he did not want it if Karen did not want hers. Ellen sued for payment, claiming that the rings had been made exactly as Jason and Karen had required and that the weight of the rings had to be what they were in order to meet those requirements. Did Ellen win the suit?

Ellen won the suit. Karen was abusing her right to personal satisfaction. The fact that the ring was heavier than she wanted was not subject to a standard of personal taste, but to a standard of functional utility. Karen could have refused her ring on a subjective basis if it had not met the specifications of the drawings. She could not, however, refuse the rings on an objective basis that it was not functional because it was heavier than she expected. Jason's personal satisfaction could not be based on Karen's personal satisfaction. The reasonable person standard would be applied here and, since the rings were made exactly as specified and would have to be their weight to be made as specified, Jason and Karen would be required to accept and pay for the rings in good faith.

10-4. Discharge by Agreement

The parties to a contract may agree to discharge all or part of their obligations under a contract either by modifying the terms of the contract or ending the contract.

A. Both parties may agree to a rescission.

Both parties may agree to rescind their contract with no performance by either party. Consideration is required for a rescission to be upheld, but the act of both parties surrendering their rights is usually allowed as consideration.

B. Both parties may agree to a novation.

Novation was discussed in Chapter 9 as a means of releasing one party from a contract and substituting a third party, in essence creating a new contract. A novation may also be used as a means between original contracting parties of discharging one contract between them and creating a new one.

C. Both parties may agree to an accord and satisfaction.

Both parties may agree to alter the terms of a contract without cancelling it altogether. An *accord* occurs when the parties agree to substitute a different performance than one stated in the original contract. A *satisfaction* occurs when the different performance has taken place. An accord and satisfaction serves to discharge the parties from the obligations to perform that were replaced.

EXAMPLE 10-5: Marine Fishery entered into a contract with Daniel to supply Daniel's pet shop with 50 fish of a rare, tropical species for $200. Soon after the contract was formed, however, Daniel contacted Marine Fishery, saying that he was having second thoughts about whether he could sell so many of the fish, as that species was very expensive. As it turned out, Marine Fishery was having a difficult time obtaining the rare fish, so they agreed to supply 200 fish of a different species for the same price and Daniel agreed to accept them. When Marine Fishery delivered the fish, however, Daniel refused to accept them, claiming that he wanted the rare fish after all, and Marine Fishery was obligated to supply them under the original terms of the contract. Marine Fishery sued to enforce the contract. Did Marine Fishery win?

Marine Fishery won. When Marine Fishery agreed to supply a different species of fish than the original contract specified, and Daniel agreed to accept them for the original contract price, an accord was formed. The accord substituted new obligations for the original ones, thereby discharging Marine Fishery from having to supply the rare species of fish. When Marine Fishery satisfied the accord by delivering the new species of fish, Daniel was obligated to satisfy his part of the accord by accepting them and paying the original contract price of $200.

D. Both parties may agree to a waiver.

A *waiver* occurs when any party to a contract agrees to discharge the other party from either part or all of his or her obligations to perform under the contract. A waiver may be expressed or implied by the actions of the party. Only a full waiver of all further obligations can discharge a contract.

EXAMPLE 10-6: Sherry borrowed $1,500 from Monroe and agreed to make payments of $200 on the first of each month until the loan was paid back. For the first three months, Sherry's payments were 7, 15, and 10 days late, respectively. Monroe was annoyed by this, but he deposited her checks into his account and said nothing. In the fourth month, Sherry's payment was 9 days late. Monroe decided that he had had enough, so he contacted Sherry and demanded that she pay the full balance of the loan at once, claiming that she had broken the terms of the contract. Sherry refused to pay the balance or any other payments on the grounds that Monroe had implied a waiver of the first of the month requirement by depositing her money, and this waiver of part of her obligations was grounds for discharging the contract. Who was right?

Neither Sherry nor Monroe was right. Monroe did imply through his acceptance of Sherry's late payments that he was waiving the obligation that Sherry make each payment on the first of the month. He could not demand full payment of the loan after demonstrating such a waiver. Sherry, however, could not refuse to make any more payments because Monroe's waiver was for only part of her obligations under the contract. All obligations under a contract must be waived in order for a contract to be discharged. She must continue to make the payments until the loan is paid back.

10-5. Discharge by Impossibility

When events occur that affect a contract to such an extent that it becomes impossible for a party or all parties to perform, the contract can be discharged. The events must occur through no fault of the parties. Performance must be truly impossible. Events that merely make performance more difficult or expensive are not sufficient to discharge a contract. Four situations are generally accepted as making a contract impossible to perform.

A. Death or incapacitating illness of a party constitutes impossibility of performance.

Death or incapacitating illness of a party can discharge a contract if the contract could only be performed by the deceased or incapacitated party. It is important to note that if parties enter into joint obligations (such as a mortgage loan granted jointly to a husband

and wife), and one of those parties dies or is incapacitated, the remaining party is still obligated to perform.

B. Illegality constitutes impossibility of performance.

Passage of a law that makes performance illegal or impossible can discharge a contract. For example, if someone contracts to have an office built in a certain area, and a zoning law is passed restricting that area to residential development, the contract can be discharged.

C. Destruction of the subject matter constitutes impossibility of performance.

Destruction of the subject matter of a contract can discharge the contract, provided that the subject matter cannot be replaced.

D. Frustration of purpose constitutes impossibility of performance.

Frustration of the underlying purpose of a contract can discharge the contract. In these circumstances, the contract is not technically impossible to perform, but some event has caused a significant departure from the basic assumptions under which the contract was made. If the frustration of purpose is only temporary, the parties are still obligated to perform once the frustration has been removed.

EXAMPLE 10-7: Frank, a farmer, contracted with Johnson Seed to have them supply a truckload of hay every month for a year for his cows and horses. Unfortunately, after six months of deliveries, Frank's barn caught on fire one night and all of his animals were killed in the fire. Frank contacted Johnson Seed shortly thereafter to let them know that he did not need any more deliveries of hay until he could replace his stock. Johnson Seed, however, refused to cancel the contract, saying that Frank must either continue to accept or at least pay for the remaining six months of deliveries. Frank sued Johnson Seed to have the contract discharged. Did Frank win?

Frank did not win. It is true that, through no fault of his own, the underlying purpose of the contract was frustrated when all of Frank's animals were killed in the fire. Frank admitted, however, that this was only a temporary frustration, in that he planned to replace his animals, at which time he would be obligated to receive the remaining six months of deliveries from Johnson Seed. Johnson Seed was incorrect, too, in their attempt to force Frank to either receive or pay for the remaining deliveries. They would be required to cease deliveries until the frustration of purpose was removed.

10-6. Discharge by Operation of Law

There are three situations that can discharge a contract by operation of law.

A. Material alteration can discharge a party from performance.

When one party to a written contract materially alters that contract without the knowledge or consent of the other party, the contract can be discharged in full or in part. A separate consideration must change hands for an alteration to be enforced. In other words, the alteration cannot substantially benefit only one party.

B. Bankruptcy can discharge a party from performance.

A bankruptcy proceeding can result in a debtor being discharged from all contractual obligations to his or her creditors. Bankruptcy will be discussed in more detail in Chapter 22.

C. The statute of limitations can discharge a party from performance.

All states have a *statute of limitations* that limits the time period during which legal actions may be taken. Different time periods are usually specified for different types of actions. If a party to a contract does not bring suit within the specified time period, the contract will be discharged.

10-7. Discharge by Breach of Contract

A *breach of contract* occurs when, without any legal excuse, a party or both parties to a contract fail to perform all or part of their obligations as specified in the contract. When a contract is breached by one party, the other party's obligation to perform can be discharged. The other party does not have to treat the breach as a discharge, however, and may choose to seek remedies for any injuries resulting from the breach of contract.

There are several situations when a party may claim that a contract has been breached by the other party and may proceed to seek any remedies available to him or her.

A. A party can claim breach of contract based on failure to perform.

When the time for performance arrives and the obligated party simply does not perform and has no legal excuse for not doing so, the other party may treat the nonperformance as a breach, is discharged from any remaining obligations of the contract, and may seek remedies.

B. A party can claim breach of contract based on anticipatory breach.

If one party clearly indicates in any way a refusal to perform when the time of performance arrives, the other party may treat the refusal as a breach of contract, is discharged from any remaining obligations of the contract, and may seek remedies. This principle is designed to protect the nonbreaching party since it would be unfair to require that party's performance in the face of the other party's blatant refusal to do so.

C. A party can claim breach of contract based on created impossibility.

If a party somehow creates a situation or event that makes it impossible for either party to perform, that party will be in breach of contract. The other party's obligation to perform is discharged and he or she may seek damages.

EXAMPLE 10-8: Sara, a politician, contracted with Kevin, a writer, to have Kevin ghostwrite her autobiography for $5,000. The contract stated that Sara would meet with Kevin over the next 3 months for not less than 25 hours in order to supply Kevin with the material he needed to write the book. Kevin, in turn, was to complete the book within six months. Kevin arranged to meet with Sara many times over the three-month period, but Sara continually cancelled the appointments and did not otherwise supply notes or information that Kevin could use in the book. At the end of the three months, Kevin sued Sara, claiming that Sara had made it impossible for him to write the book and demanding the $5000. Did he win?

Kevin won the suit. By continually cancelling her appointments with Kevin within the specified three months, Sara was not only in breach of contract for her failure to perform, but through her failure to perform, she had created a situation that made it impossible for Kevin to perform by writing the book within 6 months. Kevin's obligation to perform would be discharged, and Sara would probably be required to pay Kevin the $5,000 as a remedy for the loss of income he suffered as a result of her breach of contract.

10-8. Remedies for Breach of Contract

When one party breaches a contract, the other party may seek a remedy. A *remedy* is intended to give the nonbreaching party the benefit he or she would have received if the contract had not been breached. There are three categories of remedies that the courts may allow to a nonbreaching party.

A. Damages may be ordered by the court.

The court may order that *damages*, or money, be paid to the nonbreaching party to recover any financial loss or injury caused by the breach. When suing for damages, the nonbreaching party must base the amount of damages caused by the breach of contract on fact. For example, a loss of profits cannot be awarded unless the profits can be estimated with reasonable accuracy. Furthermore, the nonbreaching party must attempt to *mitigate damages.* In other words, it is the responsibility of the nonbreaching party to prevent damages from occurring or increasing after a breach has occurred if it is within his or her power to do so. The court will not allow recovery of losses that could have been avoided. There are four categories of damages, any or all of which may be awarded by the court.

1. *Compensatory damages* may be awarded for incurred losses, whether direct or indirect. Indirect, or *consequential*, damages, may only be granted if the breaching party knew or had reason to know that the losses would be incurred as a result of the breach. The formula for determining the amount of compensatory damages is to award the value of the unfulfilled obligations minus the cost to the nonbreaching party of fulfilling his or her obligations.

2. *Nominal damages*, often $1 or less, may be awarded when there is no real loss. In these cases, the nonbreaching party generally sues just to avoid the appearance of being responsible in any way for the breach or its results.

3. *Liquidated damages* may be awarded if the contract contained a liquidated damages clause that specified an amount to be paid in case of a breach. The liquidated damages must be reasonable, however, and must apply to situations where damages would be difficult to measure. If not, the court will ignore a liquidated damages clause and use its own judgment in determining damages.

4. *Punitive damages* are intended to punish the breaching party and usually are only awarded in cases involving fraud or misconduct of a serious nature.

B. Specific performance may be ordered by the court.

In some cases, such as contracts involving a truly unique item, money would not be a sufficient remedy for the injuries caused to the nonbreaching party. The court may order the *specific performance* of the contract, in essence not allowing the breach of contract. The court would almost never order specific performance of a contract involving personal services, on the basis that it is practically impossible to force a person to render services.

EXAMPLE 10-9: Charles, an art collector and dealer, telephoned one of his clients, Tanya, when he acquired a small sketch by a renowned French artist. He knew that Tanya was interested in this artist's works and, sure enough, she agreed to purchase the sketch for $2,000. When Tanya went to pick up the sketch, however, Charles informed her that he had had a change of heart and wanted to add the sketch to his own collection. Tanya insisted that he fulfill their contract and sell her the sketch. Instead, Charles offered to pay her the $2,000 and call it even. Tanya sued to force Charles to sell her the sketch. Did she win?

Tanya won. In this case, the contract involved a truly unique, irreplaceable item. Damages would not be sufficient to remedy the injury caused to Tanya by Charles's breach. The court would likely order the specific performance of the contract, in essence not allowing Charles to breach his contract with Tanya.

C. Rescission and restitution may be ordered by the court.

Under some circumstances, such as failure of the original consideration, the court may allow a full *rescission*, or cancellation of the contract. *Restitution* would be required, meaning that the parties would have to return any benefits received from each other up to the time of the breach.

RAISE YOUR GRADES

Can you explain . . . ?

☑ the different types of contractual conditions, express and implied, and how they affect the discharge of a contract

☑ how substantial performance differs from satisfactory performance and how each affects the discharge of a contract

☑ the various ways that the parties to a contract may agree to discharge all or part of their obligations to perform

☑ when it is generally accepted that performance of a contract is impossible

☑ the situations that can discharge a contract by operation of law

☑ when a party may claim that a contract has been breached by another party and how the breach affects the nonbreaching party's obligation to perform

☑ the three categories of remedies that the courts may allow to a nonbreaching party and how those remedies are determined

SUMMARY

1. The parties to a contract are discharged from their obligations to perform by full performance of the terms of the contract.
2. There are many ways other than full performance that the parties to a contract can be discharged from their obligations to perform.
3. There are five types of expressed and implied conditions that, if not present, can discharge the parties to a contract from their obligations to perform: conditions precedent; conditions subsequent; concurrent conditions; implied-in-fact conditions; and implied-in-law conditions.
4. There are several circumstances when it may be necessary to determine if performance or nonperformance is sufficient to discharge either party from its obligations to perform: when a tender of performance is refused; when substantial performance of the contract terms has been given with minor variations; when a specific time of performance that is vital has not been met; and when personal satisfaction of the party receiving performance is required.
5. There are four ways that the parties to a contract may agree to discharge all or part of their obligations to perform: rescission; novation; accord and satisfaction; and waiver.
6. The parties to a contract can be discharged from their obligations to perform when, through no fault of their own, events occur that make performance impossible.
7. Four situations that are generally accepted as making performance impossible are: death or incapacitating illness of a party whose existence or performance was essential to the contract; passage of a law that makes performance illegal; destruction of a contract's subject matter when that subject matter cannot be replaced; and occurrence of an event that frustrates the underlying purpose of the contract.
8. Three situations that can discharge a contract by operation of law are: material alteration of a contract by one party without the knowledge or consent of the other party; a bankruptcy proceeding that discharges a debtor from obligations to his or her creditors; and the running out of the time period, or statute of limitations, during which legal action must have been taken.
9. A breach of contract occurs when, without any legal excuse, a party or both parties to a contract fail to perform all or part of their obligations as specified in the contract.
10. A party's obligation to perform can be discharged when the other party breaches the contract.
11. A party may claim that the other party has breached a contract when the other party fails to perform when the time to perform arrives, clearly indicates that he or she will not perform when the time to perform arrives, or creates a situation that makes performance impossible. In all three situations, the nonbreaching party can be discharged from the obligation to perform and seek remedies for the breach.
12. When one party breaches a contract, the other party may seek a remedy that gives the benefit he or she would have received if the contract had not been breached.
13. There are three categories of remedies that the courts may allow to a nonbreaching party: damages, or money payment; specific performance of the contract; or rescission and restitution. The court will not allow recovery of damages that could have been avoided by the nonbreaching party.
14. When awarding damages to a nonbreaching party, the court may allow compensatory damages, nominal damages, liquidated damages, or punitive damages.

RAPID REVIEW   Answers

True or False

1. A condition is an expressly stated or implied situation or event upon which the performance of a contract is dependent. [Section 10-2]   *True*

2. A condition subsequent determines when a party's obligation to perform will arise under a contract. [Section 10-2]   *False*

3. If one party's performance is a condition precedent, that party must perform his or her obligations under the contract before the other party is required to perform. [Section 10-2]   *True*

4. If a debtor offers to repay a loan by working for the creditor instead of paying cash, and that tender of performance is refused, the debtor can be discharged from the obligation to repay the loan. [Section 10-3]   *False*

5. A performing party cannot be held liable for minor deviations from a contract so long as the deviations were not deliberate avoidance of the contract terms. [Section 10-3]   *False*

6. A party is not required to pay for the partial performance of the other party and may sue for damages caused by the partial performance. [Section 10-3]   *False*

7. A time of performance clause is always upheld in court. [Section 10-3]   *False*

8. The reasonable person standard is applied to satisfactory performance of matters pertaining to mechanical utility, merchantability, or operative fitness. [Section 10-3]   *True*

9. Consideration is required for a rescission of a contract. [Section 10-4]   *True*

10. If a party does not satisfy an accord, then he or she must satisfy the original obligations of the contract. [Section 10-4]   *False*

11. If a contract is made to sell a valuable antique, and the antique is somehow destroyed, then the selling party must pay a sum equal to the value of the antique to the buying party. [Section 10-5]   *False*

12. If, for any reason, the underlying purpose of a contract is frustrated, the contract is discharged. [Section 10-5]   *False*

13. A party to a contract may sue the other party for damages at any time. [Section 10-5]   *False*

14. A breach of contract occurs when a party or both parties fail to perform any of their obligations as specified in the contract, and have no legal excuse for not doing so. [Section 10-7]   *True*

15. An anticipatory breach has occurred when one party to a contract feels certain that the other party may not perform. [Section 10-7]   *False*

16. Consequential damages may be awarded even if the performing party had no knowledge of the consequential loss that the breach would incur. [Section 10-8]   *False*

17. Liquidated damages are only awarded if they are reasonable and apply to situations where compensatory damages would be difficult to measure. [Section 10-8]   *True*

18. Punitive damages are always awarded to a nonbreaching party as punishment of the breaching party. [Section 10-8]   *False*

19. Specific performance would likely be granted in a case where a party refused to provide a personal service as specified in the contract. [Section 10-8]   *False*

SOLVED PROBLEMS

PROBLEM 10-1 What are the five types of contractual conditions and how do they affect the obligations to perform of the parties to a contract?

Answer: (1) A condition precedent provides that a party is obligated to perform only if or when some fact or event takes place.

(2) A condition subsequent provides that a party is obligated to perform unless or until some fact or event takes place.

(3) A concurrent condition provides that a party is obligated to perform if and when the other party performs at about the same time.

(4) An implied-in-fact condition is any condition implied by the circumstances of the contract. If not met, the parties are not obligated to perform.

(5) An implied-in-law condition is implied in any contract to the effect that the performance or means of performance will not violate the law. If not met, the parties are not obligated to perform.

[Section 10-2]

PROBLEM 10-2 Explain how (1) tender of performance, (2) substantial performance, (3) time of performance, and (4) satisfactory performance can affect the obligations to perform of the parties to a contract.

Answer: (1) A tender of performance can discharge a party from the obligation to perform if it is refused by the other party, except when the tender is offered as payment of a debt.

(2) Substantial performance can discharge a party from further obligations to perform, but that party can be held liable for any minor deviations from the terms of the contract.

(3) Failure of a party to perform within a stated time of performance can discharge the other party from the obligation to perform if time is shown to be "of the essence."

(4) Satisfactory performance subjects one party's performance to the approval of the other party before the performing party can be discharged from the obligation to perform.

[Section 10-3]

PROBLEM 10-3 Amber entered into a contract to purchase 5 acres of farm land from Nick for $10,000. Amber then applied at her bank for a loan of the $10,000. Before they would agree to loan her the money, her bank wanted a title search done that, when completed, showed that Nick did not really own the land—his brother did. The bank refused to lend Amber the money, and Amber contacted Nick, refusing to buy the land. Nick, however, insisted that his brother had given him permission to sell the land, and sued Amber to enforce the contract. Did he win?

Answer: Nick did not win. Their contract contained an implied-in-fact condition that the land belonged to Nick. Since this implied-in-fact condition was not present, the parties were discharged of their obligations to perform. Amber could contact Nick's brother and contract with him to buy the land if she wished, but she was not obligated to purchase it from Nick when she discovered that the implied-in-fact condition was not present. [Section 10-2]

PROBLEM 10-4 Claude, the owner of a seafood restaurant, placed an order for twice his usual amount of flounder and shellfish in anticipation of a busy Fourth of July weekend. He made it clear to his supplier, Sea Products, that he needed the order filled *before* the Fourth of July weekend. As it turned out, Sea Products delivered only the usual amount of flounder and shellfish on the Thursday before the weekend, and said that they would deliver the rest of the order on the following Wednesday. Claude, however, told them that he would not accept or pay for the rest of the order on Wednesday, as he would no longer need it. Sea Products sued Claude, claiming that their tender of performance had been refused, releasing them from the obligation to deliver the rest of the order, and demanding damages in the amount of the rest of the order for breach of contract. Did Sea Products win?

Answer: Sea Products did not win. Ordinarily, if a tender of performance is refused, the performing party is discharged from the obligation to perform and may seek a remedy for any loss incurred. In this case, however, Sea Products was aware that a specific time of performance (before the Fourth of July weekend) was "of the essence" and indeed, was the only reason why the double order was placed to begin with. Since they did not perform by the specified time, Claude could discharge his obligation to accept the rest of the order and, in fact, could even seek damages himself, if he could substantiate a loss of business due to Sea Products' breach of the time specification. [Section 10-3]

PROBLEM 10-4 Steve contracted with Dougherty Painting to have the outside of his white house painted a pale yellow for $500. Dougherty Painting sent Emily to do the job, but on her third day of work, she fell off the ladder, breaking the wrist of the arm that she painted with. When no one showed up on the fourth day to continue the paint job, Steve contacted Dougherty Painting to find out why. They claimed that they had a backlog of painting commitments, that only Emily could do the job for him, and since Emily was incapacitated, Steve would just have to wait the six weeks for Emily to recover and finish the job. Steve, however, said that it was not acceptable to him to wait that long, especially since his house was now part pale yellow and part white, and that he was going to find another company that would complete the job. Dougherty Painting sued Steve for breach of contract. Did Dougherty Painting win?

Answer: Dougherty Painting did not win. Incapacitation can discharge a party from the obligation to perform only if the contract *must* be performed by the incapacitated person. In this case, Dougherty Painting had other employees who could complete the job just as well as Emily, and Steve should not have been required to wait for Emily's recovery. Also, a time of performance was not specified, but since the job had been started, and the house was part pale yellow and part white, it was not unreasonable for Steve to expect the job to be completed right away. Dougherty Painting should have had someone else complete the job, despite their many commitments. [Sections 10-3 and 10-5]

PROBLEM 10-5 Arthur had a contract with Lartex Corp. to supply concrete for the foundations of a new office building the company was building for $1,000. When the preparations for pouring the slab were finished, however, and Steve left to make his first delivery, he discovered that the road he would normally take to get to the construction site was washed out, and he would have to take a detour that would almost double his mileage for the deliveries. In light of this, Arthur asked Lartex Corp. to pay him $1,500 for the deliveries, since he had not realized at the time the contract was formed that it would take so much time and that his mileage costs would be so high. Lartex Corp. refused and insisted that Arthur continue the deliveries as agreed for $1,000. Instead, Arthur sued to have the contract discharged, claiming impossibility of performance. Could Arthur have the contract discharged?

Answer: Arthur could not have the contract discharged on the ground of impossibility of performance. It is true that, through no fault of his own, it was going to take longer and cost more to deliver the concrete than Steve had anticipated. Nonetheless, this fact did not make his performance truly impossible, only more time consuming and expensive. Events that merely make performance more time consuming or expensive are not sufficient to discharge a contract. Arthur would be required to continue delivering the concrete for the agreed upon price of $1,000. [Section 10-5]

PROBLEM 10-6 John, a local farmer, contracted with Sara to make daily deliveries of fresh eggs to Sara's store for a certain price per dozen. After several weeks of daily deliveries, however, John sprained his back while working on the farm, which made it painful for him to drive much. Sara agreed, therefore, to allow John to deliver the eggs every other day until his back got better. What type of change is this and is it enforceable?

Answer: John and Sara have made a material alteration of their contract by mutual assent. Consideration is necessary for a material alteration to be enforceable. In other words, a material alteration cannot substantially benefit only one party. In this case, although it would seem that only John is benefitted by delivering the eggs every other day, a court probably would find that Sara will benefit in the long run by John's rapid recovery, and that adequate consideration is therefore present. [Section 10-6]

PROBLEM 10-7   Adam, a builder, contracted with Sam to build a carport onto Sam's house for $3,000. A week before Adam was to begin work, however, he received a letter from Sam stating that Sam no longer wanted the carport built and was cancelling the contract. Could Adam sue Sam for breach of contract?

Answer: Adam could sue Sam for breach of contract on the basis of anticipatory breach. Normally, a party cannot sue another party for breach of contract until the time of performance actually arrives and the other party fails to perform. Sam, however, had clearly indicated with his letter that he no longer wanted the carport and, in fact, was attempting to cancel the contract. In a situation like this, it would be unfair to Adam to have to show up prepared to begin work when he already knew that Sam no longer wanted the work done. Adam was therefore discharged from his obligation to perform when he received Sam's letter, and could go ahead and sue without waiting for the time of performance to arrive. [Section 10-7]

PROBLEM 10-8   Kathy, a jewelry sales representative, was having trouble with her car, so she took it to Carl's Auto Shop to have the engine worked on. When she went to pick up the car, she was told that the car was running fine, and paid $155 for the engine work. She then left for an important meeting with a store owner in another city to whom she hoped to sell her jewelry line. As it turned out, the car broke down before she got to her meeting and she had to call another car shop to tow her car and repair it again. Later, Kathy attempted to schedule a new appointment with the store owner, but was told that they had already decided to carry another line of jewelry. Kathy was very upset and decided to sue Carl's Auto Shop for damages of $155 for the improper repair work, and $500 for the loss of her commission on the sale she was unable to make because of her car breaking down. Would the court award her these damages?

Answer: Kathy would probably get only the $155 for the improper repair work. When suing for damages, a party must base the amount of damages on fact. The $155 that Kathy paid to Carl's Auto Shop was a direct loss, easily proven by the fact that the car required further repair work after they had assured her it was in good shape. The $500, however, was an indirect or consequential loss, not easily proven. Whether Kathy had made it to her appointment or not, there was no way to prove that the store would have bought her line of jewelry instead of the other. Furthermore, for indirect compensatory damages to be awarded, the party at fault (in this case, Carl's Auto Shop) would have to be aware that a loss would occur as a result of their failure to fix the car properly. Carl's Auto Shop was unaware of this possibility and would not be held liable for it. They would only be held liable for the $155 for the improper repair work. [Section 10-8]

PROBLEM 10-9   Trester Construction had a three-year contract with Rodale Foundry to purchase nails for $10 a case. After two years of shipping nails, however, Rodale Foundry informed Trester Construction that it was going to quit producing nails and would therefore be unable to fulfill the rest of the contract. Trester Construction had to have nails, so it immediately contacted another supplier who agreed to supply nails for $10 a case also. Trester Construction then filed suit against Rodale Foundry for breach of contract, seeking the cost of the unfulfilled contract amount. Would Trester Construction be awarded damages by the court?

Answer: Trester Construction would not be awarded damages by the court. Trester Construction had the right to seek a remedy in the form of damages, but they also had the responsibility of mitigating any damages that resulted from the breach of contract. They were able to mitigate the damages by immediately finding another company that would supply the nails for the same price as Rodale Foundry. Consequently, there were no economic damages and the court would not award any. [Section 10-8]

11 AGENCY

THIS CHAPTER IS ABOUT

- ☑ **Creation of the Agency Relationship**
- ☑ **Authority of Agents to Bind Principals**
- ☑ **Duties and Liabilities of the Agent to the Principal**
- ☑ **Duties and Liabilities of the Principal to the Agent**
- ☑ **Liability of Principals and Agents to Third Parties**
- ☑ **Termination of Agency**

11-1. Creation of the Agency Relationship

The legal concept of agency came about because the demands of conducting business became so complex that people began to employ others to conduct business for them. An *agency relationship* occurs when one party (the *agent*) acts in behalf of and under the control of another party (the *principal*). The creation of an agency relationship generally does not require a formal written agreement in order to exist. There are several circumstances that the court recognizes as creating an agency relationship.

A. An agency relationship can be created by agreement.

The principal and the agent can enter into a mutual agreement that clearly sets forth the *express authority* of the agency. Express authority also carries with it an *implied authority* to take whatever actions are necessary to carry out the purpose of the agency, except when such authority is expressly limited by the agreement.

EXAMPLE 11-1: Dillon asked Lynn, a friend of his who sold cars, to sell his car for him, which she agreed to do for no commission. Lynn was able to sell the car, but she deducted $20 from the amount she gave Dillon for having the car cleaned and for running an ad in the local paper for several weekends. Dillon, however, demanded the $20, claiming that Lynn had no authority to do those things, and reminding Lynn that she had agreed to take no commission. Was he right?

Dillon was not right. Lynn had the express authority to sell Dillon's car, but she also had the implied authority to do whatever was necessary to carry out that purpose. Having the car cleaned and placing ads in the local paper could not be conceived of as being beyond the scope of her implied authority. Furthermore, the $20 was not deducted as commission, but only for the expenses she incurred *for* Dillon in selling the car.

B. An agency relationship can be created by ratification.

A principal is not normally bound by any action of an agent beyond the scope of the agent's authority. However, if the principal confirms such an act, whether through express or implied action or inaction, then the principal has *ratified* the act of the agent, making it binding on the principal. Such ratification generally binds the principal from the time the act was performed, rather than from the time of ratification. A principal who has ratified the acts of an agent cannot later repudiate those actions. There are several circumstances that must exist for a ratification to create an agency relationship.

1. If the agent's actions involve a third person, no ratification can exist if the third person was aware that the agent was not authorized to act in that capacity.

2. The principal must have full knowledge of all the important circumstances and facts of the action at the time of ratification.
3. The agent must have intended to act for the principal at the time of the performance.
4. The principal must have been in existence at the time of performance.

EXAMPLE 11-2: Ron, a stockbroker, had been buying and selling stocks for Elaine without her prior approval for years. Although Elaine had never expressly granted Ron this authority, she was pleased with Ron's judgments because he had usually made money for her. Unfortunately, one day Ron bought a large number of shares for Elaine in a new company that, through unusual circumstances that could not be foreseen, went out of business. Consequently, Elaine lost a large amount of money. Elaine was very disturbed about this and decided to sue Ron for the amount of her losses, claiming that she had never given him the authority to act as her agent. Was she right?

Elaine was not right. It is true that Elaine had never expressly given Ron the authority to act as her agent, but an agency relationship was created through Elaine's silence. In other words, Elaine had implied ratification of Ron's judgment and actions on her behalf by allowing him to act for her for so long without repudiation. Elaine could not reap the benefits of Ron's actions for years, and then try to retain the right to repudiate those actions because they suddenly became unprofitable. Elaine would just have to accept her losses and decide whether or not she wanted to continue to let Ron act as her agent.

C. An agency relationship can be created by estoppel.

Estoppel is a legal ban preventing a person from repudiating something when that person's prior actions or words have indicated the opposite. An *agency by estoppel* occurs when a person allows another person to act for him or her to such an extent that a third person would reasonably conclude that an agency relationship exists. The court will not allow a person to create the impression of an agency relationship and then deny the existence of that relationship later.

EXAMPLE 11-3: Joe and Terry ran a service station as partners. Terry also ran a house painting business out of the same building. A sign hung next to their service station sign that advertised the house painting business also. Diane, who had used the service station for years and had often heard Joe and Terry refer to each other as "partners for life," pulled in one day when Terry was out and talked to Joe about having her house painted. Joe told her that Terry would paint her house for $350. Diane agreed to the amount, gave Joe her address, and left. The next night, Terry called Diane and informed her that he had gone by her house that afternoon and the job would cost $500. Diane told Terry that his partner, Joe, had already said that it would cost $350 and insisted that Terry paint the house for this price. Terry denied that Joe was his partner in the house painting business. Does Terry have to paint the house for $350?

Terry has to paint the house for $350. Diane was led to believe that Joe and Terry were partners in all business run out of their station because the business signs hung together and she had heard them say often that they were "partners for life." It was therefore reasonable for her to believe that Joe could act as Terry's agent. Because Diane relied on this belief and would suffer a loss if Terry denied that Joe was his agent, the court would say that an agency relationship existed by estoppel and would not allow Terry to deny the relationship.

D. An agency relationship can be created by necessity.

An *agency by necessity* occurs when it becomes necessary for a person to act for another person in an emergency situation without the express authority to do so. The situation must be truly an emergency, or a situation where the person acting for another reasonably believes that an emergency exists. Such an agent's authority ends when the emergency situation is over and the principal has been informed of the actions taken on his or her behalf.

EXAMPLE 11-4: Randy and Michael, who were roommates, were driving home one night when they were hit by an oncoming car. Randy was shook up by the accident but otherwise felt fine. Michael, however, appeared to be unconscious and was bleeding from the head. Randy immediately ran to a nearby house and called an ambulance that came and took Michael to the hospital. Randy arrived at the hospital later and signed Michael's name to the necessary forms to ensure payment of the hospital services and ambulance fee. As it turned out, Michael was not seriously injured and he was released from the hospital after a couple of hours. While Randy was driving Michael home, he told Michael about the papers he had signed for him. Michael, however, got angry and insisted that, although he would pay the medical bills, he would not pay for the ambulance service since he really didn't need it and that Randy had no right to sign anything stating that he would. Was he right?

Michael was not right. Randy acted in Michael's behalf because it was an emergency situation and Michael could not act for himself. Randy acted correctly in assuming that it was an emergency because Michael was unconscious at the time and bleeding from the head. There was no way that Randy could have realized that the extent of Michael's injuries weren't as serious as they appeared. Therefore, an agency relationship was created by necessity and Michael would be bound by Randy's actions.

11-2. Authority of Agents to Bind Principals

The authority of an agent is usually defined when the agency is created. Whether defined or not, however, two types of agent authority are considered binding on a principal.

A. Acts performed through actual authority are binding on the principal.

Express and implied authority (see Section 11-1A) together make up the *actual authority* granted to an agent by a principal.

B. Acts performed through apparent or ostensible authority are binding on the principal.

Apparent or *ostensible authority* is the authority that an agent has due to the manner in which the agent is held out to the public by the principal. An example of apparent authority is the doctrine of estoppel (see Section 11-1C).

C. There are some important rules that limit apparent authority.

Four rules are generally accepted as limiting an agent's apparent authority. Any acts by the agent that violate these rules usually are not binding on the principal.

1. The express authority to sell goods does not include the apparent authority to extend credit to the purchaser.
2. The express authority to sell on credit does not include the apparent authority to collect money after delivering the goods.
3. The express authority to possess goods does not include the apparent authority to sell those goods.
4. The authority to borrow money in the principal's name is never considered an apparent authority. Such authority can only be express.

11-3. Duties and Liabilities of the Agent to the Principal

An agent's relationship with a principal is fiduciary in nature. There are many duties that a fiduciary relationship carries with it that, if breached, can hold the agent liable to the principal for any damages caused by the breach.

A. The agent has a duty to follow the principal's instructions in matters pertaining to the agency.

The agent cannot refuse to follow the principal's instructions if they are reasonable. Furthermore, the agent must carry out the principal's instructions with diligence and reasonable care. The court determines reasonable care by the reasonable person standard; in other words, the agent must exercise the same care that an average person would exercise under the same or similar circumstances. An agent also must not act beyond the scope of the principal's instructions.

B. The agent has a duty to keep the principal informed of all facts pertaining to the agency.

The agent must account to the principal for all profits and other advantages derived from the agency and all facts relating to the agency that come to the agent's attention. For example, if the agent informs the principal of an offer to purchase real estate, and then receives a better offer, the agent must inform the principal of the better offer.

C. The agent has a duty to be loyal to the principal's interests.

The purpose of an agency relationship is to benefit the principal. There are several things that an agent cannot do because they would be detrimental to the principal's interests.

1. The agent cannot take advantage of the agency relationship by receiving benefits beyond those agreed to by the agent and principal.
2. The agent cannot represent several principals with conflicting interests unless the principals are fully informed of and consent to the arrangement.
3. The agent cannot engage in competition with the principal's interests unless the principal is fully informed of and consents to the competition.

EXAMPLE 11-5: Mark, a writer, was busy working on his book one day and asked a neighbor, Kate, if she would drive to his travel agent's office and pick up a plane ticket to New York that he needed that evening. Kate agreed to pick up the ticket for $10. While Kate was at the travel agent's office, the agent asked Kate to deliver a free ticket to Mark that Mark had won for traveling so much on one airline. When Kate returned to Mark's, however, she delivered the New York ticket but kept the free ticket and didn't tell Mark about it. Mark found out about the free ticket when he contacted his travel agent the next week to arrange other flight plans. Can Mark make Kate return the free ticket?

Mark can make Kate return the free ticket. An agency relationship existed between Mark and Kate by mutual agreement. The fiduciary nature of the agent-principal relationship placed certain duties on Kate in acting as Mark's agent. For one thing, Kate had the duty of informing Mark of any facts pertaining to the purpose of the agency, including any profits or advantages derived from the agency—in this case, the free ticket. Furthermore, Kate had the duty to be loyal to Mark's interests. She could not take advantage of the agency relationship by receiving benefits beyond those agreed to by her and Mark—in this case, $10. Therefore, Kate had breached her fiduciary duties as Mark's agent and would be required by the court to return the free ticket to Mark.

11-4. Duties and Liabilities of the Principal to the Agent

The principal has two main duties to the agent that, if breached, can hold the principal liable to the agent for any damages caused by the breach.

A. The principal has a duty to compensate the agent according to the terms of the agency agreement.

Compensation includes payment for the agent's services and reimbursement of reasonable expenses incurred by the agent through the exercise of the agent's actual authority. In some cases, compensation may not clearly be set forth in the agency agreement.

1. If the agency agreement does not specify the amount of payment, the agent must be paid an amount equal to the reasonable value of his or her services.
2. If the agency agreement specifies that an agent take a draw from profits of the agency, that draw is normally considered a salary unless specifically identified as a loan in the agreement. This distinction is important because if the draw is not considered salary for services rendered, then the agent may be forced to return the money when the agency is terminated.

EXAMPLE 11-6: Ahmad, a dealer in rare cars, agreed to sell his friend's three-year-old Chevrolet for a commission of $200, even though it was not a rare car. In order to sell the car, Ahmad placed ads in the local newpaper for $25, in a newspaper across the country for $30, and in a national car enthusiast magazine for $50. He had the car washed and waxed for $25 and replaced the plastic floor mats with new carpeting at a cost of $125. He was able to sell the car locally, and submitted a bill for $455 to his friend. His friend, however, said that she would only pay him $250 for the commission, the local ad, and the cost of having the car cleaned. Ahmad threatened to sue for the remaining $205 on the basis that he was entitled to reimbursement of the expenses he incurred in order to sell the car. Could he win if he sued?

It is doubtful that Ahmad could recover the remaining $205 if he sued his friend. It is true that his friend had a duty to compensate Ahmad for the agreed upon commission of $200 and for expenses incurred by Ahmad through the exercise of his actual authority; however, expenses incurred must be reasonable to be reimbursed. Although Ahmad may normally have conducted nationwide marketing programs to sell his rare cars, his friend's car certainly did not warrant such a campaign. It was not reasonable, therefore, to advertise in a faraway newspaper and in a national magazine. Furthermore, it is highly unlikely that a three-year-old car needed to have plastic floor mats replaced by all new carpeting in order to sell it. Therefore, Ahmad had acted beyond the scope of his authority and would not be able to recover the $205 for the unreasonable expenses.

B. The principal has a duty to indemnify the agent.

Indemnification is a guarantee against any loss or liability. The principal, therefore, must guarantee that the agent will not incur any loss or liabilities while acting within the scope of his or her authority in the principal's behalf.

EXAMPLE 11-7: Lisa, an independent truck driver, contracted to deliver a load of canned goods to a grocery store by a specific date. A penalty of $200 was set in the contract for every day of late delivery. Unfortunately, Lisa got the flu and was not well enough to pick up the shipment and deliver it on time. She got a friend of hers, Alex, to agree to pick up the goods and deliver them for her for $200. Alex picked up the goods, but on his way to deliver them, the truck broke down through no fault of his own, and Alex had to pay $100 to have the truck repaired in time to make the delivery. Alex informed Lisa of these events. When Alex returned the truck and the money to Lisa and asked her for $300, however, Lisa refused to reimburse him for the cost of repairs, claiming that their agreement was for $200. Was Lisa correct not to pay Alex the additional $100?

Lisa was not correct. She had a duty to indemnify Alex for any liabilities incurred while he was acting in her behalf. Alex had fulfilled his duties by carrying out Lisa's instructions and keeping her informed of what was going on. He could not, therefore, be held responsible for the cost of repairs to Lisa's truck. Lisa would have to pay Alex the additional $100.

11-5. Liability of Principals and Agents to Third Parties

An agent often is empowered to contract with third parties in behalf of the principal. Either the principal or the agent can be held liable by third parties for a breach of contract, depending on the circumstances.

A. The principal generally is liable to third parties.

The principal is liable for all commitments made by his or her agent within the scope of the agent's actual or apparent authority. The third party, however, may have a choice of who to hold liable, depending on whether the principal is disclosed, partially disclosed, or undisclosed.

1. A principal is a *disclosed principal* when the third party knows of the existence of an agency and knows the identity of the principal. In such cases, the disclosed principal is liable, and the agent is not.
2. A principal is a *partially disclosed principal* when the third party knows of the existence of an agency but does not know the identity of the principal. If the third party is unable to find out who the principal is after a breach, then the third party may hold the agent liable.
3. A principal is an *undisclosed principal* when the third party is completely unaware that an agency existed at the time of contracting. The third party may hold the agent liable for any breach.

B. The principal is liable for any torts committed by the agent.

Under the doctrine of *respondeat superior*, a principal is liable to third persons for any torts committed by the agent while the agent is acting within the scope of the agency. The "superior must respond" means that the superior, in this case the principal, must pay for damages caused by someone acting in the superior's behalf. The agent, however, can still be held liable to the principal for such damages.

C. An agent generally is not liable to third parties.

An agent generally can be held liable to third parties for a breach of contract in only five situations.

1. An agent is liable if the agent knows that the principal is not competent and knows that the third party is unaware of this incompetence.
2. An agent is liable when the agent joins the principal as a joint obligor.
3. An agent is liable if the agent signs a contract in his or her own name and does not indicate that the signature is given for a principal.

4. An agent is liable if the agent acts for a partially disclosed or undisclsed principal and the third party chooses to hold the agent liable.
5. An agent is liable for damages resulting from any acts performed outside the scope of the agent's actual or apparent authority.

EXAMPLE 11-8: Nadine, a literary agent, had represented Luke, an author, for over 30 years. She knew that, unfortunately, Luke had been suffering from senility lately, and it was getting worse. Luke's publisher was unaware of his condition, so when his contract with them expired, they contacted Nadine, who went ahead and renegotiated the contract, acquiring an advance of $10,000 for a new three-book contract. Unfortunately, Luke's condition began to worsen shortly thereafter, so his relatives had him committed to a home for constant care. They used the advance money for part of the payment for the home, unaware that it had been advanced for three books that Luke never wrote. When the publisher found out about Luke's condition and his commitment, they contacted Nadine and demanded their advance money back. Nadine, however, informed them that she was not responsible and that they would have to sue Luke or his family for the money. Was she right?

Nadine was not right. An agent can be held liable if he or she contracts for a principal knowing that the principal is not competent and knowing that the third party is unaware of the principal's incompetence. In this case, Nadine knew that Luke would be unable to write the books because of his worsening senility. She also knew that the publisher was unaware of his condition, or they would not have advanced so much money toward the completion of the books. Nadine, therefore, would be liable for the return of the $10,000 to the publisher.

11-6. Termination of Agency

No formalities are necessary for termination of an agency relationship to take place.

A. An agency can be terminated through the actions of the parties or by law.

1. *Unilateral decision.* An agency may be terminated by either party at any reasonable time by communication of that decision to the other party, unless there exists an agency contract that provides otherwise.
2. *Contractual conditions.* An agency may be terminated by the parties because of conditions contained in the agency contract, such as a time limit, or occurrence of a specified event.
3. *Changes in circumstances.* An agency may be terminated because of a substantial change in the circumstances under which the agency was formed, such as a sudden change in business conditions of which both parties are aware.
4. *Termination by law.* An agency may be terminated by law because of death of the principal or agent, illegality of the subject matter, or impossibility of performance.

B. Notice of termination should be given to third parties.

Apparent agency exists when an agent continues to act for a principal after termination, and third parties have every reason to believe that the agent still has this authority. In such cases, the principal can still be held liable for the agent's actions, even though the agency has been terminated.

1. The principal is responsible for notifying third parties that an agency relationship is terminated. Notification serves to protect the principal from any further liability for the agent's actions.
2. Notification may be actual or constructive. *Actual notice* consists of personal oral or written communication with the third parties. *Constructive notice* consists of an announcement in a general-circulation newspaper. Whether actual or constructive notice will be required depends on the facts and circumstances of each case.

RAISE YOUR GRADES

Can you explain . . . ?

☑ the difference between express and implied authority
☑ how the doctrine of estoppel is an example of apparent authority

☑ how acting for a disclosed, partially disclosed, or undisclosed principal can affect the liability of an agent

☑ how indemnification serves to protect an agent from loss or liability

☑ the doctrine of *respondeat superior*

☑ how a principal can still be held liable for the actions of an agent after termination of the agency relationship

SUMMARY

1. An agency relationship occurs when one party (the agent) acts in behalf of and under the control of another party (the principal).

2. An agency relationship can be created by mutual agreement between the principal and agent.

3. An agency relationship can be created by a principal's express or implied ratification of an agent's acts.

4. An agency relationship can be created by estoppel, meaning that a person is not allowed to deny the existence of a relationship if that person's actions or words have indicated otherwise.

5. An agency relationship can be created by necessity, meaning that a person may act for another in an emergency situation.

6. Actual authority consists of an agent's express authority (authority actually granted by a principal) and implied authority (authority necessary to carry out the purpose of an agency).

7. Apparent authority is the authority that an agent has due to the manner in which the agent is held out to the public by the principal. There are limits to an agent's apparent authority.

8. Acts performed by an agent through either actual or apparent authority are binding on the principal.

9. An agent's relationship with a principal is fiduciary in nature, meaning that an agent must diligently carry out the principal's instructions, must keep the principal informed of all facts pertaining to the agency, and must be loyal to the principal's interests. A breach of any of these fiduciary duties can hold an agent liable to the principal.

10. A principal must compensate an agent according to the terms of the agency agreement and must indemnify the agent against any loss or liability incurred while acting in the principal's behalf. A breach of either of these duties can hold the principal liable to the agent.

11. The principal generally is liable to third parties for any damages caused by a breach of contract entered into by an agent while the agent was acting within the scope of his or her actual or apparent authority.

12. If a principal is partially disclosed or undisclosed, a third party may hold the agent liable for a breach of contract.

13. Under the doctrine of *respondeat superior*, the principal is liable for any torts committed by an agent while the agent is acting within the scope of the agency.

14. An agent generally is not liable to third parties for a breach of contract entered into for a fully disclosed principal.

15. An agent can be held liable if the agent enters into a contract for a principal knowing that the principal is incompetent, if the agent is a joint obligor with the principal, if an agent signs a contract without revealing that an agency exists, or if the agent is working for a partially disclosed or undisclosed principal.

16. An agency can be terminated by unilateral decision, by contractual conditions, by changes in circumstances that affect the purpose of the agency, or by operation of law.

17. Notice of termination of an agency should be given to third parties or else, because of apparent agency, a principal can still be held liable for any further acts by an agent with third parties who have every reason to believe that an agency still exists.

RAPID REVIEW	Answers

True or False

1. Agreement is always necessary for an agency relationship to be created. [Section 11-1] *False*

2. Ratification by a principal of an unauthorized act performed by an agent is binding on the principal from the time the act was performed. [Section 11-1] *True*

3. A person may create the impression that an agency relationship exists, but would not be held liable for the agent's actions since no agency agreement was actually formed. [Section 11-1] *False*

4. The way in which a principal holds an agent out to the public may give the agent apparent authority. [Section 11-2] *True*

5. An agent may not extend credit, collect money, sell goods, or borrow money in a principal's name without the express authority to do so. [Section 11-2] *True*

6. An agent is entitled to any unforeseen benefits accrued while acting for a principal. [Section 11-3] *False*

7. An agent can be held liable to the principal for any damages that result from the agent's not keeping the principal informed of all facts pertaining to the agency. [Section 11-3] *True*

8. A principal can hold an agent liable for any losses incurred as a result of the agent's unauthorized actions. [Section 11-3] *True*

9. A principal does not have to reimburse an agent for unreasonable expenses. [Section 11-4] *True*

10. A draw taken by an agent must always be returned to the principal after termination of an agency. [Section 11-4] *False*

11. As long as a contract made by an agent was authorized, a principal, whether disclosed, partially disclosed, or undisclosed, is the only one who can be held liable by third parties for a breach of the contract. [Section 11-5] *False*

12. Although a principal is liable to third parties for any torts committed by an agent while acting within the scope of the agency, the agent can still be held liable to the principal for such torts. [Section 11-5] *True*

13. An agent is not liable to third persons under any circumstances. [Section 11-5] *False*

14. It is the agent's responsibility to inform third parties that an agency relationship has been terminated. [Section 11-6] *False*

15. Only personal notification to third parties serves to protect a principal from liability resulting from acts of an agent after the agency has been terminated. [Section 11-6] *False*

SOLVED PROBLEMS

PROBLEM 11-1   Calvin, a small business owner, mentioned to a friend of his, Kathleen, that he had bought new office equipment and was trying to sell his old equipment for $3,000. He described the equipment to Kathleen and asked her to see if she could sell his old equipment. In exchange, he would give her $200. About two weeks later, Kathleen did find a buyer and contracted in Calvin's name for the person to buy the equipment for $3,000. When she contacted Calvin, however, he informed her that he had already sold the equipment. When Kathleen informed the buyer of this, the buyer claimed that he was going to sue Calvin to enforce the contract. Would the buyer win the suit?

Answer: The buyer would win the suit against Calvin. By asking Kathleen to sell his equipment, Calvin created an agency relationship, investing her with actual authority to sell the equipment. By failing to notify Kathleen of his desire to terminate the agency, Calvin remained liable for her acts performed within the scope of the agency. [Sections 11-2 and 11-6]

PROBLEM 11-2 Ruth bought a small apartment complex and gave her nephew, Nick, the authority to reside at the complex, collect rent, and act as the manager. Her nephew was also allowed to draw a salary equal to 5% of the rents collected each month. As tenants moved in, Nick informed them all that he was the owner's nephew, that they should pay rent to him, and, without Ruth's knowledge, that they must pay $1,000 as a security deposit that he kept for himself. Unfortunately, Ruth began to have financial problems and was unable to continue paying for the complex, so she sold it and Nick moved out. When the residents asked the new owner about the status of their security deposits, the new owner informed them that they would have to ask Ruth for the money. Ruth, however, claimed that Nick was responsible for returning the deposits, since she had never given him the authority to collect security deposits. Could the residents sue Ruth?

Answer: The residents could sue Ruth. The tenants could reasonably conclude that Nick had the authority to collect security deposits since he lived there, was the owner's nephew, and collected rents. They could therefore sue Ruth on a strong claim of apparent authority. Ruth would be required to return the money to the residents, but then Ruth could hold her nephew liable for the return of the money to her for several reasons. First, Nick should not have collected money that he was not expressly authorized to collect. Second, he would not be allowed to benefit from any profits resulting from the agency other than those agreed to (the 5% draw). Also, Nick would be liable to Ruth for the damages resulting from his breach of their fiduciary relationship; i.e., acting beyond the scope of his authority, not informing Ruth of profits resulting from the agency, and disloyalty to Ruth's interests. [Sections 11-2 and 11-3]

PROBLEM 11-3 Assume that Nick, from the previous problem, had been asked to act only as property manager for Ruth's apartment complex. He was instructed to take good care of the property and to respond promptly to tenant complaints or problems. Nick had been informed by tenants several times of a loose hinge on the entrance gate to the complex, and he kept promising to fix it. Instead, he put it off until, one day, a tenant's child was swinging on the gate and the gate fell off, landing on and breaking the child's arm. Could Nick be liable as a result of the accident?

Answer: Nick could be liable to Ruth if Ruth has to pay legal damages to the tenant. Ruth could sue Nick for reimbursement, since Nick had a duty to diligently follow Ruth's intructions and to exercise reasonable care when acting for her. Nick was instructed to respond promptly to tenant complaints, and there was no excuse for his not repairing the gate hinge when he was first informed of it. In other words, he was not diligent in performing his duties, nor did he exercise reasonable care in protecting Ruth's interests. [Section 11-3]

PROBLEM 11-4 Fred had been working for years to secure shipment contracts for Amy, who ran a small trucking company. One day, Fred signed a contract with the Deer Company in his own name, agreeing that goods would be picked up and delivered for the company by a certain date. Fred did not inform the Deer Company at the signing of the contract that he was acting for Amy's trucking company. As it turned out, Amy's trucking company was unable to pick up and deliver the goods by the specified date, and, consequently, the Deer Company was charged a penalty for the late delivery. The Deer Company brought suit against Fred for the penalty that they had incurred as a result of the breach of contract. Did they win?

Answer: The Deer Company won its suit against Fred. Normally, only the principal is liable to a third party for any damages resulting from the actions of an agent acting within the scope of his or her authority. Fred, however, made two mistakes when contracting with the Deer Company that made him liable to them. He did not disclose that he was acting as an agent for Amy's trucking company, even verbally. Also, he signed his own name to the contract, rather than the name of Amy's company. There was no way that the Deer Company could have known that Fred was representing someone else and they could therefore hold him liable for the damages that resulted from the breach. [Section 11-5]

PROBLEM 11-5   Assume that Fred, from the previous problem, had been fired by Amy after many years of acquiring contracts for her. After a month or so, Fred was in bad financial condition, so he went to a couple of his old accounts that had a history of bad credit, signed contracts with them in the name of Amy's company, and insisted that he had to collect the payment up front for shipments because of their bad credit histories. Of course, Amy was unaware of the contracts, and was surprised when she was served with notices that these companies were suing her for the return of their money. Amy claimed that the agency had been terminated when Fred entered into those contracts, and she was no longer responsible for his actions. Was she right?

Answer: Amy was not right. Amy never notified the accounts that Fred was no longer her agent. The accounts, therefore, had every reason to believe that Fred was still authorized to act as Amy's agent. They could hold Amy liable for Fred's actions due to this apparent agency. Amy could have protected herself from liability for Fred's actions after termination of the agency if she had notified the accounts of the termination. Amy would be held liable to the companies for the return of the money, but she could then sue to recover the money from Fred because he had acted without her authority. [Section 11-6]

PROBLEM 11-6   Beth appointed Craig as her agent to sell an antique desk for her. Craig arranged to sell the desk to an antique dealer. Unfortunately, when the antique dealer attempted to arrange a time to pick up the desk, he was told that Beth had died. The dealer contacted the executor of Beth's estate, who claimed that she was unaware of the transaction and would not sell the desk. The dealer insisted that the desk had to be sold. Was the dealer correct?

Answer: The dealer was not correct. An agency relationship is terminated by law upon the death of the principal or agent. In this case, the death of Beth would make the contract unenforceable. Beth's executor would not have to sell the desk. [Section 11-6]

12 PARTNERSHIPS

THIS CHAPTER IS ABOUT

- ☑ The Uniform Partnership Act
- ☑ Creation of a Partnership
- ☑ Rights, Duties, and Liabilities of Partners to Each Other
- ☑ Authority of a Partner to Bind Other Partners
- ☑ Liabilities of Partners to Third Parties
- ☑ Dissolution of a Partnership
- ☑ Winding Up
- ☑ Limited Partnerships

12-1. The Uniform Partnership Act

To try and unify a legal approach to partnerships, the Uniform Partnership Act (UPA) was developed and adopted by most states with some modifications on a state-by-state basis. Because of the UPA's general usage throughout the United States, the partnership law discussed in this chapter will be based largely on it. The provisions of the UPA are not mandatory, but rather are applied in the absence of any proven agreement to the contrary between the partners.

12-2. Creation of a Partnership

The UPA defines a *partnership* as the association of two or more people who agree to establish and run a business for profit as co-owners. Mere co-ownership does not constitute a partnership. The intent of the parties is essential in determining whether or not a partnership exists.

A. Two elements are necessary for a partnership to exist under the UPA.

All partners must have an equal say in the management and control of the partnership business. Furthermore, all partners must share equally in the profits and losses of the partnership business. A partnership is not considered to include a particular individual just because that person receives profits as payment for a debt, wages, rent, annuity, or interest.

EXAMPLE 12-1: Emily, Lynn, and Brandon formed a partnership to co-own and operate a bakery. Emily contributed $12,000, and Lynn and Brandon contributed $6,000 apiece. Consequently, when the partnership agreement was written, Emily was given the right to receive 50% of all profits, while Lynn and Brandon were to receive 25% each. After several years of successful operations, Lynn and Brandon decided that they were dissatisfied with their percentage of profits and planned to sue Emily to overturn the agreement and institute an equal share of the profits as specified in the UPA. Would they win such a suit?

Lynn and Brandon would not win the suit. The UPA is not mandatory in nature, but rather a set of guidelines that can be applied by the court in cases where no agreement exists between the partners. In this case, there is a written partnership agreement granting Emily 50% of all profits and Lynn and Brandon 25% of all profits. This existing partnership agreement would prevail in a court of law.

B. An agreement to form a partnership can be written or oral.

No formalities are required for a partnership to be formed. Under some circumstances, however, an agreement may be required to be in writing to comply with law. For example, if the business of a partnership cannot be carried out within one year, the agreement must be written in order to comply with the Statute of Frauds.

12-3. Rights, Duties, and Liabilities of Partners to Each Other

Under the UPA, partners have certain rights and duties that can hold the partners liable to each other if violated. Of course, any agreement to the contrary of these provisions would prevail in a court of law.

A. Partners have the right to co-own all partnership property.

Partners are said to be *tenants in partnership* concerning all partnership property. The right to possess and use all partnership property for partnership purposes is limited in several ways.

1. A partner may not assign the right to ownership of partnership property.
2. A partner's ownership of partnership property cannot be used as collateral by his or her individual creditors.
3. A partner's right to ownership of partnership property passes to remaining partners at his or her death.

EXAMPLE 12-2: Betsy and Jay were partners in a business venture to buy and lease office buildings. According to their partnership agreement, Betsy was to purchase the office buildings from partnership funds and Jay was to run the leasing end of the business. Betsy put all of the buildings that she bought in her own name. After several years, Betsy and Jay began to have serious differences of opinion, so they decided to end the partnership. At that time, Betsy claimed that she wanted the proceeds from the sale of any buildings because it had been her responsibility to purchase them and they were all in her name. Was she right?

Betsy was not right. Under the UPA, partners have the right to co-own all partnership property unless specified otherwise in the partnership agreement. Furthermore, the fact that the buildings were in Betsy's name did not grant her sole ownership because she had used partnership funds to purchase them, and they had been used for partnership purposes. Jay would be considered a tenant in partnership and would be allowed his share of the proceeds from the sale of the office buildings.

B. Partners have the right to share equally in the management of partnership business.

All partners have the right to participate equally in management unless specifically stated otherwise in the partnership agreement. Under the UPA, a majority of the partners is sufficient to make management decisions. A unanimous vote, however, is required before:

- the capital structure of the business may be changed
- the partnership can enter into a new type of business
- a new partner can be admitted
- the location of the business may be changed
- a partnership debt can be compromised
- the assets of the partnership can be disposed of or made the subject of litigation that could affect the partnership's ability to continue business

C. Partners have a right to all partnership information.

In certain circumstances, partners may demand a formal accounting of or inspection of the partnership records. This right continues for a reasonable time after dissolution of the partnership. At the death of a partner, the deceased partner's legal representatives also continue to have the right of inspection for a reasonable amount of time.

D. Partners' duties to each other are fiduciary in nature.

A fiduciary relationship carries with it the duties to be loyal to the interests of the partnership, to use reasonable care and skill in the performance of all partnership business, and to keep accurate records of any transactions performed that pertain to partnership business. Consequently, a partner may not profit from partnership business at the expense of the other partners, may not show gross negligence in the performance of partnership business, and may not refuse to inform the other partners of all facts pertaining to the partnership. Each partner can be held liable to the other partners for a breach of the fiduciary relationship.

EXAMPLE 12-3: Mike, Dale, and Tricia were partners in the ownership and operation of a discount clothing outlet. In the partnership agreement, Tricia was to actually work in the store, but they were all to share in any business decisions. Tricia, however, often ordered merchandise when sales representatives came in without keeping records of her transactions and without informing Mike and Dale. Mike received the bills for all purchases and realized one day that the partnership was in financial trouble with a lot of bills for merchandise that he was unaware had been bought. He and Dale confronted Tricia, who admitted what she had been doing. Is Tricia liable to Mike and Dale if the business fails as a result of her actions?

Tricia could be held liable to Mike and Dale on several grounds. First of all, Mike and Dale had the right to share in the management of the business. No agreement had been made to the contrary. Even though Tricia was in the store on a day-to-day basis, this did not give her the right to make business decisions without consulting Mike and Dale. Also, Mike and Dale had the right to all partnership information. Consequently, Tricia had the duty to keep accurate records of all transactions that involved partnership business, which she did not do. Furthermore, Mike and Dale may be able to show that Tricia was negligent in her conduct of partnership business, as her unauthorized purchasing had compromised the business and put it into financial difficulty. Tricia was violating the rights of Mike and Dale and violating her fiduciary relationship with them.

12-4. Authority of a Partner to Bind Other Partners

The authority of a partner to bind all partners is based largely on the laws of agency (see Chapter 11).

A. Each partner is both a principal and an agent of the partnership.

A partner is a principal in the sense that all partnership business is conducted presumably for the benefit of the partners. Each partner is also an agent of the partnership in the sense that each partner has the power to bind all partners through express, implied, and even apparent authority in the course of conducting partnership business.

B. Courts often interpret implied and apparent authority of partners in a broader sense than that of agents.

If a partnership agreement limits the authority of one of the partners and that partner exercises the prohibited authority anyway, then all partners would most likely be bound by that action on the basis of apparent authority unless they could prove that the third party had reason to know that the partner did not have that authority, or unless the action was not related to partnership business. This is because third parties entering into an agreement with an actual partner would even more strongly believe that that partner had such authority than if that partner were merely an agent of the partnership.

EXAMPLE 12-4: George and Monica were partners in an accounting firm. In their partnership agreement, George had sole authority to hire employees. One day, Juan, a recent graduate with a degree in finance, entered the accounting offices and talked to Monica about a job. Monica was impressed by Juan, so she hired him on the spot and had him sign an employment contract. When George found out about the hiring, he was very upset because, although they needed help, he had wanted to hire someone with experience. He insisted to Monica that he would not hire Juan. Can he refuse to hire Juan?

George cannot refuse to hire Juan. Juan had no knowledge of the partnership agreement and had every reason to believe that Monica, as a partner, had the authority to bind the partnership to an employment contract. Furthermore, the hiring was obviously related to partnership business. George would therefore be bound to hire Juan due to apparent authority.

12-5. Liabilities of Partners to Third Parties

Partners are generally liable to third parties for all business transactions of the partnership that involve third parties.

A. Partners are jointly liable for all debts and contracts of the partnership.

Joint liability means that all partners are held equally liable for damages to third parties resulting from conduct of the partnership business. A suit brought by a third party for collection of a debt or breach of contract by a partnership must name every partner in the suit. Liability ends for a partner upon death, but the remaining partners are still liable for the deceased partner's portion of the debt.

B. Partners are jointly and severally liable for torts committed in the course of partnership business.

Several liability means that a third party may hold individual partners liable for torts committed by a partner or employee while conducting partnership business. A single partner may even be sued when that partner neither committed the tort nor had knowledge of its commitment. The only exception to this is that if the tort is one that involves malicious intent, the partner being sued must be shown to have had such intent. A judgment can only be enforced against the partner or partners actually named in the suit. If a partner pays for damages caused by another partner's tort, that partner may seek reimbursement from the partner at fault.

EXAMPLE 12-5: Charlene and David were partners in a small brokerage business. David had been drinking a lot lately, and Charlene was beginning to get concerned about its effects on the business, since David was coming in late, making mistakes, and creating other problems. One day, Charlene received notice that one of David's clients was suing the partnership for gross negligence in the handling of his account. When Charlene confronted David, he admitted that the client had given him specific instructions to carry out that he had failed to do. Consequently, the client had lost a lot of money. Charlene told David that she was going to tell the client about his drinking problem and have him sued for being individually responsible. Could she do this?

Charlene could tell the client anything she liked, but it would only be more detrimental to the partnership's position. The client has the choice of suing Charlene and David as a partnership or each individually because partners are jointly and severally liable for any torts committed by a partner while conducting partnership business. For Charlene to tell the client about David's drinking problem would only indicate that she was aware that his problem could lead to negligent conduct, showing her to be even more liable by virtue of her knowledge.

C. A person may be held liable to third parties based on partnership by estoppel.

A person can be liable to third parties who have dealt with a partnership if that person presents or allows another to present him or her as a partner. Like agency law, this is based on the doctrine of estoppel—the person would not be allowed to deny partnership if his or her previous actions indicate otherwise.

EXAMPLE 12-6: Warren took out a loan with City Bank to begin a new business. To help secure the loan, he told the bank that he was a partner with his friend, Tommy, when in fact, Tommy merely owned the building that Warren was going to rent for his business. Warren told Tommy what he had done and Tommy asked him never to do that again, but he did not advise the bank that he was not a partner with Warren. Several years later, Warren's business failed and he defaulted on the loan. Tommy received notice that he was being sued, along with Warren, for collection of the debt. Tommy immediately informed the bank that he was not a partner because he had never received any profits from the business or participated in its management. Must the bank drop Tommy's name from the suit?

The bank does not have to drop Tommy's name from the suit. By allowing himself to be presented as a partner, Tommy can be held liable to the bank as a partner by estoppel. The court would not allow Tommy to deny partnership when his previous actions clearly indicated otherwise; i.e., he failed to notify the bank at the time of the loan that he was not a partner, even though he knew that the bank had partially relied on that fact when extending the loan to Warren.

12-6. Dissolution of a Partnership

Dissolution is defined by the UPA as a change in the relation of the partners caused by any partner withdrawing from the partnership, whether through death or voluntary withdrawal.

A partner has the power to withdraw at any time. The partnership may continue after dissolution, or it may start the winding up process that leads to termination of the business.

A. Dissolution does not automatically terminate the business.

A partner, however, may demand the termination of the business upon withdrawal, so long as the partner has not withdrawn in violation of the partnership agreement or so long as there is not a partnership provision allowing for the continuation of the business after withdrawal of a partner. If the business is to continue after dissolution, the partners must settle on compensation to the withdrawing partner for his or her interest in the partnership.

B. Dissolution can occur by act of the partners without violation of the partnership agreement.

A rightful dissolution that does not violate the partnership agreement can occur in four ways:

- when partners mutually agree to end the partnership
- when the partnership was formed for a particular purpose or time period and that purpose or time period is reached
- when the partnership agreement allows a partner to withdraw at will
- when the partnership agreement allows for expulsion of a partner

C. Dissolution can occur by act of the partners with a violation of the partnership agreement.

A partner who leaves wrongfully becomes liable to the remaining partners for any damages resulting from the withdrawal, may not demand the winding up of the business, and may not receive further benefits from the business.

EXAMPLE 12-7: Dee, who worked as an accountant, was also a partner with Chad in a distributor business. Their partnership agreement stated that the partnership was to exist for at least a three-year period. After two years, however, Dee accepted a promotion at work and informed Chad that she was leaving the partnership because she no longer had time for it. She asked that he end the business or, if he wanted to continue it, that he pay her 25% of the continuing profits because of the time and capital she had invested in the business. Did Chad have to do as she asked?

Chad was not obligated to do what Dee asked. Dee had the right to withdraw from the partnership at any time, but not the right to demand a dissolution settlement because she was violating the partnership agreement. Her dissolution was wrongful, and therefore, she was not entitled to further profits from the business. Nor could she demand the termination of the business. Furthermore, if her wrongful dissolution resulted in damages to Chad or the business in some way, then she might be held liable for those damages.

D. Dissolution can occur by operation of law.

Dissolution occurs by operation of law when:

- a partner dies
- the partnership business becomes bankrupt
- the partnership or business of the partnership becomes illegal

E. Dissolution can occur by order of the court.

There are several grounds that exist for dissolving a partnership by court order. A partner may petition the court for dissolution on any of these grounds:

- when a partner is found to be insane or of unsound mind
- when a partner persists in conduct that is harmful to the carrying on of the business
- when a partner continually and willfully breaches the partnership agreement
- when a situation exists where the business can no longer continue for a profit

F. Dissolution ends the actual authority of the partners to bind the partnership.

The only remaining authority that partners have after dissolution is that necessary for the winding up of the affairs of the business. If the business is to continue after dissolution, the remaining partners must exercise good faith in not binding the withdrawing partner to any further partnership business.

G. A withdrawing partner or the partnership should notify third parties of the dissolution.

In some circumstances, partners can still bind the partnership by apparent authority after a dissolution. Notice of dissolution by a withdrawing partner serves to protect that partner from liabilities that may result from being held out as an apparent partner to third parties. When dissolution is to lead to termination, notice serves to protect each partner's liability for any actions resulting from another partner's use of apparent authority.

1. Actual notice of dissolution must be given to creditors.
2. Constructive notice is sufficient for other third parties who have dealt with the partnership.

EXAMPLE 12-8: Amos signed a note to borrow $20,000 for his construction firm from City Bank, a bank that had extended loans to the company in the past. Unknown to the bank, however, Amos's partner in the business, Leon, had recently retired. If Amos defaults on the loan, could the bank enforce the debt against both Amos and Leon?

If the bank relied in good faith on the belief that Leon was still a partner in the company, then Leon could be held liable along with Amos for the debt as the result of being held out as an apparent partner. If Leon had given notice to the bank of his retirement, it would have served to relieve him of any liability.

12-7. Winding Up

If dissolution is to lead to termination of the partnership business, the winding up process begins. *Winding up* is the completion of any unfinished business and the liquidation and distribution of all assets.

A. Winding up results in termination of the partnership and its business.

If disputes arise about how to wind up the business, a partner may petition the court to appoint a receiver to control the winding up process.

B. The UPA has established the order of distribution of assets.

The liabilities of a partnership are settled by the distribution of assets in the following order:

• debts owed to creditors other than partners
• debts owed to partners other than for capital and profits
• debts owed to partners for their capital investments
• remaining assets distributed to partners as profits

C. Partners are severally liable for outstanding obligations of the partnership after termination.

Partnership creditors have first claim to partnership assets. If there are not enough partnership assets to pay the debt, they may then claim individual assets of solvent partners. Individual partner creditors, however, have first claim to partners' individual assets.

EXAMPLE 12-9: Elaine and Brian had wound up their partnership business, but had not paid Smith Company for goods they had ordered while their business was still operating. There were no partnership assets left to pay for the goods, so Smith Company sued Elaine and Brian as individuals for the amount owed. As it turned out, both of them owed a lot of money to individual creditors as well. Could Smith Company collect its money?

Smith Company was entitled to sue Elaine and Brian individually since there were no partnership assets left to pay for the goods. The individual creditors, however, would have first claim to their personal assets, so Smith Company could not collect from either Elaine or Brian until after their individual creditors were paid.

12-8. Limited Partnerships

It is important to distinguish between an ordinary partnership and a limited partnership. A *limited partnership* is formed by the association of one or more general partners and one or more limited partners.

A. A limited partnership usually is formed to permit a partner to invest without full liability.

A *general partner* has the power to manage the partnership business and has unlimited liability for partnership debts, just as in an ordinary partnership. A *limited partner*, however, cannot participate in the management of the partnership business and can be held liable only up to the amount of his or her contribution to the partnership.

B. There are certain requirements for the formation of a limited partnership.

A certificate must be filed with the appropriate government official. Without proper filing of this certificate, those who join a partnership with the intention of being a limited partner may find themselves liable as a general partner. The certificate must include:

• the nature, location, and terms of the partnership business
• the names and addresses of all partners and their identification as general or limited partners
• a description and value of all capital contributions of each partner
• an agreement as to whether new partners may join the association and whether limited partners may assign their interests to others

C. The rights and liabilities of a limited partner are the same as general partners with some exceptions.

Normally, a limited partner is liable for partnership debts only up to the amount actually invested in the partnership. Violation of any of the following guidelines, however, might result in a limited partner losing his or her limited liability status.

1. A limited partner's name may not be used in the partnership title.
2. A limited partner can contribute only cash or property to the partnership, not services.
3. A limited partner has no right to take control of the partnership business.

EXAMPLE 12-10: Marlo, Ted, and Jorge formed a limited partnership to operate Ted's Poultry Farm with Marlo as a general partner and Ted and Jorge as limited partners. Over the course of the business, Ted and Jorge visited the poultry farm often and advised Marlo on what breed of hens to buy and other things, although Marlo did not always agree with them. Jorge even helped crate eggs occasionally for shipment. After several years, the business failed and partnership creditors sought to have the court rule that Ted and Jorge were liable as general partners. Would they win their suit?

The court probably would rule for the partnership creditors that Ted and Jorge were general partners. Limited partners cannot use their names in the partnership title and cannot contribute services to the business or participate in management decisions. In this case, however, Ted allowed his name to be used in the business title, which could have been relied on by the creditors to indicate Ted's interests as a general partner. Also, both Ted and Jorge often participated in management decisions, which only general partners are allowed to do. Furthermore, Jorge even contributed services by helping out that could be construed as participating in the business, which only general partners are allowed to do. Ted and Jorge therefore conducted themselves more like general partners than limited partners, and most likely would lose their limited liability status.

D. Dissolution of a limited partnership is the same as ordinary partnerships with some exceptions.

1. The withdrawal of a limited partner does not dissolve a limited partnership, although withdrawal of a general partner does.
2. The liabilities of a limited partnership are settled by the distribution of assets in the following order:

   • debts owed to creditors other than general or limited partners
   • debts owed to limited partners for their share of profits
   • debts owed to limited partners for their capital investments

- debts owed to general partners other than for capital or profits
- assets distributed to general partners as profits
- assets distributed to general partners for their capital investments

RAISE YOUR GRADES

Can you explain . . . ?

☑ why the UPA was developed and how it is applied by the courts
☑ why co-ownership alone does not constitute a partnership
☑ how the formation of an ordinary partnership differs from the formation of a limited partnership
☑ how property can be in one partner's name but still be owned by all partners
☑ the fiduciary relationship between partners
☑ how the authority of partners to bind other partners is similar to agency law
☑ how dissolution can affect the continuation of a partnership business, both for ordinary and limited partnerships
☑ how a general partner's liability differs from that of a limited partner

SUMMARY

1. The UPA was developed and adopted by many states as provisions that the court may apply in the absence of agreements to the contrary between partners.
2. A partnership is the association of two or more people who agree to establish and run a business for profit as co-owners.
3. For a partnership to exist, the partners must share in the management, control, profits, and losses of the partnership business.
4. An agreement to form a partnership can be written or oral, unless required to be in writing by law.
5. Partners have the right to co-own all partnership property, to share equally in the management of partnership business, and to have access to all partnership information.
6. A fiduciary relationship exists between partners that carries with it the duties to be loyal to the interests of the partnership, to use reasonable care and skill in the performance of all partnership business, and to keep accurate records of any transactions performed that pertain to partnership business.
7. Partners can bind other partners through the exercise of express, implied, and apparent authority while conducting partnership business. Implied and apparent authority are often interpreted more broadly for partners than for agents.
8. Partners are jointly liable for all debts and contracts of the partnership. This means that all partners must be named in a suit against the partnership and all partners are equally liable for damages resulting from a suit.
9. Partners are jointly and severally liable for torts committed in the course of partnership business. This means that third parties may hold either all, some, or one partner liable for torts committed by partners or employees of the partnership. If the tort is one that involves malicious intent, however, a single partner being sued must be shown to have had such intent.
10. A person can be liable to third parties who have dealt with a partnership if that person presents or allows another to present him or her as a partner. This is based on the doctrine of estoppel.
11. Dissolution is a change in the relation of the partners caused by any partner withdrawing from a partnership, whether through death or voluntary withdrawal.
12. A partnership may continue after dissolution, or it may start the winding up process that leads to termination of the business.

13. Dissolution can occur by act of the partners without violation of the partnership agreement, by act of the partners with a violation of the partnership agreement, by operation of law, or by order of the court.

14. A partner who dissolves a partnership wrongfully becomes liable to the remaining partners for any damages resulting from the withdrawal, may not demand the winding up of the business, and may not receive further benefits from the business.

15. Third parties should be notified of a dissolution so that remaining partners will not be liable for further actions of a withdrawing partner based on apparent authority, and so that the withdrawing partner will not be liable for past actions of the partnership based on apparent partnership.

16. Winding up is the completion of any unfinished business and the liquidation and distribution of all assets.

17. Upon termination, the liabilities of a partnership are settled by the distribution of assets first to creditors other than partners, then to partners other than for capital and profits, then to partners for their capital investments, and finally to partners as profits.

18. Partners are severally liable for outstanding obligations of the partnership after termination.

19. A limited partnership is the association of one or more general partners and one or more limited partners. A general partner has the power to manage the partnership business and has unlimited liability for partnership debts. A limited partner, however, cannot participate in the management of the partnership business and can be held liable only up to the amount of his or her contribution to the partnership.

20. A certificate of limited partnership must be filed with the appropriate government agency in order for a limited partnership to be formed.

21. Limited partners may not use their names in the partnership title, may not contribute services to a partnership, and may not take any control of the partnership business. If they do, they may lose their limited liability status.

22. The withdrawal of a limited partner does not dissolve a limited partnership, although withdrawal of a general partner does.

23. The liabilities of a limited partnership are settled by the distribution of assets first to creditors other than general or limited partners, then to limited partners for their share of profits, then to limited partners for their capital investments, then to general partners other than for capital or profits, then to general partners as profits, and finally to general partners for their capital investments.

RAPID REVIEW   Answers

True or False

1. A partnership does not exist if the partners are not sharing equally in the management and profits of the partnership business. [Section 12-2]		*False*
2. Partners are said to be *tenants in partnership* concerning all partnership property. [Section 12-3]		*True*
3. A partner's right to ownership of partnership property passes to his or her heirs at death. [Section 12-3]		*False*
4. The majority of the partners rules in making all management decisions concerning partnership business. [Section 12-3]		*False*
5. A partner may not profit from partnership business at the expense of the other partners. [Section 12-3]		*True*
6. The authority of a partner to bind all partners is based largely on the laws of agency. [Section 12-4]		*True*
7. Joint liability means that all partners are held liable for damages to third parties resulting from conduct of the partnership business. [Section 12-5]		*True*

8. Only a partner or partners who committed a tort or were aware of a tort may be held liable for that tort. [Section 12-5]   *False*

9. A partner has the power to dissolve a partnership at any time. [Section 12-6]   *True*

10. When a partnership business becomes bankrupt, then the partnership is said to be dissolved by operation of law. [Section 12-6]   *True*

11. A partner may petition the court for dissolution of a partnership on many grounds. [Section 12-6]   *True*

12. Dissolution ends the actual authority of the partners to bind the partnership. [Section 12-6]   *True*

13. A withdrawing partner's liability for partnership obligations ends upon withdrawal. [Section 12-6]   *False*

14. The winding up process leads to termination of the partnership and the partnership business. [Section 12-7]   *True*

15. Partners remain jointly liable for any outstanding obligations of a partnership after termination. [Section 12-7]   *False*

16. An agreement to form a limited partnership may be written or oral. [Section 12-8]   *False*

17. A limited partner is liable for partnership debts only up to the amount invested in the partnership. [Section 12-8]   *True*

18. A limited partner may participate in all management decisions, but may not contribute services to a partnership. [Section 12-8]   *False*

SOLVED PROBLEMS

PROBLEM 12-1   Lauren worked for Aris and David, partners in a hardware store business, as their store manager. She was allowed to use her judgment in handling day-to-day interactions and problems with customers, although she had to always follow the management guidelines and policies that Aris and David had given her. Her wages were based on a flat salary plus 5% of any profits of the store. Over the years, Aris and David gained confidence in Lauren's ability to run the store and allowed her to make more and more decisions about its management. They also upped her share of the profits to 10%. Unfortunately, Aris and David began to get many complaints from customers about Lauren's behavior with customers. They tried talking with her, but the negative reports continued. Aris and David did not understand why Lauren was behaving this way, but they decided to fire her for fear of losing customers. When confronted, however, Lauren claimed that they could not fire her because she was now a partner, based on her sharing in management decisions and in profits. Was Lauren correct?

Answer: Lauren was not right. First of all, Lauren was never a co-owner of the store, and co-ownership is not established by sharing of profits alone. Second, a partnership is not considered to exist on the basis of profits received as wages, which was what her share of the profits was intended to be. Also, her participation in management decisions was no more than authority granted to her by Aris and David, not her right as a partner. Furthermore, intention of the parties is essential in determining whether or not a partnership existed in this situation. Aris and David would most likely have no problem proving that it was never their intention to have Lauren as a partner in the business, but rather their hope that she would become a valuable employee. The court would look at intention as well as the facts in deciding if a partnership existed. [Section 12-2]

PROBLEM 12-2   Brenda, Darren, and Edgar ran a farm as partners. Brenda and Darren wanted to change the type of fertilizer that they used on most of their crops, but Edgar insisted that it would be a poor decison and that a unanimous decision was necessary in order to make the change. Was Edgar right? What if Brenda and Darren wanted to sell the farm and buy a bottling plant. Would they be able to force their decision on Edgar?

Answer: Edgar was not right to believe that a unanimous decision was necessary to change the type of fertilizer being used on the crops. The majority rules when making decisions on the day-to-day management of a partnership business. However, unanimous decisions are required for some partnership decisions, and one of them is when a decision is to be made that would enter the partnership into a new type of business. In this case, to sell the farm would also mean a change in the location of the business which also requires a unanimous decision of the partners. Therefore, Brenda and Darren would not be able to force Edgar to sell the farm and buy a bottling plant. A unanimous decision would be required. [Section 12-3]

PROBLEM 12-3   Gretchen and Lily were partners in a legal practice. It was almost Christmas one year, and Gretchen decided that she needed extra cash. She began taking clients after regular business hours and not telling Lily about them. Lily went by the office one night for some papers she had forgotten and discovered Gretchen there with a client whom she was unfamiliar with. Gretchen admitted what she had been doing when Lily confronted her the next day, but she insisted that she could do anything that she wanted to on her own time. Was Gretchen correct?

Answer: Gretchen was not correct. One of the duties that Gretchen owed to Lily was the duty of loyalty to the interests of the partnership. Consequently, Gretchen may not profit from partnership business at the expense of her partner, Lily. Since the partnership business was to practice law and Gretchen was practicing law outside of the partnership, she had breached this fiduciary duty. Gretchen would be required to return any money she had made to the partnership and split it according to her agreement with Lily. [Section 12-3]

PROBLEM 12-4   Kimberley, Dwayne, and Connie had been operating a small paint supply store for almost three years. Unfortunately, their business had not been very successful. They had barely broken even the first two years and it looked like the current year was going to end with a loss. Kimberley and Dwayne wanted to dissolve the partnership and terminate the business before they had any further losses, but Connie was insisting that termination required unanimous decision, and that if they withdrew from the partnership, she would sue them both for damages. Can Kimberley and Dwayne do anything to terminate the partnership without Connie's agreement?

Answer: Connie was correct that, in the absence of any agreement to the contrary, a partnership cannot be dissolved rightfully without the mutual agreement of all partners. In a situation like this, however, Kimberley and Dwayne can petition the court for dissolution on the grounds that the business can no longer continue for a profit. If the court agrees that this is the case, then the partnership would be dissolved by order of the court. This would serve to avoid further losses and would protect Kimberley and Dwayne from any liability to Connie for their withdrawal from the business. [Section 12-6]

PROBLEM 12-5   Greg, Martha, and Nancy were partners in a business to sell the lumber from some land that they had bought together. All of the lumber was sold in five years, so they agreed to dissolve and wind up the partnership business. Initially, Greg had contributed $10,000 to the venture, Martha had contributed $5,000, and Nancy had invested $5,000 also. In addition, Martha had loaned the business $5,000 to purchase special machinery for the business. The partnership's assets were $40,000 upon termination, but they had outstanding debts of $10,000. How must they distribute the assets of the partnership?

Answer: According to the provisions of the UPA, they must first pay the partnership creditors the $10,000, which will leave them with $30,000 in assets. Next, they must repay Martha the $5,000 loan she made to the partnership, which leaves them with assets of $25,000. The partners are then entitled to a return of their initial capital investment, which means that $10,000 must be distributed to Greg, and $5,000 each to Martha and Nancy. This leaves a balance of $5,000 in profit, which must be distributed equally among the partners. Each partner will therefore receive a profit of $1,666.66. [Section 12-7]

PROBLEM 12-6 Keith, a partner in a painting business, went in to purchase paint from a paint wholesaler that the partnership also dealt with. While he was there, he told the owner that the paint was to be used to paint his house and asked that the owner bill him for the paint at his home address. As it turned out, Keith did not pay for the paint. The paint wholesaler sued the partnership for the amount owed. Would it win its suit?

Answer: The paint wholesaler would not win its suit. A court would not find that Keith bound his other partners to the amount owed for the paint after clearly stating that his purchase was not related to partnership business. [Section 12-4]

MIDTERM EXAMINATION

(Answers begin on page 117.)

TRUE-FALSE

T F 1. The term "law" is used to refer to a system of principles and rules of conduct.

T F 2. State legislative bodies create ordinances, and local governmental bodies create statutes.

T F 3. If the defendant feels the plaintiff has no valid cause of action, the defendant may decide not to answer the complaint and file a demurrer instead.

T F 4. A valid contract is one that meets all the legal prerequisites and is enforceable in a court of law.

T F 5. A bilateral contract occurs when a promise is given in exchange for a requested act.

T F 6. An invitation to trade is a valid offer.

T F 7. The offeror has control over the offer and may revoke it at any time prior to acceptance.

T F 8. In most cases, silence is not a proper form of assent.

T F 9. Like acceptances, the notice of a rejection of an offer is binding at the time it is mailed.

T F 10. The UCC does not treat an acceptance containing additional terms as a rejection of the offer.

T F 11. A unilateral mistake will not prevent the formation of an enforceable contract even though one party knows of the other party's mistake.

T F 12. A misrepresentation does not give one party the right to seek rescission of a contract if it is done innocently; that is, without any intent to deceive.

T F 13. Usually, the courts evaluate the adequacy of the consideration exchanged by the parties to a contract.

T F 14. A benefit received prior to a promise cannot serve as consideration.

T F 15. Under the UCC, no consideration is necessary for modification of a written contract if the change is mutually agreeable to all parties involved.

T F 16. A minor has the right to disaffirm a contract at any time before reaching the age of minority, and has no duty to return the consideration received under the contract.

T F 17. When a person is declared legally insane, that person's current contracts are considered to be voidable.

T F 18. A contract may be considered an illegal bargain even though the acts contemplated under it are not expressly prohibited by law.

T F 19. As a rule, revenue-producing statutes are enforceable, while regulatory statutes are not.

T F 20. Under the Statute of Frauds, oral contracts are unenforceable.

T F 21. A conveyance of an interest in real property must comply with the Statute of Frauds.

T F 22. Contracts for the sale of goods over $250 must comply with the Statute of Frauds.

T F 23. Written contracts are protected by the parol evidence rule.

T F 24. A donee beneficiary is one to whom a contract is intended to bestow a gift.

T F 25. A condition precedent provides that a party to a contract must perform, but may discontinue performance if some fact or event takes place.

T F 26. A concurrent condition is an event or occurrence that extinguishes a contractual duty.

T F 27. There are two separate tests for satisfactory performance, one involving objective standards and the other personal taste or preference.

T F 28. If one party to a bilateral contract repudiates the agreement, indicating refusal to perform when the time of performance arrives, the other party may treat the action as a present material breach of the contract. This is known as anticipatory breach.

T F 29. A principal may be prevented from denying the existence of an agency relationship if he or she has created a set of circumstances that led a third party to reasonably believe such a relationship existed.

T F 30. Apparent authority results from the manner in which an agent is held out to the public by the principal.

T F 31. Actual notice of an agency relationship may be given through a newspaper of general circulation.

T F 32. Each partner owes fellow partners a fiduciary duty of good faith and loyalty.

T F 33. Partners are individually liable for all contracts and liabilities of the partnership.

T F 34. A dissolution may be caused by operation of law, by an order of the court, or by an act of the partners.

MULTIPLE-CHOICE

1. *Stare decisis* means

    (a) let the decision stand   (c) let the judges speak
    (b) let well enough alone   (d) let the court decide

2. Which of the following is *not* an area of substantive law?

    (a) contracts   (c) civil procedure
    (b) torts   (d) property

3. Which of the following actions can be brought in a federal district court?

    (a) an action between citizens of two different states, involving more than $10,000
    (b) a suit brought under a federal statute
    (c) a suit involving a federal question, where the value of the matter exceeds $10,000
    (d) all of the above

4. A contract which is implied-in-law is also called

    (a) an express contract   (c) a severable contract
    (b) a quasi contract   (d) a bilateral contract

5. When an offeree makes a definite counteroffer to the offeror, it acts to

    (a) limit the offeree's power of acceptance
    (b) destroy the subject matter of the contract
    (c) reject and terminate the original offer
    (d) add new terms to the offer

6. Substantial change in the common law of contracts has been made by the

   (*a*) Uniform Commercial Code   (*c*) Uniform Penal Code
   (*b*) Uniform Probate Code   (*d*) Uniform Trade Code

7. If an offeree receives an offer through the mail, and mails a reply to the offeror, the reply acts as a valid acceptance when

   (*a*) it is received by the offeror
   (*b*) the letter is deposited
   (*c*) the offeror acknowledges it
   (*d*) it is received at the offeror's place of business

8. Which of the following is *not* a topic involving the reality of mutual assent?

   (*a*) duress   (*c*) misrepresentation
   (*b*) mistake   (*d*) irrationality

9. Misrepresentation allows the innocent party to seek rescission of a contract in case of

   (*a*) innocent misrepresentation   (*c*) a and b
   (*b*) fraud   (*d*) none of the above

10. *Scienter* is

    (*a*) justifiable reliance
    (*b*) knowledge of the falsity of a statement or act
    (*c*) intent to deceive
    (*d*) misrepresentation

11. The proper test for determining whether or not duress *has* occurred is to determine whether

    (*a*) a reasonable person's will would have been overcome by the threat
    (*b*) the particular person involved had his or her free will overcome by the threat
    (*c*) the threat was potentially life threatening
    (*d*) the threat was intentional

12. Which of the following will serve as consideration for a bargain?

    (*a*) a preexisting duty
    (*b*) a legal detriment incurred in exchange for the bargain
    (*c*) partial payment of an undisputed debt
    (*d*) a past benefit

13. An agreement in which a buyer agrees to buy all he or she needs of a given product from a seller is called

    (*a*) an output contract   (*c*) a requirements contract
    (*b*) an exclusive dealing contract   (*d*) an approval contract

14. A minor may be held liable in quasi contract for the reasonable value of certain goods needed to maintain his or her station in life. In general, these goods are referred to as

    (*a*) necessities   (*c*) requisites
    (*b*) expenses   (*d*) dependents

15. Which of the following is usually held to *lack* the capacity to contract?

    (*a*) corporations   (*c*) aliens
    (*b*) intoxicated persons   (*d*) senior citizens

16. If an employment contract contains unreasonable limits on the employee's actions after employment has been terminated, the contract may be

    (*a*) illegal due to being contrary to public policy
    (*b*) enforceable regardless of the restrictions
    (*c*) voidable at the option of the employee
    (*d*) voidable at the option of the employer

17. *In pari delicto* means that both parties

    (a) are innocent   (c) may sue to enforce the contract
    (b) are equally at fault   (d) may void the contract

18. A collateral contract binds one party to

    (a) put up collateral value as consideration for a loan
    (b) delegate duties under the contract to a third party
    (c) answer for the debt, default, or miscarriage of another party
    (d) perform in exchange for collateral

19. Which of the following is *not* required for a writing to be sufficient?

    (a) both parties must sign the contract
    (b) the subject matter of the contract must be described
    (c) both parties must be identified in the contract
    (d) the material terms and conditions of the agreement must be described

20. A contract is usually assignable unless

    (a) the assignment will materially alter the duty of the obligor
    (b) it involves personal services
    (c) it contains a provision prohibiting assignments
    (d) all of the above

21. The implied warranties of an assignor do *not* include

    (a) the assignor will not try to defeat or impair the assignment
    (b) the assigned right actually exists
    (c) the obligor will perform his or her obligations
    (d) the assigned right is subject to no defenses

22. A person who is benefited by a contract that was not entered into for that purpose is called

    (a) a creditor beneficiary   (c) an incidental beneficiary
    (b) a donee beneficiary   (d) a favored beneficiary

23. Which of the following is not a type of contractual condition?

    (a) implied-in-law   (c) express
    (b) restrictive   (d) implied-in-fact

24. In order to discharge a contract, the performing party's performance must be

    (a) substantial   (c) partial
    (b) complete   (d) entire

25. A contract may be discharged by operation of law through

    (a) impossibility of performance (c) material alteration
    (b) frustration of purpose   (d) all of the above

26. An agent may perform some act without the authority to do so, and the principal may later confirm the act. This is known as

    (a) ratification   (c) acknowledgment
    (b) authorization   (d) confirmation

27. An agency relationship may be created by

    (a) agreement   (c) necessity
    (b) estoppel   (d) all of the above

28. An agent is *not* liable to a third party when the agent

    (a) acts for an incompetent principal
    (b) commits a tort within the scope of the agency

(c) signs a negotiable instrument in his or her own name

(d) keeps money that has been collected for the principal

29. Usually, an agency is terminated

(a) by the bankruptcy of the agent

(b) by extraneous events

(c) either by the parties or by operation of law

(d) by the bankruptcy of the principal

30. A partnership is established by

(a) a voluntary agreement between the partners

(b) co-owning property

(c) sharing gross profits

(d) sharing in management

31. Generally, a partnership is *not* entitled to

(a) share in the net profits

(b) rights in the specific partnership property

(c) a right to compensation

(d) a right to participate in management

32. A partner has a duty to fellow partners to

(a) use reasonable care and skill in performance of partnership business

(b) act in good faith and loyalty

(c) provide information to fellow partners

(d) all of the above

33. For the torts committed by partners or employees in carrying out partnership business, all partners are

(a) jointly liable

(b) jointly and severally liable

(c) individually liable

(d) not liable

34. A withdrawing partner discharges any subsequent liabilities and terminates apparent authority when he or she

(a) gives notice to third parties of the dissolution

(b) dissolves the partnership

(c) receives her/his share of partnership assets

(d) is discharged by the remaining partners

FILL-IN-THE-BLANK

1. The doctrine of following an established precedent set by a previous judicial decision is called _____ _____ .

2. Negligence and strict liability are dealt with under the law of _____ .

3. A civil lawsuit begins with the filing of a(n) _____ and _____ .

4. A sworn statement consisting of answers to questions put to a prospective witness is called a(n) _____ .

5. A(n) _____ is a promise or set of promises for the breach of which the law gives a remedy, or the performance of which the law in some way recognizes as a duty.

6. The three essential elements of a valid offer are _____ , _____ , and _____ .

7. An overt manifestation of assent to the terms of an offer in a manner requested or authorized by the offeror is called a(n)_____ .

8. In legal terms, a(n) _____ is an erroneous belief concerning the actual facts involved in a transaction.

9. A relationship in which one party has a special reason to rely on the opinion of another party because that party holds a position of trust or confidence is called a(n) _____ _____ .

10. When one party has a dominant relationship with another and forces the weaker party into an agreement through persuasion or the abuse of a close relationship, that party has exerted _____ _____ .

11. A(n) _____ involves a bargain and a legal detriment to the promise.

12. An agreement that creates no real mutuality of obligation between the parties is a(n) _____ .

13. Courts sometimes apply the doctrine of _____ _____ when the promisor fails to keep a promise and knows or has reason to know that the promise will be relied on by the promisee and an injustice will result.

14. _____ is the ability to enter into legally binding contracts.

15. A minor's power to affirm a contract after reaching the age of majority is called _____ .

16. A(n) _____ clause is sometimes used in a contract to avoid one party's liability in case of a negligent act.

17. A loan agreement that sets an interest higher than that established by state statutes is considered _____ .

18. For a contest to constitute a(n) _____ , it must include a prize, some form of consideration, and an element of chance.

19. The UCC uses the term "_____" to describe an agreement that is unenforceable and unfair.

20. The _____ _____ _____ prevents the introduction of extraneous oral evidence to alter or modify the written terms of a contract.

21. The transfer of a right or duty created under contract is called a(n) _____ .

22. A(n) _____ beneficiary is benefited by a promisee's intention to discharge an obligation she or he owes to a third party.

23. A predetermined situation or event that must take place before the duty to perform arises under a contract is called a(n) _____ .

24. A(n) condition _____ exists when one party is required to fully perform before demanding the other party's performance in return.

25. The language typically used to denote that the time of performance expressed in a contract is to be strictly complied with is that time is _____ _____ _____ .

26. _____ _____ is a remedy available to the court when damages will not be a sufficient redress under the circumstances of the contract.

27. _____ is a relationship in which one party authorizes another party to act on his or her behalf and under his or her control.

28. In an emergency, someone who acts for an injured person in getting medical help can be termed an agent by _____ .

29. A(n) _____ principal is one who a third party knows the identity of and knows an agency relationship exists.

30. The association of two or more people to establish and run a business for profit through some sort of voluntary agreement as co-owners is a(n) _____ .

31. Partners are said to be _____ in partnership concerning all partnership property.

32. When any partner leaves or a new partner joins a partnership, a(n) _____ is said to occur.

33. Even though the actual authority of all partners is terminated upon the dissolution of a partnership, the partnership can still be held liable for the act of a partner through the doctrine of _____ _____ .

34. _____ _____ is the completion of unfinished business and the liquidation of all assets of a partnership.

PROBLEMS

1. John's house needed a few repairs. He contracted with Elaine to paint his house and clean out the gutters on his roof. Elaine went out to John's house and painted the exterior according to the terms of the contract. While going up on the roof to clean out the gutters, Elaine noticed that John's chimney was in bad shape. The mortar was crumbling and a potential fire hazard existed. Consequently, Elaine also repaired John's chimney, along with the tasks required by the contract. When presented with the bill, however, John refused to pay for the extra work. Does Elaine have a recourse?

2. Home Furnishings, a wholesaler of furniture, entered into an agreement to purchase sofas from Kelly Furniture Manufacturer. The price stated in the contract was $150 per unit, and a total of 500 units were to be purchased by Home Furnishings during the upcoming year. Home Furnishings included no exact terms of delivery or time schedule in the contract, and the goods to be purchased were described only as "sofas." Is this agreement definite enough to be considered a contract?

3. Sarah was looking for a wedding present for a close friend and stopped by Leona's Antiques. There she found a broach that Leona told her was solid ivory and at least 200 years old. Sarah eagerly purchased the broach. Upon later examination, however, the broach turned out to be solid plastic and made in Korea. Has Sarah been defrauded out of her money?

4. Drake's car was in desperate need of some maintenance. He took it to Mike's Garage, since Mike was a long-time friend. The car needed a complete valve job, some new spark plugs, and a fan belt. Drake didn't have enough money to pay the normal rate that Mike charged, but they struck a bargain. If Mike fixed Drake's car, Drake would pay back a loan he had previously gotten from Mike before the date it was due, and with additional interest. Does a valid contract exist?

5. Jo-Jo wanted to rent a car from Jake's Rent-A-Car. He was only 15, however, and the minimum age to rent a car was 18. He intentionally misrepresented his age and got the car anyway. He used the car for two weeks before returning it to Jake's. When Jake's sent a bill to him, he refused to pay it, claiming that as a minor, he could disaffirm the contract at any time. Can Jake's recover the rental price from Jo-Jo?

6. Annette collected Renaissance art. At an art auction, she met a man who said that he would sell her a Renaissance work that he had for $100,000. Annette agreed and the deal was put in writing, even though Annette had read that the particular work of art had been stolen from a private collection several months earlier. As it turned out, the man did not deliver the work of art, so Annette sued to enforce the contract. Will Annette win her suit?

7. Claude agreed to sell Buster a shipment of leather goods that Buster would subsequently retail in his sporting goods store. They set up the deal over the telephone, and the total

amount of goods to be purchased had a net worth of $1,300. The goods were delivered, but the contract was never placed in writing. Has the Statute of Frauds been violated?

8. Jerome bought a house from Reliable Realty, for which he gave a down payment and a note for the balance of the purchase price. Reliable later assigned the note to the First National Bank. A few weeks later, Jerome declared bankruptcy, and thus was unable to repay the note. First National Bank then sued Reliable Realty to recover the amount. Will this action be successful?

9. Lewis needed a supply of hay to feed his horses during the winter. Clark had a large supply and agreed to sell Lewis a set amount for a fixed price. Unfortunately, the barn where Clark stored his hay burned down one night in late August, before the contract had been performed. Consequently, Clark refused to supply Lewis with the hay, claiming that performance on his part had been impossible. Is Clark right?

10. Andy was in the habit of stopping at his mother's insurance office every day after school. While waiting for his mother, he would sit at the reception desk doing office work and greeting clients as they came in. One day, a client came in and paid an insurance premium to Andy, who assured him that the payment would be credited. Unfortunately, the payment was later lost, and Andy's mother asked the client to repay the amount, claiming that her son had no authority to accept payments. Will the client have to repay the premium?

11. Carl, Steve, and Larry entered a partnership and created Fun Time, Inc., a distributor of video games and other amusements. Burt contacted Steve and sought to rent a number of games. Steve said, "Don't tell Larry or Carl, but I've got some reconditioned games here that I'll rent to you cheap." Burt entered a contract with the partnership, but soon found out why he had gotten such a good deal. The games had faulty wiring and one shorted out, causing a fire that destroyed Burt's bar. Burt sued the partnership. Is the partnership liable?

ANSWERS TO MIDTERM EXAMINATION

TRUE-FALSE

1. T [Section 1-1]
2. F [Section 1-3]
3. T [Section 1-6]
4. T [Section 2-2]
5. F [Section 2-2]
6. F [Section 3-2]
7. T [Section 3-3]
8. T [Section 3-5]
9. F [Section 3-3]
10. T [Section 3-7]
11. F [Section 4-2]
12. F [Section 4-3]
13. F [Section 5-1]
14. T [Section 5-2]
15. T [Section 5-3]
16. F [Section 6-4]
17. F [Section 6-5]
18. F [Section 7-2]
19. F [Section 7-2]
20. T [Section 8-1]
21. T [Section 8-2]
22. F [Section 8-2]
23. T [Section 8-3]
24. T [Section 9-6]
25. F [Section 10-2]
26. F [Section 10-2]
27. T [Section 10-3]
28. T [Section 10-7]
29. T [Section 11-1]
30. T [Section 11-2]
31. F [Section 11-6]
32. T [Section 12-3]
33. F [Section 12-5]
34. T [Section 12-6]

MULTIPLE-CHOICE

1. a [Section 1-2]
2. c [Section 1-4]
3. d [Section 1-5]
4. b [Section 2-2]
5. c [Section 3-3]
6. a [Section 3-4]
7. b [Section 3-5]
8. d [Section 4-1]
9. c [Section 4-3]
10. b [Section 4-3]
11. b [Section 4-4]
12. b [Section 5-1]
13. c [Section 5-2]
14. a [Section 6-4]
15. b [Section 6-5]
16. a [Section 7-2]
17. b [Section 7-4]
18. c [Section 8-2]
19. a [Section 8-3]
20. d [Section 9-2]
21. c [Section 9-4]
22. c [Section 9-7]
23. b [Section 10-2]
24. a [Section 10-3]
25. c [Section 10-6]
26. a [Section 11-1]
27. d [Section 11-1]
28. b [Section 11-5]
29. c [Section 11-6]
30. a [Section 12-2]
31. c [Section 12-3]
32. d [Section 12-3]
33. b [Section 12-5]
34. a [Section 12-6]

FILL-IN-THE-BLANK

1. stare decisis [Section 1-2]
2. torts [Section 1-4]
3. summons, complaint [Section 1-6]
4. deposition [Section 1-6]
5. contract [Section 2-1]
6. intention, definiteness, communication [Section 3-2]
7. acceptance [Section 3-5]
8. mistake [Section 4-2]
9. fiduciary relationship [Section 4-3]
10. undue influence [Section 4-5]
11. consideration [Section 5-1]
12. illusory promise [Section 5-2]
13. promissory estoppel [Section 5-3]
14. capacity [Section 6-1]
15. ratification [Section 6-3]
16. exculpatory [Section 7-2]
17. usurious [Section 7-3]
18. lottery [Section 7-3]
19. unconscionable [Section 7-2]
20. parol evidence rule [Section 8-4]
21. assignment [Section 9-1]
22. creditor [Section 9-7]
23. condition [Section 10-2]
24. precedent [Section 10-2]
25. of the essence [Section 10-3]
26. specific performance [Section 10-8]
27. agency [Section 11-1]
28. necessity [Section 11-1]
29. disclosed [Section 11-5]
30. partnership [Section 12-2]
31. tenants [Section 12-3]
32. dissolution [Section 12-6]
33. apparent authority [Section 12-6]
34. winding up [Section 12-7]

PROBLEMS

1. Elaine has a recourse for receiving payment for her work. Even though the chimney repairs were neither expressly nor implicitly required by the contract, Elaine might be able to recover in quasi contract. She repaired a potentially dangerous flaw, and her acts were not radically beyond the scope of what she was contracted to do. Elaine's best argument is that John should not be allowed to be unjustly enriched by her actions. If the court agrees that Elaine's actions were in John's best interests and within the scope of the contracted services, she can recover the reasonable value of her extra services. [Section 2-2]

2. This agreement would fail for lack of definiteness under general contract law, but sofas are considered to be goods under the UCC. Thus, the common law of contracts will not apply here. Under the UCC, a valid contract has been formed, one that includes both price and quantity specifications. The intent to contract is present, and the contract will not fail for indefiniteness even though the subject matter of the contract is sparsely described. [Section 3-5]

3. It is possible that Sarah has been defrauded out of her money. Three of the necessary elements of fraud are present; Leona falsely represented a material fact about the broach which Sarah justifiably relied on to her resulting injury. The other element remaining to be proven is Leona's knowledge of the falsity of her statement or her intent to deceive Sarah. If this intention can be proven, then Leona is guilty of fraud. [Section 4-3]

4. A valid contract exists between Drake and Mike. Normally, a preexisting duty does not act as binding consideration since it imposes no new detriment to the promise. However, Drake agreed to pay additional interest and tender payment before the originally agreed upon due date. Neither of these acts was encompassed in the parties' previous loan agreement, and both act as valid consideration for the contract. [Section 5-2]

5. Jake's Rent-A-Car probably can recover the rental price from Jo-Jo. Jo-Jo changed the normal rules controlling disaffirmation by minors by intentionally misrepresenting his age. Furthermore, in most states, he would not be allowed to disaffirm a contract that had been fully executed unless he could return the other party's consideration. The use of a car for two weeks is not something that can be easily returned, so Jo-Jo would probably be held liable for the rental price despite his minority. [Section 6-4]

6. Annette will not win her suit. One of the elements that must be present for a contract to be valid and enforceable is legality of purpose. In this case, the contract involved acceptance of stolen goods, which Annette was aware of. Thus, the contract was illegal, and therefore void and unenforceable. [Section 7-3]

7. The Statute of Frauds has not been violated because this situation falls within an exception to the Statute contained in the UCC that pertains to the sale of goods over $500. Under the UCC, if the buyer accepts the goods, then the contract is enforceable, even though it was never placed in writing. [Section 8-2]

8. This action will not be successful. An assignor makes a number of implied warranties to an assignee. Included among these are warranties that the assigned right exists, is subject to no defenses, and that the assignor will take no actions to defeat or impair the assignment. However, there is no warranty that the obligor will in fact pay or perform as required. Thus, the First National Bank may not recover from Reliable Realty. [Section 9-4]

9. Clark is probably not right. The doctrine of impossibility may only discharge the contract when performance cannot be done through *any* means, no matter if the means available is more expensive or troublesome. In this case, destruction of the hay can discharge Clark only if it cannot be replaced. Clark may still be able to buy hay from a third party and resell it to Lewis, thus performing the contract. [Section 10-5]

10. The client probably will not have to repay the premium because he can argue that an agency by estoppel existed between Andy and his mother. By letting her son sit at the

reception desk doing office work and greeting clients, the mother created a situation where the client could reasonably conclude that an agency relationship existed. The court will not allow a person to create this impression and then deny the existence of that relationship later. [Section 11-1]

11. The partnership is not liable. The general rule is that a partnership is liable for any act of an individual partner committed in the course of conducting business. In this case, however, Steve cannot be said to have had proper authority from the partnership for his actions. His statements to Burt, asking him to keep the other partners in the dark about their deal, would prove that Burt had reason to know that Steve was not acting on behalf of the partnership. Burt could seek a recourse only against Steve. [Section 12-4]

13 *CORPORATIONS*

THIS CHAPTER IS ABOUT

- ☑ **Nature of Corporations**
- ☑ **The Process of Incorporation**
- ☑ **Defective Incorporation**
- ☑ **Foreign Corporations**
- ☑ **Financing of Corporations**
- ☑ **Merger and Consolidation**
- ☑ **Dissolution of Corporations**

13-1. Nature of Corporations

A *corporation* is a business organization created under state law to pursue some lawful purpose.

A. Ownership of a corporation is vested in individuals with limited liability.

A corporation's owners, known as shareholders, are distinct from the corporation and therefore are not liable for the corporation's debts, obligations, or misconduct beyond the amount that they have invested.

B. A corporation exists as a separate legal entity from the people who own it.

As an entity, a corporation may sue, be sued, make contracts, hold property, and conduct all other business on its own behalf. It is also entitled to most of the guarantees of the Constitution and Bill of Rights. A court might ignore the corporate entity only in cases where fraud is involved or if it is necessary for justice to be served. In such cases, the shareholders or directors can be held liable for corporate actions.

EXAMPLE 13-1: Northern Distributors, Inc., was a shipping corporation licensed in the state of Iowa. State officials had received reports that the corporation was a front for an illegal smuggling operation. Without getting a warrant, the state had Northern Distributors, Inc., raided and seized their books. When the case came to court, however, Northern Distributors, Inc., sought to have the case dismissed on the basis of illegal search and seizure. Could they do this?

Since the state did not obtain a search warrant, Northern Distributors, Inc., could have the case dismissed. A corporation exists as a legal entity and is entitled to many of the rights guaranteed by the Constitution. In this case, Northern Distributors, Inc., had the right to the protection of the Fourth Amendment, which bars illegal search and seizure.

C. A corporation exists in perpetuity.

Shareholders may transfer their interests in a corporation at any time, including upon death, with no effect on the existence of the corporation.

D. Corporations are classified as public, private, or quasi-public.

How a corporation is classified plays a part in determining how it is financed and how it is regulated by the state.

1. A *public corporation* is organized to serve some governmental function. Public corporations usually are funded with taxes.

2. A *private corporation* is created to earn profits for its owners (profit corporation) or to raise money for charitable purposes (nonprofit corporation).

3. A *quasi-public corporation* is formed to provide some public service. These corporations receive some special privileges to help them serve the public, but are also more strictly regulated so that they cannot violate the public trust.

13-2. The Process of Incorporation

The authority to form a corporation is granted by each state. A corporation can exist only by complying with the statutory requirements of the state in which it is being formed.

A. A promoter begins the incorporation process.

A *promoter* is any person who takes part in the formation of a new corporation. A promoter's duties can range from looking for capital investors to entering into contracts for the corporation before it is legally created. This can pose legal problems because a corporation that does not yet exist cannot contract for anything. There are several rules established that generally are applied to the actions of promoters.

1. *Fiduciary relationship.* A promoter has a fiduciary relationship with the future corporation and its investors. This means that the promoter must act in the best interest of the corporation, must disclose all facts to the corporate investors, and must not profit at the expense of the investors. The promoter can be held liable to the corporation once it exists for a breach of this fiduciary relationship.

2. *Promoter liability.* If for some reason a corporation is not formed or fails to perform contracts entered into by a promoter with third parties, then the promoter generally is held liable to third parties. An exception sometimes occurs when the contract includes a provision releasing the promoter from liability in the event of either of these circumstances.

3. *Corporate liability.* A corporation, once it exists, is liable for any contracts formed by promoters once it ratifies those contracts, either expressly or impliedly.

EXAMPLE 13-2: Larry, a promoter for a corporation not yet formed, entered into an employment contract on behalf of the corporation to hire Jeanine as its general manager for a period of two years. When the corporation was legally created, Jeanine began work as the contract had specified. Conflicts developed, however, between Jeanine and the board of directors of the corporation, so the board of directors fired her after eight months. Jeanine threatened to sue the corporation and Larry for breach of contract. Could she do this?

Jeanine could sue the corporation for breach of contract but she could not sue Larry. Once a corporation ratifies a contract entered into by a promoter, the promoter is relieved of liability for its performance. The corporation had ratified the contract once it actually put Jeanine to work, therefore releasing Larry from liability.

B. Articles of incorporation must be filed with the proper state official before a corporation can be formed.

Most states require that *articles of incorporation* be filed with the Secretary of State. If the articles conform to the provisions of state corporate law, the secretary must file them and issue a certificate of incorporation. Most states require that the articles include:

- the name of the corporation (which must not be similar to that of any other corporation and must include the words "corporation," "incorporated," "company," "limited," or an abbreviation thereof)
- the location of the principal office
- the purpose of the corporation
- information regarding the corporation's capital structure and stock issues
- the name of the corporation's registered agent
- the names and addresses of the incorporators

EXAMPLE 13-3: A proposed corporation calling itself Mobile Oil filed an application for incorporation in the state of Alabama. Their articles of incorporation were complete and in full compliance with

Alabama's requirements for corporate formation within the state. Despite this, the request for incorporation was denied. Why?

Alabama probably denied this request for incorporation because the proposed corporate name is obviously similar to that of an internationally known oil company, which is not allowed. Furthermore, the proposed corporate name did not contain any term indicating that it was incorporated, such as corporation or limited. Such a term is required in corporate names in most states.

C. Bylaws should be adopted to regulate the internal operation of the corporation.

Bylaws are provisions that are written to set forth any procedures for corporate administration, management, and internal operation. There are several guidelines for the establishment of bylaws and their application.

1. The bylaws must not contradict state law or the articles of incorporation.
2. Bylaws are initially set forth by the original directors or shareholders.
3. Shareholders have the right to amend, repeal, or make bylaws unless stated otherwise in the articles of incorporation.
4. Bylaws are binding on the officers, directors, and shareholders of a corporation, but usually not on third parties.

13-3. Defective Incorporation

A corporation formed in strict compliance with all statutory provisions is called a *de jure corporation*. It exists in law and its status as a corporate entity cannot be challenged by states or individuals. Occasionally, however, a corporation may not have complied strictly with all procedural requirements for corporate formation. There are two circumstances in which the court will deem that a corporation does indeed exist, despite its noncompliance with state regulations.

A. A corporation may exist as a de facto corporation.

A *de facto corporation* is said to exist when the shareholders have made a good-faith attempt to organize a corporation, but have somehow failed to strictly comply with all statutes for corporate formation. The corporation exists in fact, if not in law, and has the same status as a de jure corporation. The purpose of the de facto corporation doctrine is to prevent third parties from wrongfully holding shareholders liable when they have acted in good faith.

B. A corporation may exist by estoppel.

A *corporation by estoppel* may exist when a third party deals with a business that is neither a de jure nor de facto corporation, yet represents itself as a corporation at the time an agreement is made. The purpose of a corporation by estoppel is to prevent third parties from being harmed by a business that later attempts to invalidate a contract because of lack of corporate status. The court will deal with the business as a corporation to the extent necessary to determine the rights of the parties in that particular situation.

EXAMPLE 13-4: A manufacturing company calling itself Rucker Corporation entered into a contract to purchase raw materials from Hollister, Inc. When the first delivery was made, however, Rucker Corporation refused to accept the shipment in violation of the contract agreement. Hollister, Inc., sued Rucker Corporation for breach of contract. When the case went to court, however, Rucker Corporation defended itself on the grounds that it was not a corporation and that, therefore, Hollister, Inc., would have to sue the individual responsible for entering the contract. Would this defense work?

It is unlikely that Rucker Corporation's defense would work. The court would probably find that Rucker held itself out as a corporation by virtue of the fact that the word "corporation" was a part of its name. On this basis, the court would probably hold Rucker Corporation liable for the breach as a corporation by estoppel; in other words, the court would estop Rucker Corporation from denying that it was a corporation and would treat it as one to the extent necessary to serve justice in this case.

13-4. Foreign Corporations

A corporation registered under the laws of one state or country is considered a *foreign corporation* in any other state or country where it does business. A foreign corporation must be authorized by a state in order to do business there.

A. There are several factors that constitute doing business.

A corporation is considered to be *doing business* if it maintains a substantial and continuous operation within a state. The courts generally have ruled that doing business does not necessarily consist of one of the following, although it may consist of several of the following:

- an isolated transaction
- maintenance of an office
- maintenance of a sales staff
- mail order transactions
- owning properties or securities within a state
- installing equipment within a state
- bringing suit or defending itself against a suit

B. States generally have nominal requirements for a foreign corporation to do business within their borders.

To do business within a state other than the one that it is incorporated in, a corporation generally must:

- file its articles of incorporation with the Secretary of State
- name an agent living within the state
- pay a filing and licensing fee
- designate a place of business within the state
- file its annual report with the state

C. Failure to register to do business within a state has several consequences.

If a foreign corporation does not register or fails to qualify for registration, it is denied the right to use the state's courts and it is denied statutory protection. As a result, it will not be able to enforce its contracts within that state until it registers.

D. The Constitution limits the rights of states to regulate foreign corporations.

State regulations will be held unconstitutional if they limit any of the following:

- the right of a corporation to use federal courts
- the right of a corporation to due process and equal protection under the Fourteenth Amendment
- the right of a corporation to contract

EXAMPLE 13-5: Western Limited, a direct mail house, was incorporated in the state of Arizona. Their catalogues were mailed to customers all over the United States and, as their business grew, they established an unregistered East Coast office in New York with an office staff of ten people and a warehouse. Orders for the states east of the Mississippi were processed in New York rather than in Arizona. A major supplier located in New York breached a contract with Western Limited, so they decided to have their corporate attorney file suit in a New York court. The attorney, however, advised them that they probably could not sue to enforce the contract in a New York state court. Why not?

If a corporation is doing business in a state, it must also be registered in that state or it is denied the use of state courts or statutory protection. In this case, Western Limited would most likely be determined to be doing business because they maintained an office, maintained a staff, owned property, and conducted mail order transactions within New York. They were not registered in New York, however, so they would not be allowed to enforce their contracts in New York courts. Upon registration and payment of all necessary late fees and other charges, they would probably be permitted access to New York courts.

13-5. Financing of Corporations

There are two ways for a corporation to be financed. The first is to issue shares of stock for a price. The second is to borrow money for the corporation's operations. These are referred to as *equity financing* and *debt financing* respectively.

A. Corporations may issue several kinds of stock.

The right of a corporation to issue stock is regulated by state law. The issuance and trading of stocks are governed by the Federal Securities Act and Securities Exchange

Act in order to prevent fraud and misrepresentation. The various kinds of stock have different rights and limitations connected with them.

1. *Common stock* entitles the owner to a portion of the corporation's profits in the form of dividends, a portion of its assets upon dissolution, and a voice in the management of the corporation.
2. *Preferred stock* entitles the owner to dividends or assets before those paid to common shareholders, but the owner has no voice in the management of the corporation.
3. *Par value stock* is any stock issued with a stated par value below which it cannot be sold.
4. *No par stock* is stock that is issued with no stated par value that can be sold at any market price.
5. *Watered stock* is any stock that is issued without its full value being paid. The owner is liable for the unpaid portion of it.
6. *Treasury stock* is any stock issued and then bought back by a corporation to be held in the corporation's "treasury."

B. Corporate stock is transferable.

Stock certificates are *negotiable instruments*, meaning that their ownership can be transferred by the owner simply endorsing them and delivering them to the new owner. This method of transfer may be restricted by the articles of incorporation or by statute. There are several rules that generally govern the transfer of stock certificates.

1. If legal restrictions to transfer stock are violated, a corporation may refuse the new owner shareholder status.
2. A shareholder must request replacement of stock certificates within a reasonable time if they are lost.
3. Forged stock certificates are of no value to the purchaser.
4. A purchaser who buys stock certificates in good faith from someone who is not empowered to sell them is considered a "holder in due course" and the purchase is valid.

EXAMPLE 13-6: Carl bought twenty shares of common stock in The Grange Company from Julie, who was executive vice president of the company. Carl did not know it, but Julie had no right to sell the stock because the bylaws of the company prohibited the sale of stock by company officers. Could the corporation refuse Carl shareholder status?

The corporation could not refuse Carl shareholder status for several reasons. In this case, it was the bylaws of the corporation that prohibited the sale, and the rights of a third party to transfer stock are not restricted by the bylaws of a corporation (see Section 13-2). Furthermore, the bylaws were not a general legal restriction, but an internal corporate restriction. Therefore, since Carl bought the stock in good faith and the transfer did not violate any legal restrictions, the purchase would be valid.

C. Dividends may be paid on corporate stock.

A *dividend* is a payment in cash or property by a corporation to its shareholders in accordance with some rate or proportion. Dividends are generally paid only from the corporation's earned surplus and after the other due expenses of the corporation have been paid.

D. Corporations may borrow money for their operations.

Corporate borrowing must be authorized by the directors or officers of the corporation. Shareholder approval is not ordinarily required. Creditors receive fixed payments of some kind plus interest. There are two kinds of debt financing available to corporations.

1. *Secured debts*, known as *bonds*, are a corporate promise to pay an indebtedness and are secured by the assets of the corporation. Holders of secured debts generally have first claim to corporate assets upon dissolution.
2. *Unsecured debts*, known as *debentures*, are like secured debts in that they are a promise to repay an indebtedness, but they are backed by the general credit rating of a corporation and not by any specific property.

13-6. Merger and Consolidation

A *merger* occurs when one corporation absorbs another corporation and the absorbed corporation ceases to exist as a distinct corporate entity. A *consolidation* occurs when two or more corporations unite to become a new corporation and their previous corporate entities cease to exist.

A. The processes for merger or consolidation are regulated by state law and the corporation's bylaws.

In general, plans to merge or consolidate require approval of the boards of directors of all companies involved and approval by a majority of the shareholders of all companies involved.

B. The successor corporation continues the operation of the old corporations.

After a merger or consolidation, the continuing or new corporation generally has the same rights, privileges, property, debts, and obligations as the corporations that ceased to exist.

EXAMPLE 13-7: The directors of Cola Company were unanimous in wanting to merge with a bottling plant to assure a supply of bottles for their products. When the shareholders voted on the proposal, however, there were not enough votes as required by the bylaws to approve the merger. The directors wanted to go through with the merger anyway. Could they do this?

The directors could not go through with the merger. Although mergers are regulated by state law and the corporation's bylaws, any plans for merging generally require the approval not only of the boards of directors of all companies involved, but also of the majority of shareholders of all companies involved. In this case, without shareholder approval, the directors would not be allowed to proceed with the merger.

13-7. Dissolution of Corporations

Dissolution of a corporation leads to termination of the corporation. The directors can wind up the corporation's business and distribute its assets, first to creditors, then to shareholders. A trustee may be appointed by the court to handle the winding up business as well. Dissolution can be voluntary or involuntary.

A. Voluntary dissolution may occur in three ways.

1. A corporation that has not begun business can be dissolved by a vote of the majority of the incorporators.
2. In most states, a corporation may be dissolved with the consent of a majority of its shareholders.
3. A corporation can be dissolved when its articles of incorporation set forth a time period for its existence and that time period has ended.

B. Involuntary dissolution may occur in two ways.

1. Shareholders may petition the court for dissolution of a corporation when:
   - they are unable to elect a board of directors
   - the board of directors is deadlocked over the management of the corporation, the shareholders are unable to break the deadlock, and injury is being caused by the deadlock
   - they can prove fraudulent or oppressive conduct of the board of directors
2. The state may petition the court for dissolution of a corporation when the corporation:
   - fails to file an annual report
   - fails to pay licensing fees
   - fails to maintain an agent
   - procures fraudulent registration
   - fails to perform its corporate function

RAISE YOUR GRADES

Can you explain . . . ?

☑ the effects of considering a corporation to be a legal entity
☑ how a corporation can exist in perpetuity
☑ the relationship between a promoter and the corporation that is to be formed that he or she represents
☑ the purpose of bylaws and how they are created
☑ the ways that a corporation can exist without meeting all statutory requirements for its formation and the reasons for deeming it existent in each case
☑ why a corporation should register in a state or country in which it is doing business
☑ the difference between equity financing and debt financing
☑ the difference between a merger and a consolidation and how each affects the status of the corporations involved
☑ the difference between voluntary and involuntary dissolution and how each can occur

SUMMARY

1. A corporation is a business organization created under state law to pursue some lawful purpose.
2. Ownership of a corporation is vested in individuals with limited liability.
3. A corporation exists as a legal entity separate from the people who own it, meaning that it is entitled to most of the guarantees of the Constitution and of the Bill of Rights.
4. A corporation exists in perpetuity, meaning that its owners can transfer their interests at any time with no effect on the existence of the corporation.
5. Corporations are classified as public, private, or quasi-public, and their classification plays a part in determining how they are financed and how they are regulated by the state.
6. The authority to form a corporation is granted by each state.
7. A promoter takes part in the formation of a new corporation by acting for the corporation to be. Any promoter has a fiduciary relationship with the future corporation and its investors, and can generally be held liable to the corporation for breaching this relationship and by third parties for the breach of any contracts entered into for a corporation that does not fulfill them. Once a corporation ratifies such contracts, however, the promoter is relieved of liability to third parties.
8. Articles of incorporation must be filed with the proper state official who, if in compliance with state requirements, will file the articles and issue a certificate of incorporation.
9. Bylaws are written by directors or shareholders of a corporation to set forth any procedures for corporate administration, management, and internal operation. They are binding on officers, directors, and shareholders of a corporation, but usually not on third parties.
10. A corporation that exists in compliance with all statutory requirements is a de jure corporation, or a corporation by law.
11. A corporation that has not complied strictly with all state requirements, but whose shareholders have acted in good faith to form a corporation, may be considered to exist as a de facto corporation, or a corporation in fact.
12. The court may consider a corporation to exist by estoppel when a business has presented itself as a corporation to third parties and the third parties suffered injury by reliance on that fact.

13. A corporation registered under the laws of one state or country is considered a foreign corporation in any other state or country where it does business, and must register to do business in that state or country in accordance with its regulations.

14. Failure of a foreign corporation to register to do business within a state can result in its being denied the right to use the state's courts and its being denied statutory protection.

15. A corporation may be financed with equity financing (issuance of stock) or debt financing (borrowing money).

16. Corporations can issue stock which is common or preferred, par value or no par value, watered or fully paid, and outstanding or treasury, any of which may be freely transferred by its owner by simply endorsing it and delivering it to the new owner. The method of transfer may be restricted by the articles of incorporation or by statute, however.

17. After all expenses of a corporation have been paid, the corporation may pay dividends of cash or property to its shareholders from its earned surplus.

18. A corporation may take out secured or unsecured loans. Holders of secured loans have first claim to a company's assets upon dissolution.

19. A corporation may change its structure by merging or consolidating with other companies. The processes for merger and consolidation are regulated by state law and the corporation's bylaws. The resulting corporation generally has the same rights, privileges, property, debts, and obligations as the corporations that were merged or consolidated with it.

20. Dissolution of a corporation leads to termination of the corporation and can be voluntary or involuntary.

21. Voluntary dissolution can occur by a vote of the majority of incorporators of a corporation that has not begun business yet, by the vote of a majority of shareholders of an operating corporation, or if a time of dissolution is stated in the articles of incorporation of a corporation.

22. Involuntary dissolution can occur when the shareholders of a corporation or the state in which a corporation is registered petition the court to dissolve a corporation and the court so orders it.

RAPID REVIEW | Answers

True or False

1. A shareholder's stock must be turned over to the corporation for its market value upon the death of the shareholder. [Section 13-1]	*False*
2. A corporation that does not yet exist can contract with third parties. [Section 13-2]	*False*
3. The name of a corporation must not be confusingly similar to that of any other corporation. [Section 13-2]	*True*
4. A business would not be allowed to incorporate if it did not submit information regarding its capital structure and stock issuance in its articles of incorporation. [Section 13-2]	*True*
5. The bylaws of a corporation must not contradict state law or the articles of incorporation. [Section 13-2]	*True*
6. A de facto corporation is a corporation that has been formed in strict compliance with all state requirements. [Section 13-3]	*False*
7. The purpose of a corporation by estoppel is to prevent third parties from being harmed by a business that later attempts to invalidate a contract because of lack of corporate status. [Section 13-3]	*True*

8. A corporation is considered to be doing business within a state   *True*
   if it maintains a substantial and continuous operation within
   that state. [Section 13-4]

9. The Constitution limits the rights of states to regulate foreign   *True*
   corporations. [Section 13-4]

10. Stock certificates are not negotiable paper. [Section 13-5]   *False*

11. A purchaser who buys stock certificates in good faith from   *False*
    someone who is not empowered to sell them must nonetheless
    return them to the seller. [Section 13-5]

12. A corporation cannot be held liable for the debts of a corpo-   *False*
    ration that it has merged with. [Section 13-6]

13. Only the directors and officers of a corporation can dissolve   *False*
    the corporation. [Section 13-7]

SOLVED PROBLEMS

PROBLEM 13-1   Charlotte, the sole owner of Westside Cleaners Company, had a contract to buy cleaning supplies from Abel, Ltd., a corporation that was owned by her friend, Kyle. Unfortunately, Charlotte's company had been having financial difficulties and, since Kyle was a friend, Charlotte had not paid his company for quite a while, thinking that he would understand. When Kyle pressed Charlotte for payment, however, she got angry and refused to pay him at all. After this falling out, Kyle sued Westside Cleaners for the breach of contract; but before the case went to court, Charlotte dissolved the corporation, paying off all of her creditors except for Kyle. Kyle then filed suit against Charlotte. Could he do this, since the breach was committed by a corporation?

Answer: Kyle would probably be allowed to sue Charlotte personally. Normally, a corporation is treated as a legal entity separate from its owners, and would be responsible as a corporate entity for any breach of contract such as this one. In this case, however, the court might ignore the corporate identity because it would be the only way that justice could be served. [Section 13-1]

PROBLEM 13-2   Brent Cain was a promoter for a corporation that was not yet formed. He entered into a contract to have Star Leasing, Inc., provide a fleet of cars for the corporation's intended sales force. He signed the contract "Brent Cain, for a North Carolina corporation to be formed." The corporation, however, was never formed. Consequently, Star Leasing filed suit for breach of contract against Brent, but Brent claimed that he was not liable because he had made it clear that he was only a representative. Was he correct?

Answer: Brent was not correct. If for some reason a corporation is not formed, and contracts have been arranged for the corporation by a promoter, then the promoter generally is liable for the failure to perform those contracts. The fact that Brent made it clear that he was signing the contract for a corporation did not relieve him of liability. The only way that he would not be held liable for the contract was if he and Star Leasing had added a written clause through mutual agreement that absolved Brent of any liability or cancelled the contract in the event of the corporation not being formed. [Section 13-2]

PROBLEM 13-3   Three women were in the process of forming a corporation to purchase land and develop a hotel on it. They asked Sam, a real estate broker, to act as their promoter in finding a suitable location for the hotel. Sam found a five-acre site that the women were pleased with, and arranged to sell it to them for $150,000. In fact, once he knew the women were interested in the site, Sam had purchased the land himself for $100,000, and consequently made a $50,000 profit when he sold it to the women. Could the women do anything about this if they found out?

Answer: The women could sue Sam for the return of the $50,000. As a promoter, Sam had a fiduciary relationship with the future corporation and its investors, the three women. Consequently Sam was obligated to act in the best interest of the corporation, to disclose all facts relating to the corporation's interests, and to not profit at the corporation's expense. He violated all three of these duties by acquiring the land himself and secretly making a $50,000 profit on its sale. A court would therefore hold him liable to the women and their corporation, once formed, for this breach of the fiduciary relationship. [Section 13-2]

PROBLEM 13-4   Rusty, owner of a small wheat supplier company, claimed that Tasty Bread Corporation still owed him $3,000 as payment for wheat deliveries he had made. He had been talking with Lucy, a vice president and 30% shareholder of the corporation, who insisted that the company did not owe him any further payments and that he would just have to sue the corporation and prove his case in court. Rusty was angry about this and, after some investigation, discovered that the corporation had not included information about its capital structure in its articles of incorporation, as required by state law. He therefore filed suit against Lucy on the basis that the corporation did not legally exist, and therefore she, as an owner, could be held liable. Would he win?

Answer: It is unlikely that Rusty would win his suit against Lucy. If it can be shown in court that the owners acted in good faith to form a corporation in strict compliance with state law, then the court would view the corporation as a de facto corporation, one that exists in fact, if not in law. Consequently, Rusty would not be allowed to sue an owner and would have to file his suit against the corporation as an entity. [Section 13-3]

PROBLEM 13-5   Arcon, Inc., was a small computer software corporation registered in the state of Arizona. The one company that it sold to in California defaulted on a payment for software services, so Arcon filed suit in a California court to seek payment. Before the case came to trial, however, the California corporation claimed that Arcon could not sue them in California because it was not registered to do business in the state. Were they correct?

Answer: The California corporation probably would not be correct. It is true that a corporation would be considered foreign if it did business in a state in which it was not registered, and would therefore be denied the right to use that state's courts to enforce its contracts. The question in this case was whether or not Arcon was "doing business" in California. The courts generally have ruled that an isolated transaction does not necessarily constitute "doing business" in a state. Since Arcon's contract with the California corporation was the only one in that state, the court probably would allow Arcon to sue for enforcement of its contract in the California court. [Section 13-4]

PROBLEM 13-6   Whitco Corporation, a landscaping company, acquired Greenland Company, a nursery, through a merger. After the merger, the Whitco Corporation received notice that it was being sued for the breach of two contracts that had been made by Greenland Company before Whitco had acquired it. Whitco officials informed the plaintiffs that those contracts had been made before Whitco bought Greenland, and that therefore they would have to sue the former owners of Greenland. Were they right?

Answer: Whitco Corporation was not right. After a merger, the successor corporation becomes liable for any outstanding contracts entered into by the company that became a part of it. Depending on the circumstances of the contract, Whitco Corporation may have to either fulfill the contracts or pay damages caused by the breach of the contracts. [Section 13-6]

PROBLEM 13-7   The board of directors of Realty Developers, Inc., was at odds over whether or not to speculate on some land in Utah. Those opposed to it believed that it would be a losing venture and jeopardize the future of the company. Those in favor of it, however, were trying to force the other directors into the purchase by voting against the opposing directors on all other corporate decisions, such that nothing was being accomplished at their meetings. Consequently, the company was beginning to flounder in other areas. The shareholders of the company were aware of the conflict and the effect it was having on business. Was there anything that they could do to resolve the problem?

Answer: The shareholders could attempt to have the issue raised and voted on at the shareholders' meeting. If this was unsuccessful or ended in another deadlock, then the shareholders could seek a majority vote to dissolve the corporation since harm is resulting from the directors' deadlock. If this vote did not garner a majority, then the shareholders could petition the court for dissolution of the corporation on the ground that the directors are deadlocked over management of the corporation and are unable to break the deadlock. In order for the court to rule for dissolution the shareholders must prove that injury is indeed being caused by the deadlock. If they cannot prove this, the court will not rule for dissolution, and the shareholders will just have to hope that the directors reach a decision. [Section 13-7]

14 MANAGEMENT OF CORPORATIONS

14-1. Powers and Liabilities of Corporations

A corporation has the express power to perform any act authorized by the state, its articles of incorporation, and its bylaws in the conduct of its business. It also has implied powers to perform any reasonable acts to promote its purpose.

A. A corporation can be liable for actions performed beyond its legal authority.

When a corporation acts outside the scope of its authority, it is said to be acting in *ultra vires*, meaning "beyond the authority." There are several consequences of ultra vires actions.

1. Shareholders may file a suit to halt ultra vires actions of the corporation.
2. The state may enjoin a corporation from continuing its ultra vires actions, or revoke its incorporation if its actions are serious enough to warrant this.
3. A corporation or third parties can recover damages, if any, from directors who order ultra vires actions.
4. Ultra vires contracts generally are enforceable, and none of the parties involved can use ultra vires as a defense for why a contract should not be enforced.

EXAMPLE 14-1: The board of directors of Hamby, Inc., entered into a contract with Holden Financial Services to receive financial counseling on the issuing of stock without the approval of a majority of the shareholders, as required by the bylaws of the corporation. What are the possible consequences of this action?

The directors performed an ultra vires act in that it was specifically prohibited in the bylaws of the corporation. The act has already been performed, so the shareholders would not benefit from seeking a court order to halt the action, particularly since ultra vires contracts generally are enforceable. Nor would the state be likely to enjoin the corporation from continuing its actions, as the contract did not violate state law and was an isolated transaction. The corporation, however, may hold the directors personally liable for either the cost of fulfilling the contract (i.e., payments for services performed) or for any damages that may result from the contract performance.

B. A corporation can be liable for torts, fraud, or criminal conduct.

Under the doctrine of *respondeat superior* (see Chapter 11), a corporation can be held liable for the torts of its directors, officers, agents, or employees if such acts are committed in the course of corporate business. Furthermore, a corporation can be held liable for fraud or criminal actions of its directors, officers, agents, or employees if committed within the scope of their employment. A corporation cannot escape liability by claiming that it prohibited such actions. It can be fined, have its property seized, or be forced into dissolution as punishment for violations of the law.

EXAMPLE 14-2: Jeans and Things Company, a manufacturer of junior sportswear, received notice that it was being sued for violations of antitrust laws committed by four of its employees. They were accused of attempting to fix prices. The board of directors of the company believed that since they had no knowledge of the price fixing and had never approved of it, then the employees should be held personally liable as acting on their own. Were they correct?

The directors were not correct. The fact that they had no knowledge of and had never approved of the price fixing did not absolve the corporation of liability for any damages that may result from the suit. The corporation could, however, hold the employees liable to the corporation for reimbursement of any damages the corporation may have to pay because of their actions.

14-2. Powers of Directors and Officers

Every corporation is governed by a board of directors elected by shareholders at an annual shareholders' meeting.

A. Directors are elected to conduct the affairs of the corporation.

A director's powers are limited only by state law, the articles of incorporation, and the bylaws of the corporation. Just like the corporation as an entity, directors also have implied powers to perform any reasonable acts to promote the business. A majority vote or unanimous written assent of the directors is needed to approve any act or proposal concerning corporate business.

B. In general, directors have four main functions.

Directors are seldom involved in the day-to-day management of a corporation, rather they serve to establish broad corporate policy and continuity. Their four main functions are:

- to protect the assets and other interests of the shareholders of the corporation
- to enforce the articles of incorporation and bylaws
- to see that the company is well managed with a sound management policy to follow
- to make certain decisions, such as dividend payments, mergers, or the pricing of corporate stock, that cannot be delegated to officers of the corporation

C. Officers are elected to make day-to-day management decisions.

The board of directors elects the officers of the corporation. A person may hold more than one office, with the exception that, in most states, the president and secretary may not be the same person. The officers are considered agents of the corporation.

1. *Actual authority.* As agents, officers have the express authority to act granted by the bylaws or the board of directors, as well as the implied authority to conduct whatever business is necessary for the purposes of their positions.
2. *Apparent authority.* Like agents, officers can bind a corporation on the basis of apparent authority, and like a principal, the corporation can ratify any unauthorized acts of its officers. (See Chapter 11 for further discussion of the agency relationship.)

EXAMPLE 14-3: James, the corporate secretary of Allen Corporation, promised a one-year employment contract to Louise for her to work for $22,000. James was aware that he was acting contrary to a corporate policy that stated that only the president could hire employees. Louise accepted the offer, but when she reported to work, she was presented with a new offer by the corporate president that was for much less than James had offered her. Louise therefore sued Allen Corporation for the salary she had been offered by James. Allen Corporation, however, claimed that James did not have the actual or apparent authority to hire anyone, that such offers were against company policy, and that Louise should have been aware that James did not have such authority. Was Allen Corporation right?

Allen Corporation was not right. Although James did not have the express authority to hire Louise for a fixed salary, Allen Corporation would nonetheless be bound by his actions on the basis of apparent authority. It would be unreasonable to believe that Louise should have questioned James's authority to hire her, as he occupied a high management position. Allen Corporation would therefore be liable to Louise for the salary that was offered to her by James.

14-3. Duties of Directors and Officers

Directors and officers have a fiduciary relationship with the corporation and its shareholders. This relationship entails specific duties.

A. Directors and officers have a duty to act with reasonable care in making decisions.

Directors' and officers' decisions must be made with reasonable care and diligence in the best interests of the corporation. In exercising reasonable care, however, directors and officers may rely on reports and opinions presented to them by those whom they reasonably believe to be competent and correct in the matters being presented.

B. Directors and officers have a duty to be loyal to the corporation and its shareholders.

Directors and officers may not profit from personal ventures that exploit their corporate position. Thus, they must not take advantage of a business opportunity that could be used by the corporation, must not compete with the corporation, and must not engage in conflicts of interest. Any director or officer who has a conflict of interest with corporate actions must report the conflict to the entire board of directors, who may then vote to approve or disapprove the action.

EXAMPLE 14-4: Sara was one of the directors of Farmers' Supply Company. The directors were discussing whether or not to enter into a contract with a harness manufacturer to receive shipments of harness for all of its stores. As it turned out, Sara was also a shareholder of the harness manufacturer. What, if anything, should she do about this?

Sara should reveal to the entire board of directors that she has an interest in the harness manufacturer and, as such, could potentially profit from the contract that Farmers' Supply is considering entering into with them. This would be evidence of her good faith in not secretly seeking profits, would avoid her being liable in the future for profiting at corporate expense, and would allow the other directors the chance to vote on the proposal, knowing of her interest.

14-4. Liabilities of Directors and Officers

In general, directors and officers are jointly and severally liable to the corporation for any losses resulting from actions that are specifically prohibited by law, by the articles of incorporation, or by the bylaws of the corporation.

A. Directors are presumed to have sanctioned any act if they were present when it was adopted.

If a director is aware of an illegal or poor decision, such as the distribution of illegal dividends, he or she must record a written dissent in the minutes of the corporation to avoid liability. Otherwise, all directors who are present for a vote for such an act can be held liable to the corporation for any damages resulting from the act.

B. Directors and officers are liable to the corporation for negligence and mismanagement.

There is no guarantee that corporate decisions will never result in a loss to the corporation. The standard used to determine personal liability of directors and officers is that they must have acted with reasonable care and in good faith in making the business judgment that resulted in a loss.

EXAMPLE 14-5: Assume that the lawsuit filed against Jeans and Things in Example 14-2 had named the directors of the corporation along with the corporation in the suit. The suit charged that they should have been aware that the four employees had been involved in price fixing, and that they were negligent in not showing the reasonable care necessary to have discovered that price fixing was going on. Would such a suit win?

The corporation would still be found liable for the employees' actions, but the directors probably would not. To prove negligence, it would have to be shown that the directors had reason to believe that price fixing was being done by some of its employees. A corporation could not possibly run smoothly if, without cause, directors were expected to suspect all employees of criminal action. Reasonable care is interpreted by the court to be the amount of care that a reasonable person would exercise under the same circumstances as the case at hand. In this case, if the directors were not aware of the price fixing, had never approved of price fixing, and had no cause to suspect price fixing, the court would not hold them personally liable.

C. Directors and officers are liable to the corporation for any breach of their duty of loyalty.

Should directors or officers benefit from their inside knowledge and position at the expense of the corporation, they may be held liable to the corporation for the return of such benefits.

D. A corporation may indemnify its directors and officers.

Most corporations indemnify their directors and officers against any losses they may incur while acting in the corporation's behalf. For example, expenses incurred in defending against lawsuits may be reimbursed if the directors or officers are found not to be liable.

14-5. Rights of Shareholders

Shareholders have certain rights as a result of owning corporate stock. Although they may not participate in most management decisions, they can participate indirectly in corporate management through their right to attend annual shareholder meetings, to suggest proposals at these meetings, and to vote on certain corporate decisions. If they cannot attend these meetings, they may vote by *proxy*, meaning that they may assign their voting power.

A. Shareholders have the right to participate in certain major corporate decisions.

Unless stated otherwise in the articles of incorporation, bylaws, or state law, shareholders have the power through their voting rights to:

- amend the articles of incorporation
- adopt, amend, or repeal corporate bylaws
- elect the board of directors of the corporation
- approve loans to officers, stock option plans, and increases in corporate stock
- approve major corporate decisions such as mergers or consolidations
- approve the dissolution of the corporation

B. Shareholders' voting rights may be cumulative or noncumulative.

Cumulative voting gives a shareholder a number of votes equal to the number of shares he or she owns multiplied by the number of directors to be elected. The purpose of cumulative voting is to give minority shareholders a chance to choose minority representation on the board by directing all their votes toward only one or a few minority candidates, thereby assuring that at least a few of their candidates will be elected. Otherwise, majority shareholders would always out-vote them for every seat. *Noncumulative voting*, or "straight" voting, gives a shareholder one vote for each share of stock he or she owns. This vote normally is used for corporate decisions other than board elections, as described above.

EXAMPLE 14-6: Donald owned 100 shares of Electronics Limited stock. At the upcoming annual shareholders' meeting, a vote was to be taken to elect five directors. How many votes can Donald cast and in what way can he cast them based on cumulative voting rights?

Donald can cast votes equal to his number of shares times the number of directors to be elected, or 500 votes. He may cast them in any way he wishes, whether it be 100 votes for each of five candidates, 500 votes for one candidate, or any other allocation of his 500 votes among one or more candidates.

C. Shareholders have preemptive rights.

When a corporation intends to issue additional corporate stock, the shareholders generally have a *preemptive right* to purchase the stock before others in proportion to the number of shares each shareholder owns at the time of the issuance. This right allows shareholders the option of maintaining their existing ratio of interest and voting power in the corporation.

D. Shareholders have the right to inspect corporate books and records.

The right to inspect the corporation's books and records is not absolute. A request to inspect must be submitted in writing and must be for a reasonable purpose related to the shareholder's interest and status in the corporation. Shareholders may resort to court enforcement of this right if a request is wrongfully denied by a corporation.

E. Shareholders have the right to receive dividends.

The right to receive dividends is enforceable only after a dividend has been declared by the corporation. Shareholders may hold either the corporation or its directors liable for failure to pay a declared dividend unless it is proven to be illegal and it is proven that the directors had no knowledge of its illegality. Holders of preferred stock have a superior right to receive dividends over holders of common stock. Only directors may decide the issuance of dividends, but shareholders may force the payment of dividends when:

- the corporation is using earnings for non-corporate purposes
- the present surplus of funds is more than adequate to pay a dividend, and the corporation has no planned use for these funds
- the directors are withholding dividend payments in an attempt to "freeze out" minority shareholders

EXAMPLE 14-7: The directors of Vision, Inc., declared a generous dividend to its shareholders at the end of a very good quarter. After declaring the dividend, however, an internal audit showed that there were more creditor obligations that had to be paid than had been realized at the time of the declaration, and that payment of the dividend would result in a default on these obligations. As a result, the directors sent out an announcement to its shareholders that they would not be paying the dividends after all. A group of shareholders threatened to sue the directors for failure to pay a declared dividend. Would they win such a suit?

  The shareholders would not win such a suit. Normally, a dividend becomes a debt to the corporation and must be paid once its directors have announced that it will be issued. Dividends, however, can only be paid after all other due and payable operating expenses of a corporation have been paid. In this case, an audit revealed that payment of the dividend would be at the expense of the creditors, making the declared dividends illegal. Furthermore, the directors were unaware of the illegality of the dividends until after the audit, so they could not be held liable for the declaration. They could, however, be held liable to creditors for issuance of an illegal dividend. The directors were therefore correct to revoke the declaration of dividend payments.

F. Shareholders have the right to dissent against corporate proposals.

Since many major corporate decisions can be made with approval of a majority of shareholders, dissenting rights developed to protect the rights of minority shareholders. Any shareholder who objects to a major corporate proposal, such as a merger, consolidation, or sale of assets, has the right to register his or her dissent in writing *before* a vote is taken on the proposal. If the proposal is approved, dissenting shareholders may demand a fair value in exchange for their shares in the corporation.

G. Shareholders have the right to file derivative suits.

Shareholders normally cannot sue for injuries to the corporation—only the corporation can sue in its own behalf. They can, however, file a *derivative suit* against the directors and officers in behalf of the corporation in an attempt to get a court order to stop ultra vires actions or actions that would injure the corporation's assets. A derivative suit may be filed only if the corporation refuses to file the suit itself.

EXAMPLE 14-8: The directors of World Travel, Inc., had made low interest loans of corporate money to relatives and business acquaintances without demanding collateral. Some of the shareholders found out about these transactions and demanded that the directors stop making these loans and repay the money to the corporation. The directors claimed that the corporation bylaws granted them the right to make loans and therefore refused to stop. Is there anything further that the shareholders may do about this situation?

  Normally, only a corporation can sue on its own behalf. In this case, however, the directors of the corporation are involved in fraudulent loans that could be detrimental to the corporation's assets. Since the directors have refused to halt their actions and certainly will not file a suit in the corporate name against their own actions, then the shareholders have the right to file a derivative suit against the directors in behalf of the corporation.

14-6. Liabilities of Shareholders

Since a corporation is viewed as a legal entity separate from its owners, shareholders are generally liable only for the amount of money they have invested in corporate stock. There are several other circumstances, however, in which shareholders can incur liability.

A. Shareholders are liable if a corporation is formed for fraudulent purposes and they are aware of it.

In such cases, the courts would ignore the corporate entity and hold shareholders liable for any damages to third parties as a result of the fraudulent actions of the corporation.

B. Shareholders are liable for the true value of watered stock.

A shareholder who receives watered, or discounted, stock is liable to the corporation or its creditors for the difference between what was paid for the stock and its true value.

C. Shareholders are liable for knowingly receiving illegal dividends.

Illegal dividends are any dividends issued at the expense of creditors or that would make the corporation insolvent. Normally, directors are liable for the payment of illegal dividends, but shareholders who knowingly receive such dividends can be liable to the corporation or its creditors for the amount received.

EXAMPLE 14-9: Lampshades, Limited, which has been owned by ten shareholders for five years, needed to raise funds. It went public and acquired a large number of shareholders by selling watered stock at a discount. After the sale, the corporation still had not raised enough money to pay its creditors. Consequently, the ten principal shareholders, who were also directors, voted to pay a generous dividend to its new shareholders, hoping that this would encourage further investment through the sale of more stock. As it turned out, this plan did not work, and the corporation was unable to pay its creditors during the next quarter. What are the liabilities of the shareholders in this situation?

The dividends issued by the ten principal shareholders in their capacity as directors were illegal because they were paid at the expense of the corporation's creditors. The shareholders were unaware that they had received illegal dividends, so they would not be liable to the corporation creditors for their return. The directors, however, would be liable to the corporation creditors for the amount paid in illegal dividends because they knew that the payment would make it impossible for them to pay their creditors unless others invested in the corporation. Furthermore, the shareholders who bought watered stock would be liable to the corporation creditors for the difference between what they paid for the stock and its true value.

RAISE YOUR GRADES

Can you explain . . . ?

☑ what ultra vires acts are and the consequences of such acts
☑ how the duties of reasonable care and loyalty apply to directors and officers of a corporation
☑ how a corporation might be liable for criminal acts of its employees but its directors might not
☑ how the shareholders of a corporation can indirectly participate in its management
☑ the rights that serve to protect minority shareholders
☑ the purpose of derivative suits
☑ the limited liability of shareholders for corporate acts

SUMMARY

1. A corporation has the express power to perform any act authorized by the state, its articles of incorporation, and its bylaws in the conduct of its business, as well as implied powers to perform any reasonable acts to promote its purpose.

2. A corporation can be liable for ultra vires acts, or actions performed beyond its legal authority. A corporation or third parties can recover damages, if any, from directors who order ultra vires actions.

3. A corporation can be liable for torts, fraud, or criminal conduct of its directors, officers, agents, or employees if committed in the course of corporate business.

4. Directors are elected by shareholders to conduct the affairs of the corporation. Their powers are limited only by state law, the articles of incorporation, and the bylaws of the corporation.

5. Officers are elected by the board of directors to conduct the day-to-day management of the corporation. They are agents of the corporation with the actual authority to bind the corporation that is granted by the bylaws or the board of directors, as well as apparent authority to bind the corporation.

6. Directors and officers have a duty to act with reasonable care and diligence in making decisions in the best interests of the corporation. They may rely on reports and opinions presented to them by those whom they reasonably believe to be competent in the matters being presented.

7. Directors and officers have a duty to be loyal to the corporation and therefore may not take advantage of their position to profit at the expense of the corporation. Any conflict of interest must be reported to the directors and shareholders of the corporation.

8. In general, directors and officers are jointly and severally liable to the corporation for any losses resulting from actions that are specifically prohibited by law, by the articles of incorporation, or by the bylaws of the corporation. They are also liable for negligence, mismanagement, and any breach of their duty of loyalty.

9. Shareholders have certain rights as a result of owning corporate stock. These include the right to attend annual shareholder meetings, the right to suggest proposals at these meetings, and the right to vote on all proposals put forth at these meetings. Voting rights may be cumulative or noncumulative. A shareholder may vote by proxy if unable to attend the meetings.

10. Shareholders have preemptive rights to purchase new issuances of stock before others in proportion to the number of shares each shareholder owns at the time of the issuance.

11. Shareholders have the right to inspect corporate books and records for a reasonable purpose related to the shareholder's interest and status in the corporation.

12. Shareholders have the right to receive dividends after they have been declared by the board of directors. Under certain circumstances, shareholders may force the payment of dividends.

13. Shareholders have the right to dissent in writing against corporate proposals before they are voted on and, if approved, to demand a fair value for their stock in the corporation.

14. Shareholders have the right to file derivative suits against the directors and officers in behalf of the corporation in an attempt to get a court order to stop ultra vires actions or actions that would injure the corporation's assets. Such a suit may only be filed if the corporation refuses to file the suit itself.

15. Shareholders are normally liable only for the amount of money they have invested in corporate stock. Shareholders can also incur liability, however, if a corporation is formed for fraudulent purposes and they are aware of it, for the true value of watered stock, and for knowingly receiving illegal dividends.

RAPID REVIEW   Answers

True or False

1. Ultra vires can be used as a defense for why a contract should not be enforced. [Section 14-1]   *False*

2. A corporation can be held liable for fraud or criminal acts committed by its directors, officers, agents, or employees in the scope of their employment, even if it specifically prohibited such actions. [Section 14-1]   *True*

3. A director may individually make any business decision so long as it is in the best interest of the corporation. [Section 14-2]   *False*

4. A corporation can ratify any unauthorized acts of its officers. [Section 14-2]   *True*

5. Directors and officers have the right to take advantage of any business opportunity that they become aware of as a result of their position in the corporation. [Section 14-3]   *False*

6. Directors and officers can always be held liable for business decisions that result in a loss to the corporation. [Section 14-4]   *False*

7. A director who disagrees with a decision passed by the board of directors must register his or her dissent orally in order to avoid future liability for the consequences of the decision. [Section 14-4]   *False*

8. Corporations may indemnify their directors and officers against any losses incurred in defending against lawsuits for corporate actions if they were indeed not liable. [Section 14-4]   *True*

9. The purpose of cumulative voting rights is to give minority shareholders a chance to choose representation on the board of directors. [Section 14-5]   *True*

10. Preemptive rights give shareholders the option of maintaining their existing ratio of interest and voting power in the corporation. [Section 14-5]   *True*

11. A corporation may refuse to allow a shareholder to inspect corporate books and records if the shareholder does not have a reasonable purpose for doing so. [Section 14-5]   *True*

12. Holders of preferred stock have a superior right to receive dividends over holders of common stock. [Section 14-5]   *True*

13. After a corporate decision has been made that a shareholder disagrees with, the shareholder may demand that the corporation pay a fair value for any stock the shareholder holds in the corporation. [Section 14-5]   *False*

14. Shareholders generally are liable only for the amount that they have invested in corporate stock. [Section 14-6]   *True*

SOLVED PROBLEMS

PROBLEM 14-1   The directors of Sunland Oil Company, an oil refinery, had been contributing a lot of money in the corporate name to a woman's campaign to be elected to the state legislature. They did this because her opponent advocated increasing taxes on oil industry profits, while she opposed such increases. The shareholders of Sunland Oil Company, however, claimed that the directors had no authority, either in the articles of incorporation or the bylaws, to use corporate assets for campaign contributions. Can they do anything to halt the contributions and, if so, what would be the outcome of their actions?

Answer: The shareholders can file a suit seeking a court order to halt what they consider to be ultra vires acts of the corporation. In this case, however, they probably would not be successful in their suit. Besides the express authority granted by the state, the articles of incorporation, and the bylaws, a corporation has the implied power to perform any reasonable act to promote its purpose. The court would probably take the view that the corporation's purpose—to make profits as an oil refinery—would conceivably be damaged by the election of a state official who vowed to increase taxes on oil industry profits. It would therefore be reasonable and serve the purpose of the corporation for the corporation to contribute to the woman's campaign, since she opposed the tax increases. The court would therefore rule that the contributions did not constitute ultra vires actions, but rather justifiable actions taken on the basis of the corporation's implied authority to promote its purpose. [Section 14-1]

PROBLEM 14-2   Ken, an assistant store manager of a branch store owned by Marvo Corporation, signed the corporate name to a contract to lease a pinball machine for two years that was to be placed in the employee lounge at the store. Ken paid for the machine each month with a cashier's check. After five months, however, the president of Marvo Corporation visited the store and saw the machine. The president immediately sent a letter to the vending company, requesting that it remove the machine since Ken had no authority to rent it. The vending company decided to sue Marvo Corporation for the remaining amount due on the two-year lease anyway, claiming that Ken's actions were binding on the corporation based on implied and apparent authority. Would the vending company win its case?

Answer: The vending company probably would not win its case. Ken did not have the express authority to contract for the corporation. The key issue here is whether or not he had the implied or apparent authority, which, if he did, would be binding on the corporation. Implied authority pertains only to actions that serve the purpose of the corporation or the officer's function in the corporation. A pinball machine in an employee lounge does not pertain to the corporation's purpose, nor to Ken's function as an assistant manager. It would therefore be unreasonable for the vending company to have relied solely on Ken's implied authority to lease the pinball machine. As to apparent authority, the fact that Ken was an *assistant* manager coupled with the fact that he was contracting for something unrelated to the business, should have led the vending company to challenge his authority to contract for the corporation. Furthermore, Marvo Corporation did not ratify Ken's actions in any way. In fact, it sought to stop the action as soon as it became aware of it. Consequently, the vending company was not reasonably justified in relying on Ken's sole authority, implied or apparent, and the corporation probably would not be held liable for the amount remaining on the contract. The vending company could, however, hold Ken liable for the breach of contract. [Section 14-2]

PROBLEM 14-3   Lana was the president of Aaron Investment Company, a corporation that bought office buildings for leasing. On her own, Lana bought old buildings that she refurbished and leased as apartments. One day, while looking at a building that she was considering buying for apartment rentals, Lana realized that the building would be ideal for the corporation to buy and rent for office use. Does Lana have any obligation to the corporation with regard to this building?

Answer: Lana would be violating her duty of loyalty to the corporation if she were to buy the building for her own use. The duty of loyalty prohibits any officer of a corporation from taking advantage of a business opportunity that could be used by the corporation. Lana must give the corporation the first right to buy the building if it wants it. If the corporation does not want it, then she would be free to purchase it for herself. [Section 14-4]

PROBLEM 14-4   The board of directors of Worthington, Inc., a metals mining corporation, voted to purchase land for a mining operation in a Central American country that was rumored to be on the verge of civil war and was economically unstable. The purchase price was a good deal, but one of the directors, Andy, felt that the venture was too risky because of the country's current turmoil. Andy cast the only dissenting vote, but he was overruled by the majority. Can Andy do anything to avoid liability if the venture fails?

Answer: Andy should have the secretary note his dissent in the minutes of the meeting because, should a lawsuit ever be filed against the directors for their actions, the law would presume that he sanctioned the purchase since he was present at the meeting when it was approved. By recording his written dissent in the minutes, however, he can avoid any future liability for the board's decision. [Section 14-4]

PROBLEM 14-5   Bill held 15% of the stock in a publishing corporation. The other 85% was owned by the directors of the corporation. Bill had not received a dividend for several years, despite the facts that the company had shown excellent profits each year and the directors were being paid increasing salaries and bonuses. Does Bill have any recourse in this situation?

Answer: Bill can probably force the directors to pay a dividend on the ground that they are attempting to "freeze out" a minority shareholder. The power of the majority shareholders as directors of the corporation imposes on them the duty to protect the interests of the shareholders in the corporation, including those of minority shareholders. In this case, the directors are abusing this power by using corporate profits to benefit themselves with high salaries and bonuses, while refusing to pay any portion of the profits in the form of dividends to Bill. Bill could therefore file a derivative action that would result in the court ordering the payment of dividends on the basis that the directors have breached their duty to protect the interests of shareholders. [Sections 14-1 and 14-5]

PROBLEM 14-6 On the advice of a broker, Carol acquired some shares of stock in Bardson, Inc. She did not know much about the corporation, so she presented the directors of Bardson with a request to review corporate records for the purpose of "evaluating the management and condition of the company." Would she be allowed to review the records?

Answer: Carol would not be allowed to review the records of the corporation. A shareholder has the right to inspect the books and records of a corporation, but only for a reasonable purpose related to the shareholder's interest and status in the corporation. If Carol could prove that she had strong reason to suspect fraud, mismanagement, or other irregularities in the corporation, then a reasonable purpose would exist for her to inspect the corporate records. Her purpose, however, of "evaluating management and the condition of the company" would not be reasonable just because she owns some shares and wants to know more about the corporation. She should review public records, such as the corporation's annual reports, for that information. [Section 14-5]

PROBLEM 14-7 Footwear Company, a shoe manufacturer, wanted to merge with a tanning firm to be certain that it would always have a supply of leather for its products. The board of directors unanimously wanted the merger, and they were certain that a vote would produce the approval of two-thirds of their shareholders, as required by the bylaws of the corporation. There was a group of shareholders, however, who were attempting to block the merger. Could they do this?

Answer: The group of shareholders probably could not block the merger. If the boards of directors of both companies approve of the merger, and the majority of shareholders approve also, as required by the bylaws, then the merger could go through. Their only recourse would be to record their dissent before the vote took place and request the fair value of their shares of stock from Footwear Company if the merger is approved. [Section 14-5]

PROBLEM 14-8 HG Personnel, Inc., was wholly owned and operated by Gretchen and Harry. For three years, they had been taking payments from clients for the purpose of obtaining employment for them. In fact, they had only found jobs for about 5% of the people who came to them, and had used most of the money to pay themselves very high salaries. At the end of the three years, they were audited by the IRS, who claimed that the corporation owed $70,000 in back taxes. Harry and Gretchen filed for corporate bankruptcy, claiming that there were not enough assets to pay the taxes. The IRS, however, filed a suit to collect the money from Gretchen and Harry as the shareholders of the corporation. Could they do this?

Answer: The IRS could collect the money from Harry and Gretchen. Normally, shareholders cannot be held liable for corporate debts. In this case, however, the court would probably ignore the corporate entity and hold Gretchen and Harry liable because it probably could be proven that they formed the corporation for fraudulent purposes. The facts that they kept most of the corporate money for themselves, only placed about 5% of their clients in jobs, and failed to pay taxes when due would strongly support this belief. The corporate entity, therefore, would be viewed as a fraud that, if allowed to stand, would constitute an injustice. [Section 14-6]

15 SALES CONTRACTS

THIS CHAPTER IS ABOUT

- ☑ **The Uniform Commercial Code**
- ☑ **Special Provisions Regulating Merchants**
- ☑ **Special Provisions Regulating the Sales Contract**

15-1. The Uniform Commercial Code

The Uniform Commercial Code (UCC) was developed and adopted by almost all states to govern commercial transactions. In particular, Article 2 of the UCC applies to contracts for the sale of goods. Of course, general contract law, as discussed in earlier chapters, applies to sales contracts unless changed or modified by the UCC. To determine when a contract falls under Article 2 of the UCC, it is important to determine what a sale is, what goods are, and what therefore constitutes a transaction that falls under Article 2 of the UCC.

A. Two elements are necessary for a sale to take place.

Article 2 of the UCC defines a *sale* as the transfer of title from a seller to a buyer for a price.

1. *Title*. Title to the goods must be transferred to the buyer. Title refers to the legal ownership of property, either personal or real. Possession of a title reflects a right to property that is legally enforceable and superior to all other claims. Passage of title will be discussed further in Chapter 16.
2. *Price*. Price must be given as consideration in exchange for the title. Price can be money or any other value that a buyer agrees to pay a seller in exchange for goods.

EXAMPLE 15-1: Frank signed a written contract to exchange two of his prize hogs for a set of tractor tires from Elaine. After the agreement was made, however, Frank decided that his hogs were worth more than the tires. He therefore informed Elaine that he wanted to pay money for the tires, claiming that the contract was not enforceable anyway since no price had been set, only an exchange of goods. Could he do this?

Frank could not attempt to void the contract on the basis that no price had been determined. Under Article 2 of the UCC, price does not have to be money. It can be anything of value that a buyer agrees to pay a seller in exchange for goods. In this case, the price for the tractor was the hogs, and vice versa, so the contract would be a sales contract and would be enforceable under Article 2.

B. Only transactions involving goods fall under Article 2 of the UCC.

Article 2 defines goods as all things tangible and movable at the time of identification to the sales contract. Thus, Article 2 does not cover contracts to provide services or sales of real property. Goods must be existing and identified in order for a sale to occur.

1. *Existing goods*. Because some confusion has occurred over what constitutes existing goods, goods have been interpreted to include specially manufactured goods, the unborn young of animals, growing crops, timber to be cut, minerals, oil, gas, and structures that are attached to land if they are severable without causing harm to the land.
2. *Future goods*. If goods are not existing and identified, then parties may still contract to sell future goods. A contract to sell future goods falls under Article 2 of the UCC.

EXAMPLE 15-2: Juan, a horse breeder, wanted to buy Flyaway, a mare that was expected to foal in one month. Flyaway's owner, Kim, wanted $7,000, which Juan agreed to pay after making it clear that the price included the foal. They agreed not to move Flyaway to Juan's stables until after the foal was born. One month later, Kim contacted Juan and told him to come after Flyaway, since she had foaled. When Juan arrived, however, he was surprised when Kim insisted that he was only to pick up Flyaway. Kim claimed that the foal had not been a part of the agreement and that there was nothing Juan could do about it since a sales contract had to be for existing goods when formed, and that the foal was not in existence at that time. Was Kim correct?

Kim was not correct. At the time the contract was formed, Juan made it clear that the price was to include the unborn foal. Furthermore, Kim was wrong in believing that the foal would not be considered existing goods at the time of the contract. To clarify confusion over what constitutes existing goods, Article 2 of the UCC defines goods to include the unborn young of animals.

C. Whether or not a transaction falls under Article 2 may depend on its purpose or definition.

In some cases, a contract may be a mixed transaction involving both a transfer of goods and a rendition of services. In other cases, a contract may appear to be a sales contract, when in fact it is not.

1. *Mixed transactions.* The courts look at the main purpose of a contract to determine if it falls under Article 2 of the UCC. If it is determined that the transaction is mainly for the sale of goods, then the *entire* contract falls under Article 2.

EXAMPLE 15-3: Alma went to her dentist to have a set of dentures fitted and made. When she received them, however, they were improperly fitted and caused sores in her mouth. Alma demanded a refund for the dentures, claiming that the goods that she had received from the dentist were not usable. The dentist, however, claimed that there had been no sale of goods, just services provided. Who was correct?

The dentist was wrong to claim that there had been no sale of goods. The transaction was mixed in that the dentist was providing services in fitting Alma with dentures, but the dentist was also providing goods for a price. The court would probably find that the transaction was mainly for the sale of goods, and Alma would be allowed to seek a remedy under Article 2 of the UCC.

2. *Other transactions.* There are several transactions that may appear to be sales but do not fall under Article 2 of the UCC by definition.

- A gift is not a sale because no price is given in exchange for the title.
- A lease is not a sale because possession of property is transferred, but the title remains with the lessor.
- A security agreement is not a sale in that it does not actually transfer title, but transfers to a creditor the right to take title if a debtor defaults on a loan.

15-2. Special Provisions Regulating Merchants

The UCC distinguishes between transactions involving merchants and those involving nonmerchants or amateurs.

A. Merchants are held to a higher standard of conduct than nonmerchants.

Article 2 defines a *merchant* as one who has or holds one's self out as having special knowledge of or skills relating to the goods involved in a transaction. This definition also includes one who employs an agent who has or is held out to have such special knowledge or skills.

B. Merchants are required to deal in a commercial standard of good faith.

Nonmerchants are required to deal in simple good faith. For merchants, however, good faith includes observing fair business practices that are consistent with reasonable commercial standards in the trade.

EXAMPLE 15-4: Melinda, a music professor at a university, contracted to sell her violin to Willy for $450. The violin did not sound good when Willy played it, but Melinda assured Willy that it just needed new strings. Willy relied on her assertion and took the violin. When he replaced the strings, however, it did not sound any better. Upon closer inspection, he realized that the wood on the back of the violin was badly warped and, consequently, there was no way that it would ever sound good. When Willy attempted to return the violin, Melinda claimed that Willy had had a chance to inspect the violin and should not have relied on her remarks alone. Was she correct?

Melinda was not correct. Under Article 2 of the UCC, a merchant is held to a higher standard of conduct than a nonmerchant. A person does not have to be a dealer of goods to be considered a merchant. A person must simply have special knowledge of or skills relating to the goods involved in a transaction. In this case, the court would probably view Melinda as a merchant because of her position as a music professor. She would therefore be expected to observe fair business practices, and be held responsible for the quality of the violin that she sold to Willy.

15-3. Special Provisions Regulating the Sales Contract

Several of the UCC provisions governing sales contracts have already been covered in earlier chapters on contracts. Refer back to them at this time to review UCC provisions that change or modify general contract laws concerning firm offers (Chapter 3), valid acceptance (Chapter 3), consideration (Chapter 5), the Statute of Frauds (Chapter 8), and assignments (Chapter 9).

One of the more important differences between general contract law and UCC provisions is that under the UCC, a contract does not necessarily fail because the contract is not specific enough. The UCC contains provisions for dealing with open or missing terms, generally on the basis of common trade practices, what has occurred in past contracts, or the circumstances of the contract.

A. Price may be left open in a sales contract.

If price is not set forth in a sales contract, the price is determined as what is reasonable at the time of delivery. On the other hand, if it is obvious that the parties had no intention of contracting unless a price was agreed on, then no contract would be formed.

B. Quantity may be left open in a sales contract.

An *output contract* binds a buyer to take a seller's entire output of particular goods. A *requirements contract* binds a buyer to buy only what he or she needs of a seller's particular goods. In both contracts, quantity generally is left open.

1. The rule of good faith applies in estimating the quantity of goods to be produced under an output contract or taken under a requirements contract.
2. If no estimate is made, no quantity may be demanded or must be taken that exceeds what would normally be expected.

EXAMPLE 15-5: Fran, who owned a poultry farm, had contracted with Seth's Grocery Store for several years to supply all the eggs that Seth needed to sell to his customers. Over the years, Fran had been delivering 50 to 100 dozen eggs a month to Seth's store. One month, however, Seth insisted that he needed 300 dozen eggs delivered because he was planning to run a special on eggs and expected business to triple. Fran told Seth that she would not be able to supply that many eggs. Seth threatened to sue for breach of contact, claiming that Fran had to supply as many eggs as he needed, as stated in the contract. Would Seth win his suit?

Seth would not win his suit. The contract formed between Fran and Seth was a requirements contract that left the quantity of eggs to be sold undetermined. Under Article 2 of the UCC, when a contract contains missing terms, those terms would be interpreted on the basis of common trade practices, what has occurred in past contracts, or the circumstances of the contract. In the case of undetermined quantity, no quantity can be demanded that exceeds what would normally be expected. Thus, in this case, Seth would not be allowed to demand delivery of 300 dozen eggs in one month since this amount would far exceed the usual amounts of 50 to 100 dozen eggs delivered in past months.

C. Time of performance may be left open in a sales contract.

If no time of performance is specified in a sales contract, a reasonable time of performance is implied. A sales contract that requires successive performances over an undetermined period of time is considered valid for a reasonable period of time. Such a contract may be terminated at any time by either party upon giving reasonable notice unless the contract provides otherwise.

EXAMPLE 15-6: Suppose that, in the situation given in Example 15-5, Fran's contract to supply eggs to Seth's Grocery contained no provision stating how or when the contract was to be terminated. After several years, Fran decided to stop selling eggs. She informed Seth of this and said that she would stop delivering eggs to Seth's store in three months. Could Seth sue for breach of contract?

Seth could not sue for breach of contract. Under Article 2 of the UCC, if performance is to be successive over an undetermined period of time, the contract would be deemed valid for a reasonable period of time. Also, if no termination time is specified in the contract, then either party may terminate the contract at any time upon reasonable notice to the other party. In this case, the court probably would find that Fran could terminate the contract for two reasons. First, she had carried out the terms of the contract over a reasonable period of several years before attempting to terminate the contract. Furthermore, she had given three months' notice to Seth, which would be considered a reasonable time for Seth to make arrangements to buy eggs from someone else.

RAISE YOUR GRADES

Can you explain . . . ?

☑ how general contract law and UCC law interact when dealing with sales contracts
☑ what constitutes a sale
☑ what distinguishes goods as defined by the UCC from other types of goods
☑ how the purpose of a contract can determine if it falls under Article 2 of the UCC
☑ why a merchant is held to a higher standard of conduct than nonmerchants
☑ why a sales contract does not necessarily fail because of missing or indefinite terms and on what basis such terms would be decided

SUMMARY

1. The UCC was developed and adopted by most states to govern commercial transactions.
2. Article 2 of the UCC applies to contracts for the sale of goods.
3. General contract law applies to sales contracts unless changed or modified by the UCC.
4. Article 2 of the UCC defines a sale as the transfer of title from a seller to a buyer for a price.
5. Price can be money or any other value that a buyer agrees to pay a seller in exchange for goods.
6. Only transactions involving goods fall under Article 2 of the UCC.
7. Article 2 of the UCC defines goods as all things tangible and movable at the time of identification to the sales contract. Thus, goods must be existing and identified in order for a sale to occur, although parties can contract to sell future goods.
8. If a transaction involves both a transfer of goods and a rendition of services, the court will look at the main purpose of the contract to determine if it is mainly a transaction for the sale of goods. If so, then the entire contract falls under Article 2.
9. A merchant is one who has or holds one's self out as having special knowledge of or skills relating to the goods involved in a transaction.
10. Merchants are held to a higher standard of conduct than nonmerchants, meaning that they are expected to deal in good faith by observing fair business practices that are consistent with reasonable commercial standards.
11. The UCC contains provisions that modify general contract law concerning firm offers, valid acceptance, consideration, the Statute of Frauds, and assignments.

12. The UCC contains provisions for dealing with open or missing terms in a contract, generally on the basis of common trade practices, what has occurred in past contracts, or the circumstances of the contract.
13. If price is left open, the price is determined by what is reasonable at the time of delivery, unless it is clear that the parties did not intend to be bound unless a price was agreed on.
14. If quantity is left open, good faith must be used in estimating the quantity of goods to be produced or taken, and no quantity may be demanded or must be taken that exceeds what would normally be expected.
15. If time of performance is left open, a reasonable time of performance is implied.
16. Sales contracts that require successive performances over an undetermined period of time can be terminated after a reasonable period of time by either party upon giving reasonable notice, unless the contract provides otherwise.

RAPID REVIEW	Answers

True or False

1. If provisions of the UCC conflict with general contract law concerning a contract for the sale of goods, then general contract law rules. [Section 15-1] — *False*

2. Possession of a title reflects a right to property that is legally enforceable and superior to all other claims. [Section 15-1] — *True*

3. Price is consideration that is given in exchange for goods. [Section 15-1] — *True*

4. A contract to sell land would fall under Article 2 of the UCC. [Section 15-1] — *False*

5. A contract with a utility company to sell gas and electricity would fall under Article 2 of the UCC. [Section 15-1] — *True*

6. A security agreement is a sale because it gives the right to take title to a creditor. [Section 15-1] — *False*

7. A person does not have to deal in goods to be considered a merchant. [Section 15-2] — *True*

8. Merchants are allowed to establish any business practices they please. [Section 15-2] — *False*

9. An output contract binds a buyer to take a seller's entire output of particular goods, no matter how much is produced. [Section 15-3] — *False*

10. Indefinite terms of a sales contract are determined through arbitration between the parties to the contract. [Section 15-3] — *False*

SOLVED PROBLEMS

PROBLEM 15-1 Jeff and Bill made an agreement whereby Jeff could have an oak tree from Bill's front yard to use for firewood in exchange for cutting it down and hauling it away himself. Was this a sales contract and, if so, why?

Answer: The agreement between Jeff and Bill constituted a sales contract. Article 2 of the UCC defines a sale as the passage of title from a buyer to a seller for a price. Price does not have to be money—it can be anything of value given by the buyer to the seller in exchange for goods. In this case, the ownership of the tree was being transferred from Bill to Jeff in exchange for Jeff's cutting down the tree and hauling it away. Furthermore, the tree was a tangible, movable item that was existent and identified at the time the contract was formed. The transaction was therefore a sale. [Section 15-1]

PROBLEM 15-2   A young couple bought a refrigerator on time from an appliance dealer. The terms of the sale provided that one missed payment would result in immediate repossession of the refrigerator and that other furniture owned by the couple would also be taken as payment for the remainder of the debt. Would this sales contract be enforceable?

Answer: The terms of this contract would not be enforceable. The court would hold the appliance dealer to a high standard of conduct as a merchant. The appliance dealer therefore would be expected to deal in good faith with the couple and to observe fair business practices that were consistent with reasonable commercial standards in the trade. In this case, should the young couple fail to make one payment, the court would probably find that the immediate repossession of the refrigerator *and* the taking of other furniture for the balance of the debt would be extreme, unreasonable, and inconsistent with the standards of good faith and fair business practices that merchants must observe. [Section 15-2]

PROBLEM 15-3   Import Grains Co. submitted a written offer to Dingo Foods, an Australian company, to buy a shipment of wheat. The offer stated that Dingo Foods had six weeks to reply. The next week, wheat prices dropped significantly in the Canadian Market, so Import Grains hoped to save money by buying from Canada instead. Thus, they telegrammed a cancellation of their offer to Dingo Foods, but the shipment was already on its way. Could Import Grains escape its previous offer?

Answer: Import Grains could not escape its offer. In general contract law, an offer can be revoked at any time prior to acceptance upon notification to the offeree. The UCC, however, provides that a firm, written offer made by a merchant cannot be revoked during the time stipulated in the offer. Furthermore, the UCC also provides that a seller can accept an offer to purchase goods by shipping the goods. Thus, a valid acceptance had already taken place due to the fact that the wheat shipment was already on its way. A sales contract therefore was already formed and binding on Import Grains Co. [Chapter 3, Sections 3-4 and 3-6]

PROBLEM 15-4   As they had done in the past, Abner, Inc., placed an order for ten boxes of bolts from Brexel Corporation. No price was specified on the order, but Abner, Inc., assumed that the price would be the same as it had been six months ago when they last ordered. When the bolts arrived however, the invoice stated that the price was $250, instead of the usual $150. Abner, Inc., refused to pay more than $150, claiming that the price should not have been any higher than it had been before. Brexel Corporation responded that the price had increased because the price of the metal for the bolts had doubled, and that Abner, Inc., must pay the current market price. Who was correct?

Answer: Brexel Corporation was correct. The UCC contains provisions for defining open or indefinite terms in a sales contract. In some instances, indefinite terms are indeed based on what has occurred in past contracts. When price is not specified, however, the UCC provides that price is determined as what is reasonable in the trade at the time of delivery. If it is true that Brexel Corporation's price increase was due to an increase in the cost of metal, and that their price was the current market standard, then Abner, Inc., would be required to pay the $250 for the bolts. [Section 15-3]

PROBLEM 15-5   The Status Motor Co. arranged with a stereo manufacturer to have a custom car stereo produced for a new line of luxury cars that it was going to manufacture. All arrangements were made over the telephone and the specific guidelines were mailed to the stereo manufacturer, who agreed to produce the stereos for $20,000. The stereo manufacturer had geared up for the special production and had produced about one-third of the order when they received notice that Status Motor Co. was cancelling the contract. The stereo manufacturer sued for breach of contract, but when the case went to court, Status Motor Co. defended itself on the grounds that there had been no written contract as required by the Statute of Frauds. Who won the case?

Answer: The stereo manufacturer won its case. It is true that the Statute of Frauds requires that contracts for the sale of goods for $500 or more must be in writing to be enforceable. There are several exceptions, however, when an oral contract for the sale of goods for $500 or more would be enforceable. One of these exceptions occurs when the goods have been custom-manufactured for the buyer, as was the case with the car stereos. A valid contract therefore existed between Status Motor Co. and the stereo manufacturer, despite the fact that the contract was not in writing. [Chapter 8, Section 8-2]

PROBLEM 15-6   Mack agreed to sell Pete's grocery story 45 truckloads of vegetables. The signed contract stated that Mack would deliver the vegetables to Pete by August 28. On July 30, however, Mack called Pete and informed him that he had planted late because of a wet spring, so the vegetables would not be ready for delivery until September 10. Pete accepted the new terms. Unfortunately, a hail storm destroyed Mack's crops on September 2. Pete sued for breach of contract, claiming that the alteration of the date to September 10 was not enforceable because no consideration had been given, and that therefore, the vegetables should have been delivered by August 28, as originally agreed upon, which was before the crop was destroyed. Would his suit be successful?

Answer: Pete's suit would not be successful for several reasons. First of all, Pete was wrong to believe that consideration was necessary in order to alter the terms of the contract. This is true in general contract law, but the UCC provides that no consideration is necessary for modification of a written sales contract if the change is mutually acceptable to the parties involved (Chapter 5, Section 5-4). On the other hand, modifications should be put in writing because the parol evidence rule normally would prevent oral testimony that contradicts the terms of a written contract. Pete was not, however, denying that the delivery date had been changed, just that it was not enforceable. Oral testimony by Pete or Mack would establish that the new delivery date was added later (Chapter 8, Section 8–4). Once that was established, then Mack would not be liable because the goods were destroyed before the delivery date, and goods must be existing in order for a sale to occur. [Section 15-1]

PROBLEM 15-7   Status Designs, a clothing manufacturer in New York, contacted Southern Cloth Company, a textile manufacturer in Georgia, to arrange to purchase 100 bolts of cotton fabric. Southern Cloth Company sent a written offer stating its terms to Status Designs. In turn, Status Designs sent a preprinted acceptance form that was signed and returned to them by Southern Cloth Company. As it turned out, the fabric was not colorfast. Although colorfastness had not been stipulated in either the written offer or the acceptance form, Status Designs demanded that arbitration on the matter be held in New York, as provided for in their acceptance form. Southern Cloth Company, however, insisted that they did not have to submit to arbitration in New York because their written offer contained no provisions for settling disputes, and because they had never expressed their consent to the new terms provided for in the acceptance form. Southern Cloth Company then demanded that arbitration take place in Georgia. Where must the dispute be settled?

Answer: The dispute would have to be settled through arbitration in New York. The UCC provides that, unlike general contract law, an acceptance forms a contract even if it contains additional terms. Unless prohibited by the terms of the offer, new terms become a part of the contract and are enforceable, so long as they do not materially alter the terms of the offer, and so long as the offeror does not reject the new terms within a reasonable period of time. In this case, Southern Cloth Company set forth no terms in its offer as to how disputes should be settled. The arbitration terms in Status Designs' acceptance form would therefore be considered a part of the contract by the court, since they certainly did not materially alter any terms of the offer, and since Southern Cloth Company did not object to the new terms before shipping the goods. [Chapter 3, Section 3-6]

16 PASSAGE OF TITLE AND RISK OF LOSS

16-1. Passage of Title

Passage of title generally is not relevant in determining the rights and responsibilities of the parties involved in a sales transaction. In any given case under the UCC, the party bearing the risk of loss or enjoying the right to exercise dominion over goods might or might not be the party who holds title to the goods. There may be areas, however, where who holds title to goods may influence the solution to a dispute. In the absence of any contractual provision to the contrary, passage of title is governed by Article 2 of the UCC.

A. Passage of title cannot occur until the goods are identified to the contract.

This requirement can be met when the goods are specifically designated to the buyer in some way by the seller.

B. In general, once identified, passage of title occurs when the seller physically delivers the goods.

The moment when physical delivery takes place usually depends on the terms of the contract.

1. *Shipment contracts.* In a shipment contract, a seller agrees to deliver the goods to a carrier, such as a trucking company, for delivery to a specified destination. Title passes to the buyer upon delivery of the goods to the carrier.
2. *Destination contracts.* In a destination contract, a seller agrees to deliver the goods directly to a specified destination. Title passes to the buyer upon delivery to the specified destination.

EXAMPLE 16-1: Roger wanted to order some shirts for his clothing store from a manufacturer. The manufacturer's payment policy was that the goods must be paid for within 30 days after receipt of title. Roger therefore wanted to delay receiving title to the goods for as long as possible. What type of contract should he try to arrange?

Roger should try to arrange a destination contract, naming his store as the specified destination. With a destination contract, he would not receive title to the goods until they actually arrived at his store. In contrast, if he were to arrange a shipment contract, he would receive title to the goods earlier, when they arrived at a designated carrier's for transport to his store.

C. In some cases, physical delivery of goods may not be required.

A sale may take place without the actual possession of the goods changing hands, as when a third party, called a *bailee*, maintains possession of the goods at all times.

1. Title passes to the buyer when the seller delivers the necessary document of title. Documents of title include warehouse receipts and bills of lading.
2. If no document of title is to change hands, then title passes to the buyer at the time of contracting.

EXAMPLE 16-2: Wickman Furniture contracted to buy 500 mattresses from a mattress manufacturer. The mattresses were in a rented warehouse and Wickman agreed to take over rental of the space in order to leave the mattresses stored there until they needed them. In January of the next year, Wickman did not include the mattresses in its stock inventory. The store was audited later that year, and Wickman received a tax bill for the inventory of mattresses. The company, however, claimed that they did not have title to the goods because they had never been delivered, and that the mattress manufacturer owed the unpaid taxes. Was Wickman Furniture correct?

Wickman Furniture was not correct. In general, passage of title to goods occurs when the seller physically delivers the goods. In this case, however, the contract did not require physical delivery of the goods, and no documents of title changed hands. Under the UCC, title therefore passed to Wickman Furniture at the time of contracting and they owe the unpaid taxes on the mattresses.

16-2. Third-Party Rights

In general, a buyer cannot acquire better title to goods than the seller has. The UCC, however, contains several exceptions to this rule.

A. A seller who has a voidable title can pass title to a good-faith buyer for value.

A *voidable title* is one that has been obtained through fraudulent means. For example, a person who purchases a car with a bad check has obtained the goods fraudulently. If the car were then passed to a buyer who was unaware that the title was not legitimately the seller's, and who paid a price that was sufficient to support a simple contract, then the good-faith buyer would have good title to the car. In such a case, the original owner would have to seek damages from the person who wrote the bad check.

B. A merchant entrusted with goods may pass title to a good-faith buyer.

If a person entrusts goods to a merchant who deals in that type of goods, and the merchant sells those goods in the ordinary course of his or her business to a good-faith buyer, then the buyer would have valid title to the goods. This rule also applies when a merchant retains possession of goods already sold and then resells them.

EXAMPLE 16-3: Leo took his radio in to be repaired at a local store that also sold new and used radios. He returned in three weeks, but the store manager was unable to find the radio. After asking around, it was discovered that one of the store's sales clerks had sold the radio to a customer, assuming that it belonged to the store's inventory. Leo insisted that the store manager find the customer and return the radio. Does the store manager have to do this?

The store manager could not make the customer return the radio. When goods have been entrusted to a merchant who ordinarily deals in those goods, and then sold by the merchant to a good-faith buyer in the ordinary course of business, then the buyer holds valid title to those goods. Leo's only recourse would be to seek damages from the store.

C. A holder of a void title cannot pass title to a good-faith buyer.

A *void title* is one that has no legal basis. For example, a merchant-seller could never pass title to stolen goods because the merchant-seller never held a legal right of possession to begin with and the original owner did nothing to facilitate the transfer. The buyer would be required to return the goods to the legal owner.

16-3. Creditors' Rights

Creditors have rights to claim title to goods that are involved in a fraudulent sale. A fraudulent sale occurs when a person sells property in an attempt to defraud his or her creditors. The creditors' rights in such a transaction can be obtained by suing either to have the transaction overturned or the property recovered by the court until all rights are settled.

A. A creditor's right to relief depends on whether the parties had the intent to defraud.

To prove fraudulent intent, the court generally looks at any or several of the following indicators:

- original owner's indebtedness when the transaction occurred
- lack of fair consideration for the transaction
- family or close relationship between the buyer and the seller
- seller's continued possession of the goods
- pending or threatened litigation involving the seller at the time of the transaction
- attempted concealment of the transaction

EXAMPLE 16-4: Elaine ran a small hair-styling shop. Unfortunately, business had not been good, so she had not paid her creditors for several months. One day, she received notice that a creditor who had sold salon hair dryers to her was suing for either the $5,000 still owed or for repossession of the goods if necessary. When the case went to court, however, Elaine claimed that she had recently sold the dryers to her mother for $500 in order to raise money, although they were still in her shop, and that the creditor would just have to wait until business was better to collect the money. Would the court allow this defense?

The court probably would not allow Elaine to claim that she no longer owned title to the goods. The transaction would be deemed fraudulent for several reasons. First of all, Elaine still owed money for the dryers when she sold them to her mother. Since $5,000 was still owed, the $500 that she received from her mother was probably not fair consideration in exchange for the goods. The fact that she sold the dryers to her mother and continued to possess and use the goods at a time when litigation was pending would also indicate that the transaction took place as an attempt to avoid repossession of the goods by the creditor. In this case, if Elaine could not pay the $5,000, the court probably would overturn the transaction and allow the creditor to repossess the goods.

B. Creditors' rights are protected in a bulk transfer.

In some cases, a person may attempt to sell an entire business to an innocent buyer with the intent of taking the money and disappearing without paying the creditors of the business. Such transactions, known as bulk transfers, are regulated by Article 6 of the UCC.

1. *Bulk transfer.* A bulk transfer is defined as a transfer that meets all of the following criteria:

   - transfer is made in a single transaction
   - property transferred is a major part of the seller's materials, supplies, merchandise, or other inventory
   - transfer is not made in the ordinary course of seller's business
   - seller's principal business is the sale of merchandise from stock

2. *Seller's duty.* The seller must give the buyer a sworn schedule of the property to be transferred and of the seller's outstanding creditors, including the amounts owed to those creditors.

3. *Buyer's duty.* The buyer must give written notice to the outstanding creditors of the pending transfer at least ten days before payment for or possession of the goods is to take place, whichever comes first.

4. *Effect of compliance.* Once the requirements of Article 6 have been met, the creditors have six months to file suit to enforce their rights under the bulk transfer law.

5. *Effect of noncompliance.* If the requirements of Article 6 are not met, then the buyer is considered to be holding the goods in trust for the seller. If the transaction is concealed, the creditors have six months from the time they find out about the transaction to file suit.

16-4. Passage of Risk of Loss

The UCC provides guidelines to determine when the risk of loss of goods passes from the seller to the buyer. The law once placed the risk of loss on whoever held title to the goods. The UCC, however, generally places the risk of loss on the party who has the most control over the goods at the time of the loss. This person may not necessarily be the person who holds title to the goods. The contracting parties may specify who has the risk of loss in the contract, either specifically or by using commonly accepted shipping terms. If the contract does not specify who bears the risk of loss or if the goods delivered are in breach of contract, then Article 2 of the UCC provides guidelines to determine who has the risk of loss.

A. In shipment contracts, risk of loss passes to the buyer upon delivery to the carrier.

Shipment contracts can be created through use of any of the following common shipment terms.

1. *FOB (free on board)*. This term means the seller must deliver the goods at his or her own risk and expense to the carrier designated. Furthermore, if the term is "FOB vessel, car, or other vehicle," then the seller must also load the goods at his or her own risk and expense.
2. *FAS (free along-side)*. This term is usually followed by a particular vessel and port to which the seller must deliver goods at his or her own risk and expense.
3. *CIF (cost, insurance, freight)*. This term means the price of the goods includes the cost of shipping and insuring them. The seller must bear the risk and expense.
4. *C&F (cost and freight)*. This term is the same as CIF except the seller does not have to insure the goods.

B. In destination contracts, risk of loss passes to the buyer upon delivery to a specific destination.

Destination contracts can be created through the use of any of the following common shipment terms:

1. *FOB destination*. This term requires the seller to bear the risk and expense of transporting goods to the buyer's destination.
2. *Ex-ship*. This term does not designate a vessel or port, but puts the risk and expense on the seller until goods are unloaded from whatever ship is used.
3. *No arrival, no sale*. This term also places the risk and expense of shipment on the seller, but if the goods do not arrive through no fault of the seller, then the seller has no further obligations to the buyer.

EXAMPLE 16-5: Seth's Grocery had a standing contract to receive shipments of eggs every week from a poultry farm. One week, the truck carrying the eggs was involved in an accident in which all the eggs were broken. If the terms of the contract were "FOB," who bore the loss of the eggs? What if the terms were "FOB Seth's Grocery?"

If the terms of the contract were FOB, then the seller was only responsible for delivering the goods to the carrier. Once the carrier was en route, the buyer bore the risk of loss; therefore, Seth would bear the loss of the eggs. If the terms were "FOB Seth's Grocery," however, then the seller was required to bear the risk of loss until the eggs arrived at Seth's Grocery; therefore, the seller would bear the loss of the eggs.

C. Risk of loss for goods not to be physically delivered can pass to the buyer in two ways.

1. If a document of title is to be delivered to the buyer, risk of loss passes to the buyer upon delivery of that document.
2. If no document of title is to be delivered to the buyer, risk of loss passes to the buyer when the bailee notifies the buyer that the buyer has the right to possess the goods. In this case, however, if the buyer is to pick up the goods upon notification, then the buyer is allowed a reasonable time to pick up the goods before risk of loss passes to him or her.

EXAMPLE 16-6: John paid for and received a receipt for a desk from Smithtown Furniture. The desk was not in stock, however, so Smithtown said that its warehouse would notify John when the desk arrived and that he could then pick up the desk by presenting proper identification to the warehouse clerk. When John did not hear from the warehouse for two months, he contacted Smithtown Furniture and was told that his desk had arrived, but that it was destroyed in a fire in the warehouse. When John asked when another desk would arrive, Smithtown claimed that it was not responsible for the loss of the desk since he already owned it by paying for it. Were they correct?

Smithtown Furniture was not correct. John's receipt was not a "document of title," but merely an acknowledgment that payment had been received. Therefore, the risk of loss was to have passed to John when the bailee (in this case, the warehouse) notified John that he could pick up the desk. Since John was never notified, the risk of loss remained with the seller, Smithtown Furniture.

D. The seller's status can determine risk of loss if the contract does not.

1. If the seller is a merchant, then risk of loss passes to the buyer upon physical delivery of the goods.
2. If the seller is a nonmerchant, then risk of loss passes to the buyer upon the seller's tendering of delivery of the goods.

EXAMPLE 16-7: Marva wanted a cassette recorder. Her neighbor, a teacher named Mike, wanted to sell his, so she paid him $75 for it. Marva told Mike that she would pick it up on Monday, when she had more time. As it turned out, Marva did not go back for the recorder until the next Saturday, only to find out from Mike that his place and been robbed the night before, and the recorder was stolen. Marva asked for her money back, but Mike insisted that it was not his fault that the recorder was stolen, and that she should have picked it up when she said she would. Did Mike have to return Marva's money?

Mike did not have to return Marva's money. Mike was not a merchant as defined by the UCC. As a nonmerchant, once he had tendered delivery of the recorder, and Marva had failed to take possession of the recorder when tendered, then Marva had to bear the loss of the recorder.

E. In a breached contract, the breaching party may have to share the risk of loss.

1. *Breach by seller.* If a seller delivers goods that do not comply with the contract, the seller has risk of loss until the defect is corrected or until the buyer accepts the goods. If the buyer discovers after acceptance that the goods do not comply with the contract, then the seller has risk of loss to the extent not covered by the buyer's insurance.
2. *Breach by buyer.* If a buyer refuses to purchase goods that have already been contracted for and identified by the seller to the contract, then the risk of loss remains with the buyer for a reasonable period of time after the breach to the extent not covered by the seller's insurance.

EXAMPLE 16-8: Timothy, the owner of a produce market, contracted to buy Kim's entire crop of lettuce. The crop was picked and crated, and Timothy was notified that the shipment would arrive the next day. Timothy, however, told Kim that he did not intend to accept the crop after all. Before Kim could find another buyer, the lettuce spoiled. Who must bear the loss?

Kim must bear only that part of the loss covered by her insurance. If her insurance covers none or only part of the loss, then Timothy must bear the rest of the loss.

16-5. Risk of Loss and Conditional Sales

There are two types of conditional sales, each of which determines when the risk of loss passes to the buyer.

A. Risk of loss passes to a buyer upon acceptance in an approval contract.

An *approval contract* exists when goods are delivered to a buyer with an understanding that the buyer may use or test them for the purpose of deciding whether or not to accept them.

1. The risk of loss does not pass to the buyer until the buyer actually accepts the goods.
2. If the goods are refused, they must be returned within a reasonable time at the seller's risk and expense. The buyer must conform with any reasonable mode of return requested by the seller.
3. If the buyer misuses the goods or retains them for an unreasonable period of time, it is assumed that the goods have been accepted and the buyer has assumed risk of loss.
4. Goods sold on approval remain subject to claims of the seller's creditors until the buyer accepts the goods.

EXAMPLE 16-9: Faye was in charge of a testing laboratory for a large drug manufacturer. She ordered ten microscopes from a company with the option of returning them if they were not sufficient for their intended purpose in the laboratory. When she received the microscopes, she was very pleased with them. Two months later, however, two of the microscopes broke down, so she contacted the microscope company and informed them that she wished to return all of the microscopes, out of fear that they would continue to break down. Did the company have to accept their return?

   The company did not have to accept the return of all of the microscopes. Faye did buy the microscopes through a "sale on approval" contract, but the buyer must return the merchandise within a reasonable time after delivery. The court probably would find that two months of use was an unreasonable time period. The manufacturer of the microscopes may be responsible for repairing or replacing the broken microscopes, but it would not be obligated to accept the return of the microscopes.

B. Risk of loss passes to a buyer upon delivery in a sale or return contract.

   A *sale or return* contract exists when goods are delivered to a buyer for resale with an understanding that the buyer may return any goods that do not sell.

   1. The risk of loss passes to the buyer upon delivery of the goods.
   2. Any goods that are returned are returned at the risk and expense of the buyer.
   3. Goods sold on a sale or return basis become subject to the claims of the buyer's creditors upon delivery.

16-6. Insurable Interest

It is a common practice for both sellers and buyers to insure their interest in goods in order to obtain security against the risk of loss. An insurable interest carries with it the right to bring suit against third persons for any damage, destruction, or unauthorized conversion of goods. Normally, no one can insure anything that does not belong to him or her. The UCC, however, provides guidelines for allowing a buyer to obtain insurance before actually holding title to goods.

A. Only the seller may insure goods before they are identified to the contract.

   Once goods are identified to the contract, the seller continues to have an insurable interest in the goods until title is turned over to the buyer.

B. The buyer and seller may insure goods once they are identified to the contract.

   Even though the seller still has an insurable interest in the goods, the buyer also has an insurable interest in those same goods without necessarily holding title to the goods yet.

C. Only the buyer may insure goods once the title to the goods has been received.

   This is true unless the seller has retained some security interest in the goods.

RAISE YOUR GRADES

Can you explain . . . ?

☑ the various ways in which title can pass in a sale of goods
☑ the rights of a buyer who receives a void or voidable title to goods
☑ how creditors' rights are protected in either a fraudulent sale or a bulk transfer
☑ in what ways the terms of a sales contract can provide for who is to bear the risk of loss during the transaction
☑ who bears the risk of loss when a sales contract does not specify who bears the risk
☑ who bears the risk of loss when a contract is breached
☑ who bears the risk of loss when the contract is a conditional one
☑ how both a buyer and seller can have an insurable interest in goods when only one of them holds title to those goods

SUMMARY

1. Once goods are identified to a sales contract, passage of title occurs when the seller physically delivers the goods. If physical delivery of the goods is not required, however, passage of title occurs either at the time of contracting or when the seller delivers the necessary document of title.
2. A seller who has a voidable title can pass title to a good-faith buyer for value.
3. If goods are entrusted to a merchant who deals in that type of goods, the merchant can pass title to a good-faith buyer for value.
4. A holder of a void title cannot pass title to a good-faith buyer.
5. In a sale of property that attempts to defraud creditors, the creditors have the right to sue either to have the transaction overturned or the property recovered by the court until all claims are settled.
6. Bulk transfers are regulated by Article 6 of the UCC. In a bulk transfer, the seller must provide the buyer with a list of all property being transferred and a list of all outstanding creditors. The buyer must notify all outstanding creditors of the impending transaction or else the buyer is considered to be holding the goods in trust for the seller's creditors.
7. During a sales transaction, the risk of loss generally is placed on the person who has the most control over the goods at the time of the loss.
8. The sales contract can specify who bears the risk of loss during the transaction.
9. In a shipment contract, risk of loss passes to the buyer upon delivery of the goods to a carrier.
10. In a destination contract, risk of loss passes to the buyer upon delivery to a specific destination.
11. If goods are not to be physically delivered, the risk of loss passes to the buyer upon delivery of a document of title. If no document of title is to be delivered, however, risk of loss passes to the buyer when the bailee notifies the buyer that the buyer has the right to possess the goods.
12. If the buyer is to pick up goods, then the buyer is allowed a reasonable period of time to pick up the goods before risk of loss passes to him or her.
13. If the contract does not specify who bears the risk of loss during a transaction and the seller is a merchant, risk of loss passes to the buyer upon physical delivery of the goods. If the seller is a nonmerchant, however, risk of loss passes to the buyer upon the seller's tendering of delivery of the goods.
14. If a contract is breached by the seller, then the seller has risk of loss until the breach is corrected or the buyer accepts the goods. However, if the buyer discovers after acceptance that the goods do not comply with the contract, then the seller has risk of loss to the extent not covered by the buyer's insurance.
15. If a contract is breached by the buyer, then risk of loss remains with the buyer for a reasonable period of time after the breach to the extent not covered by the seller's insurance.
16. In an approval contract, risk of loss does not pass to the buyer until the buyer actually accepts the goods. However, if the buyer misuses the goods or retains them for an unreasonable period of time, it is assumed that the goods have been accepted and the buyer has assumed the risk of loss.
17. In a sale or return contract, the risk of loss passes to the buyer upon delivery of the goods and any goods that are returned are returned at the risk and expense of the buyer.
18. Once goods are identified to a sales contract, both the buyer and seller have an insurable interest in those goods in order to obtain security against the risk of loss.

RAPID REVIEW   Answers

True or False

1 A buyer can never acquire better title to goods than the seller has. [Section 16-2]   *False*

2. Intent to defraud must exist for a court to overturn a sales transaction in favor of a creditor. [Section 16-3]   *True*

3. A seller must notify all outstanding creditors of an impending bulk transfer. [Section 16-3]   *False*

4. The question of who holds title to goods at any given time is important under the UCC to determine who bears the risk of loss of the goods during the sales transaction. [Section 16-4]   *False*

5. The question of when the parties to a sales transaction bear the risk of loss can be set forth by the shipping terms specified in the contract. [Section 16-4]   *True*

6. The risk of loss for goods that are not to be physically delivered always passes to the buyer at the time of contracting. [Section 16-4]   *False*

7. A nonmerchant seller need only tender delivery of goods for the risk of loss to pass to the buyer. [Section 16-4]   *True*

8. If goods are accepted by a buyer who later discovers that they do not comply with the contract, then risk of loss passes back to the seller until the defects have been corrected. [Section 16-4]   *False*

9. The buyer must bear the expense and risk of returning any goods bought in either a sale or return or a sale on approval. [Section 16-5]   *False*

10. In a sale or return, the buyer's creditors can make claim against the goods in the hands of the buyer. [Section 16-5]   *True*

11. Buyer and seller can never have a simultaneous insurable interest in the goods being sold. [Section 16-6]   *False*

12. Identification of goods to a contract does not create an insurable interest for the buyer. [Section 16-6]   *False*

SOLVED PROBLEMS

PROBLEM 16-1 Rick contracted to buy nails from Harmon Supply. The contract specified that the nails were to be delivered FOB to Dick's business address. Harmon Supply shipped the nails by rail and mailed a bill of lading to Rick. The bill of lading arrived before the nails. Did title pass when the bill of lading arrived?

Answer: Title did not pass when the bill of lading arrived. The receipt of a document of title by a buyer constitutes passage of title only when delivery is to be made under the contract without physically moving the goods. In this case, however, the contract specified that the nails were to be delivered FOB to Rick's place of business, making it a destination contract. In destination contracts, title passes to the buyer upon delivery to the specified destination, so title would not pass to Rick until the nails arrived at his business address. [Section 16-1]

PROBLEM 16-2 Al wrote a check to purchase a new reel-to-reel tape deck from Sal's Stereo Shop for $450. The next day, he sold the tape deck to the Hi-Fidelity Store, another nearby retailer of new and used stereo equipment, for $200. The owner of the Hi-Fidelity Store, Judy, did not ask for any evidence of title, even though the tape deck appeared to be new and was obviously worth much more than she paid. As it turned out, Al's check bounced at Sal's Stereo Shop. Sal was unable to track down Al, but he noticed the deck in the window of the Hi-Fidelity Store on his way to work one day. He went in and explained the situation to Judy, but she claimed that, as a good-faith buyer, she did not have to return the tape deck. Sal sued for repossession of the deck. Did he win the suit?

Answer: Sal won the suit. Al held a voidable title to the tape deck in that he obtained the tape deck fraudulently by writing a bad check for it. Normally, a seller who has a voidable title can pass title to a good-faith buyer for value. The key issue in this case is whether or not Judy was a good-faith buyer. Under the UCC, Judy would be considered a merchant because she dealt in goods of the kind that she acquired. As a merchant, she would be held to a higher standard of good faith than a nonmerchant and must be consistent with fair business practices and commercial standards of the trade. Therefore, the court would find that, as a merchant, her suspicions should have been aroused. She should have at least requested evidence of valid title from Al since the tape deck was obviously new and yet Al was willing to accept less than half its true value. Judy therefore would not be considered a good-faith buyer and would be required to return the tape deck to Sal. [Section 16-2]

PROBLEM 16-3   Andy, a wheat farmer, sold, harvested, and delivered his entire crop of wheat to a bakery. Unfortunately, Andy had been having bad years due to the depressed wheat market. Consequently, the creditor who held the loans on Andy's farm equipment sought to repossess the wheat on the basis that the sale had not complied with Article 6 of the UCC. Would the court overturn the transaction and allow the creditor to repossess the wheat from the bakery?

Answer: The court would not overturn the transaction. Article 6 of the UCC applies only to transactions known as bulk transfers. The wheat sale, however, did not meet all the criteria necessary to be considered a bulk transfer under the UCC. The transfer was made in the ordinary course of Andy's business and his principal business was not the sale of merchandise from stock. It was not necessary, therefore, that the sale meet the provisions of Article 6. The creditor would have to use other assets to secure payment of the amount still owed on Andy's farm equipment. [Section 16-3]

PROBLEM 16-4   Amanda had a dining room set that she kept stored at a nearby warehouse because it did not fit into her new apartment. She had a warehouse receipt stating "for delivery to Amanda Cooper." She advertised the set for sale and sold it to Craig, turning over the warehouse receipt endorsed by her to read "for delivery to Craig Basso." Three weeks later, Craig went to pick up the set, only to find out that it had been badly damaged the week before when a heavy rainstorm caused the warehouse to flood. He immediately contacted Amanda and asked for his money back. Did Amanda have to return his money?

Answer: Amanda did not have to return Craig's money. In this case, the goods were held by a bailee, the warehouse, to be delivered without being moved by Amanda. Once Craig accepted the warehouse receipt directing the warehouse to deliver the dining room set to him upon request, then he assumed the risk of loss for any damage to the set. [Section 16-4]

PROBLEM 16-5   Maggie bought a car on Friday from a local car dealer. The dealer was to put a radio in the car and Maggie was to pick up the car the following Tuesday. On Monday, however, Maggie was called out of town on a business trip, and was unable to return for the car until the following Thursday. When she did return, she was told that the car had been stolen from the dealer's lot on Wednesday. Maggie demanded either another car or the return of her down payment. The dealer, however, claimed that delivery had been tendered and that it was her loss for not returning for the car on Tuesday as she had agreed. Consequently, Maggie stopped payment on the down-payment check, and the dealer filed suit for the cost of the car. Who won the suit?

Answer: Maggie won the suit. The dealer would be considered a merchant under the UCC. As a merchant, then regardless of the fact that delivery of the car had been tendered, the dealer still bore the risk of loss until the car was physically delivered to Maggie. The dealer would have to either provide Maggie with a new car to meet the terms of the contract or return her down payment. [Section 16-4]

PROBLEM 16-6   Carmen Paper Works had specially manufactured and printed 2,000 party napkins for a catering company in compliance with a valid contract between the two companies. Without giving a reason, however, the catering company refused to accept the napkins when they were delivered, so Carmen Paper Works stored the napkins in its warehouse. Shortly thereafter, the warehouse was flooded when a water main burst and the napkins were ruined. Carmen Paper Works had no insurance on the napkins, so it sued the catering company for the cost of the napkins. Did Carmen Paper Works win the suit?

Answer: Carmen Paper Works won the suit. The fact that, without reason the catering company refused to accept the goods that it had contracted to have specially manufactured and printed constituted a breach of the contract. Consequently, the catering company would have the risk of loss for a reasonable period of time after the breach to the extent not covered by Carmen Paper Works's insurance. Since the flood occurred shortly after the breach, the court probably would find this to be within a reasonable period of time. Furthermore, since Carmen Paper Works had no insurance, the catering company would be responsible for the entire contract amount. [Section 16-4]

PROBLEM 16-7   Edgar bought a refrigerator from an appliance dealer, but said that he did not want the refrigerator delivered until the house that he was building was completed in about four months. The dealer, however, said that they did not have the room to store the refrigerator for that long. Consequently, Edgar asked that the refrigerator be delivered to a warehouse for storage and that he would pay the storage fee. The dealer agreed to this. Unfortunately, the warehouse was destroyed in a fire three months later. Edgar asked for his money back, claiming that the dealer was still responsible for the refrigerator since he had never received physical delivery of it at his new house. Was Edgar correct?

Answer: Edgar was not correct. He would have to bear the loss because, in this case, the agreement was that the goods would be delivered to a bailee, the warehouse, for holding for delivery to Edgar upon demand. The dealer, therefore, had fulfilled its obligation of delivery according to the terms of the agreement, particularly since Edgar was even paying the storage fee. [Section 16-4]

PROBLEM 16-8   Lannie ordered a selection of fall dresses for his clothing store on a sale or return contract. After the dresses arrived, Lannie filed for bankruptcy and all of his inventory was seized by the court. The dresses had not been paid for yet, so the manufacturer attempted to reclaim them, claiming that Lannie did not own the dresses since they had not been paid for and could be returned. Would the manufacturer get the dresses back?

Answer: The manufacturer would not get the dresses. In a sale or return contract, the goods become subject to the claims of the buyer's creditors upon delivery. The manufacturer would have to seek compensation from the settlement of Lannie's business affairs. [Section 16-5]

17 PERFORMANCE AND REMEDIES

17-1. Duty to Perform

The parties to a sales contract have a duty to perform in compliance with the terms of the contract, just as in general contract law. Article 2 of the UCC contains guidelines for the enforcement of rules governing performance. In general, however, inherent in all sales contracts is the duty that all parties deal with each other in good faith and within standards of commercial reasonableness. Furthermore, merchants are always held to the higher standard of using ordinary commercial standards of fair dealing and honesty.

17-2. Seller's Duties

In general, the seller is obligated to tender delivery of conforming goods to the buyer.

A. The method of delivery of goods need not be specified in the contract.

If the contract does not specify the time and place of delivery, the UCC provides the following guidelines.

1. Delivery must be tendered within a reasonable time.
2. Delivery must be made at seller's place of business or at seller's residence.
3. Goods must be tendered for delivery at a reasonable hour, upon reasonable notice to the buyer, and must be held for a reasonable amount of time for the buyer.

EXAMPLE 17-1: Alicia had a destination contract to receive 50 bolts of cloth from a manufacturer at her upholstery shop. The carrier delivered the goods to her shop, but he arrived after hours and left the cloth outside without notifying Alicia. During the night, a thunderstorm ruined the material. When contacted, the manufacturer insisted that the risk of loss had passed to Alicia upon delivery. Was the manufacturer correct in this case?

The manufacturer was not correct. Normally, since this was a destination contract, the risk of loss would have passed to Alicia when the cloth was delivered to her shop. In this case, however, the seller tendered delivery at an unreasonable hour without giving notice to Alicia. Alicia could therefore seek a remedy for the damage to the cloth.

B. The method of delivery may be specified by the shipping terms of the contract.

1. *Shipment contracts.* The seller must make a reasonable contract for the shipment of the goods with a carrier, deliver the goods to the carrier, deliver a document to the buyer allowing the buyer to take possession of the goods, and give the buyer prompt notice of the shipment.

2. *Destination contracts and contracts not requiring physical delivery of the goods.* The seller must either give the buyer a negotiable document of title allowing the buyer to take possession of the goods, or must give the buyer a nonnegotiable document of title or written direction to the bailee to turn over the goods to the buyer.

C. In general, the UCC requires substantial performance of the contract.

In theory, the UCC allows the buyer the right to void the contract if the goods or the tender of delivery do not conform *in all respects* to the terms of the contract. This is known as the *perfect tender* rule. In reality, substantial performance by the seller is allowed in many cases because of several exceptions to this rule that are found throughout Article 2.

1. *Seller's right to cure.* If nonconforming goods are delivered to the buyer prior to expiration of the required time of delivery, then the seller may repair, replace, or make a price adjustment for the nonconforming goods.

    (*a*) The seller must give the buyer notice of his or her intention to correct the defect.

    (*b*) If a buyer rejects nonconforming goods that the seller reasonably believed the buyer would accept, then the seller is allowed a reasonable time to tender conforming goods, upon notice to the buyer, even if the time of performance has expired.

EXAMPLE 17-2: The Fitness Center had a contract to purchase athletic equipment from Physical Distributors. Physical Distributors delivered the goods one week before shipment was due. Upon inspection, however, The Fitness Center noticed that some of the weights that had been ordered were missing and rejected the shipment. Could they do this?

The Fitness Center could not reject the shipment without first notifying Physical Distributors of the defect and giving them a chance to cure it, particularly since the time of performance had not expired. Physical Distributors, upon receiving notice of the defect, would have to give The Fitness Center notice of its intention to cure the defect. If The Fitness Center did not receive such notice, then it could seek a remedy for the nonconforming delivery.

2. *Improper shipment.* The buyer cannot reject conforming goods that have been improperly shipped if no material delay or loss has resulted.

3. *Substituted method of delivery.* The seller may substitute a different means of delivery for the one required by the contract if the method agreed upon becomes impracticable or impossible.

4. *Installment contracts.* If delivery is to be made in several installments at different times, the buyer cannot reject a nonconforming installment unless the defect substantially impairs its value and cannot be cured.

    (*a*) The seller must give notice that the defect can be cured.

    (*b*) The buyer cannot claim breach of contract because of one or more nonconforming installments unless they substantially impair the entire contract.

EXAMPLE 17-3: Rick ordered 12 law books from Publishing House, to be delivered once a month for one year. After the first three deliveries, Rick received an accounting book instead of the correct law book. Can Rick hold Publishing House in breach of contract?

Rick cannot hold Publishing House in breach of contract. He can reject the nonconforming accounting book and Publishing House would be required to correct the defect. A buyer cannot claim breach of contract, however, because of just one or more nonconforming deliveries on an installment contract. If Publishing House does not correct the defect or continues to deliver the wrong books, then the entire contract would be substantially impaired and Rick could claim breach of contract and seek a remedy.

5. *Commercial impracticability.* The UCC provides that the seller does not have to perform if the occurrence of an unforeseen event causes performance to become impracticable or impossible. It should be noted, however, that the court applies this rule sparingly. For instance, an increase in the cost of performance does not dismiss the seller from the obligation to perform.

6. *Partial performance.* If commercial impracticability only partially affects the seller's ability to perform, the seller must perform to the extent possible. Furthermore, if

more than one buyer is involved, then the seller must fairly and reasonably distribute performance to the buyers.

7. *Destruction of identified goods.* If goods identified to the contract are destroyed, the seller need not perform. If the goods are only partially destroyed, however, the buyer may choose either to void the contract or accept the goods with a price adjustment.

17-3. Seller's Remedies

The seller has a number of remedies available in case of breach by the buyer or buyer's insolvency.

A. The seller may hold a lien on the goods until the purchase price is paid.

A *lien* is a charge or encumbrance imposed on property by a creditor to secure a debt and insure payment by a debtor. The seller may retain possession of goods until the purchase price is paid, in essence placing a lien on the goods. This right may be waived or lost by:

- an express agreement of the parties
- payment or tender of payment by the buyer
- unconditional and voluntary delivery of the goods to the buyer or the buyer's bailee or agent
- an act by the seller inconsistent with the existence of the lien. For example, if the transaction is a sale for credit, the seller may not impose a lien until the credit period expires or the buyer becomes insolvent.

B. The seller may withhold delivery to the buyer.

The seller may withhold delivery if the buyer breaches the contract, wrongfully rejects or revokes his or her acceptance, or becomes insolvent.

C. The seller may stop delivery to the buyer.

The seller may stop the goods in the hands of a carrier or bailee once the buyer has breached the contract. There are certain limitations to this right.

1. Shipment must be a large one that would greatly harm the seller should payment not be forthcoming.
2. Seller may stop shipment regardless of size if the buyer is insolvent.
3. Seller must give timely notice of the stoppage to the buyer's bailee and pay any additional freight charges that may result.
4. The seller may not stop delivery once the buyer has taken physical possession of the goods, or buyer's bailee has acknowledged that the goods are being held for the buyer.

EXAMPLE 17-4: Rodney's drug store had been receiving deliveries from a distributor of 100 comic books a month. Each delivery was soon followed by a bill for $25. After mailing the seventh delivery, the distributor's subscription department notified the shipping department that Rodney had not paid for the last three months' deliveries. The shipping department immediately attempted to stop the delivery. Could they do this?

It is unlikely that the distributor would be allowed to stop the delivery of 40 comic books. First of all, the shipment must be a large one that would greatly harm the seller should payment not be forthcoming. A delivery of 40 comic books delivered by mail would not be considered a large shipment. Also, it is unlikely that the $100 due for the unpaid deliveries plus the one in transit would be substantially harmful to the distributor. The distributor would have to seek other means of collecting the unpaid amount.

D. The seller may reclaim goods from the buyer.

If the seller finds out that a buyer is insolvent after goods are delivered, the seller may reclaim the goods within ten days of the buyer's receipt of the goods. There is no time limit to the seller's right to reclaim if the buyer has misrepresented his or her solvency in writing within the three months prior to delivery. The right to reclaim is lost, however, if the buyer has resold the goods to a good-faith purchaser for value.

E. The seller may identify goods to the breached contract.

If goods have not been identified to the contract yet and the buyer breaches, the seller may identify the goods to the contract and seek appropriate remedies. The seller may identify finished goods that conform to the contract or unfinished goods.

1. The seller must make a reasonable effort to mitigate damages by trying to resell finished goods.
2. In the case of unfinished goods, the seller must use good judgment and make a reasonable effort to mitigate damages by either completing the manufacture of the goods, identifying them to the contract, and seeking to resell them, or ceasing manufacture immediately and seeking to resell the unfinished goods for salvage value.

EXAMPLE 17-5: A printing company had a contract to print 2,000 pamphlets for an insurance company. The pamphlets included the insurance company's policies, name, and logo. After about 200 pamphlets had been printed, however, the printing company received notice from the insurance company to cancel the contract. The printing company completed printing all 2,000 pamphlets, then sued the insurance company for the full contract price. Would the printing company receive the full contract price?

The printing company would not receive the full contract price. Upon receiving notice that the insurance company was cancelling the contract, the printing company had a duty to attempt to mitigate the damages. Since the goods were unfinished when the contract was breached, it had two choices. Under the UCC, the company could complete the printing job, identify the goods to the contract, and attempt to resell them, but *only* if it was commercially reasonable to do so. In this case, it was not commercially reasonable to complete the printing job because it was highly unlikely that the printing company could resell a product tailored to a particular company's business. The printing company should have ceased production immediately. Because it did not cease production and therefore mitigate damages, the printing company probably would receive the full contract price for the 200 pamphlets that had been printed before notification of the breach, but only its lost profits on the 1,800 pamphlets that it printed after notification of the breach. Since the court would have awarded the same amount of lost profits to the printing company whether or not the 1,800 pamphlets were printed, the company cost itself much time and expense by completing the project.

F. The seller may resell the goods.

If the seller has properly retained possession of goods via withholding, stoppage in transit, or reclamation, and the buyer has breached or repudiated the contract, the seller may resell the goods.

1. A resale must be carried out in good faith in a commercially reasonable manner.
2. The seller must give the buyer reasonable notice of the resale, unless the goods are perishable and time is of the essence.
3. After resale, the seller may seek to recover the difference between the resale price and the contract price and any incidental damages incurred.
4. The seller is not liable to the buyer for any profits made on the resale.
5. The resale purchaser takes possession free from any claims of the previous buyer.

G. The seller may recover the full purchase price of the goods and incidental damages.

The seller may recover the full purchase price plus incidental damages in only three situations.

- when the buyer has the goods but has not paid for them
- when the breach occurs after the goods have been identified and the seller has been unable to resell them despite taking reasonable steps to do so
- when conforming goods are lost or damaged within a commercially reasonable time after risk of loss has passed to the buyer

EXAMPLE 17-6: Furniture Mart ordered eight television stands from a manufacturer. When the goods arrived, they were accepted in good condition and stored in the company's warehouse. Payment for the stands was due in 60 days. Unfortunately, a small fire in the warehouse damaged the stands two weeks after they arrived. Furniture Mart believed that it should not have to pay for the stands since they had been damaged before it could sell them. Was Furniture Mart correct?

Furniture Mart was not correct. It had to pay the manufacturer for the stands, even though they were damaged before being sold. The stands had been delivered and accepted in good condition, ending the seller's obligations and passing the risk of loss to Furniture Mart.

H. The seller may cancel the contract and sue for damages.

If the buyer breaches the contract, the seller may cancel the contract and seek any appropriate remedies for the breach. The measure of damages is the difference between the contract price and the market value of the goods at the place and time of tender, plus any reasonable incidental damages, minus any expenses saved. If this formula is inadequate to give the seller justice, then the seller may also recover lost profits. This alternative is most often applied in cases involving standard-priced, readily available goods.

17-4. Buyer's Duties

In general, the buyer is obligated to accept the goods and tender payment for them in accordance with the contract of sale.

A. The buyer may inspect the goods prior to acceptance or payment.

Inspection must occur at a reasonable place and time and in a reasonable manner.

1. The buyer must pay any expense of an inspection, but may recover the expense if the goods are nonconforming.
2. The right to inspect goods before payment does not exist if the contract calls for delivery COD (collect on delivery) or if payment is to be made upon presentation of documents of title before the buyer receives the goods. Payment before inspection does *not* constitute acceptance of the goods, however.

B. The buyer must accept goods that conform to the contract.

Acceptance can be express or implied.

1. The buyer may expressly indicate that the goods conform to the contract or that they are acceptable despite any nonconformities.
2. An implied acceptance may be indicated by the action or nonaction of the buyer. For example, if the buyer has an opportunity to reject the goods and does not, the goods will be deemed accepted by implication.
3. The performance of some act by the buyer that is inconsistent with the seller's continued ownership of the goods will be considered an acceptance.

EXAMPLE 17-7: Steve, the owner of a construction firm, ordered walnut doors for a home he was building. The doors arrived and were installed by Steve. The buyers of the home, however, saw the doors after installation and informed Steve that they wanted oak doors, not walnut. Consequently, Steve took the doors down and attempted to return them to the manufacturer. Does the manufacturer have to take back the doors?

The manufacturer does not have to take back the doors. Steve had accepted the doors when he installed them, as this was an act inconsistent with the seller's continued ownership.

C. The buyer may reject nonconforming goods, either in whole or in part.

When nonconforming goods are delivered, the buyer may accept all the goods and seek damages, accept some of the goods, or reject all of the goods.

1. The buyer should notify the seller of the nonconforming goods in order to give the seller a chance to cure.
2. The buyer must follow the seller's reasonable instructions for returning or disposing of the rejected goods.
3. To mitigate damages, the buyer must attempt to sell goods that are perishable if the seller has no way of immediately taking the goods.

D. The buyer may revoke an acceptance of goods.

A buyer may revoke acceptance only if he or she was unaware that the goods were nonconforming when accepted.

1. The buyer must prove that the defect is of a type that would be difficult to discover.
2. The defect must substantially impair the value of the goods to the buyer for the buyer to revoke acceptance.
3. The buyer may revoke acceptance if the seller promised to correct any nonconformity but failed to do so within a reasonable period of time.
4. The buyer must notify the seller of revocation within a reasonable time after the defect is discovered or should have been discovered, and before any substantial change in the goods not caused by the defect can occur.

EXAMPLE 17-8: Marie bought a new motorcycle from Bob's Cycle Shop. When she got home, she noticed that the motorcycle was leaking oil. She contacted Bob, who had her bring it in and assured her he would fix it. As it turned out, over the next six months, the motorcycle continued to have problems. It even broke down on the highway three times and had to be towed in, causing Marie to be late for work. Each time something happened, Marie diligently followed Bob's instructions to bring the motorcycle in. Each time he fixed it, Bob assured her that it was as good as new. After the six months, the motorcycle broke down again on the highway, and this time, Marie told Bob that she no longer wanted the motorcycle and wanted either a new one or her money back. Bob refused, claiming again that it was fixed. Marie decided to sue to get her money back. Would Marie win her suit?

Marie probably would win her suit. Bob had many chances to fix the motorcycle, but despite his efforts, it still did not work properly, therefore substantially impairing its value to Marie. Even though six months had elapsed since the original sale, Marie's revocation probably would be deemed to be made within a reasonable period of time because she had been assured after each repair that the motorcycle was working properly and had no reason to doubt Bob's word until it had failed as many times as it did.

E. Payment must be made at the time and place that the buyer receives the goods.

This rule applies *only* when no specific provisions governing payment are contained in the contract. Payment must be in cash or any other commercially acceptable value, unless specified otherwise. If the contract specifies payment on a credit basis, but does not state the time at which the credit will be given, the credit period is calculated from the date of shipment.

17-5. Buyer's Remedies

A number of remedies are available to a buyer should a seller breach a contract. Rejection and revocation under certain circumstances concerning nonconforming goods have already been discussed. There are other remedies also available, depending on the circumstances of the breach.

A. The buyer may seek substitute goods.

Comparable to the seller's right to resell is the buyer's right to purchase goods elsewhere that a seller has either failed to deliver or has delivered in nonconformance with the contract. This concept is known as *covering*.

1. The measure of damages that can be sought against the seller is the difference between the cost of covering and the contract price.
2. The buyer is not obligated to cover and may seek the difference between the contract price and the market price at the time of the breach, plus any consequential damages, minus any expenses saved.

EXAMPLE 17-9: Tricia, the owner of a grocery store, had contracted to buy 2,000 pounds of a local farmer's broccoli crop for 10¢ a pound. The farmer later informed Tricia, however, that he had decided to sell the broccoli to someone else for more money instead. Tricia immediately contracted with an out-of-state farmer to buy 2,000 pounds of his broccoli for 20¢ a pound. What damages may Tricia collect from the farmer who breached the first contract?

Tricia may collect the difference between the original contract price and the covering cost, which is 10¢ a pound or $200 for 2,000 pounds. She may also collect any consequential damages such as increased shipping costs she may have had to pay because of buying the broccoli out of state.

B. The buyer may have a right to recover goods if the seller becomes insolvent.

If the buyer has not received goods yet for which at least one payment has been made, and the seller becomes insolvent within ten days of receipt of that first payment, then the buyer may recover the identified goods by tendering the unpaid balance of the purchase price to the seller.

C. The buyer may seek specific performance of the sales contract.

Specific performance may be ordered by the court in cases where the goods involved are unique or where other remedies would not give justice to the buyer.

D. The buyer may recover possession of identified goods if the seller is wrongfully withholding them.

If the buyer is unable to obtain cover for the seller's goods and the seller is wrongfully withholding them, the court may order *replevin*, which gives the buyer the right to possess the goods.

E. The buyer may retain a security interest in rejected goods.

The buyer, upon rightful rejection or revocation of the goods, retains a security interest in the goods to the extent of any payment made on the purchase price and reasonable expenses for receipt and inspection. The buyer may hold the goods and resell them to recover this security interest upon any breach by the seller.

F. The buyer may cancel the contract and sue for damages.

The buyer's right to cancel the contract in case of the seller's breach is the same as the seller's right to cancel. The measure of damages depends on the circumstances of the breach.

1. In case of nondelivery or repudiation, the measure of damages is the difference between the contract price and the market price at the time the buyer learns of the breach.
2. In cases where the buyer accepts goods and then seeks damages based on nonconformity, the measure of damages is the difference between the value of the goods as accepted and the value they would have had if they had been delivered as warranted.
3. Consequential damages are recoverable if they were foreseeable and could not have been prevented by the buyer. They may include any reasonable costs of inspection, storage and reshipment of the goods, or the cost of obtaining cover.
4. Any costs saved by the seller's breach or by covering are deducted from the damages.

EXAMPLE 17-10: Herb, a horse breeder, contracted to buy 20 mares from another breeder for $20,000. Five of the mares contracted for were with foal. As it turned out, the breeder repudiated the contract. Herb therefore sued for the $20,000, plus $5,000 for the unborn foals, plus another $15,000 for the future foals of the other mares, which he had intended to breed. Would he receive this amount of damages?

Herb would not receive the amount he was asking in damages. Herb would be entitled to the difference between the contract price and the market value of the mares at the time of the breach. He would also be entitled to the difference between the contract price and market value of the five unborn foals, as they were also identified to the contract. He could not collect any damages for the future foals of the other mares, however, because, despite his intentions to breed them, there would be no conceivable way to foresee how many foals would or would not actually have been born, due to many unforeseeable circumstances that could affect the outcome. Consequential damages must be foreseeable and provable within reason in order to be awarded by the court.

17-6. Other Remedies

The buyer and seller may expressly limit, modify, or specify remedies or measures of damages to be used in case of breach by including them in the contract. The court will not enforce remedies expressed in a contract, however, if they are unreasonable or unsuitable to the circumstances of the breach. Other remedies available to the nonbreaching party as discussed earlier would be applied.

17-7. Anticipatory Breach and Assurance of Performance

Much like general contract law, if one party clearly repudiates performance of the contract before performance is due, the other party may treat the repudiation as a breach.

A. The nonbreaching party may choose one of three courses of action.

1. The nonbreaching party may wait for performance for a commercially reasonable time. If the nonbreaching party waits longer than a commercially reasonable time, then any damages incurred cannot be recovered if they could have been avoided.
2. The nonbreaching party may seek any remedy available for breach without waiting for performance.
3. The nonbreaching party may suspend his or her performance in anticipation of any acts by the other party.

B. Either party may retract repudiation before performance is due.

If the nonbreaching party has already changed his or her position somehow in reliance on the repudiation, however, the repudiation cannot be retracted.

C. Either party may demand assurance of performance.

Anticipatory breach must be absolute. In cases where a party is not sure of the other party's intention or ability to perform, that party may demand assurance of performance in writing from the other party.

1. The demanding party may suspend his or her own performance if it is commercially reasonable to do so until receiving the assurance.
2. Assurance must be given within a reasonable time, not to exceed 30 days.
3. Failure to provide assurance constitutes a repudiation of the contract.

RAISE YOUR GRADES

Can you explain . . . ?

☑ how the *perfect tender* rule applies to the performance of the seller in a sales contract

☑ how commercial reasonableness affects the seller's choices in a case of buyer's breach concerning unfinished goods

☑ what is meant by *mitigating damages* and how mitigation affects either party's right to collect damages

☑ the buyer's choices of action when delivered nonconforming goods

☑ the measure of damages applied when a seller repudiates a contract as opposed to when a seller delivers nonconforming goods that are accepted by the buyer

☑ what a nonbreaching party may do if certain of an anticipatory breach by the other party and what a nonbreaching party may do if uncertain of an impending breach

SUMMARY

1. The UCC contains guidelines governing performance of a sales contract.
2. In general, the seller is obligated to tender delivery of conforming goods to the buyer.
3. If the method of delivery is not specified in the contract, then: (*a*) delivery must be tendered within a reasonable period of time at the seller's place of business or residence; (*b*) tender must be made at a reasonable hour, upon reasonable notice to the buyer; and (*c*) the goods must be held for a reasonable period of time for the buyer.

4. If the method of delivery is specified as a shipment contract, then the seller must: (*a*) make a reasonable contract with and deliver the goods to a carrier; (*b*) deliver a document to the buyer allowing the buyer to take possession of the goods; and (*c*) give the buyer prompt notice of the shipment.

5. If the method of delivery is specified as a destination contract or a contract not requiring physical delivery of the goods, then the seller must do one of the following: (*a*) give the buyer a negotiable document of title allowing the buyer to take possession of the goods; or (*b*) give the buyer a nonnegotiable document of title or written direction to the bailee to turn over the goods to the buyer.

6. The *perfect tender* rule allows a buyer to void a contract if the goods or the tender of delivery do not conform in all respects to the terms of the contract. There are several exceptions to the rule, as follows:

   (*a*) The seller has the right to cure any defects in the goods if the time of performance has not expired, upon notice to the buyer.

   (*b*) The seller has the right to cure nonconforming goods within a reasonable time if the seller reasonably believed that the buyer would accept the goods.

   (*c*) The buyer cannot reject conforming goods that were improperly shipped if no material delay or loss has resulted.

   (*d*) The seller may substitute a different means of delivery if the agreed upon method of delivery becomes impracticable or impossible.

   (*e*) The buyer may not void an installment contract on the basis of one or more nonconforming installments unless they substantially impair the entire contract.

   (*f*) The seller does not have to perform if an unforeseen circumstance makes performance impracticable or impossible.

   (*g*) If performance by the seller is partially affected by impracticability, the seller must perform to the extent possible and distribute goods fairly if more than one buyer is affected.

   (*h*) The seller need not perform if goods identified to the contract are destroyed through no fault of the seller after risk of loss has passed to the buyer.

7. The seller has many remedies available in case of breach by the buyer or buyer's insolvency. Depending on the circumstances and under certain limitations, the seller may: (a) hold a lien on the goods until the purchase price is paid; (*b*) withhold delivery to the buyer; (*c*) stop delivery of goods in the hands of a carrier or bailee; (*d*) reclaim goods from the buyer; (*e*) identify goods to the contract; (*f*) resell the goods; (*g*) recover the purchase price of the goods plus incidental damages; or (*h*) cancel the contract and sue for damages.

8. The measure of damages if the buyer breaches a contract is the difference between the contract price and the market value of the goods at the place and time of tender, plus any reasonable incidental damages, minus any expenses saved. In some cases, the seller may also be able to recover lost profits.

9. In general, the buyer is obligated to accept conforming goods and tender payment for them in accordance with the contract.

10. The buyer may inspect goods prior to acceptance or payment. If the contract requires payment upon or before delivery, payment does not constitute acceptance.

11. The buyer must accept conforming goods. Acceptance may be express or implied.

12. The buyer may reject nonconforming goods, either in whole or in part, but must notify the seller of the defect to give the seller a chance to cure.

13. The buyer may revoke an acceptance of goods if he or she can prove that the defect substantially impairs the value of the goods and that the defect was difficult to detect upon first acceptance. The buyer may also revoke acceptance if the seller fails to cure defects as promised within a reasonable period of time.

14. When no provision for payment is made in the contract, payment must be made at the time and place that the buyer receives the goods.

15. The buyer has many remedies available in case of breach by the seller or seller's insolvency. Depending on the cirumstances and under certain limitations, the buyer may: (*a*) seek substitute goods, known as *covering;* (*b*) seek specific performance of the contract;

(c) recover possession of identified goods wrongly withheld, known as *replevin;* (d) retain a security interest in rejected goods; or (e) cancel the contract and sue for damages.

16. The measure of damages if the seller breaches a contract generally is the difference between the contract price and the market price or cost of covering at the time the buyer learns of the breach. If accepted goods are nonconforming, the measure of damages is the difference between the value of the goods as accepted and their value as warranted. The buyer may also be able to recover any reasonable consequential or incidental damages minus any expenses saved as a result of the breach.

17. In the case of anticipatory breach, either party may wait for performance for a commercially reasonable period of time or suspend performance and seek any remedy available for the breach.

18. Repudiation may be retracted if the other party has not changed his or her position in reliance on the repudiation.

19. If either party is unsure of the other party's intention or ability to perform, assurance of performance may be demanded in writing. Adequate assurance must be given within 30 days or the contract is considered to be repudiated.

RAPID REVIEW   Answers

True or False

1. The buyer may void a contract if the seller's tender of delivery does not conform in all respects to the terms of the contract. [Section 17-2]	*False*
2. The buyer may cancel an installment contract if an installment is nonconforming. [Section 17-2]	*False*
3. If a seller has a contract to deliver 1000 bats to each of two buyers, and 1000 bats are destroyed, the seller must still deliver 500 bats to each buyer. [Section 17-2]	*True*
4. The seller must pay any additional freight charges that may result from stopping delivery of goods to a buyer. [Section 17-3]	*True*
5. The seller may never reclaim goods from a buyer once they are in the buyer's possession. [Section 17-3]	*False*
6. The seller need not notify the buyer of an intention to resell goods that the buyer had contracted for. [Section 17-3]	*False*
7. Lost profits are most often awarded to a seller in cases involving standard-priced, readily available goods. [Section 17-3]	*True*
8. If a buyer has an opportunity to reject goods and does not, the seller may assume that the goods have been accepted. [Section 17-4]	*True*
9. Both the seller and buyer must attempt to mitigate damages after a breach of contract. [Sections 17-2 and 17-4]	*True*
10. The buyer is obligated to cover if a seller breaches in order to mitigate damages. [Section 17-5]	*False*
11. The court never orders specific performance of the contract by the seller when the seller breaches. [Section 17-5]	*False*
12. Consequential damages are recoverable if they were foreseeable, could not have been prevented, and were provable within reason. [Section 17-5]	*True*
13. The court will always enforce any remedies specified in a sales contract. [Section 17-6]	*False*

14. The demanding party must always suspend his or her perfor-   *False*
mance if awaiting assurance of performance from the other
party as an effort to mitigate damages. [Section 17-7]

SOLVED PROBLEMS

PROBLEM 17-1   Margaret, the owner of a hardware store, ordered 100 hammers from a
tool manufacturer. The manufacturer did not have the exact model in stock that Margaret
ordered, so they substituted a comparable model for the same price. When Margaret received
the hammers, however, she rejected them as nonconforming and informed the manufacturer
that she was cancelling the contract. Could she do this?

Answer: Margaret could not cancel the contract. The manufacturer delivered the different model of
hammer under the reasonable belief that Margaret would accept it. Margaret had the right to reject
the nonconforming model, but she also had the obligation to give the manufacturer a reasonable time
to deliver the conforming goods before she could cancel the contract. [Section 17-2]

PROBLEM 17-2   Marvin, the owner of a bookstore, ordered 300 books from a publishing
company. The order specified that the books would be sent by mail. The books arrived on
time by UPS instead, so Marvin wrote the publisher that he was not going to pay for the
books because the company had not conformed with the contract in all respects. The publisher
responded by demanding payment or the return of the books at Marvin's expense. Who was
correct?

Answer: The publishing company was correct. One of the exceptions to the *perfect tender* rule is that
a buyer cannot reject conforming goods that have been improperly shipped if no material delay or loss
has resulted. Since no material delay or loss resulted from the shipment of the books by UPS, and
since the books were the correct ones ordered, then Marvin was obligated to pay for them. Furthermore, even if a material delay or loss had allowed Marvin to reject the goods rightfully, he would not
be allowed to keep them without payment. [Section 17-2]

PROBLEM 17-3   Nadine, a building contractor, agreed to build a home for a couple for
$90,000. The contract contained no clause for escalating costs. As it turned out, Nadine was
unable to acquire some of the building materials for the price she had thought she could.
Consequently, it was going to cost her $10,000 more than she had realized to build the house.
She told the couple that unless they agreed to pay the extra $10,000, she would cancel the
contract on the basis of commercial impracticability. Could she do this?

Answer: Nadine could not cancel the contract on the basis of commercial impracticability. As a building contractor, she should have foreseen the possibility of escalating costs and had a clause included in
the contract to cover such a possibility. It is unlikely that a court would allow her to cancel the contract
because performance ended up being more expensive than she realized. Nadine would have to accept
the agreed upon price of $90,000. [Section 17-2]

PROBLEM 17-4   Bates Furniture was holding a set of living room furniture for Beth, who
had put $500 down and was supposed to return within a week with the remaining $1,000 of
the purchase price. As it turned out, Beth did not return within a week, nor did she return
telephone calls that Bates Furniture made to her place of work. After a month, Bates Furniture finally sent Beth a letter informing her that they were going to resell the furniture if
she did not pay for it within ten days. When she did not respond, Bates Furniture resold the
furniture for $1,000, after making reasonable efforts to sell the furniture at a higher price.
Several days later, Beth returned and demanded the return of her $500 deposit. Did Bates
Furniture have to return the money?

Answer: Bates Furniture did not have to return the $500. Beth had clearly breached the contract
when she did not return within a week to pay the remaining $1,000 for the furniture. Furthermore,
Bates Furniture ended up giving her an extra month of time to come up with the money. The breach

gave Bates Furniture the right to resell the furniture, which it informed Beth that it was doing. If anything, Beth should leave well enough alone because, if it wanted to, Bates Furniture could sue her for damages. The damages would be the difference between the contract price ($1,500) and the resale price ($1,000), or $500, plus any incidental damages, such as storage costs or lost profits. Although Beth's down payment would offset the first $500 worth of damages, the court would require her to pay the incidental damages. [Section 17-3]

PROBLEM 17-5 Carlos, the owner of a construction firm, ordered 10,000 square feet of gold carpet to be installed in an apartment complex he was building. The carpet was delivered by the carpet company to a warehouse for storage. Three months later, some of the apartments were completed enough to begin installing the carpet. Upon unrolling the first roll of carpet, however, the installers noticed that the color was not uniform and, in fact, seemed stained in many places. They informed Carlos, who had all of the rolls of carpet inspected, only to discover that they were all blotchy in color. Carlos then notified the company from whom he bought the carpet that he was rejecting the carpet and expected the company to replace it. The company, however, responded that his acceptance of the carpet had been implied by the fact that he had not reported the defect until three months after delivery. Who was correct?

Answer: The court may find that the carpet company was correct in assuming that Carlos had accepted the carpet when it did not hear from him for three months after delivery. Carlos, however, had the right to revoke his inspection if he could prove that the defect was difficult to discover or that inspection had occurred at a reasonable time. Obviously, it should not have been difficult to discover that the carpet was not uniform in color if it had been inspected entirely upon delivery. Inspection, however, may occur at any reasonable time and, in this case, the court probably would find that it was reasonable and standard under the circumstances that the carpet not be inspected until it was unrolled for installation, particularly since it was delivered to a warehouse for storage, as the carpet company was aware. At the time of installation, all of the rolls were inspected and found to be unsuitable. The court therefore would allow Carlos to revoke his implied acceptance and seek any remedy legally available to him. [Section 17-4]

PROBLEM 17-6 Maggy, the owner of a bakery, was notified on June 3 that a farmer from whom she had contracted to buy five tons of wheat would not be able to deliver because his wheat crop was not as large as he had anticipated. The contract price was to have been $7,500. When notified of the repudiation, five tons of wheat was selling for $9,000 on the market. Maggy did nothing about the breached contract for a long time, but in December, she contracted to buy five tons of wheat for $10,500. She then brought suit against the farmer for the difference between the contract price and the covering cost. Would she get this amount in damages?

Answer: Maggy would not get this amount in damages. In cases of repudiation by the seller, the buyer has the right to wait for performance by the seller for a commercially reasonable period of time and to seek cover. In this case, however, the farmer's wheat crop was not going to get any larger, so it was not reasonable for Maggy to wait until December to seek cover. At the time of the breach, five tons of wheat cost $9,000. By December, the price had climbed to $10,500. When Maggy intended to cover, she should have done so immediately after the breach in order to mitigate damages. The court would only give her the difference between the contract price ($7,500) and the market value of the wheat at the time of the breach ($9,000), or $1,500. [Sections 17-5 and 17-7]

PROBLEM 17-7 Suppose that the contract between Maggy and the farmer in Problem 17-6 had included a provision that, in case of the farmer's breach, the farmer would have to pay the full contract price plus the full price of covering. Would this remedy be enforceable?

Answer: This remedy would not be enforceable. The parties to a contract have the right to expressly specify remedies for breach in the contract. The court will not enforce any remedy expressed in a contract, however, that is unreasonable or unsuitable to the circumstances of the breach. Since the normal remedy for this breach would be the difference between the contract price and the market value at the time of the breach, or just $1,500, the court probably would find that to impose the full contract price of $7,500 plus the covering cost of $10,500, or $18,000, would be unreasonable and unsuitable to the circumstances of the breach. [Section 17-6]

PROBLEM 17-8   Ace Electric had been selling electrical supplies to Bret's electrical repair business for years. Their contract specified that each delivery was to be followed by payment within 30 days. Bret had fallen behind in his payments for several months, until $5,000 was owed to Ace Electric, despite its many requests for payment. Finally, Ace Electric sent a letter stating that no more deliveries would be made until the $5,000 was paid, and that all future deliveries would be sent COD. Bret paid the $5,000, but when Ace Electric's next delivery arrived, he refused to pay for it at the time, so the carrier returned the shipment. Bret then sued Ace Electric for breach of contract. Did he win his suit?

Answer: Bret did not win his suit. Bret's failure to pay for successive deliveries for several months constituted a breach of contract. Ace Electric was therefore justified in demanding payment for the amount due before any more deliveries would be made. Furthermore, since Ace Electric was justifiably unsure of Bret's future intention to pay on time, it had the right to demand the new terms of sending all future deliveries COD as assurance of performance. [Section 17-7]

18 WARRANTIES AND PRODUCT LIABILITY

THIS CHAPTER IS ABOUT

☑ **Liability**
☑ **Warranties**
☑ **Disclaimers of Warranties**
☑ **Product Liability**

18-1. Liability

Anyone who purchases a product has expectations of that product as to its quality and fitness for its intended use. When goods do not meet these expectations, the question arises as to the seller's or manufacturer's liability. Liability is established on the basis of:

• express and implied warranties
• negligence
• strict liability

18-2. Warranties

A *warranty* is the responsibility that a seller or manufacturer assumes for the product being sold. Article 2 of the UCC covers two kinds of warranties.

A. Express warranties are created by the seller.

An *express warranty* arises when a seller makes a direct representation to the buyer regarding the goods to be sold, either orally or in writing. Representations can be made through an outright promise regarding the goods, a description of typical performance, technical specifications, or the use of a model or sample. Such representations are usually made during the course of the negotiations of sale and may be included in the contract.

1. *Basis of the bargain.* No matter how the representation is made by the seller, it must form the "basis of the bargain" for it to be an express warranty. The buyer must rely on the representation in making the decision to purchase the goods.
2. *Sales talk.* Not all statements of the seller give rise to express warranties. If the seller is merely giving a personal opinion, affirmation of value, or praise, this is considered "sales talk" and is not regarded by the court as a direct representation of the nature of the goods.
3. *Application.* Whether or not a representation is considered an express warranty by the court often depends on the status of the buyer and seller. If a seller deals in the goods and has specific knowledge of and experience with them, and the buyer does not, a statement might be considered an express warranty. On the other hand, if the buyer is also a dealer or has specific knowledge of and experience with the type of goods being purchased, the same statement might be considered an expression of opinion.

EXAMPLE 18-1: Hillary, who knew nothing about cars, purchased a used car from a dealer after he assured her that the car had been overhauled completely and was in excellent working condition. Within three weeks of the purchase, however, the electrical system failed. Hillary had the car towed to the dealer, who repaired the system and presented Hillary with a bill for $320. Hillary refused to pay it, claiming that an express warranty existed for the condition of the car. Was she correct?

Hillary was correct. An express warranty need not be in writing to be binding on the seller. The dealer made a direct, oral representation to Hillary that the car was in excellent working condition. There would be no doubt that this representation was "a basis of the bargain," in that Hillary relied on the representation in making the decision to purchase the car. An express warranty was therefore created and the dealer would be responsible for the failure of the electrical system such a short time after the purchase.

EXAMPLE 18-2: Suppose that Hillary was a competent mechanic and, despite the dealer's claim that the car was in excellent working condition, she had thoroughly examined the car herself before purchasing it. Would the dealer still be responsible for the failure of the electrical system?

In this case, a court might find that since Hillary had specific knowledge of and experience in car mechanics, and had conducted an inspection of the car for herelf, the dealer's statement would not constitute an express warranty since she had not relied on it in making her decision to purchase the car.

B. Implied warranties are created by law.

Because today's merchandising seldom allows a buyer to inspect goods carefully before buying them, the law imposes responsibility on the seller for the quality and fitness of goods, particularly if the seller is a merchant. Warranties imposed by law are known as *implied warranties*. The UCC establishes two types of implied warranties.

1. *Implied warranty of merchantability.* If the seller is a merchant who deals in the goods being sold, then an implied warranty exists that the goods are reasonably fit for the ordinary purpose of such goods. This warranty does not extend to sellers who are not merchants. Along with fitness for ordinary purpose, other standards of merchantability, when applicable, are that the goods:

   - must be adequately packaged and labeled
   - must conform to any statements made on the package or label
   - must be of a consistent kind and quality within a unit
   - must, if fungible, be of the average quality described in the contract
   - must conform to the description in the contract so as to be acceptable to others in the trade

EXAMPLE 18-3: Monroe bought a new toaster at an appliance store but it did not work properly when he got it home. Is the appliance store responsible for the defective toaster? What if Monroe had bought a used toaster at a neighbor's garage sale and it didn't work properly? Would the neighbor be responsible for the defective toaster?

The new toaster bought at an appliance store would carry an implied warranty of merchantability that it was reasonably fit for the ordinary purpose it was intended for. The store, as a merchant, would therefore be responsible for the defective toaster and would either have to repair it, exchange it for one that works, or take it back and refund the purchase price to Monroe. The used toaster bought at a neighbor's garage sale, however, would not carry an implied warranty of merchantability unless the neighbor also happened to be a merchant that dealt in toasters, which is unlikely. In this case, Monroe would be responsible for repairing the defective toaster himself.

2. *Implied warranty of fitness for a particular purpose.* In some cases, the seller knows or has reason to know of a particular purpose for which the buyer intends to use a product, and knows that the buyer is relying on his or her knowledge to select the product for that purpose. When these two conditions exist, an implied warranty of the fitness of that product for the particular purpose exists. The important point here is that the buyer must be relying on the seller's knowledge or experience to choose the product. Unlike the implied warranty of merchantability, the seller does not have to be a merchant to make an implied warranty of fitness for a particular purpose.

EXAMPLE 18-4: Bernie went to a stereo shop to purchase new speakers for his stereo. He was interested in a particular pair and asked a sales representative if they could carry 100 watts per channel. The sales representative assured him that the model could carry 100 watts per channel. Bernie bought the speakers, but when he hooked them up to his system, they blew out. It was later determined that the speakers were designed to carry only 50 watts per channel. Was the stereo shop responsible for the speakers?

The stereo shop was responsible for the speakers. An implied warranty of merchantability that the speakers were reasonably fit for ordinary use was not violated. In this case, however, an implied warranty of fitness for a particular purpose was also created when the sales representative told Bernie that the speakers could carry 100 watts per channel. When Bernie asked this particular question, the sales representative had reason to know that Bernie's system needed speakers with at least this much power. The speakers turned out not to be fit for this particular purpose, so the store was responsible.

18-3. Disclaimers of Warranties

Often, the seller attempts to exempt or limit his or her responsibility for express or implied warranties. Such disclaimers are scrutinized warily by the court because of the possibility of the buyer's not being aware of the disclaimer. The seller must therefore meet strict guidelines for a disclaimer to be upheld by the court. Even so, the court will often overlook disclaimers if they appear unreasonable, against the intent of the parties, or to fail in their essential purpose.

A. Disclaimers of express warranties must not contradict express warranties given.

An express warranty is difficult to disclaim. The court will often find that a disclaimer is inconsistent if the contract for sale or the conduct of the seller clearly indicates that express warranties were made. In many cases, the seller has made oral representations and the written contract disclaims them. The court seldom enforces disclaimers of this nature, particularly if the oral representations were relied on by the buyer and were a part of the "basis of the bargain."

EXAMPLE 18-5: Sam, a farmer, was at a farm equipment dealer's one day because he wanted to buy a new tractor. He could not afford a new tractor of the type he wanted and was going to wait. The dealer finally convinced him to buy a used one, however, after promising him that the engine had been rebuilt by the service staff and the body had been repainted. The dealer also promised that she would guarantee the tractor to run properly for up to a year. Sam signed a contract to make payments for a year and took the tractor home. Unfortunately, within three months, the paint had begun to peel and the tractor shut off every time he tried to pull something heavy. When Sam contacted the dealer about the problems, she told him to read the back of his contract. Although Sam was unaware of it, the back of the contract read, "No warranties exist as to the condition of any used equipment sold by this dealership." Sam decided to sue anyway for breach of warranty. Would he win his suit?

Sam probably would win his suit. This was a case where the seller made oral, express warranties, but the written contract disclaimed them. Sam could testify in court as to his original intention to purchase a new tractor and to his ultimate decision to purchase a used one on the basis of the dealer's representations as to the used tractor's fitness. Furthermore, Sam could also explain the dealer's oral guarantee of the tractor for one year and of his unawareness of the disclaimer in the contract. If the court chose to believe Sam, it probably would overlook the disclaimer on the basis that it was inconsistent with the evidence of express warranties given, and perhaps even fraudulent.

B. Disclaimers of implied warranties must be clear or prominent and conspicuous.

The seller must expressly and clearly mention merchantability in order to disclaim an implied warranty of merchantability. The disclaimer need not be in writing, but if it is, it must be prominent and conspicuous. A disclaimer of a warranty of fitness for a particular purpose must be in writing and must be clear, prominent, and conspicuous.

1. *Language.* Language such as "as is" or "with all faults" is considered sufficient to call the buyer's attention to a full disclaimer of both merchantability and fitness.
2. *Conspicuousness.* The standard of conspicuousness is that a reasonable person who is to be affected by the disclaimer ought to be able to notice it. Factors such as the size of type, placement within the contract, and contrasting color or type are considered by the court. The court is likely to overlook even a conspicuous disclaimer when the buyer has been personally injured, or when the buyer holds an unequal bargaining position due to lack of knowledge, expertise, or economic power.
3. *Buyer's inspection.* If the seller provides the goods and the buyer inspects them fully or refuses to inspect them, then no implied warranty exists for defects that the inspection should have revealed.

4. *Other disclaimers.* Implied warranties can also be disclaimed by course of dealing, course of performance, or usage of trade.

18-4. Product Liability

Under the general rule of contract law known as *privity of contract,* a person cannot sue to enforce a contract that he or she is not a party to, and cannot sue to enforce a contract against third parties who are not parties to the contract. Under strict application of this doctrine, a person would have no cause of action for defective goods unless that person had actually purchased the goods. Furthermore, even a person who suffered injury from defective goods would only be allowed to sue the seller and not the manufacturer, since technically the manufacturer was not a party to the contract. Today, however, the privity of contract rule has been abolished in most product liability cases, and most courts allow a person to recover damages from the retailer, the manufacturer, and even the distributor, if such an action is justified.

There are three theories of product liability used by consumers to bring the manufacturers and processors of defective products into a lawsuit. They involve both the concepts of warranty discussed previously and elements of the law of torts.

A. Product liability can be established on the basis of breach of warranty.

In most states, a buyer may sue both the retailer and the manufacturer if injury results from a product by breach of its warranty. The UCC even extends this right to any injured third party who may "reasonably be expected to use, consume, or be affected by the goods and who is injured in person by breach of the warranty." Furthermore, the seller is not allowed to disclaim responsibility for such injury.

EXAMPLE 18-6: Patsy purchased a new lawn mower from Handy Hardware. The warranty that came with the lawn mower stated that it was "guaranteed against defects in material or workmanship for a period of 120 days." Two weeks after she bought the lawn mower, Patsy loaned it to a neighbor, Phillip. Unfortunately, the blade came off while Phillip was mowing, and he suffered a serious cut on his foot. Could Phillip recover damages for breach of warranty?

In most states, even though Phillip did not have privity of contract, he would be allowed to sue the hardware store, the manufacturer, or both for breach of warranty. The key to whether he could collect damages would be whether or not the court considered him to be a person "reasonably expected to use . . . the goods." If the court found it reasonable that Patsy would loan the lawn mower to a neighbor, then Phillip would be able to recover damages.

B. Product liability can be established on the basis of negligence.

The courts have found that a manufacturer owes a duty to the community to exercise the due care of a reasonable person in producing a product that will not cause harm to any person. This care includes proper safeguards in the manufacturing process, proper warnings of any known defects or hazards concerning the product, and proper representations as to the quality of the product and its fitness for a particular purpose. Failure to exercise due care can lead to product liability on the basis of negligence.

1. *Res ipsa loquitur.* In a suit for negligence, it would be difficult for an injured party to prove the conditions existing within a company at the time a defective product was made. The doctrine of *res ipsa loquitur* requires the injured party only to show that the defect that caused the injury was within the responsibility of the manufacturer, therefore putting the burden of proof on the manufacturer to show that it did exercise due care under the circumstances.
2. *Disclaimers.* The manufacturer's duty of care extends to all persons who may be injured by the product, and no disclaimer in a contract is allowed to exclude this duty.
3. *Defenses.* In some states, if a person fails to use due care in handling the product or proceeds in the face of a known hazard and injury results, the manufacturer is not held negligent. The former defense is called *contributory negligence,* the latter *assumption of risk.* In states that follow the *comparative negligence* doctrine, the person's own negligence would merely reduce the amount of damages assessed against the negligent manufacturer.

EXAMPLE 18-7: Suppose that Phillip, who borrowed the lawn mower from Patsy in Example 18-6, was pushing the lawn mower across a gravel driveway and a rock had caused the blade to come loose and injure his foot. Would Phillip be able to recover damages on the ground of negligence?

Phillip could bring suit against the manufacturer for negligence, claiming that proper safeguards were not present to prevent the injury. The manufacturer, however, could argue that this was a case of contributory negligence, in that Phillip did not exercise due care in using the lawn mower when he pushed it across gravel with the blade spinning. Some courts would take contributory negligence into consideration and not award damages to Phillip. Courts following the comparative negligence doctrine would simply reduce the amount of Phillip's award.

C. Product liability can be established on the basis of strict liability.

An injured party may not always be able to recover damages on the basis of breach of warranty or negligence. An injured party may be barred from recovering for breach of warranty if they would not "reasonably have been expected to use, consume, or be affected by" the product or if the warranty had run out. Contributory negligence or assumption of risk on the injured party's part may effectively limit or bar recovery for negligence. In such cases, product liability can be assessed due to *strict liability* in tort. Strict liability holds manufacturers liable for defects in products they put on the market that cause injury to anyone, regardless of the manufacturer's fault or lack of fault.

1. *Tort law.* The essential aspects of strict liability are found in tort law. They are:
   - the seller must be in the business of selling the product
   - the defect must have been present at the time the product left the manufacturer
   - the product must be unreasonably dangerous; that is, dangerous to a degree not to be expected by an average person

2. *Application.* Strict liability is being applied in various ways in different states. Some courts only allow an injured person to collect for injuries resulting from a product's intended purpose. Other courts have held manufacturers accountable for injury caused through use of a product in an unintended way and even through use of a product that has been changed by the user.

3. *Defense.* Under strict liability, no defense of reasonable care, privity of contract, or contributory negligence is effective. The defenses of assumption of risk or lack of unreasonable danger may be effective.

EXAMPLE 18-8: Don was walking on the sidewalk when Eve was mowing her lawn. The lawn mower blade hit a rock that, despite a safety shield, hit Don's eye, causing serious injury. The lawn mower was five years old, with no existing warranties. If Don wanted to sue the manufacturer for damages, on what grounds would he have the best chance of success?

No warranties remained on the lawn mower, so there is no cause of action for breach of warranty. A safety shield was present on the lawn mower, so to sue on the ground of negligence might mean that the manufacturer could successfully defend on the basis of due care. Don's best approach would be to sue on the ground of strict liability, claiming that the lawn mower was unreasonably dangerous.

RAISE YOUR GRADES

Can you explain . . . ?

☑ how express and implied warranties are created and the difference between the two

☑ the difference between an implied warranty of merchantability and an implied warranty of fitness for a particular purpose

☑ why disclaimers of warranties may be difficult to uphold in court

☑ the three theories of product liability that a person may use to recover damages from the manufacturers and processors of defective products

☑ why strict liability is sometimes imposed by the court even though a manufacturer may not have been at fault in the manufacture of a product

SUMMARY

1. When goods do not meet a buyer's expectations, liability of the seller or manufacturer is established on the basis of warranties, negligence, or strict liability.
2. A warranty is the responsibility that a seller or manufacturer assumes for the product being sold.
3. An express warranty arises when a seller makes a direct representation to the buyer regarding the goods to be sold, either orally or in writing, and the representation forms a basis of the bargain.
4. Warranties imposed by law are known as implied warranties.
5. An implied warranty of merchantability exists on any goods sold by a merchant and means that the goods are reasonably fit for their ordinary purpose.
6. An implied warranty of fitness for a particular purpose exists on goods sold by any seller who knows or has reason to know that a buyer is relying on his or her knowledge to select goods for a particular purpose.
7. Disclaimers of express warranties need not be in writing, but must be conspicuous if they are.
8. Disclaimers of implied warranties must be in writing and must be conspicuous.
9. Any disclaimer, oral or written, will not be upheld if the court finds it to be unreasonable, inconsistent with the intent of the parties, or failing in its essential purpose.
10. Any sale of goods that bear the terms "as is" or "with all faults" is sufficient to disclaim all implied warranties.
11. If the buyer inspects the goods or refuses to inspect them, then no implied warranty exists for defects that the inspection should have revealed.
12. The UCC provides that not only the buyer, but any person "reasonably expected to use, consume, or be affected by" a product may attempt to recover damages for breach of warranty.
13. The failure of a manufacturer to exercise due care to produce a product that will not cause harm to any person can lead to product liability on the basis of negligence. This duty cannot be disclaimed.
14. A manufacturer can defend against a charge of negligence by seeking to prove that due care was exercised, that the injured party did not use due care in handling the product, or that the injured party proceeded in the face of a known danger that led to the injury.
15. Strict liability exists in tort law and can be used to hold manufacturers liable for defects in products they put on the market that cause injury to anyone, regardless of the manufacturer's fault or lack of fault.
16. For strict product liability to be assessed, tort law requires that the seller be in the business of selling the product, that the defect be present at the time the product left the manufacturer, and that the product be unreasonably dangerous.
17. Assumption of risk or lack of unreasonable danger are the only defenses available to a manufacturer charged with strict product liability.

RAPID REVIEW   Answers

True or False

1. A merchant's statement that his bicycles are "the best in town" creates an express warranty. [Section 18-2]   *False*

2. A merchant who provides a sample of the product being sold and says that the goods, when delivered, will "conform in every way" to the sample creates an express warranty. [Section 18-2]   *True*

3. A casual person who sells a tape recorder to his neighbor is bound by an implied warranty of merchantability. [Section 18-2]   *False*

4. If an inexperienced buyer bought bricks to build a fireplace from a neighbor who was told of the buyer's purpose, then an implied warranty of fitness for a particular purpose would exist. [Section 18-2]

True

5. A written disclaimer printed in small type among several paragraphs on the back of a contract would nonetheless be upheld by the court. [Section 18-3]

False

6. If a person carefully inspected a bicycle before deciding on it and then found a scratch on it after taking it home, that person could still hold the seller responsible on the basis of an implied warranty of merchantability. [Section 18-3]

False

7. Under the UCC, privity of contract is an important concept in determining when a person injured by a product may recover damages for breach of warranty. [Section 18-4]

False

8. To take advantage of the doctrine of *res ipsa loquitur,* an injured party must show that the defect that caused injury was within the responsibility of the manufacturer. [Section 18-4]

True

9. Assumption of risk is a defense available against negligence whenever an injured party has failed to use due care in handling the product that caused injury. [Section 18-4]

False

SOLVED PROBLEMS

PROBLEM 18-1 Sheila went to a local hardware store to purchase a chain saw. When asked for a lightweight saw, the clerk who was helping her showed her the lightest chain saw in the store and said, "as far as I know, this is the lightest weight chain saw on the market." Several days after the purchase, and after using the chain saw several times, Sheila saw a chain saw in a different store that was at least ten pounds lighter than the one she had purchased. She therefore took the chain saw she had purchased back to the hardware store and demanded a refund, claiming breach of an express warranty. Did the store have to refund her money?

Answer: The store did not have to refund Sheila's money. Sheila was shown the lightest weight chain saw that the store carried. Although she relied to some extent on the clerk's judgment, the clerk's statement that it was the lightest weight chain saw on the market would be considered personal opinion, or sales talk, and would not be deemed to have created an express warranty, particularly since the clerk prefaced the statement with the words, "as far as I know." [Section 18-2]

PROBLEM 18-2 Walter needed several drill bits to use on steel. He was not very knowledgeable about bits, so he told a clerk what he wanted the bits for. The clerk selected bits for him and said that they would work for his purpose. As it turned out, the bits broke when Walter tried to use them. He took the bits back to the store, explained what happened to the store manager, and said that he wanted to exchange the bits for ones that would work. The store manager pointed out that the package the bits came in specifically stated that they were for use on wood only and refused to exchange them. Was there a breach of warranty in this case?

Answer: There was a breach of warranty in this case. The package did expressly state that the bits were to be used for drilling wood only. The clerk, however, created an implied warranty of fitness for a particular purpose when she selected the bits for Walter and promised that they would work on steel. This implied warranty was breached and the store must exchange the bits for Walter or refund his money. [Section 18-2]

PROBLEM 18-3 Shelly wanted to buy a home computer. She liked two models and read all of the manufacturer's brochures on each one. She finally decided to buy one of the models on the basis of its brochure explicitly stating the memory capacity and function capabilities that she wanted. When she began to use the computer, however, she found that its capabilities were well below what the brochure indicated and that it did not have the stated memory capacity either. Unfortunately, when she looked for her purchase contract in order to take the computer back, she noticed a large, printed disclaimer of all warranties, express or implied. Would this disclaimer be upheld?

Answer: The disclaimer would not be upheld. An advertising brochure is distributed with the purpose of convincing people to buy a product on the basis of the information given in the brochure. The brochure, by making explicit statements about the computer's capabilities and memory capacity, created an express warranty and an implied warranty of merchantability. It clearly set forth what could be expected by the buyer to be the computer's ordinary purpose. The court would therefore find that the disclaimer was in conflict with the warranties expressed in the brochures. [Sections 18-2 and 18-3]

PROBLEM 18-4   Kate ordered a coat from a mail-order catalogue on the basis of a picture of the coat. When the coat arrived, however, it was green instead of blue as pictured. Kate wrote to the company that she wanted to return the coat, but the company wrote back that the front of their catalogue included a disclaimer stating that actual colors of items may vary slightly due to printing quality. Kate looked and, sure enough, there was a heading entitled "Terms of the Sale" and buried in the eighth paragraph was the disclaimer. Would this disclaimer be upheld?

Answer: This disclaimer probably would not be upheld. The picture would serve as an express warranty that the item being ordered would conform to the picture. In this case, the catalogue did state that actual colors may vary slightly, but it also stated that variation would be due to printing quality. Since the company was aware that color might not be exactly as pictured, it should have provided some sort of description saying that the coat was green. Furthermore, the disclaimer itself was not conspicuous and appeared under a misleading heading. [Sections 18-2 and 18-3]

PROBLEM 18-5   Elizabeth was interested in buying a used car that was advertised in the paper. The owner of the car, a home mechanic, showed her a detailed maintenance record that indicated that the car had been well taken care of. The last entry showed that the oil had been changed by the owner and five quarts of new oil put in the car a week ago. Elizabeth bought the car on the basis of this record. Unfortunately, about a week later, the car stopped on the highway. After having it towed and inspected, a service person told her that, although there were no leaks or other problems, the oil had run dry. Repair would cost $800. Elizabeth had the car repaired and then sued the previous owner for recovery of the cost on the ground of breach of warranty. Would she win her case?

Answer: Elizabeth would win her case. An express warranty was created when the previous owner showed Elizabeth the maintenance record, therefore guaranteeing the accuracy of the information. Elizabeth relied on this record to make her decision, therefore making the information a basis of the bargain. When this information failed, the warranty was breached. [Sections 18-2 and 18-3]

PROBLEM 18-6   Marvin bought retread tires for his car that came with a guarantee of performance and quality for up to 20,000 miles. The guarantee was also limited to replacement of the tires as remedy for breach of the warranty. Unfortunately, one of the rear tires blew out after 12,000 miles. The car veered into a tree, causing serious injury to Marvin as well as damage to the car. Marvin sued the retread company to recover all damages, but they raised the defense in court that their liability was strictly limited to replacement of the tire. Would this defense work?

Answer: This defense would not work. The court would recognize that a purchaser of the tires would rely on the guarantee of performance for 20,000 miles for the purpose of safety as well as for the purpose of getting new tires in case of defect. When serious bodily harm and damage to the car resulted before the 20,000 miles had expired, the court would find the limited remedy to be unreasonable and against the intent of the purchase. [Section 18-3]

PROBLEM 18-7   Marshall bought a chemical pesticide to spray on plants in his yard. The bottle contained many warnings and explicit directions for proper use of the product. One of the warnings was "do not inhale." Marshall followed all of the instructions for use and tied a scarf around his face while spraying the product. Nevertheless, he was overcome by the fumes and required hospitalization and treatment for a week. After recovering, Marshall brought suit against the manufacturer of the product on the ground of strict liability. The company's defense was that they had provided proper warnings and that Marshall had assumed the risk of use of the product and should have worn a face mask to avoid injury. Who won?

Answer: Marshall won the case. Strict liability is applied in cases where harm results from a product that is found to be unreasonably dangerous; that is, the danger exceeds what would be expected by an average person. Marshall had followed all of the instructions for use of the product as far as they went. In the absence of specific instructions as to how to avoid inhalation, he tied a scarf around his face. The court would find that an average person would reasonably believe that this was sufficient to prevent harmful inhalation. An average person would certainly not be expected to know that a special face mask was necessary to avoid harm. The defense of assumption of risk would therefore fail and Marvin would recover for damages. [Section 18-4]

*19*COMMERCIAL PAPER

THIS CHAPTER IS ABOUT

☑ **Definition and Importance of Commercial Paper**
☑ **Types of Commercial Paper**
☑ **Requirements for Negotiability**
☑ **Rules of Construction**

19-1. Definition and Importance of Commercial Paper

Commercial paper is the general term for a number of special types of contracts for the payment of money. In some cases, the commercial paper is a promise to pay money; the most common paper of this kind is the promissory note. In other cases, the commercial paper is an order to pay money; the most common paper of this kind is the check. There are several reasons why commercial paper is important for conducting business in today's marketplace.

A. Commercial paper can be transferred from one party to another.

The main importance of commercial paper is that it can be transferred from one party to another much more easily than other kinds of contracts. Ordinary contracts in which a promise is exchanged for consideration can, of course, be assigned, but the assignee's rights in such cases are generally limited by whatever legal defenses existed between the original contract parties. With commercial paper, however, this is not the case, so parties are normally much more willing to accept transfers of such paper in the course of business.

B. Commercial paper can be negotiable.

In many cases, commercial paper is "negotiable," or acceptable in place of money in trade. Such paper is called a *negotiable instrument*. For most purposes, commercial paper must meet certain requirements of the Uniform Commercial Code (UCC) to qualify as a legitimate negotiable instrument. These requirements are discussed in Section 19-3.

C. Commercial paper can be used as a credit device.

Another important use of some kinds of commercial paper is as credit devices. For example, a promissory note can be given in exchange for a loan.

19-2. Types of Commercial Paper

The chief types of commercial paper that are promises to pay money are promissory notes and certificates of deposit. The chief types that are orders to pay money are drafts, including checks.

A. A promissory note is a promise to pay money.

A *promissory note* is formally defined as a written instrument whereby a first party unconditionally promises to pay a stated sum of money to a second party. A promissory note is therefore most often a two-party instrument. The party who promises to pay is called the *maker* of the note. The party to whom the note is payable is called the *payee*. To be negotiable, a note must be made payable to the *bearer* (the party in physical possession of it) or to *order;* that is, "to the order of" a named party or other agency.

The note can be made payable *on demand;* that is, whenever the payee presents it for payment; or it can be made payable at some definite future time. Some promissory notes are payable in installments.

The promissory note is used mainly as a credit instrument. Lenders frequently have borrowers sign promissory notes to cover the amount to be repaid. Two special kinds of promissory notes are the following:

1. A *mortgage note* is one whereby a borrower promises to repay a loan for which real property has been pledged as security.
2. A *collateral note* is one whereby a borrower promises to repay a loan for which personal property has been pledged as security.

B. A certificate of deposit is a promise to pay money.

A *certificate of deposit* (CD) is an instrument that a bank issues acknowledging that a certain sum has been deposited and promising to repay that sum, normally with interest, when the holder of the certificate presents it after a stated period has elapsed.

C. A draft is an order to pay money.

A *draft* is formally defined as a written instrument whereby a first party unconditionally orders a second party to pay a stated sum of money to a *payee* (usually a third party, sometimes the first party). A draft is therefore most often a three-party instrument. Drafts are also called *bills of exchange.* The party who orders the payment is called the *drawer.* The party who is ordered to pay is called the *drawee.* A draft can be made payable to the bearer or to order.

Like notes, drafts can be made payable on demand (called a *sight draft*) or at some definite future time (called a *time draft*).

Two common types of drafts are checks and bank drafts.

1. A *check* is a written order by a bank customer (the first party) to the bank (the second party) to pay a stated sum of money to a third party (or sometimes to the first party, as when a depositor writes himself a check to "cash"). Checks are payable on demand.

   • A special kind of check is the *cashier's check,* which the bank itself writes directing payment from its own funds to a party designated by a customer who has paid the bank an equivalent amount.

2. A *bank draft* is an instrument whereby one bank orders another bank to pay a stated sum of money as directed.

EXAMPLE 19-1: Beverly was going to buy ten acres of land. She planned to pay part of the purchase price by personal check and finance the rest with a mortgage. What types of commercial paper will she be using to purchase the land?

Beverly will be using two different types of commercial paper to purchase the land. The check is a draft and the mortgage is a form of promissory note.

19-3. Requirements for Negotiability

For commercial paper to qualify as a legitimate negotiable instrument, it must meet certain requirements of the UCC. The purpose of these requirements is to ensure the reliability of the instrument so that purchasers will willingly accept it in trade. Commercial paper that fails to meet these requirements is not considered a valid negotiable instrument for most purposes. Transactions involving such paper are governed instead by the law of contracts. Articles 3 and 4 of the UCC set forth the requirements for negotiability.

A. A negotiable instrument must be in writing.

The instrument must take the form of a written document, although no particular form is required. The instrument can be handwritten, printed, typewritten, or written down in any other manner. As with other written agreements, the parol evidence rule applies.

B. A negotiable instrument must be signed by the maker or drawer.

The instrument must be signed by the party who is promising or ordering payment. In the case of notes, this is the maker; in the case of drafts, the drawer.

C. A negotiable instrument must contain a promise or order to pay.

1. A promise to pay must be more than a mere acknowledgment of a debt (for example, an I.O.U.); it must represent a current undertaking to pay that debt.

2. An order to pay must be more than a mere request; it must contain a requirement to tender a stated payment.

D. The promise or order to pay must be unconditional.

The promise or order to pay cannot be contingent on the occurrence of some event or some other action by any of the parties. A promise to pay "when able" is usually considered conditional. A promise or order to pay is also considered conditional if it states that payment is to be made from a specific fund.

EXAMPLE 19-2: Janet made a written note promising to pay $400 to the order of the Greengrass Landscaping Company in return for landscaping her yard. The fee was payable 30 days following completion of the job. Under UCC rules, can Greengrass use Janet's note as a negotiable instrument?

Under UCC rules, Greengrass cannot use Janet's promise as a negotiable instrument since it does not meet the requirement of being unconditional; that is, Janet will only pay if Greengrass does the work. The promise is not a valid negotiable instrument, and its use is governed instead by the law of contracts.

E. The payment must be a sum certain in money.

The payment must be a *sum certain;* that is, a sum whose total is fixed even though it may be payable in installments or subject to interest. Also, the payment must be in money rather than, for example, goods or stocks.

F. A negotiable instrument must state a definite time of payment.

1. The stated time of payment can be any of the following:

   - on demand (whenever the payee presents the instrument for payment)
   - within a stated period after the payee presents the instrument for payment ("after sight")
   - on or before a stated date
   - at the end of a fixed period after a stated date
   - at a definite time subject to optional acceleration or extension

2. If the time of payment is made contingent on the occurrence of some event that may never happen or that may happen at some time not yet known, the instrument is not negotiable.

EXAMPLE 19-3: Emily made a written note promising to pay $1000 to the order of her nephew Max on the day that Max marries. Is this note a negotiable instrument?

Under UCC rules, Emily's note is not a negotiable instrument since it fails to state a definite time of payment. Max may never marry and, in any case, the date of his wedding, even if announced, could be changed.

G. A negotiable instrument must be made payable to order or bearer.

The use of phrases such as "pay to the bearer" or "pay to the order of" indicate that the instrument is negotiable and does not have to be paid to a specific party. That is, if an instrument is payable "to the order of Jane Doe," payment can be made to Jane Doe or to anyone whom Jane Doe orders to be paid. An instrument that is payable "to Jane Doe" is not negotiable.

1. An instrument that is payable "to the order of" a specific party is called *order paper.*

2. An instrument that is payable to the bearer is called *bearer paper.*

H. A negotiable instrument may not require any other act besides the payment of the sum certain.

An instrument whereby the holder can require some other act besides the payment of money, such as the delivery of goods, is not negotiable.

19-4. Rules of Construction

Any negotiable instrument is likely to be transferred from one party to another, so the terms written on the instrument need to be clearly understood by all parties. As a result, the following *rules of construction* have been established to govern the writing and interpreting of the terms of negotiable instruments.

A. Printing *versus* typing *versus* handwriting

A negotiable instrument can sometimes be ambiguous because it contains printing along with subsequent typewritten or handwritten entries. When this is the case,

- typewritten terms take precedence over printed terms
- handwritten terms take precedence over typewritten and printed terms

B. The sum in words *versus* the sum in figures

A negotiable instrument can sometimes inadvertently be made out to show a different sum in figures from the one shown in words. When this is the case, the sum shown in words takes precedence over the one shown in figures. If the words are ambiguous, however, the sum shown in figures takes precedence over the one shown in words.

EXAMPLE 19-4: Jeff's careless aunt sent him a check on which she had written "$100" in the space for the sum in figures, and "ten and 00/00 dollars" in the space for the sum in words. Which sum can Jeff collect?

Since the sum shown in words is clear and unambiguous, it takes precedence over the sum shown in figures, so Jeff can collect only ten dollars.

RAISE YOUR GRADES

Can you explain . . . ?

☑ why commercial paper is considered a special kind of contract
☑ how commercial paper differs from ordinary contracts
☑ why not every commercial paper qualifies as a legitimate negotiable instrument
☑ what purpose is served by the UCC requirements for negotiable instruments
☑ why an instrument that is not payable to the bearer or to order is not negotiable
☑ how notes are used as credit instruments
☑ how the law treats commercial paper that fails to qualify as a negotiable instrument
☑ why an instrument that fails to state a definite time of payment is not negotiable
☑ why rules of construction are necessary for negotiable instruments

SUMMARY

1. Commercial paper is the general term for a number of special types of contracts for the payment of money.
2. The main importance of commercial paper is that it can be transferred from one party to another much more easily than other kinds of contracts.
3. When commercial paper qualifies under UCC requirements as a negotiable instrument, it can be acceptable in place of money in the course of trade.
4. Another important use of some kinds of commercial paper is as credit devices.
5. In general, commercial paper contains either a promise to pay money or an order to pay money.

6. Common types of commercial paper are promissory notes, certificates of deposit, and drafts, including checks.

7. A check is a written order by a bank customer to the bank to pay a stated sum of money to a third party.

8. The UCC sets requirements for negotiable instruments to ensure their reliability so that purchasers will willingly accept them in trade.

9. Commercial paper that fails to meet the requirements for negotiable instruments is governed by ordinary contract law.

10. Under UCC requirements, a negotiable instrument must: (*a*) be in writing; (*b*) be signed by the party who is promising or ordering payment; (*c*) contain an unconditional promise or order to pay a sum certain in money; (*d*) state a definite time of payment; (*e*) be payable to order or bearer; and (*f*) not require any other act besides payment of the sum certain.

11. On a negotiable instrument, typewritten terms take precedence over printed terms, and handwritten terms take precedence over either typewritten or printed terms.

12. When the sum in figures on a negotiable instrument contradicts the sum in words, the sum in words takes precedence unless those words are ambiguous.

RAPID REVIEW   Answers

True or False?

1. Commercial paper is always a promise to pay money. [Section 19-1]	*False*
2. Any commercial paper is negotiable; that is, acceptable in place of money in trade. [Section 19-1]	*False*
3. In most cases, a promissory note is a two-party instrument. [Section 19-2]	*True*
4. A promissory note must always be made payable to the order of a named party or other agency. [Section 19-2]	*False*
5. In most cases, a draft is a two-party instrument. [Section 19-2]	*False*
6. A negotiable instrument must be signed by the maker or drawer. [Section 19-3]	*True*
7. A simple I.O.U. can be a legitimate negotiable instrument. [Section 19-3]	*False*
8. A promise to pay "when able" is usually conditional and thus cannot be a legitimate negotiable instrument. [Section 19-3]	*True*
9. A negotiable instrument need not state a definite time of payment. [Section 19-3]	*False*
10. If an instrument is payable "to the order of Jane Doe," payment can be made to Jane Doe or to anyone whom Jane Doe orders to be paid. [Section 19-3]	*True*
11. An instrument that is payable "to Jane Doe" is not negotiable. [Section 19-3]	*True*
12. A negotiable instrument may not require any other act besides the payment of the sum certain. [Section 19-3]	*True*
13. In a negotiable instrument, typewritten terms take precedence over handwritten terms. [Section 19-4]	*False*
14. In a negotiable instrument that shows different sums in figures and in words, the sum shown in figures always takes precedence. [Section 19-4]	*False*

SOLVED PROBLEMS

PROBLEM 19-1   Harry borrowed $100 from Jill. In return, he gave her a piece of paper on which he had written "I.O.U. $100—Harry." Is this piece of paper a negotiable instrument?

Answer: Harry's I.O.U. is definitely not a negotiable instrument because it fails to meet several UCC requirements. First and foremost, it hardly represents a current undertaking by Harry to pay his debt; it is nothing more than an acknowledgment of that debt. Also, it fails to state a definite time of payment, and nothing in it makes it payable to the bearer or to order. On all these counts, it fails to qualify as a negotiable instrument. [Section 19-3]

PROBLEM 19-2   Elliot wanted to make sure that his niece Lucy would be provided for if her parents died. He therefore wrote a note promising to pay $10,000 to the order of Lucy within ten days after the death of her last surviving parent. Is Elliot's note a negotiable instrument?

Answer: Elliot's note does not qualify as a negotiable instrument because it fails to state a truly definite time of payment. It is certain, of course, that Lucy's parents will someday die and thus, in principle, Elliot is bound to pay sooner or later. However, the times of those deaths are by no means certain, so the note as written fails to fulfill the UCC requirement that it include a definite time of payment. [Section 19-3]

PROBLEM 19-3   Hester borrowed $350 from Charlie. In return, she wrote a note promising to repay the $350 to the order of Charlie as soon as she was able. Is Hester's note a negotiable instrument?

Answer: Hester's note fails to qualify as a negotiable instrument because her promise to pay is subject to a condition; she will pay only if and when she is able. The note therefore violates the requirement that the promise to pay must be unconditional. [Section 19-3]

PROBLEM 19-4   Ted made a written note promising to pay $125 to the order of Angela's Bookkeeping Service in return for preparing his taxes. The note was payable 30 days following completion of the work. Can the bookkeeping service use Ted's note as a negotiable instrument?

Answer: Ted's note cannot be used as a negotiable instrument since payment is subject to a condition; that is, Ted will only pay if the bookkeeping service prepares his taxes. The note therefore fails to fulfill the UCC requirement that the promise to pay must be unconditional. Since the note cannot be a negotiable instrument, the law will treat it instead like an ordinary contract. [Section 19-3]

PROBLEM 19-5   Robert's promissory note to Whitney read as follows: "I promise to pay Whitney Smith $250 within 30 days from the date of this note. (signed) Robert Wells." Does this note qualify as a negotiable instrument?

Answer: Robert's note does not qualify as a negotiable instrument because it fails to meet the requirement that the sum be payable to the bearer or to order. If Robert promises to pay the $100 only to Whitney and not to the bearer of the note or to whomever Whitney orders to be paid, then anyone but Whitney who comes into possession of the note has no guarantee of collecting the $250. [Section 19-3]

PROBLEM 19-6   On the negotiable promissory note that Mickey's Hardware Store sent to South Coast Distributors, the printed phrase "payable 30 days from date" had been crossed out and replaced with the handwritten phrase "payable 3 months from date." When is the note payable?

Answer: Under the rules of construction that apply to negotiable instruments, handwritten terms always take precedence over printed terms and also over typewritten terms. Hence, the note is payable three months from its date, not thirty days. [Section 19-4]

PROBLEM 19-7   When Francine wrote a check to the dry cleaner, she inadvertently wrote "223 00/00" in the space for the sum in figures and "twenty-three and 00/00" in the space for the sum in words. Can the dry cleaner collect the higher amount?

Answer: The dry cleaner cannot collect the higher amount because, under the rules of construction governing negotiable instruments, when the sum in figures on an instrument contradicts the sum in words, the sum in words takes precedence as long as the words are clear and unambiguous. Hence, in this case, the dry cleaner can collect only $23. [Section 19-4]

PROBLEM 19-8   Roger wrote a note promising to pay $65 to the order of the North Gulf Finance Company. The note further specified that the money was payable on Friday, June 20, and that it was to be taken from Roger's paycheck for that week. Does Roger's note qualify as a negotiable instrument?

Answer: Roger's note does not qualify as a negotiable instrument because it specifies that the payment is to be made from a specific fund—Roger's paycheck for the week of June 20. Under UCC rules, this makes Roger's promise conditional; that is, the money is collectible only if Roger does indeed collect a paycheck that week. Hence, the note violates the UCC requirement that the promise to pay must be unconditional. [Section 19-3]

PROBLEM 19-9   Harold wrote a note promising to give 100 shares of the Pennsylvania Pyrite Company to Laura or to order within thirty days of the date of the note. Does Harold's note qualify as a negotiable instrument?

Answer: Harold's note does not qualify as a negotiable instrument because it violates the UCC requirement that payment for a negotiable promissory note must be a sum certain in money. In this case, payment is to be stock shares rather than money. Furthermore, the value of those shares is most likely constantly changing, so there is no question of a sum certain. [Section 19-3]

PROBLEM 19-10   On April 1, Ginny wrote a note promising to pay $90 to the order of Reuben's Repair Service. The note specified that the money would be payable in three installments of $30 each, due on May 1, June 1, and July 1. Does Ginny's note qualify as a negotiable instrument?

Answer: Ginny's note does qualify as a negotiable instrument since it fulfills all of the UCC requirements for negotiability. The fact that it is payable in installments does not make the total sum any less certain or the time of payment any less definite. [Section 19-3]

20 *TRANSFER OF NEGOTIABLE INSTRUMENTS*

THIS CHAPTER IS ABOUT

☑ **Negotiation**
☑ **Indorsement**
☑ **Holder in Due Course**
☑ **Checks and Banking**

20-1. Negotiation

Negotiation is the process whereby the "holder" of an instrument (the party to whom that instrument is currently payable) transfers that instrument to a second party in a manner that makes that second party a new holder of the instrument. The method of negotiation depends on whether the instrument is bearer paper or order paper. (Recall from Chapter 19 that bearer paper is any instrument made payable to the "bearer," whereas order paper is any instrument made payable "to the order of" a specific party.)

A. Bearer paper can be negotiated by simple delivery by the transferor.

The transferee will qualify as the new holder of the bearer paper by virtue of simply possessing it.

B. Order paper can be negotiated by delivery and indorsement by the transferor.

Only if both conditions are met will the transferee qualify as a new holder. If order paper is delivered but not indorsed, the transferee *cannot* qualify as a new holder of that instrument by virtue of simply possessing it.

20-2. Indorsement

An *indorsement* is a signature or other written indication by the present holder of a negotiable instrument (or that holder's authorized agent) whereby that holder transfers that instrument to a new holder. The indorsement is written on the instrument, usually on the back, or on another paper firmly attached to the instrument.

A. Indorsement gives several guarantees to the new holder.

Indorsement is written assurance that the indorser has negotiated the instrument to the new holder. Indorsement also generally makes the indorser liable for payment of the instrument if the maker or drawer fails to pay. A party who acquires a properly indorsed instrument thus has this further guarantee of the instrument's value.

B. There are five general rules of indorsement.

1. *Entire sum certain.* The indorsement must convey the entire sum certain represented by the instrument; the sum may not be split in any way.
2. *Wording.* No special words of negotiability are needed other than those already shown on the face of the instrument.
3. *Form of signature.* In general, the indorser should sign his or her name exactly as it is shown on the instrument. However, if the name shown on the instrument is misspelled or wrong, the indorser may sign the name either in the correct form or in the form shown on the instrument. Some transferees will require the indorser to sign the name both ways.

EXAMPLE 20-1: An acquaintance wrote Susan Sterling a check payable "to the order of Susan Stirling." How should Susan indorse the check?

Susan can indorse the check by signing either "Susan Stirling" or "Susan Sterling." If she deposits the check in a bank, however, the bank would probably require her to indorse the check both ways.

4. *Agent indorsement.* If an instrument is payable to a business, corporation, or some other organization, the indorsement may be made by a properly authorized agent of that organization (for example, an officer of a corporation) using her or his own name, the name of the organization, or both.

5. *Joint and several indorsement.* If an instrument is payable to two or more parties, the instrument may specify whether it is payable to all the parties jointly or to each party separately. If nothing is specified, the instrument is considered payable to all parties jointly. An instrument that is payable to several parties jointly must be indorsed by all the parties in order to be negotiated. An instrument that is payable to each of several parties separately may be indorsed and negotiated by any one of those parties. (*Note:* This rule does not apply when the parties are partners or when one party is authorized to act for all of the parties.)

EXAMPLE 20-2: How must a check be indorsed if it is made payable "to the order of Joe Alton and Linda Sibert" or "to the order of Joe Alton or Linda Sibert?"

In the first case, the payees are payable jointly, and both must indorse the check in order to negotiate it. In the second case, the payees are payable separately, and either can indorse the check and negotiate it.

C. There are four main kinds of indorsements.

1. *Blank indorsement.* In a blank indorsement, the indorser merely signs his or her own name; no attempt is made to specify to whom the instrument is payable. This kind of indorsement makes the instrument payable to the bearer; when order paper (such as a check) is indorsed in this manner, it becomes bearer paper. It can then be negotiated simply by delivery; no further indorsements are necessary. ·

2. *Special indorsement.* In a special indorsement, the indorser signs his or her own name and specifies to whom, or to whose order, the instrument is payable. For example, on a check payable to her order, Jeanne Wallace might write the special indorsement "Pay to Steven Wong, Jeanne Wallace" or "Pay to the order of Steven Wong, Jeanne Wallace." This kind of indorsement makes the instrument payable to the order of the specified party; in other words, the instrument becomes (or remains) order paper and is negotiable further only if indorsed by the specified party and delivered to the transferee. Bearer paper indorsed with a special indorsement is thus thereby converted to order paper. (Note that in contrast to the wording on the face of an instrument, a special indorsement need not include the words "the order of" for the instrument to remain negotiable.)

3. *Restrictive indorsement.* In a restrictive indorsement, the indorser specifies the use to be made of the instrument. A restrictive indorsement does not affect an instrument's negotiability, whereas a condition imposed by the maker or drawer of an instrument makes that instrument unnegotiable (see Section 19-3). There are five main types of restrictive indorsements.

   (a) *Indorsement for deposit.* This kind of indorsement indicates that the instrument is to be deposited. An example is "For deposit only to the account of Lawrence Zinn."

   (b) *Indorsement of collection.* This kind of indorsement indicates that the instrument is to be received by the indorsee, usually as part of a bank's collection process. An example is "for collection only."

   (c) *Indorsement prohibiting further negotiation.* An example of this kind of indorsement is "Pay to Deborah Glynn only."

   (d) *Trust indorsement.* This kind of indorsement indicates that the indorser intends the instrument to benefit or be used by a party other than the one to whom it is payable. An example is "Pay to Irene Gordon in trust for Ray Gordon."

(*e*) *Conditional indorsement.* This kind of indorsement indicates that it will become effective only if a stated condition is satisfied. An example is "Pay to John Murray upon delivery of Order #486."

4. *Qualified indorsement.* In a qualified indorsement, the indorser adds words to disclaim or limit his or her liability if the party who is primarily liable for the instrument—the maker or drawer—fails to make payment. Qualified indorsements commonly include the words "without recourse."

20-3. Holder in Due Course

In general, the *holder* of an instrument is the party to whom that instrument is currently payable. A party can become the holder of an instrument if the instrument is issued to that party or if the instrument is bearer paper, or by delivery and indorsement by the transferor if the instrument is order paper.

However, a party to whom an instrument is transferred under certain legally specified conditions can qualify for the preferred status of *holder in due course.* This kind of holder can take title to the instrument free of most claims and defenses from other parties, even if those claims and defenses could have been asserted successfully against the transferor. A holder in due course is thus virtually assured of being able to convert the instrument into cash.

A transferee who does not qualify as a holder in due course is subject to the same claims and defenses as the transferor of the instrument.

A. There are several requirements to qualify as a holder in due course.

To qualify as a holder in due course, a party must first qualify as a holder; that is, be in possession of an instrument that includes any necessary indorsements. Next, the party must have acquired the instrument under certain conditions.

1. *Value.* The party must have given "value" (not necessaily the same as consideration) in exchange for acquiring the instrument. A party gives value by, for example, extending a loan in return for a note or delivering goods in return for a check. A party who is given or who inherits an instrument does not give value for it and thus cannot qualify as a holder in due course.

2. *Good faith.* The party must have acquired the instrument honestly. A party who acquires an instrument through an illegal or fraudulent transaction cannot qualify as a holder in due course, nor can one who knowingly acquires an instrument that has been stolen, forged, or altered. If the acquiring party takes the instrument in good faith, it does not matter whether or not the party who is transferring the instrument has acted in good faith.

3. *Defenses and adverse claims.* The party must have acquired the instrument without any notice of defenses against its negotiability or adverse claims to its ownership. There are four situations in which this situation commonly arises.

   (*a*) *Voidable or discharged instrument.* If the acquiring party has notice that the obligations of any party to the instrument are voidable or have been discharged, the acquiring party cannot qualify as a holder in due course. For example, if a party acquires an instrument knowing that an indorsement on that instrument was obtained under duress, the acquiring party cannot become a holder in due course.

   (*b*) *Altered instrument.* If there are visible alterations or forgeries in the instrument, the acquiring party is deemed to have received notice that there may be defenses and claims against the instrument. Consequently, the acquiring party cannot qualify as a holder in due course.

EXAMPLE 20-3: Marian wrote a check for $8 to the order of Jerry, her neighbor, to pay him for shoveling snow. Jerry, however, rather sloppily altered the check by changing "eight" dollars to "eighty" dollars and "$8" to "$80." Jerry then took the check to a hardware store and attempted to negotiate it to pay for an electric drill. Will the store owner qualify as a holder in due course if she accepts the check?

If Jerry's alterations are indeed rather sloppy and clearly visible, the store owner will be deemed to have received notice that there might be a defense against the check's negotiability; i.e., Marian's defense that she is liable only for the $8 original amount. Consequently, the store owner will not qualify as a holder in due course if she takes the check.

    (c) *Incomplete instrument.* If some important term on an instrument has been left blank, the acquiring party is deemed to have received notice that there may be defenses or claims against the instrument. Consequently, the acquiring party cannot qualify as a holder in due course.

    (d) *Instrument improperly negotiated by a fiduciary.* If the instrument is payable to a fiduciary (such as a trustee) on behalf of a beneficiary, the acquiring party is deemed to have received notice that the fiduciary may be attempting to negotiate the instrument improperly to the fiduciary's own benefit, and that the intended beneficiary may raise a claim. Consequently, the acquiring party cannot qualify as a holder in due course.

4. *Overdue or dishonored instruments.* The party must have acquired the instrument without any notice that it was overdue or had been dishonored.

- An instrument is *overdue* if it was due to be paid on a certain date and no payment was made. (An instrument that is payable on demand is usually considered to be due within thirty days.)
- An instrument is *dishonored* if it was presented for payment and payment was refused. (For example, a check that failed to clear because of insufficient funds is dishonored.)

    Not every party who acquires an overdue or dishonored instrument does so knowingly. However, a party is deemed to have notice of the overdue or dishonored status if that status is apparent from the instrument itself, or if notice was given by another party, or if the status could be inferred from the facts and circumstances surrounding the transaction.

B. A holder in due course has certain rights.

In contrast to an ordinary holder, a holder in due course has the advantage of being able to acquire title to a negotiable instrument free of most claims and defenses from other parties to that instrument. In other words, none of those specified claims and defenses may be used by another party to the instrument as grounds for not paying a holder in due course. Consequently, a holder in due course is far more assured of being able to convert an instrument into cash than is an ordinary holder.

Specifically, holders in due course are not subject to "limited" (or "personal") defenses. However, they may be subject to "universal" (or "real") defenses, which have to do with the validity of the instrument itself.

1. *Limited ("personal") defenses.* A holder in due course is not subject to limited (personal) defenses that may be asserted by another party to the instrument. There are two broad categories of limited defenses involving negotiable instruments.

    (a) *Failure of consideration.* A party who fails to receive proper consideration for an instrument may not assert that failure as a defense against payment to a subsequent holder in due course.

EXAMPLE 20-4: Susan asked Joe the bricklayer to build her a patio. In exchange, she gave him a promissory note payable to his order on April 1, the day the patio was expected to be finished. Joe's work was so shoddy, however, that Susan decided to find out if she could avoid payment of the note. In the meantime, though, Joe had negotiated the note to Southside Bank, which had qualified as a holder in due course. Can Susan avoid payment of the note?

Susan cannot avoid payment of the note since Southside Bank is a holder in due course and therefore not subject to a defense like Susan's, which is based on failure to receive proper consideration. Susan will have to pay Southside the full amount of the note. However, she can seek to recover that amount in a separate action against Joe.

(*b*) *Fraud in the inducement.* If a party is induced to sign an instrument because of fraudulent representations, that party may not assert the fraud as a defense against payment to a subsequent holder in due course. This rule applies only so long as the signing party was aware at the time of the signing that the instrument was indeed an instrument.

2. *Universal ("real") defenses.* A holder in due course may be subject to universal (real) defenses that may be asserted by another party to the instrument. There are six categories of universal defenses involving negotiable instruments.

(*a*) *Minority.* A party who signs an instrument while a minor may assert that fact as a defense against payment to a holder in due course.

(*b*) *Fraud in the essence.* A party who unwittingly signs an instrument after being fraudulently informed that it is something other than an instrument may assert that fact as a defense against payment to a holder in due course.

(*c*) *Illegality.* A party who signs an instrument that is void under the law because of its connection with illegal conduct may assert that fact as a defense against payment to a holder in due course.

(*d*) *Forgery.* A claim that the signature on an instrument was forged may be asserted as a defense against payment to a holder in due course.

(*e*) *Duress.* If a party signs an instrument under such duress that by general legal principles the transaction would be void (and not merely voidable), that fact may be asserted as a defense against payment to a holder in due course.

(*f*) *Material alteration.* If the instrument is fraudulently altered by one of the parties in a way that changes the contractual obligations of any party, that fact may be asserted as a defense against payment to a holder in due course. (Note, however, that the holder may enforce the instrument in its original terms.)

20-4. Checks and Banking

Checks are by far the most frequently used negotiable instruments, hence it is vital to understand the rights and duties of the parties who issue them, as well as those of the banks who are expected to honor them.

A. Checks must go through a collection process in order to be settled.

A *check* is a draft drawn on a bank and payable on demand, normally from assets kept on deposit with the bank by the drawer. The drawer's bank is the primary agent in the *collection process*, which is the chain of events that a check goes through before a final settlement is made. There are three steps in the collection process.

1. *Presentment.* The party to whom the check is payable (sometimes the original payer, sometimes a party to whom the check has been negotiated, sometimes a bank that has received the check as a deposit) presents the check for payment by the drawer's bank. (Presentment will be discussed further in Chapter 21.)

2. *Sufficient funds.* If the check is properly drawn and there are sufficient funds in the drawer's account to pay it, the bank has a duty to pay the check and a final settlement is made.

3. *Insufficient funds.* If there are not sufficient funds in the drawer's account, the bank may *dishonor* the check, or refuse to pay it. There are several rules that govern the handling of dishonored checks.

(*a*) Under the *bad check laws* enacted in many states, if a dishonored check is not made good within a given period of time, it will be assumed that the check was drawn with the intent to defraud, and the drawer will be subject to criminal prosecution.

(*b*) If a check is dishonored, the drawer becomes liable for payment to the holder.

(*c*) A dishonored check sometimes may be presented again later to the drawee bank in the hope that the drawer's account will by then contain sufficient funds to cover it.

(*d*) In some cases, instead of dishonoring a check for insufficient funds, a bank may pay it and thus create an overdraft in the drawer's account. The drawer then owes the bank the amount of the overdraft, and the bank may deduct that amount from the drawer's subsequent deposits.

B. The drawee bank has certain duties.

1. A bank has the duty to pay on demand every check properly drawn by a depositor up to the amount of the funds credited to that depositor's account. If a bank fails to fulfill this duty (for example, by wrongfully dishonoring a check), it is liable for damages to the depositor.
2. A bank has the duty to be familiar with a depositor's authorized signature in order to be able to detect forgeries. If a bank pays such a check, it is liable to the depositor; however, it may seek recompense either from the forger or from subsequent indorsers.

C. The drawee bank has certain rights.

1. A bank has the right to charge a depositor's account for every properly payable check issued by that depositor.
2. A bank has the right not to pay any check that is more than six months old. Such a check is called a *stale check*.
3. If a depositor issues an *incomplete check*, that is, one with the amount left blank for another party to fill in, the bank has the right to pay the check as completed and charge the depositor's account accordingly unless the bank receives notice that the completion was improper.

EXAMPLE 20-5: Ned gave his friend Oscar a check to buy a few groceries. Ned completed the check in every way except for the amount, trusting Oscar to fill that in for whatever the groceries cost. Oscar, however, filled in the amount of $200 and pocketed the change. Is Ned's bank liable if it charges the check to Ned's account?

Even though Oscar disobeyed Ned's wishes, Ned's bank would normally honor this check unless notified that the check has been improperly completed. If there is no such notice, the bank has the right to charge the check to Ned's account and incurs no liability for doing so.

4. If a depositor's check is altered by another party—in most such cases, the alteration consists of increasing the amount of the check—the bank generally cannot charge the check to the depositor's account, but only up to the amount the depositor originally wrote. Any sum beyond that amount that is paid out by the bank from the depositor's account must be reimbursed to the depositor. The bank may, however, seek recompense for that excess sum from the party who altered the check or from subsequent indorsers.

D. The depositor has certain duties.

1. The depositor has the duty to keep sufficient funds in an account to cover the checks that he or she writes.
2. The depositor has the duty to report to the bank all unauthorized alterations or signatures on his or her canceled checks. In most cases, if the depositor does not report a forgery or unauthorized alteration within one year, the bank cannot be required to recredit the depositor's account for the amount of the improper check.

E. The depositor has certain rights.

1. The depositor has the right to expect the bank to pay on demand every check properly drawn by the depositor up to the amount of the funds credited to the depositor's account.
2. The depositor has the right to stop payment on a check. The depositor can stop payment by an oral or written *stop payment order* to the bank. However, the order must be given soon enough for the bank to have a reasonable amount of time to comply with it; in other words, before the bank has paid the check. There are several rules governing stop payment orders.

(a) An oral stop payment order is valid only for fourteen days. A written stop payment order is valid for six months.

(b) If the bank pays a check that is subject to a stop payment order, the bank is liable to the depositor for any loss the depositor suffers as a result of that payment. However, it is the depositor's responsibility to prove any such loss.

(c) Depositors most often stop payment when a check is lost or stolen or when the payee fails to deliver some contract consideration (for example, merchandise) for which the check is meant as payment.

(d) When a check is meant as payment for some contract consideration but the payee fails to deliver that consideration, the drawer has a perfect right to stop payment on the check. However, if the payee negotiates the check to a holder in due course, failure of consideration can no longer be used as a defense against payment, and the drawer will have to pay the holder in due course (see Section 20-3B).

RAISE YOUR GRADES

Can you explain . . . ?

☑ the significance of an indorsement on a negotiable instrument

☑ how indorsement can convert order paper into bearer paper and bearer paper into order paper

☑ the difference between a holder and a holder in due course

☑ the main advantage of being a holder in due course

☑ what takes place during the check collection process

☑ what may happen to the drawer if a check is dishonored for insufficient funds

☑ what may happen when a check that has been altered by some other party is presented at the drawer's bank for payment

☑ what circumstances may oblige a party who writes a check for merchandise to pay that check even though the merchandise is not delivered

SUMMARY

1. Negotiation is the process whereby the holder of an instrument transfers that instrument to a second party in a manner that makes that second party a new holder of the instrument.

2. If the instrument is bearer paper, simple delivery is all that is required for negotiation.

3. If the instrument is order paper, negotiation requires delivery to the transferee and indorsement by the transferor.

4. An indorsement is a signature or other written indication by the present holder of a negotiable instrument whereby that holder transfers that instrument to a new holder.

5. Indorsement generally makes the indorser liable for payment of the instrument if the maker or drawer fails to pay.

6. If on the face of the instrument the indorser's name is wrong or misspelled, the indorser may sign the name either in the correct form or in the form shown on the instrument.

7. An instrument that is payable to several parties jointly must be indorsed by all the parties in order to be negotiated. An instrument that is payable to each of several parties separately may be indorsed and negotiated by any one of those parties.

8. A blank indorsement is a simple signature; an instrument with this kind of indorsement remains or becomes bearer paper.

9. A special indorsement consists of a signature and words specifying to whom the instrument is payable. An instrument with this kind of indorsement remains or becomes order paper.

10. A restrictive indorsement specifies the use to be made of the instrument.

11. A party to whom an instrument is transferred under certain legally specified conditions can qualify for the preferred status of holder in due course.

12. A holder in due course can take title to an instrument free of most claims and defenses from other parties. This kind of holder is virtually assured of being able to convert the instrument into cash.

13. To qualify as a holder in due course, a party must have (*a*) qualified as a holder, (*b*) given value in exchange for the instrument, (*c*) acquired the instrument in good faith, (*d*) acquired the instrument without any notice of defenses against its negotiability or adverse claims to its ownership, (*e*) acquired the instrument without any notice that it was overdue or had been dishonored.

14. A holder in due course is not subject to limited ("personal") defenses that other parties may assert against payment of the instrument. Such defenses include failure of consideration and fraud in the inducement.

15. A holder in due course may be subject to universal ("real") defenses that other parties may assert against payment of the instrument. Such defenses include minority, fraud in the essence, illegality, forgery, duress, and material alteration.

16. A check is a draft drawn on a bank and payable on demand, normally from assets kept on deposit with the bank by the drawer.

17. If the check is properly drawn and there are sufficient funds in the drawer's account to pay it, the bank has a duty to pay the check; otherwise, the bank may dishonor the check.

18. A bank normally cannot charge a depositor's account for checks that have been altered by some other party or on which the signature has been forged.

19. If a depositor issues an incomplete check, the bank has the right to pay the check as completed.

20. A depositor has the right to stop payment on a check.

RAPID REVIEW   Answers

True or False?

1. If an instrument is order paper, simple delivery is all that is required for negotiation. [Section 20-1]   *False*

2. An indorsement generally will make the indorser liable for payment of the instrument if the maker or drawer fails to pay. [Section 20-2]   *True*

3. If an instrument is payable to a corporation, a properly authorized officer of that corporation can indorse it. [Section 20-2]   *True*

4. An instrument that is payable to each of several parties separately must be indorsed by all the parties in order to be negotiated. [Section 20-2]   *False*

5. An instrument that is indorsed with a blank indorsement becomes or remains bearer paper. [Section 20-2]   *True*

6. A special indorsement is one that specifies the use to be made of the instrument. [Section 20-2]   *False*

7. A party who inherits an instrument can qualify as a holder in due course. [Section 20-3]   *False*

8. A party who knowingly acquires an instrument that has been stolen cannot qualify as a holder in due course. [Section 20-3]   *True*

9. If an instrument contains visible alterations or forgeries, a party who acquires it cannot qualify as a holder in due course. [Section 20-3]   *True*

10. A party who fails to receive proper consideration for an instrument may assert that failure as a defense against payment to a holder in due course. [Section 20-3]   *False*

11. A party who signs an instrument while a minor may not assert that fact as a defense against payment to a holder in due course. [Section 20-3]   *False*

12. If a bank fails to pay a check that is properly drawn and for which there are sufficient funds in the depositor's account, the bank is liable to the depositor for damages. [Section 20-4]   *True*

13. A bank is not responsible for detecting forged signatures on the checks of its depositors. [Section 20-4]   *False*

14. A bank has the right not to pay any check that is more than six months old. [Section 20-4]   *True*

15. If a bank in good faith pays a depositor's check that has been altered by another party, the bank has the right to charge the depositor's account for the full amount of the check. [Section 20-4]   *False*

SOLVED PROBLEMS

PROBLEM 20-1   Kathleen wrote a check payable "to the order of Matthew Weiss." Matthew indorsed the check by signing "Matthew Weiss" on the back. What effect does this indorsement have on further negotiation of this check?

Answer: By simply signing the check, Matthew has indorsed the check with a so-called "blank" indorsement. This means that the check, which had been order paper, is now bearer paper and thus Matthew can negotiate it to any other party simply by delivering it to that party. [Section 20-2]

PROBLEM 20-2   Phil wrote a check payable to "cash." He then gave the check to Martin as payment for a debt. Martin wished to use the check as partial payment for his rent, so he indorsed it to his landlady by writing "Pay to the order of Laurie Stein, Martin Caine" on the back. What effect does this indorsement have on further negotiation of this check?

Answer: By specifying to whom the instrument is payable, Martin has indorsed the check with a so-called "special" indorsement. This means that the check, which had been bearer paper because it was payable to "cash," is now order paper. As a result, if Laurie wishes to negotiate the check further, she must now indorse it herself; simple delivery to a new holder is no longer sufficient. [Section 20-2]

PROBLEM 20-3   Robin Meyer was collecting money for her block association. One of her neighbors sent her a check that read "Payable to the order of Robin Myer." How should Robin indorse this check?

Answer: Robin can indorse the check by writing her name either the correct way or the incorrect way shown on the check. If she deposits the check in a bank account, however, the bank will most likely require her to indorse it by writing both "Robin Meyer" and "Robin Myer." [Section 20-2]

PROBLEM 20-4   A check was made payable "to the order of Grace Samuels or Jackie Benson or Art Klein." How many of these parties need to indorse this check in order for it to be negotiated?

Answer: Since the names of the payees are connected by the word *or*, the payees are payable separately and indorsement by any one of the three will be sufficient for the check to be negotiated. If the names had been connected by the word *and*, the payees would have been payable jointly, and all three would have had to indorse the check in order for it to be negotiated. [Section 20-2]

PROBLEM 20-5   The roof on Ray's house needed fixing. Walter agreed to do the job, and in return, Ray gave Walter a promissory note payable to Walter's order on May 15, the day the work was expected to be finished. On June 1, Walter approached Norma and offered to negotiate Ray's note to her in payment for a debt. Norman examined the note and found no indication that it had yet been paid. What would be Norma's situation if she accepted Walter's offer?

Answer: Ray's note is overdue since it was to be paid on May 15 and no payment has yet been made. Since this fact is apparent from the face of the instrument, Norma is deemed to have notice of it. Furthermore, since an overdue note is considered likely to have some defense or adverse claim against it, Norma is deemed to have notice of this circumstance as well. (It is very possible that Walter has failed to fix Ray's roof, and Ray is asserting this failure of consideration as a defense against paying the note.) Since this is the case, if Norma accepts Ray's note from Walter, she cannot legally qualify as a holder in due course. She can only be an ordinary holder and, as such, she too would be subject to whatever defense has so far prevented payment of the note. [Section 20-3]

PROBLEM 20-6 Betty wrote a check for $7 to the order of Stuart, a taxi driver, to pay for a ride to the station. After Betty left his cab, however, Stuart altered her check by changing "seven" dollars to "seventy" dollars and "$7" to "$70." Whereas Betty used a blue pen, Stuart made his changes in red. Stuart then took the check to a garage and attempted to negotiate it for some badly needed repairs to his cab. What would be the garage owner's situation if he accepted the check?

Answer: Stuart's alterations to Betty's check are clearly visible since Betty wrote in blue and Stuart wrote in red. Consequently, under the law, the garage owner would be deemed to have received notice that there might be some defense against the check's negotiability; i.e., Betty's defense that she is liable only for the $7 original amount. As a result, if the garage owner took the check, he would not qualify as a holder in due course. He could only be an ordinary holder and, as such, he too would be subject to Betty's defense. [Section 20-3]

PROBLEM 20-7 Julia needed a new sofa. She saw one she liked in Russell's Furniture Store, but Russell told her that he was out of stock in that model. However, he told her that he was expecting a new shipment on September 1. Julia then wrote Russell a promissory note for the price of the sofa, payable September 1. On that day Julia called the store and was told that no sofas had arrived, nor were any expected. She immediately decided to try to avoid payment of the note. The week before, however, Russell had negotiated the note to the West River Bank under circumstances permitting the bank to qualify as a holder in due course. Can Julia avoid payment of the note?

Answer: Julia cannot avoid payment of the note since the West River Bank has qualified as a holder in due course and therefore is not subject to a defense like Julia's, which is based on Russell's failure to supply consideration for her note. Julia now has no choice but to pay the bank the full value of the note and then seek to recover that sum from Russell in a separate proceeding. [Section 20-3]

PROBLEM 20-8 Rick, an unscrupulous salesman, was selling jewelry door to door. When he came to the home of Anna, a recent immigrant who could not read English, he told her that she had won a piece of jewelry as a free gift. He then had her sign a paper that he said signified acceptance of the "gift." The paper, however, was actually a promissory note obligating Anna to pay $380 in ten installments. Later that day, Rick negotiated Anna's note to Midcity Bank under circumstances that permitted the bank to qualify as a holder in due course. Must Anna pay the bank?

Answer: Anna probably will not have to pay since she signed the note unwittingly after being fraudulently informed that it was something other than a note. She can therefore assert the defense of "fraud in the essence" against payment of the note, and this defense is a universal ("real") defense that can be asserted even against a holder in due course like Midcity Bank. [Section 20-3]

PROBLEM 20-9 Mel gave his friend Rita a check to take to the drugstore to pay for a prescription. He completed the check in every way except for the amount, which he left blank because he was not sure what the prescription would cost. Rita promised to fill in the amount for him when she made the purchase. At the store, however, when the druggist presented a bill for $47, Rita filled in "$150" on the check and kept the change for herself. How will Mel's bank treat this check?

Answer: If Mel finds out what Rita has done, he can ask his bank to stop payment on the check. Otherwise, however, the bank will honor the check even though someone other than Mel filled in the amount—and with a sum that was greater than Mel wished. The bank will pay the full $150 and has the right to charge Mel's account accordingly, and it will incur no liability by doing so. [Section 20-4]

PROBLEM 20-10   Ellen wrote a check for $9, payable to the order of her friend Bernard. With great care, Bernard altered the check so that "$9" read "$90," and "nine dollars" read "ninety dollars." He then deposited the check in his own account, and his bank presented the check to Ellen's bank for payment. Ellen's bank failed to spot the alteration and paid the $90. When Ellen received the cancelled check, however, she spotted the change right away and reported it to her bank. What must the bank do for Ellen?

Answer: Under the law, although the bank has paid the altered check in good faith, it can charge Ellen's account only up to the amount she originally wrote; that is, $9. If the bank has charged $90 to her account, it must reimburse to her all but the $9; that is, $81. The bank can then seek to recoup that $81 from Bernard. [Section 20-4]

21 PRESENTMENT, LIABILITY, AND DISCHARGE

THIS CHAPTER IS ABOUT

☑ **Presentment**
☑ **Contractual Liability**
☑ **Warranty Liability**
☑ **Liability for Fraudulent Instruments**
☑ **Discharge**

21-1. Presentment

Presentment is a demand on the maker or drawee of a negotiable instrument to accept the instrument or tender the cash value that it represents. Article 3 of the UCC sets forth the requirements for presentment.

A. Presentment can be made in several ways.

1. *Clearinghouse.* The instrument can be paid by a third party acting as a clearinghouse, such as a bank, that cashes or deposits checks and other drafts.
2. *Mail.* The instrument may be mailed to the party to whom presentment is required. The time of presentment is not the time of mailing but the date of receipt by the receiving party.
3. *Specified location.* The instrument can specify the location where presentment must be made. If no place is specified, presentment can be made at the place of business or residence of the party expected to accept the instrument or tender payment.

B. The time of presentment must be reasonable and in accordance with the instrument.

The UCC provides specific guidelines for when presentment of an instrument must be made because the time of presentment can affect the liabilities of the parties involved, as will be discussed later.

1. Presentment must be made on or before a due date that is specified on an instrument.
2. An instrument made payable on demand must be presented for payment or acceptance within a reasonable time after its date of issue. The court determines reasonable times on the basis of the nature of the instrument, usage of trade, or circumstances of each case.
3. In the case of checks, a reasonable time of presentment is specified as within 30 days of the date of issuance or date of the check, whichever is longer. A check indorsed to another party should be presented within seven days of the date of indorsement.

EXAMPLE 21-1: Meredith wrote a check to Karl for $100 as payment for a table she bought from him. She asked Karl not to cash the check for two weeks so that she would have sufficient funds to cover it. Three weeks later, Karl indorsed the check and mailed it to Jan as payment for work that Jan had done for him. Jan was on vacation and did not return and deposit the check until two weeks later. When she did deposit the check, it was dishonored for insufficient funds. She contacted Karl, who reimbursed her in cash. Karl then sought reimbursement from Meredith, but she claimed that the delay in presenting the check released her from the debt. Was she correct?

Meredith was not correct. Normally, a check should be presented within 30 days and an indorsed check should be presented within seven days of indorsement. In this case, however, the court would look at the circumstances of the case to determine that presentment was not delayed unreasonably. Meredith's request that the check be held and Jan's absence when the check was mailed to her would justify the delay in presentment. In fact, Meredith's defense would likely be considered an attempt to avoid her debt. Meredith would owe Karl the $100.

C. Notice of dishonor must be given if an instrument is dishonored.

At presentment, a negotiable instrument is either accepted, paid, or dishonored. If it is dishonored, notice of dishonor must be given to any secondary parties involved in the transaction in order to establish any liability they may have for the dishonoring. Liability will be discussed in Sections 21-2 and 21-3.

1. Notice of dishonor may be given by any reasonable means.
2. Notice must be given by midnight of the third business day after dishonor occurs.
3. Notice must be given by midnight of the next business day if the holder or indorser is a bank.
4. Notice is considered to be given when it is sent, whether or not it is received or acknowledged.

21-2. Contractual Liability

Any party who signs a negotiable instrument, whether as maker, drawer, drawee, or indorser, becomes contractually liable for the instrument. A signature can be any word, mark, or name indicating a person's signature. The status of the signer determines the contractual liability the signer assumes.

A. The maker of a note and the drawee of a draft are primary parties.

A maker's or drawee's signature:

- binds him or her to pay in accordance with the terms of the instrument
- attests that the payee has the capacity to indorse
- guarantees that, if the instrument is incomplete, payment will be made upon authorized completion

B. Drawers and indorsers are secondary parties.

The contractual liability of secondary parties does not arise unless the primary party fails to pay. In the case of indorsers, primary liability cannot arise unless the rules of presentment and notice of dishonor are complied with. If the primary party fails to pay, every indorser becomes liable to the holder. In turn, the indorsers are liable to each other in the order that they signed the instrument.

EXAMPLE 21-2: Shirley wrote a check to Carlos. Carlos indorsed it over to Frank. Frank indorsed it over to Lori. When Lori attempted to deposit the check, however, it was dishonored. What was the liability of all of the parties to the check?

Shirley had primary liability for the check. Upon proper notice of dishonor, however, Carlos and Frank became liable as secondary parties for payment of the check when Shirley failed to pay. Lori could try to collect from Frank, and Frank could then collect from Carlos, who could then seek to collect from Shirley. Lori could also choose to try and collect directly from Carlos. If she chose to do this, however, Frank would have no liability to Carlos since he indorsed the check after Carlos. Carlos could still attempt to recover payment from Shirley in this case.

C. An agent can bind a principal to primary liability for a negotiable instrument.

There are several rules that an agent must follow when signing a negotiable instrument for a principal or else the agent can be held personally liable for payment.

1. The agent must clearly indicate that he or she is signing for a principal. This can be done by either signing the principal's name only, or signing the principal's name along with his or her own name, or signing his or her own name along with the word "agent."
2. The identity of the principal must be revealed.
3. The agent must have the authority to bind the principal. If the authorized agent is an officer of an organization and the organization's name appears anywhere on the instrument, then the organization is bound, not the officer.

D. An accommodation party assumes equal liability with the party being signed for.

An *accommodation party* is any person who signs a negotiable instrument for the purpose of lending credit to a party to the instrument. If the instrument is dishonored, an accommodation party becomes primarily liable for it, but may in turn collect from the party for whom he or she signed.

21-3. Warranty Liability

In addition to contractual liabilities that arise from the signatures of parties, negotiable instruments carry certain implied warranties. There are two categories of implied warranties.

A. Implied warranties are made by a transferor of a negotiable instrument.

Any party who transfers a negotiable instrument in exchange for consideration makes five warranties to all good-faith holders or transferees that come after her or him. These warranties are not limited by the manner of presentment or notice of dishonor that play a part in determining the contractual liability of secondary parties.

1. The transferor has good title to the instrument.
2. All signatures on the instrument are valid or authorized.
3. There are no material alterations on the instrument.
4. There are no present defesnses against the transferor.
5. The transferor has no notice of any insolvency of the maker, drawer, or drawee of the instrument.

EXAMPLE 21-3: Harvey stole a 30-day promissory note held by Janet and forged Janet's name to indorse it. He then sold it to his friend Bill, who was unaware of the forgery, and who indorsed it over to Gladys. Gladys then presented the note for payment. She was informed at that time that the note had been cancelled after the theft was discovered by Janet, and that Harvey was the thief. When Gladys demanded payment from Bill, however, Bill refused to pay, claiming that he was innocent of any wrongdoing, and that she should seek recovery from Harvey. Would this defense hold up in court?

Bill's defense would not hold up in court. When Bill transferred the note to Gladys, he made an implied warranty that Janet's signature on the note was valid. As a result, Bill would be liable to Gladys for the amount of the note. His own lack of knowledge about the theft would be irrelevant.

B. Implied warranties are made upon presentment of a negotiable instrument.

Any party who presents a negotiable instrument to a party who accepts or tenders payment in good faith makes three implied warranties.

1. The party presenting the instrument has good title or is authorized to receive payment for someone who has good title.
2. There are no material alterations on the instrument.
3. The presenting party has no knowledge of any unauthorized signature by the maker or drawer.

21-4. Liability for Fraudulent Instruments

In general, a person is not liable for payment of a negotiable instrument on which his or her name has been signed without authorization or approval. The forged signature acts as the signature of the forger, though, and the forger is liable for payment, even though his or her own name is not signed. There are three exceptions to this rule.

A. Negligence does not excuse a person from paying a holder in due course.

If a party is negligent in writing or signing a negotiable instrument and alteration or unauthorized signature results, that party is liable to a holder in due course. The negligent party is responsible for going after the person who altered or wrongfully signed the instrument.

EXAMPLE 21-4: Oscar made a check out for $100 as payment of a debt to his bookie. He neglected to write the amount out on the check, so the bookie changed the numbers to read "1,000" and wrote the amount in, copying Oscar's handwriting. When Oscar received the cancelled check, he demanded that the bank return $900 to his account because the check had been materially altered by the bookie. Would the court make the bank return the money?

It is unlikely that a court would make the bank return the money to Oscar's account. The court would probably find that Oscar was negligent in not writing in the amount of the check, leaving alteration easy to accomplish without any crossing out or erasing. The signature on the check was valid and the bank would have no cause to suspect that the check had been altered. Oscar's only recourse would be to go after the bookie for return of the money.

B. The indorsement of an impostor is effective.

If a person poses as someone else and a drawer makes a check out to the impostor, any indorsement by the impostor is deemed effective. The reasoning behind this rule is that the drawer is in the best position to determine the identity of a payee, rather than later holders. The drawer is responsible for going after the impostor.

C. The indorsement of a fictitious payee is effective.

The fictitious payee situation occurs most often in cases of business fraud. For instance, an employee makes a company check out to a fictitious payee, indorses the check, and pockets the money, or an employee has the employer make out the check without knowledge that the payee is fictitious or that the check is to be used to the employee's benefit. In either case, the indorsement by the fictitious payee is effective, making the company responsible for going after the wrongdoer, rather than later holders. Again, the reasoning behind this rule is that the company is in the best position to determine that the fraud is going on.

21-5. Discharge

There are several ways that the parties to a negotiable instrument may be discharged from their liability.

A. Discharge can occur by payment or satisfaction.

The most obvious method of discharge is payment or satisfaction of the debt represented by the instrument.

1. If payment is made in full by the party primarily liable for the debt, the payor and all other parties to the instrument are discharged from liability.
2. If partial payment is made by one of a number of parties liable for the debt, the payor is discharged from his or her part of the debt, and the other parties remain liable for the rest.
3. If payment is made in full by a secondary party, all other parties are discharged from liability to the payee, but they may remain liable to the secondary party who paid the debt.

B. Discharge can occur by cancellation or renunciation.

The holder of a negotiable instrument can discharge the obligated party by cancelling the instrument in several ways.

1. The holder may cancel the instrument in any intentional manner made plain and apparent on the instrument. For example, the holder may strike out the obligated party's signature or write some term indicative of the intent to cancel, such as "void," "paid," or "cancelled."
2. The holder may intentionally destroy the instrument. Unintentional destruction of an instrument does not discharge the obligated parties.
3. The holder may surrender the instrument to the obligated party.

C. Discharge can occur by impairment of recourse or collateral.

There are several circumstances where a party may be discharged because the holder of a negotiable instrument has somehow impaired his or her right of recourse to enforce the instrument.

1. If a holder discharges an indorser from liability by striking that indorser's signature, then any indorser who signs subsequent to the discharged indorser is also discharged from liability, since their right of recourse against that indorser has been impaired.

2. If a holder unjustifiably impairs collateral that an obligated party also held an interest in, then that obligated party is discharged from liability. This is most often the case when an accommodation party is relying on collateral to back up his or her credit guarantee.

EXAMPLE 21-5: Reuben wanted to take out a loan for $1,000 from County Bank to buy a motorcycle. County Bank would not loan him the money on his credit rating, so a friend of his, Joy, signed the note as an accommodation party. As it turned out, Reuben defaulted on the payments, and County Bank gave notice to Joy that they expected payment from her. Joy asked why they did not repossess the motorcycle and was told that the bank had reached an agreement with Reuben earlier whereby Reuben would sell the motorcycle and give the proceeds to the bank. Instead, Reuben had sold the motorcycle and left with the money. Consequently, Joy refused to pay on the ground that the collateral had been impaired. Would this defense hold up in court?

This defense would be upheld by the court. As an accommodation maker, Joy was discharged from liability for the debt when the holder, County Bank, gave permission to Reuben to sell the motorcycle, thus giving up their interest in the motorcycle as collateral. As a consequence of this action, the bank was also giving up Joy's right of recourse to recover against the motorcycle as collateral without her knowledge or consent. More than likely, she had relied on the motorcycle as collateral for the loan herself when she decided to sign as an accommodation party. The bank would be found to have unjustifiably impaired the collateral for the loan, and Joy would be discharged from liability.

D. Discharge can occur by material alteration of the instrument.

A fraudulent and material alteration acts to discharge any party whose rights or duties under the instrument are therefore changed. That party, however, remains liable to any subsequent holder in due course.

EXAMPLE 21-6: Andy signed a 60-day promissory note to pay Aiken Furniture $300 for a chair. The note was sent to the accounting department of the store where someone filled in the date, the agreed-upon interest rate, and Andy's telephone number. A copy was sent to Andy. When the note came due, Andy refused to pay, claiming that he was discharged from liability because the note was altered after he signed it. Was Andy correct?

Andy was not correct. For an alteration to discharge a party from liability, it must change the contract of one of the parties to the instrument. In this case, filling in the date, the agreed-upon interest rate, and Andy's telephone number did not change the agreement that Andy had made. Thus, the alteration was not material, and Andy was liable for the amount of the note.

E. Discharge can occur when the rules of presentment and notice of dishonor are not followed.

If there is an unexcused delay in the presentment of an instrument or if timely notice of dishonor is not given to secondary parties, then those secondary parties are discharged from liability for the instrument. If the instrument contains a waiver of the rules of presentment and dishonor, however, then secondary parties can be held liable.

F. Discharge can occur by compliance with a restrictive indorsement.

If a party to a negotiable instrument restricts the method or means of payment in any way, the party who pays must comply with the restriction in order to be discharged from liability for the instrument.

RAISE YOUR GRADES

Can you explain. . . .?

☑ why the rules of presentment and notice of dishonor are important when negotiating an instrument

☑ the difference between the contractual liability of a primary party and a secondary party to a negotiable instrument

☑ how an agent can be held personally liable for a negotiable instrument when signing for a principal

☑ when the rules of presentment and notice of dishonor do not serve as a defense against liability for a negotiable instrument

☑ the effect of negligence on liability for a forged or altered instrument

☑ what is meant by "material alteration"

SUMMARY

1. Presentment is a demand on the maker or drawee of a negotiable instrument to accept the instrument or tender the cash value that it represents.
2. Presentment can be made in several ways, but it must comply with any specifications made on the instrument.
3. The time of presentment must be reasonable and in accordance with the instrument.
4. Notice of dishonor must be given by any reasonable means by midnight of the third business day after dishonor occurs. Banks must give notice of dishonor by midnight of the next business day. Notice is considered to be given when it is sent.
5. Any party who signs a negotiable instrument becomes contractually liable for that instrument.
6. Makers and drawees are primary parties and warrant that they will pay in accordance with the terms of the instrument, that the payee has the capacity to indorse, and that, if the instrument is incomplete, it will be paid upon authorized completion.
7. Drawers and indorsers are secondary parties and warrant that they will pay a negotiable instrument if the primary party fails to pay and, in the case of indorsers, if the rules of due presentment and notice of dishonor are followed. In that case, every indorser becomes liable to the holder, and the indorsers become liable to each other in the order that they signed the instrument.
8. Authorized agents can bind a principal to primary liability for a negotiable instrument, but they must clearly indicate that they are signing for a principal and reveal the principal's identity. Otherwise, they can be held primarily liable for the instrument.
9. An accommodation party is anyone who signs a negotiable instrument for the purpose of lending credit to a party to the instrument and becomes primarily liable for the instrument along with the other party. An accommodation party can, however, collect from the party for whom he or she signed.
10. A transferor of a negotiable instrument warrants that he or she has good title, that all signatures are valid or authorized, that there are no material alterations on the instrument, that there are no present defenses against the transferor, and that he or she has no notice of any insolvency of the maker, drawer, or drawee of the instrument.
11. Any party who presents a negotiable instrument warrants that he or she has good title, that there are no material alterations on the instrument, and that he or she has no knowledge of any unauthorized signature by the maker or drawer.
12. In general, a person is not liable for an instrument on which his or her name has been signed without approval. Negligence or the indorsement of an impostor or fictitious payee may bar that person from this defense.
13. Discharge of liability for payment of an instrument can occur by payment or satisfaction, cancellation or renunciation, impairment of recourse or collateral, material alteration, failure to comply with the rules of presentment and notice of dishonor, or compliance with a restrictive indorsement.

RAPID REVIEW   Answers

True or False?

1. Delay in presentment of an instrument may be excused if it   *True*
   is due to circumstances beyond the control of the holder. [Section 21-1]

2. Notice of dishonor must be given in writing and mailed to all secondary parties to an instrument. [Section 21-1]   *False*

3. The drawee of a draft is released from liability if the holder does not make due presentment. [Section 21-2]   *False*

4. The holder of a dishonored instrument must seek payment of the instrument from any indorsers in the order in which they signed the instrument. [Section 21-2]   *False*

5. An agent who is authorized to sign a negotiable instrument and who clearly reveals the principal's identity and the agency relationship can bind the principal to primary liability for the instrument. [Section 21-2]   *True*

6. Implied warranties do not arise from the signatures of the parties to an instrument, but rather from the acts of transferring or presenting an instrument. [Section 21-3]   *True*

7. A party who presents a check for payment with knowledge that the maker's signature is forged is contractually liable for the instrument. [Section 21-3]   *False*

8. A person can never be held liable for payment of an instrument on which his or her name has been signed without authorization or approval. [Section 21-4]   *False*

9. Impairment of recourse can serve as a defense for an accommodation party against liability for an instrument. [Section 21-5]   *True*

10. If a holder strikes an indorser's name from an instrument, then any indorser who signs subsequent to that indorser's name has had their right of recourse impaired. [Section 21-5]   *True*

11. A maker who writes "for deposit only to Account #21851" on a check and indorses it to a bank has placed a restrictive indorsement on that check that the bank must comply with or it can be held liable for the amount of the check. [Section 21-5]   *True*

SOLVED PROBLEMS

PROBLEM 21-1   Howard forged his brother's name, Leroy, to a 30-day promissory note payable to Glenda. Glenda, unaware of the forgery, indorsed the note and sold it to Mildred. Two months passed before Mildred presented the note to Leroy for payment. Leroy refused to pay, claiming that his name had been forged by Howard. A week later, Mildred gave notice to Glenda that the note had been dishonored. Glenda refused to pay. Mildred then contacted Howard, who refused to pay on the basis of unreasonable delay in presentment. Discuss the liability of Howard for payment of the note to Mildred.

Answer: Howard would not be successful in his defense of undue presentment. He would be held liable as the maker of the note, even though his own name was not signed to the note. As a maker, he would be contractually liable as a primary party for the note. The defense of undue presentment is not available to makers, only to indorsers. Mildred would be allowed to collect on the note from Howard. [Section 21-2]

PROBLEM 21-2   Creative Enterprises, a contracting agency for authors, owed $2000 to Hilltop Publishers. After much prodding by the publishers, Carmen, the president of the agency, sent a check for the amount. Although the check was to be drawn from the account of Creative Enterprises, there was no indication of this on the check and Carmen had signed just his own name to the check. As it turned out, the check was dishonored, and Hilltop Publishers filed suit against Carmen for the amount of the check. Carmen defended on the ground that he signed the check as an agent of the company, and did not intend to be personally bound by it. Who won the case?

Answer: Hilltop Publishers won the suit. The rules are very clear regarding the personal liability of agents. An agent can be held personally liable for an instrument if the instrument does not name the principal represented or otherwise indicate that the agent signed in a representative capacity. Thus, in this case, Carmen was personally liable for the amount of the check. [Section 21-2]

PROBLEM 21-3 Parker wrote a check for $1,000 to Ruth. Ruth attempted to cash the check at her bank, but the bank called Parker's bank and was told that there were insufficient funds to cover the check. Consequently, Ruth's bank refused to cash the check. Later, Ruth indorsed the check over to Trudy as payment for a debt. When Trudy tried to cash the check, her bank also refused to cash it, after calling Parker's bank. A week later, Trudy told Ruth about the dishonoring, but Ruth refused to pay because she had not been given proper notice of dishonor. Would Trudy be able to recover from Ruth, even though proper notice of dishonor was not given?

Answer: Trudy would be able to recover from Ruth. Notice of dishonor within three business days of the time of dishonor is required to hold an indorser contractually liable for a check. In this case, however, Trudy could recover from Ruth on the ground of breach of implied warranty. Ruth had knowledge when she transferred the check that Parker was insolvent. A defense of lack of proper notice of dishonor would not be effective against a charge of breach of implied warranty. [Section 21-3]

PROBLEM 21-4 Myrtle stole a pocketbook belonging to Vera. Vera's checkbook was in the pocketbook, so Myrtle had a cashier's check drawn against Vera's account the next day. Later that day, she indorsed the check and cashed it at another bank. The next day, Vera called the bank president and informed him that she wanted to void the series numbers of the stolen checks. The president told her that a cashier's check had already been issued for $200. Vera demanded that the bank return the money to her account. The bank refused to, saying that she would have to attempt to find and prosecute Myrtle to get the money back. Who was correct?

Answer: Vera was correct in demanding that the bank return her money. Myrtle was an impostor when she had a cashier's check issued at Vera's bank. The law provides that any drawer who makes a check out to an impostor is in the best position to determine the true identity of the impostor. Thus, in this case, the bank would have to return the $200 to Vera's account and go after Myrtle to recover the money. [Section 21-4]

PROBLEM 21-5 Barney signed a promissory note as an accommodation party along with Linda, the maker. The note was payable to Sherry. The note specified that the rules of presentment and notice of dishonor were waived. Sherry indorsed the note and sold it to Margaret. Margaret eventually indorsed the note over to Jimmy. When the note came due, Linda said that she couldn't pay it for another month, so Jimmy filed suit against Barney, Sherry, and Margaret to recover the money. Would any of these parties have a defense against liability for payment?

Answer: The only party who could defend against liability would be Barney as an accommodation party. By granting an extension of time to Linda, Barney was discharged from liability due to impairment of his right of recourse. Sherry and Margaret, however, would have no defense against liability as indorsers because the note contained a provision waiving their defense of delay in presentment or lack of notice of dishonor, both of which are the only defenses available to an indorser against liability for a dishonored instrument. [Section 21-5]

PROBLEM 21-6   Suppose that the promissory note from Problem 21-5 had not contained the provision that the rules of presentment and notice of dishonor were waived. Would this change the liability of Sherry and Margaret for payment of the note?

Answer: The extension of time that was granted by Jimmy to Linda would not affect the liability of Sherry and Margaret. It would be deemed a reasonable delay under the circumstances. Sherry and Margaret may be able to defend, however, on the ground that Jimmy did not comply with the rules for giving notice of dishonor. [Section 21-5]

22 SECURED TRANSACTIONS AND BANKRUPTCY

THIS CHAPTER IS ABOUT

☑ **Creation of a Secured Interest**
☑ **Perfected Security Interests**
☑ **Priorities of Creditors**
☑ **Default**
☑ **The Bankruptcy Act**
☑ **Liquidation (Chapter 7)**
☑ **Reorganization (Chapter 11)**
☑ **Adjustment of Debts (Chapter 13)**

22-1. Creation of a Secured Interest

Article 9 of the UCC deals with secured transactions. Any transaction in which a debtor gives a creditor an interest in personal property or fixtures in order to secure payment or performance of a debt is a *secured transaction*. The property given as security is known as *collateral*. All secured transactions have three basic elements that operate to create an enforceable security interest between the parties.

A. A security agreement must exist between the parties.

The *security agreement* describes the transaction and demonstrates the intent of the parties to create a security interest.

1. The security agreement must be in writing unless the creditor has possession of the collateral.
2. The writing must reasonably identify and describe the collateral. It should also specify under what terms the debt is to be paid and what constitutes default.
3. The debtor and the creditor must sign the agreement to be bound by its terms.

B. Some form of value must be given in exchange for the security interest.

The creditor must give sufficient consideration to support a simple contract. In most cases, this value is in the form of a direct loan or the extension of future credit.

C. The debtor must have rights in the collateral.

The debtor must have some type of present or future ownership interest in the collateral.

EXAMPLE 22-1: Ralph borrowed $5,000 from a local bank. As collateral, Ralph offered and the bank accepted the interest that Ralph would acquire in his uncle's farm upon his uncle's death. A security agreement was written setting forth the terms of payment and describing the location and interest in the collateral. Both Ralph and the bank representatives signed the security agreement. Did an enforceable security interest exist between Ralph and the bank?

An enforceable security interest did exist between Ralph and the bank. All of the requirements for an enforceable security interest were met in that a written security agreement stating the terms of payment and describing the collateral was signed by both parties. Also, the loan was given as value for the security interest. The possibility exists, however, that the bank would be unable to enforce the security interest until long after Ralph defaulted on the loan, because the bank could take no action against the collateral until Ralph actually received his interest in the farm.

22-2. Perfected Security Interests

Other parties (such as other creditors or buyers of the collateral) could conceivably make claims against the same collateral that is used as a security interest. A creditor can protect his or her interest in collateral by creating a *perfected security interest* that serves as public notice of the existence of the security interest.

A. A perfected security interest can be created by filing a financing statement with the proper authorities.

A *financing statement* must include the names and addresses of the debtor and the creditor, a description of the collateral involved, and the signature of the debtor.

B. The place of filing depends on the type of collateral being used as a security interest.

Depending on the type of collateral, filing may be required with the county recorder in the county of the debtor's residence or the county where the collateral is located, or centrally with the Secretary of State.

C. Filing perfects the security interest for five years.

During the last six months of a filing, a *continuation statement* may be filed extending the perfected security interest for another five years, and may be filed every five years thereafter until the obligation is fulfilled by the debtor. An exception is collateral for mortgage loans, which are valid from the time of filing until the loan is paid. In the case of consumer goods used as collateral, a *termination statement* must also be filed within one month (or ten days, if requested by the debtor) of fulfillment of the obligation.

D. A perfected security interest is automatic if the creditor has possession of the collateral.

In some cases, the creditor may retain possession of the collateral until the obligation is fulfilled by the debtor. In such cases, a perfected security interest is automatic, and no financial statement need be filed.

EXAMPLE 22-2: Greta gave her watch to a pawnbroker as collateral for a $50 loan. She was supposed to return in one week to repay the debt and get her watch back. Did the pawnbroker have to file a financing statement in order to perfect his security interest in the watch?

The pawnbroker did not have to file a financing statement. The security interest in the watch was automatically perfected because the pawnbroker had possession of the collateral.

22-3. Priorities of Creditors

As mentioned earlier, claims may be made by third parties against collateral held by a creditor. The rights and priorities of such claimants are set forth in Article 9 with regard to unperfected security interests, perfected security interests, and conflicting claims against such interests.

A. An unperfected security interest has the lowest priority against other claims.

1. A perfected security interest will prevail over an unperfected security interest.
2. A lien creditor will prevail over an unperfected security interest. A *lien creditor* is anyone to whom a court grants possession or control of a debtor's property so it can be used to satisfy a debt.
3. A buyer or transferee will prevail over an unperfected security interest if he or she gives value for the collateral without knowing of the security interest.
4. When collateral is used for more than one unperfected security interest, the first creditor to attach the collateral has priority. *Attachment* is a seizure of a debtor's property granted by the court for use in satisfying a later judgment.

B. A perfected security interest has the highest priority against other claims.

1. A creditor with a perfected security interest will prevail over all subsequent buyers. An exception to this rule is that a buyer in the ordinary course of business takes free of any security interest, even if he or she is aware of the security interest, so long as he or she is not aware that the purchase is in violation of the security agreement.

EXAMPLE 22-3: A bank had loaned Musicland, a wholesaler of musical instruments, $50,000 to finance its inventory. The bank took a security interest in the inventory as collateral for the loan and perfected it by filing a financing statement. Musicland sold a piano out of its inventory to Barbara, who wanted her son to take piano lessons. Musicland later defaulted on its payments to the bank. Could the bank claim its security interest in the piano sold to Barbara?

The bank could not claim its security interest in the piano sold to Barbara. Barbara was a buyer in the ordinary course of business. Thus, she took the piano free of the bank's security interest, even though Musicland defaulted on the loan. The reason for this rule is obviously that consumers should not be expected to investigate whether a security interest exists on every item they wish to purchase.

2. A lien upon goods created by statute prevails over a perfected security interest unless the law expressly provides otherwise.
3. When collateral is used for more than one perfected security interest, priority is established as to which security interest was filed first or, if filed on the same day, which security interest was granted perfection first.

22-4. Default

In general, any breach of the security agreement constitutes a *default*.

A. A creditor has several options available in case of debtor's default.

After default, the creditor may either:

• sue the debtor for what is owed
• take possession of the collateral as satisfaction of the obligation
• take possession of the collateral, sell it, and either sue for any deficiency or return any surplus to the debtor

B. A creditor must comply with Article 9 concerning repossession or resale of collateral.

A creditor can be liable to the debtor if any harm results from the improper repossession or sale of collateral. Thus, the UCC is specific as to the procedure to be followed for such action.

1. Repossession may not take place if the security agreement states otherwise.
2. The creditor may take possession if it can be done without disturbing the peace.
3. If repossession by the creditor would disturb the peace, the creditor must seek court action to repossess the collateral.
4. If the collateral is intangible, such as negotiable instruments, the creditor may give notice to have payments made or performance given to him or her.
5. A sale of the collateral may be public or private and must be handled in a commercially reasonable manner.
6. Notice of the sale must be given to the debtor unless the goods are perishable or rapidly declining in value.
7. After the sale, the proceeds must be distributed first to cover any reasonable costs of repossession and sale, then to satisfy the debt, then to the debtor if there is any surplus.
8. If the sale does not cover the costs of the repossession, sale, and debt, the creditor may sue the debtor for any deficiency.

EXAMPLE 22-4: Wally had taken a loan for $30,000 to purchase cooking equipment for his restaurant. The equipment was taken as security for the loan and was perfected by the bank. Wally defaulted on the loan when he still owed $21,000. The bank repossessed the equipment and gave notice to Wally that the equipment would be sold in a private sale. At the time, the equipment was valued at $25,000. Wally assumed that the equipment was being sold to another restaurant. Instead, he received notice that he was being sued for a deficiency of $11,000 plus costs that remained after the sale, and that the bank had purchased the equipment itself for $10,000 without attempting to find any other buyers. Will Wally have to pay the deficiency?

It is unlikely that Wally will have to pay the deficiency. The court would find that the bank did not conduct the sale in a commercially reasonable manner. Not only did the bank make no attempt to contact any bona fide buyers, but it purchased the equipment itself for an amount well below what the equipment was worth. Since the bank was certainly not in the restaurant business, it would appear that the bank purchased the equipment with the intent of collecting the deficiency from Wally and then reselling the equipment again for its true value. Consequently, Wally would be harmed by the bank's improper sale and the deficiency amount and costs remaining on the loan would probably be dismissed as damages.

22-5. The Bankruptcy Act

Bankruptcy is a legal proceeding that allows relief to individuals, businesses, and governmental organizations in the event that they are unable to pay their debts. Proceedings are held in federal court and are based on the federal Bankruptcy Act. The Act governs four kinds of bankruptcy, three of which regulate bankruptcy proceedings for individuals and businesses. These three will be discussed briefly.

22-6. Liquidation (Chapter 7)

In a *liquidation* proceeding, the debtor (whether an individual or a business) must turn over all assets to a court-approved trustee for liquidation and distribution of the proceeds to the debtor's creditors.

A. The filing of a petition with the bankruptcy court initiates the proceedings.

The filing of a petition for bankruptcy puts an automatic stay on any present or future action against the debtor regarding his or her debts. The petition must include a list of all creditors and a list of all assets of the debtor. Filing can be voluntary or involuntary.

1. *Voluntary petition.* A voluntary petition may be filed by an individual, a partnership, or a corporation.
2. *Involuntary petition.* When twelve or more creditors have claims against a debtor, then three of them can file a petition for involuntary bankruptcy against the debtor, provided their debts total at least $5,000 more than the value of any collateral. If there are fewer than twelve creditors, any one can file a petition for involuntary bankruptcy if the debt is $5,000 more than any collateral. Involuntary petitions cannot be filed against some types of businesses, such as banks.

B. An order for relief must be issued to continue the proceedings.

If a debtor files a voluntary petition or does not contest an involuntary petition for bankruptcy, an order for relief is automatic. If a debtor contests an involuntary petition, the bankruptcy court hears the case to decide if an order for relief should be issued.

C. A trustee is appointed to take control of the debtor's assets.

The court may appoint an interim trustee to immediately take control of the debtor's property or business. A meeting is then held with the creditors and debtor to select a permanent trustee, who must be approved by the court, and to question the debtor about his or her financial affairs. The trustee's duties are:

- to set aside any property that state or federal statutes allow the debtor to keep
- to collect all remaining assets and liquidate them
- to examine all creditors' claims for validity and for purposes of establishing priorities among them
- to pay outstanding debts to the extent possible, with the power to sue or be sued as the representative of the debtor's estate

D. The debtor can be discharged from remaining debts after the bankruptcy proceedings.

The debtor must be honest in all dealings with the bankruptcy court. If it is found at any time that the debtor is lying about financial affairs or hiding assets, then the court can cancel the bankruptcy and the debtor becomes liable to all claims of creditors for all debts again. If the debtor has acted honestly with the court, all debts can be discharged with the exception of a few types of debts that are not dischargeable by law, such as federal taxes.

EXAMPLE 22-5: Brad filed a voluntary petition for bankruptcy under Chapter 7 of the Bankruptcy Act. During an investigation into Brad's financial affairs, however, the trustee discovered that within the three weeks prior to Brad's filing for bankruptcy, Brad had sold a car valued at $6,000 to his daughter for $50, had transferred stock certificates valued at over $25,000 to his son "for his college education," and had put other property in his children's names as well. What will be the likely result of these actions?

These actions would be viewed as an attempt to hide assets from the bankruptcy court. Although Brad's intentions may very well have been good to give something to his children before all of his assets were liquidated, nonetheless, the court would either order that the transactions be voided and the assets turned over to the trustee, or that the petition for bankruptcy be dismissed, submitting Brad to the full claims of all of his creditors.

22-7. Reorganization (Chapter 11)

Chapter 11 of the Bankruptcy Act governs the reorganization of businesses faced with financial difficulties. In a *reorganization*, a plan is formulated between the debtor and the creditors to reduce, adjust, pay, or discharge outstanding debts, while avoiding liquidation and continuing the business.

A. Initiating a reorganization proceeding is the same as for a liquidation proceeding.

The rules for initiating a bankruptcy proceeding under Chapter 11 are the same as those for Chapter 7 regarding voluntary and involuntary filing of petitions and issuance of an order for relief.

B. The debtor must file a plan for satisfying all debts.

After the entry of an order for relief, the debtor or trustee has 120 days to file a plan for handling the claims of creditors. The plan must classify all claims and specify how each class will be satisfied.

C. The plan is submitted to creditors for approval.

In general, each class of creditors must approve the plan by a two-thirds majority. If approved by the creditors, the court must then confirm the plan as fair and reasonable to all concerned. Either the debtor or a trustee, if warranted by the court, continues to manage the business and must abide by the plan.

EXAMPLE 22-6: An involuntary petition for bankruptcy under Chapter 11 was filed by the creditors of Melinda's construction company. Despite Melinda's protest, an order for relief was issued by the court. At the meeting between the creditors, the trustee, and Melinda, the creditors complained that a big reason for Melinda's current financial difficulties was that her bookkeeping practices were so poor that many accounts owed to Melinda had never even been billed. What, if anything, can the trustee do about this situation?

The trustee can propose to the bankruptcy court that Melinda's business should be turned over to the trustee for management in order to straighten out the bookkeeping and collect on accounts owed. Most likely, if Melinda's poor bookkeeping were taken as evidence of mismanagement and a contributing factor to the poor state of her financial affairs, the court would order the trustee to take over the business.

22-8. Adjustment of Debts (Chapter 13)

Adjustment of debts allows individual debtors who have regular incomes to develop a plan to satisfy their debts. In essence, the plan protects debtors from the claims of creditors while they pay their debts in installments. This plan benefits both debtors and creditors in that debtors can retain possession of property and creditors generally recover more of the debt owed to them than they would get as a result of liquidation proceedings.

A. The proceedings can only be initiated by voluntary petition.

Only an individual who owes secured debts of less than $350,000 and unsecured debts of less than $100,000 can file a petition for protection under Chapter 13.

B. The debtor must submit a plan for satisfaction of debts.

Unlike Chapter 11, only the debtor may file a plan for the payment of debts not to exceed a three-year period, unless the court approves a longer period of time. The plan is subject to confirmation by the court. If the debtor fails to file an acceptable plan, the court may dismiss Chapter 13 proceedings and the debtor loses protection from any actions by creditors. The debtor may either seek a composition or an extension of debts.

1. A *composition of debts* is an arrangement where the amount owed is reduced.
2. An *extension of debts* is an arrangement granting the debtor a longer period of time to pay debts.

C. The court can discharge all debts after performance of the plan.

The court can discharge all debts covered by the plan. The court may even discharge the debts without completion of the plan if the court regards the failure as due to circumstances beyond the debtor's control. If the debtor defaults on the plan, however, the court can dismiss the Chapter 13 protection, and creditors may proceed with full claims against the debtor.

EXAMPLE 22-7: Bruce had a monthly income of $900 and very few assets. His rent was $300 a month, other living expenses cost him $250 a month, and he had monthly payments due to creditors of $150, $75, and $90, on a total debt of $7,380. Unfortunately, Bruce was laid off from his job for two months and fell behind in his payments to creditors. At the same time, he found out that his rent was going up to $350 a month. He filed for protection under Chapter 13 after receiving notice of actions against him by his creditors. What sort of plan could Bruce submit to the court?

Bruce's rent and other living expenses are fixed at $600 a month. He could submit a plan asking for an extension of his debts whereby he would agree to pay the three creditors $95, $45, and $65 a month respectively over a three-year period, rather than over the shorter period that the payments are scheduled for. At the end of the three-year period, the total debt of $7,380 would be paid in full. The bankruptcy court could, in its discretion, confirm this plan as being offered in good faith and being fair to all concerned.

RAISE YOUR GRADES

Can you explain . . . ?

☑ the three elements necessary to create an enforceable security interest
☑ why a creditor should perfect his or her security interest
☑ the actions available to a creditor if a debtor defaults on a loan
☑ how a creditor can lose the right to seek a deficiency judgment against a debtor
☑ the difference between the relief available under Chapters 7, 11, and 13 of the Bankruptcy Act
☑ the possible consequences of a debtor's failure to act in good faith in dealing with a bankruptcy court

SUMMARY

1. Article 9 of the UCC deals with secured transactions. A secured transaction is any transaction in which a debtor gives a creditor an interest in personal property or fixtures in order to secure payment of a debt.
2. In order to create an enforceable security interest, a security agreement must exist between the parties, some form of value must be given in exchange for the security interest, and the debtor must have some type of present or future ownership rights in the collateral.
3. A perfected security interest serves as public notice of the existence of a security interest.
4. A financing statement must be filed with the proper authorities to perfect a security interest. If the creditor has possession of the collateral, perfection is automatic.
5. Filing generally perfects the security interest for five years. A continuation statement may be filed to extend the perfected security interest for another five years. In the case of consumer goods used as collateral, a termination statement must also be filed when the debt is fulfilled.

6. The UCC establishes the priorities of third-party claimants against the same collateral.

7. A perfected security interest, a lien creditor, and a buyer or transferee who is unaware of the security interest will prevail over an unperfected security interest. When collateral is used for more than one unperfected security interest, the first creditor to attach the collateral will prevail.

8. A buyer in the ordinary course of business and a lien created by statute will prevail over a perfected security interest. When collateral is used for more than one perfected interest, the first creditor to file a financing statement or be granted perfection will prevail.

9. In general, any breach of the security agreement constitutes a default.

10. Upon default, a creditor may sue the debtor for the amount owed, take possession of the collateral as satisfaction of the debt, or take possession of the collateral, resell it, and either sue the debtor for any deficiency or return any surplus to the debtor.

11. The UCC sets forth specific guidelines for the repossession and resale of collateral by a creditor. Failure to observe these procedures can result in the creditor's being liable to the debtor for any harm that may result.

12. The Bankruptcy Act allows relief to individuals, businesses, and governmental organizations if they are unable to pay their debts.

13. In a liquidation proceeding (Chapter 7), the debtor must turn over all assets to a court-approved trustee for liquidation and distribution of the proceeds to the debtor's creditors.

14. Bankruptcy proceedings are initiated by the filing of a petition with the bankruptcy court that puts an automatic stay on any present or future actions of the debtor's creditors. The petition must include all creditors and a list of all assets of the debtor and can be voluntary or involuntary.

15. An order for relief is issued by the bankruptcy court.

16. If the debtor has acted in good faith with the bankruptcy court, all remaining debts can be discharged with the exception of a few that are not dischargeable by law.

17. A reorganization proceeding (Chapter 11) is initiated in the same way as a liquidation proceeding, but a plan is then formulated between the debtor and the creditors to reduce, adjust, pay, or discharge outstanding debts while avoiding liquidation and continuing the business.

18. An adjustment of debts proceeding (Chapter 13) can only be initiated voluntarily by an individual with regular income and with limited debts. A plan is developed to satisfy all debts, generally within a three-year period, either by reducing or extending the debt. Upon completion of the plan, all remaining debts can be discharged.

RAPID REVIEW   Answers

True or False

1. A security agreement need not include the terms under which a debt is to be paid in order to be enforceable. [Section 22-1]	*False*
2. A financing statement need not include the terms under which a debt is to be paid in order to perfect a security interest. [Section 22-2]	*True*
3. A creditor with a perfected security interest will prevail over all subsequent buyers. [Section 22-3]	*False*
4. Upon default, a creditor may take possession of collateral if it can be done without disturbing the peace. [Section 22-4]	*True*
5. A sale of collateral may be public or private and must be handled in a commercially reasonable manner. [Section 22-4]	*True*
6. Upon default, a creditor may file an involuntary petition for bankruptcy against a debtor. [Section 22-6]	*False*
7. An order for relief is automatic unless a debtor contests an involuntary petition for bankruptcy. [Section 22-6]	*True*
8. In a reorganization proceeding, a trustee is appointed by the court to run the debtor's business. [Section 22-7]	*False*

9. A plan for satisfying debts under a reorganization proceeding must be approved by all creditors of the business. [Section 22-7]

False

10. In an adjustment of debts proceeding, a debtor must file an acceptable plan evidencing a good-faith effort to satisfy all debts. [Section 22-8]

True

SOLVED PROBLEMS

PROBLEM 22-1   Harvey, a farmer, agreed to buy a used pickup truck for $3,500 from his neighbor, Jean. Jean let him take the truck after Harvey gave her $1,500 as a down payment and promised to pay the remaining $2000 when he sold his crops at the end of the year. Unfortunately, Harvey's crop yield was low that year because of little rain, so he was barely able to cover his operating costs, much less pay Jean the $2,000. He offered to pay Jean another $1,000 now and the other $1,000 in six more months, but Jean insisted that she was taking the truck back. Could Jean do this?

Answer: Jean could not take the truck back. Jean did not establish an enforceable security interest in the truck by executing a security agreement between she and Harvey. Nor did she have possession of the truck when Harvey defaulted, which would have given her an automatic security interest in the truck. Jean's only recourse would be to either accept Harvey's tender of performance or sue him for the $2,000. [Section 22-1]

PROBLEM 22-2   Beverly purchased a washer, dryer, refrigerator, dishwasher, and stove on credit from an appliance dealer. For each purchase, she signed a security agreement giving the terms for payment and giving the appliances as collateral for the loans. The appliance dealer perfected the security interests by filing financing statements. Beverly completed payment for the appliances one year later. A year after that, she applied for credit to purchase a new car and was turned down for the loan. The bank she was trying to borrow from had discovered the five secured interests against loans filed with the county recorder, none of which had she put on her credit application. The bank had therefore assumed that she was not being honest about debt liability. Could Beverly do anything about this situation?

Answer: Beverly could seek penalties against the appliance dealer. In cases where consumer goods are put up as collateral and perfected by filing a financing statement, a termination statement must also be filed upon satisfaction of the debt. Since the appliance dealer did not do this and, as a result, Beverly was turned down for credit, the appliance dealer would be subject to penalties under the law. [Section 22-2]

PROBLEM 22-3   Rhonda bought a desk and typewriter from a business supply store on credit, signing a security agreement that gave the business supply store an unperfected security interest in the property. A year later, a judgment was entered against Rhonda for failure to repay a different loan, and a lien was placed on the desk and typewriter, as well as other items of furniture for satisfaction of the debt. Later, Rhonda also fell behind in her payments to the business supply store. Would the store be allowed to repossess the desk and typewriter?

Answer: The business supply store would not be allowed to repossess the desk and typewriter. It held an unperfected security interest in the desk and typewriter that was secondary to a lien creditor's claim to the property. A situation like this represents why it is advisable that a creditor perfect his or her security interest in property. [Section 22-3]

PROBLEM 22-4   Denise borrowed $7,000 from Auto Credit Corp. to buy a new car. Auto Credit Corp. kept a secured interest in the car in case of default. Unfortunately, Denise was laid off from her job and she fell behind on the payments. Consequently, Auto Credit Corp. repossessed the car. At the time, the car had a market value of $5,000. Auto Credit Corp. notified Denise that they were reselling the car. Over a year later, however, Denise received notice that she was being sued for a deficiency remaining after the sale, and found out that Auto Credit Corp. had waited a year to sell the car and had then sold it to an employee for $2,500. Will Denise have to pay the deficiency?

Answer: Denise will not have to pay the deficiency. Article 9 of the UCC imposes certain standards on creditors for the repossession and resale of collateral. The purpose for these rules is much like the obligation of mitigating damages of a nonbreaching party to a contract. In this case, holding the car for another year caused the car to drop further in value than it had at the time of repossession. Furthermore, selling the car to an employee for $2,500 might be seen as an unfair sale, unless it could be shown that the credit company tried to get other buyers. The sale would therefore be seen as not being conducted in a commercially reasonable manner, and Denise would not have to pay the deficiency because of the harm caused by this. [Section 22-4]

PROBLEM 22-5   Aurora, the owner of a pet shop, had fallen behind in her payments to pet food companies, pet suppliers, pet care products suppliers, and other creditors. Together, her creditors held unsecured amounts of $12,000 outstanding against the business. Furthermore, her store had been operating at a loss for three years. What can the creditors do to try and collect the amounts owed to them.

Answer: The creditors have several options. They could each sue the business individually for the amount owed. Since Aurora's business had been operating at a loss for three years, however, it is unlikely that they could collect the full amounts. If there are at least 12 creditors, three of which hold at least $5,000 in unsecured debts, then they could file a petition for involuntary bankruptcy against Aurora's business. If they believe that her business can be made profitable, their best chance of recovering the full amount would be to file under Chapter 11 for a reorganization proceeding. Under Chapter 11, Aurora's business would continue and they might realize a higher payback of the amount owed. If it appears that Aurora's business is not salvageable, they might file under Chapter 7, calling for the liquidation of the business and a distribution of the proceeds in as fair a manner as possible. [Sections 22-6 and 22-7]

PROBLEM 22-6   Curtis had been paying his creditors according to a court approved plan under Chapter 13 for about 2½ years. Unfortunately, with only six months to go on the plan, he suffered an accident at work and was put on temporary disability income that was well below his usual take-home pay. Consequently, he was unable to complete the payment plan. Would the bankruptcy court revoke the protection of Chapter 13 and allow Curtis' creditors to go after him?

Answer: The court would not revoke Curtis' protection under Chapter 13. In a Chapter 13 proceeding, all debts are usually discharged upon full completion of the payment plan. In this case, however, a discharge would still be granted by the court because Curtis' failure to complete the plan was due to circumstances beyond his control. [Section 22-8]

23 REAL PROPERTY, ESTATES, AND TRUSTS

THIS CHAPTER IS ABOUT

☑ **Real Property**
☑ **Possessory and Nonpossessory Interests in Real Property**
☑ **Concurrent Ownership of Real Property**
☑ **Transfer of Ownership by Deed**
☑ **Other Methods of Acquiring Ownership**
☑ **Estates**
☑ **Wills**
☑ **Trusts**
☑ **Intestate Succession**

23-1. Real Property

Real property, also known as *realty*, is generally of a fixed and permanent nature, such as land, buildings, trees, shrubs, and minerals found in the earth. *Personal property*, also known as *personalty*, is generally movable and lacking a permanent physical location. Items of personal property may be treated as real property, as in the case of fixtures. *Fixtures* are items of personal property that are attached to real property in such a way that they are considered to be a part of the real property.

EXAMPLE 23-1: Valerie had been renting an apartment for several years. She had put in a window air-conditioner, laid an oriental carpet in the bedroom, and had built bookshelves into the walls of the living room. Would Valerie's landlord have the right to demand that she leave any of this property when she moves out?

Although the air-conditioner, the carpet, and the bookshelves were all purchased by Valerie and were her personal property, the bookshelves could conceivably be considered real property that would have to remain in the apartment when Valerie moves out. The facts that the shelves were built in (as opposed to a free-standing shelf unit) and that damage to the walls could occur if she removed them are strong arguments for considering the shelves a fixture that has become a part of the apartment itself.

23-2. Possessory and Nonpossessory Interests in Real Property

A variety of interests can be created in real property other than just those of the owner.

A. A person may have a possessory interest in real property.

1. *Fee simple absolute*. This is the highest form of ownership and possession. It grants the owner and his or her heirs all interests in the land forever with no restrictions. A person who owns land in fee simple may grant rights on the land to others without giving up absolute ownership.
2. *Life estate*. A person who has a life estate interest in real property has absolute possession of the land, but only for her or his lifetime or the lifetime of someone else. Such a person's rights in the property are limited to the extent that she or he may not do anything that would cause permanent harm to the land.

3. *Leasehold.* A leasehold grants possession to a tenant, but ownership remains with the landlord. A tenant is restricted from causing any harm to the property and is subject to losing possession at any time called for by the landlord or the lease agreement.

B. A person may have a nonpossessory interest in real property.

1. *Easement.* An easement gives a person a limited right to use someone's land for a specific purpose but not to actually occupy or possess the land in any way. Easements can be created in many ways, either express or implied, and can be affirmative or negative.

   (*a*) An affirmative easement is the right to make specific uses of property, such as a utility company's right to run power lines over someone's property.

   (*b*) A negative easement is the right to restrict someone who holds adjoining property from making certain uses of that property, such as restricting a neighbor from building within 20 feet of the joint property line.

EXAMPLE 23-2: Frances owned 50 acres of farmland fronted by one highway and surrounded on three sides by woods. She sold the back 20 acres to Kelly, knowing of Kelly's intention of building a home on the land. After the sale, Kelly went out to the property, only to find that the only access road, which went through Frances' property, now had a gate across it that was locked. When confronted, Frances said that Kelly could not cross her land to get to the back property. Could Frances deny Kelly the use of the road?

Frances could not deny Kelly the use of the road. Easements can be created in many ways. In this case, Kelly would be granted an implied easement to use the road by necessity. In other words, Kelly cannot be denied the beneficial use of her land and Frances would have to allow Kelly an easement to cross her property.

2. *License.* A license gives a person the right to use another's land also, but for a limited and specific purpose, such as the right to hunt or fish on another's land. A license can be revoked at any time by the owner of the property.

3. *Profit.* A profit gives a person the right to acquire a possessory interest in another's land, such as the right to take minerals or timber from land. An easement is generally implied to give that person the ability to take the profit.

23-3. Concurrent Ownership of Real Property

Two or more people, known as *cotenants*, may have an ownership interest in the same realty at the same time. Different states recognize various types of cotenancies, but there are three main types.

A. Several people may share a tenancy in common.

A *tenancy in common* exists when each tenant is considered to share an undivided interest in real property. The shares do not have to be equal, but regardless of the size of the shares, each tenant may occupy the whole property, subject to the rights of the other tenants. Each cotenant may sell or mortgage his or her share in the property at any time or, upon death, the interest passes to his or her heirs.

B. Several people may share a joint tenancy.

A *joint tenancy* exists when an undivided interest in real property is conveyed at one time to two or more people by a single document that specifies that they are to be joint tenants. The significant characteristic of a joint tenancy is the right of survivorship. Upon the death of a joint tenant, his or her interest passes immediately to the remaining joint tenants and is not subject to the debts of the decedent. A joint tenancy can be severed by any one or more of the joint tenants at any time. When this happens, it becomes a tenancy in common, and the right of survivorship is lost.

EXAMPLE 23-3: Simon and James, who were close friends, bought a farm together. Two documents were drawn up indicating that they had an equal interest in the farm. Although not specified in the documents, they agreed between them that, if one of them died, the other would get the entire farm. Would the court uphold this desire?

The court would only uphold this desire if it were put in writing in a will. By law, Simon and James have a tenancy in common because the documents for their interests in the farm were drawn up separately and they were not named as joint tenants. Should one of them die, his interest would go to his heirs. To create a joint tenancy, which would carry the right of survivorship, one document should have been prepared naming them as joint tenants in the land.

C. A husband and wife may share a tenancy by the entirety.

A *tenancy by the entirety* can exist only between a husband and wife. It is just like a joint tenancy in its creation with the same undivided interest in property and the right of survivorship. The difference is that it cannot be severed without the consent of both parties.

23-4. Transfer of Ownership by Deed

The requirements for transferring ownership of real property are set forth by each state. In general, all states require that ownership can only be transferred by sale or by gift through the proper execution and delivery of a deed. A *deed* is a written instrument whereby the property owner, called the *grantor*, conveys her or his interest in the property to another, called the *grantee*.

A. A deed must include certain information.

Each state sets forth its requirements for the proper execution of deeds. In general, however, a deed must:

- be in writing
- identify the grantor and the grantee
- state consideration given
- identify the property with reasonable certainty
- be signed by the grantor

B. There are three main types of deeds.

1. In a *general warranty deed*, the grantor warrants the title against any defects or encumbrances arising before or after his or her ownership of the property.
2. In a *special warranty deed*, the grantor warrants only against any defects or encumbrances arising after his or her acquisition of the property.
3. In a *quitclaim deed*, the grantor makes no warranties concerning title, and merely transfers to the grantee whatever interest, if any, he or she has in the property.

EXAMPLE 23-4: Lucy bought a small home on a ⅓-acre lot from Marvin. They were old friends, so they conducted the transaction themselves. Lucy just gave Marvin the money and Marvin gave her a general warranty deed to the property. A couple of months later, however, Lucy accidentally opened a letter that was addressed to Marvin from the state. The letter said that the state would move forward on its lien on the property and seize it the next week if Marvin did not pay the back taxes he owed. Does Lucy have any recourse against Marvin for the fact that a lien existed on the home when he sold it to her?

If Lucy loses the home, she can seek damages from Marvin because he gave her a general warranty deed to the property. By giving her this deed, Marvin warranted that no encumbrances, such as a tax lien, existed on the property. Since a tax lien did exist, Lucy would be entitled to damages from Marvin for breach of warranty.

C. Deeds must be delivered and recorded to be valid.

Title to property passes upon actual or constructive delivery of a valid deed to the grantee. Furthermore, to avoid conflicts that may arise over ownership interests in the same property, all states require that a deed be recorded in the required office in the county where the property is located. This serves as public notice of ownership.

23-5. Other Methods of Acquiring Ownership

There are other methods by which ownership of real property can be acquired without the execution of a deed.

A. Ownership may be acquired by adverse possession.

Every state has a statute of limitations establishing a fixed period of time in which an owner must assert his or her right of ownership over a trespasser who has possession of his or her property. If an owner does not take action to remove one who has been occupying his or her property within the stated time period, the owner loses that right and title passes to the trespasser by *adverse possession*. To establish ownership by adverse possession, the trespasser must actually occupy the property continuously during the statutory period, to the exclusion of all others, and in a way that is open and hostile to the owner's rights.

EXAMPLE 23-5: Anna and David were friends and neighbors. One year, Anna erected a fence between their property that actually extended about three feet onto David's property. David did nothing about this and Anna mowed the three-foot strip, planted flowers, and generally maintained the strip along with her property for 20 years. At that time, David sold the property to Paul. In the many papers of conveyance, Paul found a surveyor's map that showed that the three-foot strip should belong to his property, so he asked Anna to move the fence. Would Anna have to move the fence?

Whether or not Anna would have to move the fence depends on the laws of the state where the property is located. If the statute of limitations for requiring an owner to assert ownership rights is under 20 years, then Anna could claim ownership of the property by adverse possession. The court would give her title to the property because she actually occupied the property that the three-foot strip was on and took care of it in an open way as though it were her own during the entire statutory period.

B. Ownership may be acquired by eminent domain.

Every state has the right to take real property for the public benefit under the laws of *eminent domain*. For example, a slum area may be taken by the state through eminent domain for the purpose of developing better housing conditions for the community. This right is limited only by the Fifth Amendment of the Constitution which requires that the private owner be justly compensated for the fair market value of the property taken.

23-6. Estates

The property that a person acquires during a lifetime, real and personal, comprises that person's *estate*. If a person does not dispose of the estate during her or his lifetime, then it will be passed on upon that person's death. The law provides that, upon death, a person's estate can be passed on by will, through formation of a trust, or according to state statute.

23-7. Wills

A *will* is a document by which a person sets forth how his or her estate is to be distributed after death.

A. Each state establishes requirements for the formation of a valid will.

In general, most states require that:

- the will must be in writing
- the person making the will must be of sound mind and of legal age
- the will must be signed by that person in the presence of two or three "disinterested" witnesses
- the witnesses must sign in the presence of each other and in the presence of the person making the will

B. A will can be amended or revoked.

A person may amend a will by adding a *codicil* to the will according to the same procedure required for the formation of a will. If a person wishes to change a will entirely, that person can revoke the old will by either destroying it or by revoking it in writing when forming a new will.

EXAMPLE 23-6: Joe's Aunt Mary had recently died. A will was found among her papers. Most of it was typed and executed in conformance to all formalities required by the state, properly signed and witnessed, and distributing her estate equitably among various relatives. At the very end, however, was a handwritten paragraph that read, "I hereby revoke the foregoing will and wish that my entire estate be liquidated and the proceeds used to establish a home for unwanted cats." It was dated two weeks before her death and was clearly signed by the aunt. Would the revocation be upheld in court?

It is unlikely that this revocation and revision would be upheld by the court. First of all, any addition, modification, or revocation to a properly executed will would also have to be properly executed according to the laws of the state in order to be enforced. Furthermore, the relatives could conceivably prove that Aunt Mary may not have been of sound mind two weeks before her death, particularly since she was revoking an equitable distribution of her estate to her family in favor of unwanted cats.

C. Upon death, a will must be probated and the disposition of the estate must be administered.

Probate is the process of submitting a will to the court to prove its validity. If executed properly, many courts will accept a will's genuineness. In some cases, testimony may be required from the witnesses or proof of the genuineness of the signatures may be required.

After being probated, if the will does not name a person to administer the disposition of the estate, the court will name an administrator, generally a close relative or friend of the decedent. The administrator is responsible for taking inventory of the estate, settling any debts or tax requirements against the estate, and then distributing the remains of the estate according to the wishes expressed in the will.

23-8. Trusts

Another way to plan the disposition of one's estate is to establish a trust. A *trust* is created when one party (the *trustor*) transfers property to another party (the *trustee*), who administers it for the benefit of a third party (the *beneficiary*). Trusts can be established during the trustor's lifetime or after, through a will. Trusts can be express or implied.

A. There are six requirements for creating an express trust.

Most trusts are express trusts; that is, trusts that are intentionally created by the trustor. The six requirements for creating an express trust are:

1. The trustor must have the same legal capacity as needed to form a contract if the trust is created during the trustor's life, or the same capacity as required to form a will, if the trust is created by a will.
2. The trustor must intend to create a trust and must conform to any formal requirements necessary for establishing that type of trust, as required by law.
3. The trustor must convey specific property that the trustor has the right to convey.
4. The trustee must be capable of administering the subject property of the trust. (An unqualified trustee does not negate an express trust. The court will appoint a qualified trustee instead.)
5. The beneficiary must be clearly identified.
6. The trust must not be created in violation of public policy or of law.

B. Implied trusts are created by law.

The law provides for the creation of implied trusts in order to correct an unfair situation. There are two types of implied trusts.

1. *Resulting trust.* If a trustor's property goes to someone that the trustor did not intend to receive it, a resulting trust is created by law that makes the person holding the property a resulting trustee for the intended beneficiary or the beneficiary's successors.
2. *Constructive trust.* If a person obtains property through fraud or other wrongdoing, a constructive trust is created by law that makes the person holding the property return it to the trustor.

EXAMPLE 23-7: Mabel's attorney, Larry, had been handling her affairs for years. He had advised her on many things, drawn up her will, and even successfully defended her against a lawsuit once. She had a lot of faith in him. One day, Mabel asked Larry to draw up the proper papers to create a trust for her grandson. She wanted some stock she owned to be held for him until he turned 21 and she wanted Larry to act as trustee. Instead, Larry drew up the papers such that the stocks were turned over to himself and, after assuring Mabel that the papers were in order, Mabel signed them. Was a valid trust created?

Despite Mabel's signature on the papers, the court would view this as a constructive trust because Larry acquired the stocks through fraud and misrepresentation, and in violation of the fiduciary relationship that he had with Mabel. He would be required by the court to return the stocks to Mabel and could be liable to her for any unlawful benefits he received, such as dividends.

23-9. Intestate Succession

A person who dies without leaving a valid will is said to have died *intestate*. In such cases, the person's estate is distributed according to the *intestate succession* laws of the state. These laws vary from state to state but, in general, they provide for the division of the estate among any remaining close relatives according to specific formulas. If the deceased had no relatives, the estate *escheats* (passes) to the state.

RAISE YOUR GRADES

Can you explain . . . ?

☑ under what circumstances personal property can become real property
☑ the difference between possessory and nonpossessory interests in land and give examples of each
☑ the difference between a tenancy in common, a joint tenancy, and a tenancy by the entirety
☑ why it is necessary to record a deed
☑ how ownership can be acquired without the execution of a deed
☑ the ways in which a person's estate can be passed on after that person's death
☑ how a trust can be created by law

SUMMARY

1. Real property, or realty, is generally of a fixed and permanent nature. Personal property, or personalty, is generally movable and lacking a permanent physical location. Fixtures are items of personal property that are attached to real property in such a way that they are considered to be a part of the real property.
2. Interests in real property can be possessory or nonpossessory. The three main types of possessory interests in real property are fee simple absolute, life estate, and leasehold. The three main types of nonpossessory interests in real property are easement, license, and profit.
3. Two or more people, known as cotenants, may have an ownership interest in the same realty at the same time. The three main types of cotenancies are tenancy in common, joint tenancy, and tenancy by the entirety.
4. In general, all states require that ownership of real property be transferred by sale or by gift through the proper execution and delivery of a deed.
5. There are three main types of deeds: a general warranty deed, warranting the title against any defects or encumbrances; a special warranty deed, warranting the title against defects or encumbrances arising since the grantor acquired ownership; and a quitclaim deed, warranting only that all interests are transferred, whether valid or not.
6. Deeds should be recorded in the required office in the county where the property is located in order to avoid conflicts that may arise over ownership interests in the same property.
7. Adverse possession is a method of acquiring property on the basis of an open and hostile, continuous occupation or use of another's property for a statutorily prescribed amount of time.

8. Eminent domain is the state's power to take real property for the public benefit. The owner must be justly compensated for the fair market value of property so taken.

9. The property that a person acquires during a lifetime, real and personal, comprises that person's estate.

10. Upon death, a person's estate can be passed on according to her or his wishes as set forth in a properly executed will. Most states require that a valid will be in writing, that the person making the will be of sound mind and of legal age, and that the will be signed by the person making it and two or three disinterested witnesses in the presence of each other.

11. A codicil can be added to a will as an amendment according to the same procedure required for the will itself.

12. A will can be revoked by destroying it or revoking it in writing when forming a new will.

13. A will must be probated to determine its validity, and then an administrator, either named in the will or appointed by the court, will inventory the estate, settle any debts or taxes against the estate, and then distribute the estate according to the wishes set forth in the will.

14. A trust is created when a trustor transfers property to a trustee, who administers it for the benefit of a beneficiary. A trust can be established during the trustor's lifetime or after, through a will.

15. Trusts can be expressly created by the trustor so long as the trustor has legal capacity, has the right to convey the specific property, the beneficiary is clearly identified, all formalities are met, and the trust does not violate public policy or law.

16. There are two types of implied trusts that are created by law—a resulting trust and a constructive trust. Both are intended to correct an unfair situation when an unintended beneficiary receives property or property is received through fraud or misrepresentation.

17. If a person dies without leaving a valid will, that person's estate is distributed to close relatives according to the intestate succession laws of the state. If there are no remaining relatives, the estate escheats to the state.

RAPID REVIEW   Answers

True or False

		Answers
1.	If the owner of a home put new windows in the home, they would be fixtures and become a part of the real property. [Section 23-1]	*True*
2.	A fee simple absolute possessory interest grants an owner of real property and his or her heirs all interests in the property with the restriction that they not cause any harm to the property. [Section 23-2]	*False*
3.	An easement can be implied if a person has a profit interest in real property because that person must be allowed to cross the land in order to have access to the profit. [Section 23-2]	*True*
4.	A tenancy in common carries with it the right of survivorship. [Section 23-3]	*False*
5.	If a joint tenant severs the joint tenancy relationship, then the joint tenancy becomes a tenancy in common. [Section 23-3]	*True*
6.	A tenancy by the entirety can be created by any cotenants who desire that their cotenancy require mutual agreement in order to be severed. [Section 23-3]	*False*
7.	Title to property passes upon actual or constructive delivery of a valid deed to the grantee. [Section 23-4]	*True*

8. The only way to acquire an ownership interest in real property is through the proper execution and delivery of a deed. [Section 23-5]

False

9. The witnesses to a will must not be named as recipients of any benefits of the will. [Section 27-7]

True

10. A will can be challenged during the probate proceedings. [Section 23-7]

True

11. A trust will be invalidated if the appointed trustee is not capable of administering the subject property of the trust. [Section 23-8]

False

12. If a person dies without leaving a valid will, then that person's estate passes to the state in which he or she lived. [Section 23-9]

False

SOLVED PROBLEMS

PROBLEM 23-1   Dolly contracted to buy some property from Max. When shown the lot, there was a trailer home on it that Max lived in. The tongue and wheels had been removed, it was set on cement blocks, and all water, sewer, and electric lines were attached to it. Dolly had met with Max several times in the trailer while working out the terms of the transaction, and each time she had made comments such as, "my furniture will fit great in here." After the sale was completed, however, Dolly discovered that the trailer home had been removed by Max. When confronted, Max claimed that the trailer was a mobile home that was his own personal property. Dolly decided to sue Max to return the trailer home on the ground that it was so attached as to become a fixture and a part of the property. Would Dolly win her suit?

Answer: Dolly would win her suit. There are several reasons why the trailer home would be considered a fixture and therefore a part of the real property by the court in this case. First of all, the tongue and wheels had been removed, the trailer had been placed on cement blocks, and all utilities had been connected. This would indicate that the trailer home had been fixed to the property in a permanent manner. The other crucial factor is that it was surely obvious to Max that Dolly believed the trailer home to be a part of the property because of her comments about arranging her furniture. Max made no effort to deny this obvious belief of Dolly's, perhaps with the intent of getting more money for the property because of her belief that the home came with it. For whatever reason, Max gave the impression that it was his intent to leave the trailer home, and the court would decide in favor of Dolly. [Section 23-1]

PROBLEM 23-2   Roger owned a building where he ran a restaurant on the bottom floor and lived on the top floor. He decided to sell the building to Amanda, who wanted a restaurant business, but he wanted to continue to live on the top floor of the building, as he had for 25 years. Roger offered to knock $10,000 off of the price of the building if Amanda would agree to let him live on the top floor for the rest of his life. Amanda agreed to this and the terms were included in the contract for sale and the deed. What type of interest does Roger have in the property?

Answer: Agreeing to let Roger live in the top floor of the building for the rest of his life gave him a possessory interest known as a life estate. This interest gave Roger the absolute right to possess the top floor for the remainder of his life, with the one restriction that he not cause any permanent harm to the property. Upon his death, Amanda will gain absolute possession of the top floor, along with the restaurant, but not until then. [Section 23-2]

PROBLEM 23-3   Floyd had been rabbit hunting for years on a friend's wooded property about five miles from his home. One year, when rabbit season began, he got a license to hunt, as he did every year, and headed for his usual hunting grounds, although he knew that his friend had moved and that someone else owned the property now. When he got to the woods, he saw signs posted in various places prohibiting trespassing, but he ignored them and entered the woods anyway. A couple of hours later, a man approached him and insisted that he leave, identifying himself as the owner of the property. Floyd argued that his hunting license gave him the right to be there. Was Floyd correct?

Answer: Floyd was not correct. Although the word "license" may appear on Floyd's hunting license issued by a government agency, it has a different meaning from the word "license" when used in a nonpossessory interest sense. In order to hunt on private property, Floyd will need his hunting license plus a license from the property owner, granting him a temporary right to use the owner's land for a specific purpose. A license can be revoked at any time by the person granting the license. In this case, Floyd was correct that his hunting license gave him the right to hunt, but it did not give him the right to hunt on someone's land if the owner chose to prohibit it. Floyd will have to find a new hunting ground. [Section 23-2]

PROBLEM 23-4   Shelly and Nancy were not related, but they were best friends and had lived together for many years. They had even purchased a home together as joint tenants. Unfortunately, Shelly became sick one year and eventually succumbed to the illness. After her death, a will was discovered in which Shelly left her interest in the house to her niece. Nancy challenged this provision in probate court. Would the provision be upheld?

Answer: If Nancy has a single document that conveyed the home to she and Shelly and named them as joint tenants at the time of purchase, then the provision in Shelly's will will not be upheld by the court. The significant characteristic of a joint tenancy is that it carries with it the right of survivorship. This right means that, upon Shelly's death, her interest in the house passed immediately to Nancy and was not subject to any other claims. If Shelley had sold or given her interest to her niece along with proper documentation during her lifetime, this would have severed the joint tenancy, and it would have become a tenancy in common. In that case, the right of survivorship would have been lost. [Section 23-3]

PROBLEM 23-5   Dan purchased ten acres of land from Porter. Porter gave him a properly executed general warranty deed to the land. Dan put the deed in a safety-deposit box at his bank. Unknown to Dan, however, Porter sold the same land to Kenneth several weeks later, also giving him a properly executed general warranty deed. Kenneth promptly recorded the deed at the county recorder's office. Who has valid title to the land?

Answer: Kenneth has valid title to the land. A case like this points out the importance of properly recording a deed to real property. Although recording is not absolutely required in all states, it is crucial to determining the rights of people who claim ownership of the same property. Although both Dan and Kenneth held properly executed general warranty deeds to the land, and although Dan purchased the land first, Kenneth's recorded deed will prevail in a court of law. Dan does have a recourse against Porter though. Porter gave Dan a general warranty deed to the land, warranting against any defects in or encumbrances to the title arising before or after his own acquisition of the land. Dan could therefore sue Porter to recover the purchase price of the land based on breach of this warranty of title. [Section 23-4]

PROBLEM 23-6   Sidney owned 20 acres of farmland. Adjacent to the back of his property was 15 acres of good farmland along a riverbed that was owned by Francesca. He had wanted to buy this land for years, but Francesca refused to sell, although she lived in another city and had never farmed the land. Sidney, however, had crossed the land often to get to the river, and had even grazed cattle there and planted a small home garden on the land off and on for 15 years, although he had gotten Francesca's permission to do so. After finding out that the statute of limitations for asserting ownership rights was only ten years in his state, Sidney decided to bring suit claiming ownership of the land by adverse possession. Would Sidney get title to the land?

Answer: Sidney would not get title to the land. There are several requirements for gaining adverse possession of property that were not evident in Sidney's case. First of all, the property being claimed must have been occupied or used continuously by the claimant during the entire statutory period. Sidney had merely crossed the land, grazed cattle, and planted a small garden "off and on" for 15 years. This was not continuous, nor was it even full use of the land. Second, the land must have been used in an open manner that was hostile to the owner's rights. The fact that Sidney got permission to use the property from Francesca was an open recognition on his part of her ownership rights, and could not be considered hostile to her rights in any way. Francesca would retain title to the land. [Section 23-5]

PROBLEM 23-7   Dean's grandfather had recently passed away. In the last few years of his life, he had been in poor health and had required 24-hour care from a live-in nurse, Gail. Unfortunately, his mind had not been as sharp during this period of failing health either, and the family knew that he had often referred to Gail as his mother and even his wife, neither of which were still living. Dean was aware that his grandfather had made him administrator of his estate and that he had kept his will in a safe in the house. To his surprise, however, he retrieved two wills from the safe and saw that his grandfather had revoked one that was beneficial to his family and left his entire estate to Gail just two months before he died. The will was witnessed by Gail and her daughter. Dean decided to challenge the validity of the will in court. On what grounds could he do this?

Answer: Dean could challenge the validity of the will on several grounds. He could seek to prove that his grandfather was not of sound mind when he executed the will. The fact that he had become dependent on Gail and had referred to her in front of family members as his mother and wife would be evidence that he was emotionally confused about her identity and relationship to him during this period of failing health. Dean could also challenge the will on the basis that the witnesses were not disinterested. It might be shown that Gail exercised undue influence over his grandfather in his weakness since she had signed the will knowing that she was its main recipient. Her daughter, too, would certainly stand to benefit from the provisions of the will if her mother inherited the estate. There is little doubt that, based on this evidence, the court would invalidate the recent will and reinstate the old will that was beneficial to the family. [Section 23-7]

PROBLEM 23-8   Raymond knew that his elderly mother was having financial problems. He wanted to help, but it was difficult to handle her financial affairs because he lived in another state. He therefore transferred property to his aunt, who lived next door to his mother, to be used to provide for her. Raymond did not think to provide for who the trust should go to upon his mother's death. Who would the benefits of the trust go to at that time?

Answer: This is a case where a resulting trust would be implied by law. The intended beneficiary of the trust was Raymond's mother. Upon her death, however, the aunt would still be holding the property, and she was never intended to be a beneficiary. She would thus become a resulting trustee, holding the property for the successors of Raymond's mother. Assuming that Raymond was the closest living relative, the trust would revert back to him. [Section 23-8]

FINAL EXAMINATION

(Answers begin on page 234.)

TRUE-FALSE

T F 1. A corporation cannot survive a change of ownership when all of the original shareholders transfer their interests.

T F 2. The state requires a copy of a corporation's bylaws to be filed with it in order for them to be valid.

T F 3. The promoters of a corporation may enter into binding contracts in the name of a corporation before the corporation itself is legally created.

T F 4. Watered stock is stock issued at a discount.

T F 5. A corporation cannot be forced to dissolve involuntarily.

T F 6. If the directors or officers of a corporation have caused it to enter an ultra vires contract that is later enjoined, they may be liable both to the corporation and to third parties for damages caused by their acts.

T F 7. The officers of a corporation are elected by the shareholders.

T F 8. It is possible for one person to hold two offices in a corporation at the same time.

T F 9. In certain circumstances, shareholders may force a corporation to pay a dividend.

T F 10. A shareholder cannot be held liable for the fraudulent purpose behind a corporation.

T F 11. For a valid sale to take place, there must be a transfer of title for the payment of consideration.

T F 12. A sale of present goods may involve the transfer of title to goods that are not in existence at the time of the contract.

T F 13. A sale of goods by a non-owner may transfer only a voidable title.

T F 14. Bulk transfers are regulated by the UCC to protect the buyer's creditors.

T F 15. An insurable interest carries a right to bring suit against third persons for any damage, destruction or unauthorized conversion of the goods.

T F 16. Under the perfect tender rule, a seller must tender conforming goods in a manner that perfectly complies with the terms of the contract.

T F 17. A seller may, through his or her own actions, waive or lose the right to impose a seller's lien upon the property sold.

T F 18. After shipment has begun, a seller no longer has a right to prevent the buyer from receiving the goods.

T F 19. If a seller becomes insolvent, the buyer may have a right under the UCC to tender payment for and recover the goods he or she has contracted for.

T F 20. A sale of goods will create an implied warranty of merchantability regardless of whether the seller regularly deals in or has any special knowledge of the types of goods being sold.

T F 21. Under the privity of contract doctrine, the party to be sued must also be a party to the agreement or the action may not be brought.

226

T F 22. In product liability, a manufacturer may be held strictly liable for an injury caused by its product despite a lack of privity and the manufacturer's best efforts to avoid the harm.

T F 23. Checks are a commonly used type of draft that can be drawn on a bank and are payable on demand.

T F 24. If a sum is expressed on the face of a negotiable instrument in both words and figures and the two amounts conflict, the sum expressed in figures will control.

T F 25. A negotiable instrument is negotiated when it is transferred to another party in such a way as to make the transferee a holder or a legal bearer of the document.

T F 26. To be a holder in due course, the transferee must receive the instrument in good faith for value, have no notice of any applicable defenses to collection of the sum certain, and have no knowledge of any defects in the instrument itself.

T F 27. If a bank honors a check that later proves to be a forgery, it may seek recovery from the forger but cannot recover from subsequent endorsers.

T F 28. A reasonable time for presentment of a check is within 30 days of its issue or the date it bears, whichever period is longer.

T F 29. An accommodation party assumes primary liability for payment of a debt.

T F 30. A security agreement must always be embodied in a writing.

T F 31. Perfecting a security interest will protect the secured party from the claims of third parties.

T F 32. A Chapter 11 bankruptcy involves a reorganization of a debtor's business rather than an outright liquidation.

T F 33. A life estate is a possessory interest in real property held by a person for life or for the life of someone else.

T F 34. The court will always negate a trust if the trustee is found to be incapable of administering the property of the trust.

MULTIPLE-CHOICE

1. Articles of incorporation must include

    (a) a description of the capital structure of the corporation
    (b) the official name of the corporation
    (c) the location of the corporation's principle office
    (d) all of the above

2. Which of the following is *not* a type of corporation?

    (a) de jure corporation   (c) per stirpes corporation
    (b) corporation by estoppel   (d) de facto corporation

3. The type of stock that usually carries no right to vote in corporate office is

    (a) preferred stock   (c) watered stock
    (b) common stock   (d) no par stock

4. Dividends are typically paid from a corporation's

    (a) earned surplus   (c) capital stock
    (b) petty cash   (d) borrowed equity

5. Preferred stock enables the bearer to be paid a dividend

    (a) after the holders of common stock are paid
    (b) before the holders of common stock are paid

    (*c*) higher in value than that paid to other shareholders
    (*d*) only upon dissolution of the corporation

6. A state may not constitutionally limit a foreign corporation from

    (*a*) gaining access to the federal courts
    (*b*) doing business within their borders
    (*c*) gaining access to state courts
    (*d*) trying to incorporate within the state

7. A corporation may *not* be dissolved by

    (*a*) a majority vote of the incorporators before beginning business
    (*b*) the demand of a shareholder
    (*c*) a court order
    (*d*) a dissolution period set forth in its articles of incorporation

8. Shareholders may participate in the management of a corporation by

    (*a*) managing the corporation's transactions
    (*b*) electing the board of directors
    (*c*) ordering mergers with other corporations
    (*d*) issuing more stock

9. A corporation derives its powers from

    (*a*) its bylaws
    (*b*) the laws of the jurisdiction in which it is created
    (*c*) its articles of incorporation
    (*d*) all of the above

10. A corporation's directors are selected by

    (*a*) the holders of preferred stock
    (*b*) its managing board
    (*c*) the shareholders
    (*d*) the officers of the corporation

11. A director or officer of a corporation is said to have a conflict of interest if he or she

    (*a*) owns stock in the corporation
    (*b*) contracts with the corporation
    (*c*) is a partner in another non-competing corporation
    (*d*) holds more than one office in the corporation

12. A security agreement differs from a sales contract because

    (*a*) there is no consideration for the security interest
    (*b*) title never actually changes hands
    (*c*) the passage of title is dependent upon the default of the debtor
    (*d*) all of the above

13. Under the UCC, a person possessing special skills or knowledge of the goods involved in a particular transaction is deemed

    (*a*) an expert   (*c*) a merchant
    (*b*) a trade specialist   (*d*) a dealer

14. Goods that are singled out or designated as the subject matter of a particular contract are said to be

    (*a*) identified   (*c*) earmarked
    (*b*) labeled   (*d*) settled

15. If a contract does not specify risk of loss, then the risk of loss shifts from the merchant to the buyer when

    (*a*) the goods are tendered   (*c*) the seller ships the goods
    (*b*) the buyer receives the goods   (*d*) the contract is signed

16. The type of delivery requiring a seller to deliver goods to a named vessel, at which time the risk of loss passes to the buyer, is called

    (*a*) FAS   (*c*) CIF
    (*b*) FOB   (*d*) COD

17. The various exceptions to the perfect tender rule do *not* include

    (*a*) goods that are more expensive to produce and deliver than at the time of contracting
    (*b*) the right to cure
    (*c*) destruction of identified goods before risk of loss passes
    (*d*) commercial impracticability

18. If no specific provisions governing payment are contained in a contract, payment is to be made

    (*a*) upon contracting
    (*b*) before the seller ships the goods
    (*c*) at the time and place the buyer receives the goods
    (*d*) when the seller ships the goods

19. A buyer *covers* when a contract made for some commodity is rejected and he or she

    (*a*) sues the seller for damages
    (*b*) finds another source for the goods
    (*c*) claims that subsequent performance is impossible
    (*d*) sues the seller for specific performance

20. An implied warranty that is imposed upon a seller when the seller has knowledge of a purpose for which the buyer intends to use a product is called an implied warranty of

    (*a*) merchantability   (*c*) fitness for a particular purpose
    (*b*) habitability   (*d*) serviceability

21. Which of the following is *not* a theory of liability used in product liability?

    (*a*) misrepresentation   (*c*) strict liability
    (*b*) negligence   (*d*) warranty

22. A negotiable instrument must contain an unconditional promise or order to pay the bearer of a third person a fixed amount of money. This amount is called the

    (*a*) sum certain   (*c*) res
    (*b*) corpus   (*d*) total sum

23. A negotiable instrument must be made payable either upon the bearer's demands or

    (*a*) within a reasonable time   (*c*) a and b
    (*b*) at a definite time   (*d*) none of the above

24. Arrange the following in the order in which they would control if placed upon the face of a negotiable instrument: (1) handwritten terms; (2) typewritten terms; (3) printed terms

    (*a*) 1, 3, 2   (*c*) 1, 2, 3
    (*b*) 3, 2, 1   (*d*) 2, 3, 1

25. A type of indorsement that requires a certain transferee's signature before the instrument may be transferred again is a

    (*a*) blank indorsement   (*c*) restrictive indorsement
    (*b*) special indorsement   (*d*) general indorsement

26. Which of the following is *not* a defense available to prevent the collection of the sum certain of a negotiable instrument?

    (*a*) material alteration   (*c*) duress
    (*b*) minority   (*d*) mistake

27. The act of presentment may be accomplished

    (a) at a specified location   (c) through the mail
    (b) through a clearinghouse   (d) all of the above

28. In general, notice of dishonor must be given to the holder of an instrument and to other potentially liable parties

    (a) the same day
    (b) by the third business day after the dishonor occurs
    (c) within a reasonable time
    (d) within two weeks

29. Which of the following is *not* a method of discharge from liability for a negotiable instrument?

    (a) impairment of collateral   (c) renunciation
    (b) cancellation   (d) avoidance

30. Which of the following is *not* a form of presentment warranty?

    (a) The party presenting the instrument has good title to it.
    (b) The transferor has no notice of any insolvency of the maker, drawer, or drawee.
    (c) There are no material alterations on the face of the instrument.
    (d) The party presenting the instrument does so in good faith.

31. If two perfected security interests conflict, the collateral will go to the one that

    (a) had been filed first   (c) had been filed most recently
    (b) seeks to recover first   (d) attaches the collateral first

32. In case of default by the debtor, the secured creditor may

    (a) sue to recover the underlying debt
    (b) enforce the security interest in the collateral
    (c) a and b
    (d) none of the above

33. Which of the following is *not* a duty of a trustee in a Chapter 7 bankruptcy proceeding?

    (a) setting aside property that the debtor is allowed to retain
    (b) examining creditors' claims for validity and for establishing priorities
    (c) discharging the debtor after distribution of proceeds to creditors
    (d) collecting the debtor's assets and liquidating them

34. The creation of a tenancy by the entirety requires the same conditions as a joint tenancy, plus a fifth condition of

    (a) survivorship   (c) concurrent ownership
    (b) marriage   (d) conveyance

FILL-IN-THE-BLANK

1. A(n) _____ is an organization created under state law as a special legal entity intended to pursue some legal purpose.

2. The document that must be filed to create a corporation is called the _____ _____ _____ .

3. A(n) _____ _____ corporation is formed when the shareholders have made a good-faith effort to incorporate, but have failed to perform the proper procedural formalities.

4. Stock certificates are a form of _____ _____ , and can be transferred by endorsement and physical delivery.

5. A corporation formed under the laws of one state is considered a(n) _____ corporation under the laws of other states.

6. A(n) _____ occurs when one corporation absorbs another, ending its existence as a separate entity.

7. A corporation acting outside of its express or implied powers is said to be acting in _____ _____ .

8. A(n) _____ right may be granted to shareholders, enabling them to buy a pro rata share of any stock offered by the corporation.

9. _____ refers to the legal ownership right to some sort of property.

10. Under the UCC, _____ are all things that are moveable at the time of identification to a contract of sale.

11. If an owner of goods _____ them to a merchant who deals in that sort of goods, the merchant may transfer good title to a third person in the ordinary course of business.

12. In a(n) _____ contract, the goods are delivered for the potential buyer's use, and the risk of loss remains with the seller until the goods are actually accepted.

13. FOB stands for _____ _____ _____ .

14. A seller may hold a(n) _____ upon property sold to secure the debt and force the buyer to tender payment.

15. The UCC provides for a seller's right to _____ goods within ten days after an insolvent buyer receives the goods.

16. Under the UCC, a buyer has the right to _____ nonconforming or improperly delivered goods.

17. _____ is a form of action whereby a buyer may recover goods from a seller who has wrongfully taken or retained them.

18. _____ warranties arise when the seller makes a direct representation to the buyer regarding the condition, quality, or performance standards of the goods to be sold.

19. The general area of the law that has abolished the rules of privity is called _____ _____ .

20. The party who promises to pay a negotiable instrument is called the _____ .

21. A negotiable instrument made payable upon the demand of the bearer is called _____ _____ .

22. A(n) _____ is a signature or other written indication representing the transfer of a negotiable instrument from the present holder to another person.

23. Under certain circumstances, a holder may become a(n) _____ _____ _____ _____ and receive a negotiable instrument free from most defenses or claims from other parties.

24. An alteration of a negotiable instrument is said to be _____ when it acts to alter the contractual obligations of the parties in any way.

25. A customer has the right to order the payor bank not to honor a check previously issued, provided the bank is given sufficient time to comply with the order. This order is known as a(n) _____ _____ _____ .

26. A negotiable instrument has been _____ when a demand has been made upon the payee, maker, or holder to accept the instrument or to tender the cash value it represents.

27. A party is _____ from liability on a negotiable instrument when her or his responsibility for the obligation the instrument represents has ended.

28. The maker of a note and the drawee of a draft are considered _____ parties to the instrument.

29. The property given as security in a secured transaction is known as _____.

30. _____ is a seizure of a debtor's property granted by the court for use in satisfying a later judgment.

31. The type of bankruptcy proceeding that requires the liquidation of all of the debtor's assets is regulated by _____ _____ of the Bankruptcy Act.

32. The type of bankruptcy proceeding that allows an individual to adjust the payment of debts is regulated by _____ _____ of the Bankruptcy Act.

33. _____ are items of personal property that become so attached to their locations that they assume the attributes of real property.

34. A(n) _____ is a special document that allows a person to direct the disposal of property after death.

PROBLEMS

1. A group of promoters formed a corporation, but there was a defect in the articles of incorporation. Can the shareholders be held liable for the corporate debts?

2. Morris was a member of the board of directors of Dex Corp. He negotiated a contract with Dex Corp. on behalf of Cooper Enterprises, a partnership that he was a member of. Morris disclosed his interest in Cooper Enterprises to Dex Corp., and a majority of its disinterested directors approved the deal. Is this contract voidable by Dex Corp.?

3. John was a retailer and Leonard was a wholesaler. Leonard agreed orally to sell John $3,000 worth of soccer balls for $15 each. A few weeks later, the parties orally agreed to modify the sale price to $13 each. Is this contract enforceable?

4. Barry ran a clothing store and ordered an assortment of men's dress shirts from Superior Mills, Inc. The parties executed a shipment contract for the goods, which were to be transported from Superior's plant in Little Rock to Barry's store in Boston. Unfortunately, the goods were destroyed in transit. Who bears the risk of loss?

5. Monica entered into a contract with Brian for the sale of goods. They agreed upon a purchase price of $50,000, and Brian agreed to extend credit to Monica in order to facilitate the purchase. Brian also decided to impose a seller's lien and retain the goods in his possession until Monica tendered the entire purchase price. May he do this under these circumstances?

6. Stan bought a few pens at Pete's Stationery Shop. When he used them at home, however, they blotted and leaked. Does Stan have a recourse?

7. Ellen made a written note promising to pay $1,000 to the order of John's Roofing Company in return for roofing her house. The amount was payable 30 days after completion of the job. Can John use Ellen's note as a negotiable instrument?

8. Andy's aunt gave him a bank draft for $100 for his birthday. Andy had no notice of any defects in the instrument itself and received it in good faith. Also, he had no knowledge of any outstanding claims or defenses against the negotiability of the instrument. Is Andy a holder in due course?

9. Several years ago, Jeff loaned his old friend Drew $150 and Drew gave him a note for that amount. Now, Jeff wanted to cancel the debt. He intended to destroy the note, but he couldn't find it. Can the debt be cancelled?

10. Albert and Betty had a security agreement. Albert gave cash value for a security interest in Betty's automobile. Betty had a valid ownership interest in the automobile, which was

already in Albert's possession. Must this security agreement be put in writing to be enforceable?

11. Jeff sold 20 acres of land to Nancy and gave her a general warranty deed, which Nancy put in her safety deposit box. Unknown to Nancy, Jeff also sold the land to Dorothy two months later, giving her a general warranty deed, which she recorded at the county recorder's office. Who has valid title to the land?

ANSWERS TO FINAL EXAMINATION

TRUE-FALSE

1. F [Section 13-1]
2. F [Section 13-2]
3. T [Section 13-2]
4. T [Section 13-5]
5. F [Section 13-7]
6. T [Section 14-1]
7. F [Section 14-2]
8. T [Section 14-2]
9. T [Section 14-5]
10. F [Section 14-6]
11. T [Section 15-1]
12. F [Section 15-1[

13. F [Section 16-2]
14. F [Section 16-3]
15. T [Section 16-6]
16. T [Section 17-2]
17. T [Section 17-3]
18. F [Section 17-3]
19. T [Section 17-5]
20. F [Section 18-2]
21. T [Section 18-4]
22. T [Section 18-4]
23. T [Section 19-2]

24. F [Section 19-4]
25. T [Section 20-1]
26. T [Section 20-3]
27. F [Section 21-3]
28. T [Section 21-1]
29. T [Section 21-2]
30. F [Section 22-1]
31. T [Section 22-2]
32. T [Section 22-7]
33. T [Section 23-2]
34. F [Section 23-8]

MULTIPLE-CHOICE

1. d [Section 13-2]
2. c [Section 13-3]
3. a [Section 13-5]
4. a [Section 13-5]
5. b [Section 13-5]
6. a [Section 13-4]
7. b [Section 13-7]
8. b [Section 14-5]
9. d [Section 14-1]
10. c [Section 14-2]
11. b [Section 14-3]
12. c [Section 15-1]

13. c [Section 15-2]
14. a [Section 16-1]
15. b [Section 16-4]
16. a [Section 16-4]
17. a [Section 17-2]
18. c [Section 17-4]
19. b [Section 17-5]
20. c [Section 18-2]
21. a [Section 18-4]
22. a [Section 19-3]
23. b [Section 19-3]

24. c [Section 19-4]
25. b [Section 20-2]
26. d [Section 20-3]
27. d [Section 21-1]
28. b [Section 21-1]
29. d [Section 21-5]
30. b [Section 21-3]
31. a [Section 22-3]
32. c [Section 22-4]
33. c [Section 22-6]
34. b [Section 23-3]

FILL-IN-THE-BLANK

1. corporation [Section 13-1]
2. articles of incorporation [Section 13-2]
3. de facto [Section 13-5]
4. negotiable instruments [Section 13-5]
5. foreign [Section 13-4]
6. merger [Section 13-6]
7. ultra vires [Section 14-1]
8. preemptive [Section 14-5]
9. title [Section 15-1]

10. goods [Section 15-1]
11. entrusts [Section 16-2]
12. approval [Section 16-5]
13. free on board [Section 16-4]
14. lien [Section 17-3]
15. reclaim [Section 17-3]
16. reject [Section 17-4]
17. replevin [Section 17-5]
18. express [Section 18-2]

19. product liability [Section 18-4]

20. maker [Section 19-2]

21. bearer paper [Section 19-3]

22. indorsement [Section 20-2]

23. holder in due course [Section 20-3]

24. material [Section 20-3]

25. stop payment order [Section 20-4]

26. presented [Section 21-1]

27. discharged [Section 21-5]

28. primary [Section 21-2]

29. collateral [Section 22-1]

30. attachment [Section 22-3]

31. Chapter 7 [Section 22-6]

32. Chapter 13 [Section 22-8]

33. fixtures [Section 23-1]

34. will [Section 23-7]

PROBLEMS

1. The shareholders probably cannot be held liable for corporate debts. If the promoters made a good-faith effort to incorporate, the court will recognize the organization as a de facto corporation with the same power to enter contracts and the same limited liability as a de jure corporation. However, to be safe, the shareholders should correct the defect at their next annual meeting. [Section 13-3]

2. This contract is not voidable by Dex Corp. It would have been voidable under the common law of corporations, since Morris is an "interested" party. However, by having the contract approved by Dex Corp.'s board of directors, Morris avoided any potential problems arising out of his conflict of interest. [Section 14-3]

3. This contract is not enforceable. Under the UCC, any agreement for the sale of goods in excess of $500 must be placed in writing. Furthermore, any subsequent modification of such an agreement must be in writing. [Section 15-3]

4. In a shipment contract, the risk of loss passes when the seller delivers the goods to the designated carrier instead of when the goods are actually given into the hands of the buyer. Thus, in this case, Barry bears the loss. [Section 16-4]

5. Brian cannot impose a lien under these circumstances. Under the UCC, the seller has a right to impose a seller's lien to ensure payment by the buyer. However, the right to do so can be waived by an inconsistent act. The extension of credit to the buyer would be such an act, and would prevent the seller from imposing a lien until the credit period has ended. [Section 17-3]

6. Stan may seek a remedy. Since Pete runs a stationery store, he may be considered a merchant of such goods, thus having some degree of knowledge about them. As a result, every sale he makes carries with it an implied warranty of merchantability, promising that the goods sold are of fair, average quality. Here, that warranty is breached. Pete must either exchange the pens or return Stan's money. [Section 18-2]

7. Under the UCC, John cannot use Ellen's note as a negotiable instrument because it is not unconditional; that is, Ellen will only pay John if the roof is done. The promise therefore is not a valid negotiable instrument. [Section 19-3]

8. Andy is not a holder in due course. Andy has not acquired the instrument through a sales transaction for which he has given present value. The status of holder in due course cannot be established without some form of consideration changing hands. [Section 20-3]

9. In order for Jeff to cancel the note, he must destroy it or make some intentional markings on the instrument itself showing that the debt is cancelled. Since he cannot locate the instrument, his best option would be to release Drew from the debt through a written renunciation. [Section 21-5]

10. This security agreement need not be put in writing to be enforceable. As a general rule, all security agreements must be in writing. The one exception is when the intended collateral is already in the hands of the secured party. Since Albert already has possession of Betty's automobile, an oral agreement is sufficient. [Section 22-1]

11. Dorothy has valid title to the land. Properly recording a deed is crucial to determining the rights of people who claim ownership of the same property. In this case, although both Nancy and Dorothy have general warranty deeds, and although Nancy purchased the land first, Dorothy's recorded deed will prevail in a court of law. [Section 23-4]

GLOSSARY

ab initio From the beginning, as an ab initio contract that is void from the beginning.

acceptance The actual or implied agreement of an offeree to be bound by the terms of an offeror's proposal, usually binding the parties to a contract.

accommodation party Any party who signs a negotiable instrument in order to lend credit to a party to the instrument.

accord and satisfaction An accord is an agreement by contracting parties to substitute a performance for one originally in the contract; a satisfaction is the actual performance of the accord, thereby discharging the contract.

actual authority Express and implied authority of an agent to act for a principal.

administrative law Rules and regulations enacted by state administrative agencies to allow them to carry out their assigned tasks.

adverse possession A means of acquiring ownership of real property by openly occupying land continuously for a statutory period of time in a manner that is hostile to the true owner's rights.

agent A party acting on behalf of and under the control of another party (the principal).

anticipatory breach A clear breach of contract before the time for performance has arrived that allows the nonbreaching party to be discharged from the contract and seek a remedy for the breach.

apparent authority An agent's authority to act for a principal based on the manner in which the principal holds the agent out to third parties; also known as ostensible authority.

appellant The party who appeals a court decision.

appellee The party who receives notice of an appeal.

articles of incorporation Documents that must be filed with a state official before a corporation can be legally formed.

assignee The party to whom an assignment of rights or interests is made.

assignment A transfer of rights or interests to a third party.

assignor The party who assigns rights or interests to a third party.

assumption of risk In a product liability suit for negligence or strict liability, the defense that the buyer of the product voluntarily assumed the risk of using it and proceeded in the face of a known hazard.

attachment Seizure of a debtor's property granted by the court for use in satisfying a creditor's later judgment.

bailee A third party who holds goods in trust for a specific purpose and for a limited time.

bankruptcy A legal proceeding that allows relief to those who are unable to pay their debts by placing their property under the control of the court and either liquidating it to pay creditors or planning a method of repayment to creditors. Bankruptcy usually results in a discharge of any remaining debts of the debtor.

bearer paper A promissory note that is payable to anyone who possesses it.

beneficiary A person entitled to receive the benefits of a contract, trust, or will, but who is not the promisee.

board of directors The group of persons elected by the shareholders of a corporation to oversee the management of the corporation.

bond A corporate promise to pay an indebtedness that is secured by the assets of the corporation; any promise in writing to pay a sum certain on the occurrence of a specified event.

breach Failure to perform or live up to legally binding obligations with no legal excuse for not doing so.

bulk transfer A single transfer of a major part of a merchant's business inventory that is not made in the ordinary course of the seller's business. The seller's principal business must be the sale of merchandise from stock.

burden of proof The obligation to prove facts in a court of law.

business judgment rule A doctrine of noninterference and acceptance of the management of corporate affairs by those entrusted with it.

bylaws Written provisions for the administration, management, and internal operation of a corporation.

codicil A properly formalized amendment to a will.

collateral An interest in property given by a debtor to a creditor to secure payment or performance of a debt.

commercial paper Various types of paper that represent cash value by containing either a promise or an order to pay money.

common law Legal principles developed through case decisions, rather than by statute, that form the basis of the law in most states.

complaint The process of initiating a lawsuit through the filing of a document with the appropriate court official that sets forth the cause of action against a party.

condition An express or implied situation or event upon which the performance of a contract depends.

consideration   The promises or performance that the parties to a contract exchange and upon which the contract is based.

consolidation   The uniting of two or more corporations into a new third corporation.

contract   A lawful and enforceable agreement based on consideration.

conveyance   An instrument, such as a deed, that transfers title to real property from one party to another. In a broader sense, any transfer of real or personal property or an interest in it.

corporation   A business organization created under state law to pursue a lawful purpose and existing as a separate legal entity from its owners.

counteroffer   A proposal by an offeree that changes the terms of an original offer in a definite way.

covering   A buyer's purchasing of goods elsewhere because a seller has either failed to deliver or has delivered not conforming to the contract.

crime   An act considered a wrong against society, such as treason, felony, or misdemeanor, for which the government can prosecute a person.

cumulative voting   The method of voting for corporate directors whereby a shareholder is given a number of votes equal to the number of shares he or she owns times the number of directors to be elected, with the choice of distributing these votes in any manner desired.

damages   Money awarded by the court as compensation for any financial loss or injury caused by another's misconduct.

debenture   An unsecured corporate promise to pay an indebtedness backed by the general credit rating of the corporation.

deed   A written instrument whereby the owner of real property (grantor) conveys his or her interest in the property to another (grantee).

de facto   In fact. Existing in fact despite failure to comply strictly with statutory requirements, as a de facto corporation.

default   The failure to perform a duty as promised in transactions such as contracts, deeds, loans, and so forth.

default judgment   Judgment for one party in a civil suit because the other party failed to respond to a summons.

defendant   The party being sued for a criminal or civil violation.

deficiency judgment   A judgment for the amount outstanding on a secured debt after the collateral has been sold and the proceeds applied to settlement of the debt.

de jure   In law. Existing in law through strict compliance with statutory requirements, as a de jure corporation.

demurrer   A defendant's filing of a response to a summons stating that the complaint fails to state a cause of action sufficient for legal action.

deposition   A sworn statement consisting of answers to questions put to a prospective witness in a judicial proceeding.

derivative suit   A suit filed by one or more shareholders in behalf of a corporation that fails to pursue the course of action itself.

disaffirm   To deny a contract, either expressly or by implication.

discharge   Release from obligation.

dishonor   Refusal to pay an instrument upon presentment.

dissolution   A change in the relationship of a partnership caused by the withdrawal of any partner, by operation of law, or by court order; an event leading to the termination of a corporation.

dividends   Payment of profits in cash or property by the directors of a corporation to shareholders according to some rate or proportion.

donee   A person to whom a gift is given.

donor   A person who gives a gift.

draft   A written instrument whereby a first party unconditionally orders a second party to pay a stated sum to a payee (third party or first party). A bill of exchange.

drawee   A party who is ordered to pay by draft.

drawer   The party who orders a payment by draft.

due care   The care that a reasonable person would exercise in a particular set of circumstances.

duress   Depriving a person of free will through force or fear.

easement   A nonpossessory interest in real property in which one has a limited right to use or benefit from another's land for a specific purpose.

escheat   The passing of property to the state when its owner dies leaving no one to inherit it.

estate   The property that a person acquires during a lifetime.

estoppel   A legal ban preventing a person from denying something when that person's actions or words have indicated the opposite, as an agency by estoppel.

eminent domain   The state's legal right to take privately owned real property for the public benefit in exchange for fair compensation to the owner.

exculpatory clause   A contract clause that disclaims liability even if the party making the disclaimer is actually at fault; generally considered unconscionable and not upheld by the court.

express authority   The clearly specified authority to act, oral or written, given to an agent by a principal.

fee simple absolute The highest right of ownership and possession of real property, in which the owner and his or her heirs are granted all interests in the land forever with no restrictions.

fiduciary relationship A relationship in which one party has reason to rely on the opinion of the other because of the latter's position of trust or confidence.

financing statement The document filed to perfect a security interest against other claimants.

fixtures Items of personal property attached to real property in such a way that they are considered part of the real property.

foreign corporation A corporation registered under the law of another state or country other than the one in which it is doing business.

fraud Knowing, intentional, or reckless misrepresentation or deceit in order to induce a person to give up some property or rights.

fraudulent conveyance Any transfer of property or property rights as a means of defrauding one's creditors.

frustration of purpose The occurrence of some circumstance that significantly changes the basic assumptions under which a contract was made, generally resulting in discharge of the contract or suspension of performance until the frustration has been removed.

general partner A partner with power to manage partnership business and unlimited liability for partnership debts.

good faith The sincere belief and intent that one's actions are legal and causing no harm to anyone.

grantee One who is sold or given real property by its owner.

grantor One who sells or gives his or her interest in real property to another.

holder One who possesses an endorsed instrument and to whom the instrument is payable.

holder in due course One who takes a negotiable instrument in good faith, for value, and with no notice of any defenses against it.

implied Communicated as an act or show of intention, rather than in written or oral form.

implied authority Unstated authority of an agent to take whatever actions are necessary to carry out the purpose of the agency.

implied warranties Warranties imposed by law for the quality and fitness of goods being sold.

indemnify To guarantee against loss or liability.

indorsement A signature or other written indication by the holder or agent of a negotiable instrument that transfers it to a new holder.

in pari delicto Both parties are equally at fault.

insolvent Unable to pay debts when due.

intestate succession The passing on of a decedent's property according to state law, rather than as provided in a will.

joint and several liability Equally and individually responsible for damages to third parties.

joint tenancy Form of cotenancy in which real property is conveyed at one time by a single document to joint tenants with right of survivorship.

lease An agreement by which the owner of real property gives a tenant the right to possess the property in exchange for rent or some other recompense.

legal capacity A legally defined level of rationality or mental competence for entering into contracts.

lessee The person who has the right to possess real property granted under a lease.

lessor The owner of real property who grants the right of possession to another under a lease.

license The nonpossessory, revocable right to use another's real property for a limited, specific purpose.

lien A charge or encumbrance imposed on property for the payment or discharge of a debt or duty.

life estate A grant of ownership interest in real property to a person for the rest of his or her life or for the life of someone else.

limited partner A partner with no power to manage partnership business and liability for partnership debts only up to the amount of his or her contribution.

limited partnership A partnership formed by the association of one or more general partners and one or more limited partners.

liquidation The conversion of assets to cash; under Chapter 7 of the Bankruptcy Act, liquidation is required for payment to creditors.

litigants The parties to a lawsuit.

maker The party who executes an instrument, promising to pay.

merchant Any seller who presents himself or herself as having special knowledge of or skills relating to the transacted goods.

merger The acquisition of one corporation by another, such that the acquired corporation becomes a part of the acquiring one.

minor Anyone under the legal age of majority, which is 21 in some states and 18 in others.

mitigation of damages The act of reducing damages caused by another party below what they otherwise would be.

mortgage A contract whereby a person's real property is designated as security for the payment of a debt.

mutual assent The reciprocal agreement between two parties to a contract required to make the contract binding and enforceable.

necessaries Such things that the court considers essential to sustain existence, such as food, clothing, and shelter.

negligence The failure of a person to exercise due care under a specific set of circumstances.

negotiable instrument Commercial paper that can be transferred by indorsement or delivery to a new holder.

noncumulative voting The method of voting whereby each shareholder receives one vote for each share of stock he or she owns.

novation A mutual agreement between all parties to a contract that cancels an existing contract and creates a new one.

obligee The party to a contract who is to receive performance of rights or duties.

obligor The party to a contract who is to perform rights or duties.

offer A legally valid proposal to form a contract.

offeree The party to whom an offer is made.

offeror The party who makes an offer to another.

ordinance A law passed by a city, town, or county for the purpose of local administration.

parol evidence rule A rule of law whereby oral testimony cannot be presented in a lawsuit to change or contradict the terms of a written contract except to clarify ambiguous terms, show that a term was added later, or prove that the contract was signed under duress or fraud.

partnership The association of two or more people who agree to establish and run a business for profit as co-owners.

payee A person to whom an instrument is made payable.

payor A person who is responsible for paying the value of an instrument.

perfection The process whereby a creditor legally protects an interest in collateral against claims by others.

performance The fulfillment of obligations required by a contract in the time and manner specified.

personal property Property that is movable and has no permanent physical location.

plaintiff The party who initiates a lawsuit by filing a complaint against another party (the defendant).

precedent A published case decision that serves as the basis of future case decisions.

presentment A demand that the maker or drawee of a negotiable instrument accept it or pay its cash value.

principal The person for whom an agent acts and from whom an agent derives his or her authority.

privity of contract A general rule that a person may not sue to enforce a contract that he or she is not a party to; of little relevance to cases of product liability.

probate The process of submitting a will to the court to prove its validity.

product liability The responsibility of a distributor of a product for harm caused by any condition or defect in the product.

profit In real property law, the right to acquire a possessory interest, such as minerals or timber, in another's real property.

promise A pledge to perform, supported by consideration, giving the person to whom the pledge is made the right to expect and claim the performance.

promisee The person to whom a promise is made.

promisor The person who makes a promise to another.

promissory note A written instrument whereby one party unconditionally promises to pay a stated sum of money to a second party.

promoter Any person who participates in the formation of a new corporation.

proxy An assignment of voting power by a corporate shareholder.

ratification The express or implied affirmation of an act that otherwise would not be binding.

real property Land and other things that are fixed and permanent, such as buildings and vegetation.

remedy The appropriate legal form of relief that an injured party may seek to enforce or compensate for a remedial right.

reorganization The rearrangement of a business' financial structure; under Chapter 11 of the Bankruptcy Act, a reorganization plan is adopted to reduce, adjust, pay, and discharge the debtor's debts while continuing the business and avoiding liquidation.

replevin Court order giving a buyer the right to recover goods wrongfully withheld by a seller.

repossession The act whereby a creditor takes possession of collateral after a debtor's default.

rescission Release from contractual obligations through mutual consent or conditions of the contract.

res ipsa loquitur The doctrine that an injured party in a product liability suit for negligence must show only that the defect causing the injury was within the responsbility of the manufacturer, placing the burden of proof on the manufacturer.

respondeat superior The superior must respond. The doctrine under which an employer is held liable for the torts of his or her employees that result in injury to third persons and that are committed within the course and scope of their employment.

revocation   In contract law, the withdrawal of an offer by the offeror before it is accepted; also, the cancellation of a document.

right of survivorship   The right to immediately acquire the interest in real property of a deceased co-owner; the distinguishing characteristic of joint tenancy.

sale   The transfer of title from a seller to a buyer for a price.

scienter   The knowing misrepresentation of fact by one party to another; an element of fraud.

secured transaction   Any transaction in which a debtor gives a creditor an interest in personal property or fixtures in order to guarantee payment or performance of a debt.

specific performance   The court-ordered remedy of performance of a contract according to its terms.

stare decisis   Let the decision stand. The doctrine that decisions of the court should stand as guidance or precedents in deciding similar cases in the future.

statute   A law enacted by a federal or state legislative body.

Statute of Frauds   A statute in each state specifying that certain types of contracts are enforceable only if they are in writing.

Statute of Limitations   A statute in each state limiting the time period after the occurrence of an event during which legal action arising from the event can be taken.

stock   The ownership interest in a corporation, usually issued in shares, carrying rights of ownership, profit sharing, and management, and represented by negotiable certificates.

stop payment order   An order by a depositor to his or her bank not to honor a specified check.

strict liability   The responsibility of a manufacturer for the harm caused to anyone by its product, regardless of the manufacturer's fault or lack of fault.

summons   In a civil lawsuit, a document served on the defendant that a response to a suit is necessary to avoid a default judgment.

tenancy   Any right to possession of real property.

tenancy in common   Ownership of real property by two or more people who each hold a separate, distinct share in the property without the right of survivorship.

tenancy by the entirety   A joint tenancy between husband and wife that cannot be severed without the consent of both.

tender   A good-faith offer to perform as required.

tort   A civil wrong resulting in an injury caused directly by the breach of a legal duty.

transferee   A person to whom a transfer is made.

transferor   A person who makes a transfer.

trust   An arrangement whereby property is transferred from one person to another for the benefit of a third party.

trustee   One who receives property from a trustor and administers it for the benefit of a third party.

trustor   One who transfers his or her property to a trustee who administers it for the benefit of a third party.

ultra vires acts   Acts performed by a corporation that are beyond the scope of the powers conferred upon it.

unconscionable agreement   An agreement in which one party, through superior bargaining power, has compelled another to accept grossly unfair terms.

undue influence   The subordination of a person's free will to the will of another, usually by taking advantage of a close or confidential relationship with the coerced person.

Uniform Commercial Code (UCC)   A uniform code created to deal with most commercial transactions, including sales of goods, commercial paper, banking, and secured transactions. The UCC has been adopted by all states except Louisiana, which has adopted portions of it.

unsecured creditor   A creditor who has no security from a debtor to repay a debt other than the debtor's promise to pay.

usury   Charging interest that is above the rate allowed by law.

void   An act that is entirely null; it has no legal standing and is not binding or enforceable, as a void contract.

voidable   That which is capable of being made void, but may also be confirmed.

waiver   A party's voluntary decision to discharge another from part or all of the obligations to perform.

warranty   A guarantee, either express or implied, as to a product's fitness and quality.

will   A document by which a person sets forth how his or her estate is to be distributed after death.

winding up   The completion of unfinished business and the liquidation and distribution of all assets after dissolution of a partnership.

INDEX